W9-BKR-327

LIBRARY IN A BOOK

JUVENILE CRIME
REVISED EDITION

Aaron Kupchik

First Edition by Jeffrey Ferro

An imprint of Infobase Publishing

Juvenile Crime, Revised Edition

Facts On File, Inc.
An imprint of Infobase Publishing
132 West 31st Street
New York NY 10001

Library of Congress Cataloging-in-Publication Data
Kupchik, Aaron.
   Juvenile crime / Aaron Kupchik. — Rev. ed.
      p. cm. — (Library in a book)
   "First edition by Jeffrey Ferro."
   Includes bibliographical references and index.
   ISBN 978-0-8160-7917-9 (alk. paper)
   1. Juvenile delinquency—United States. 2. Juvenile delinquents—United States.
I. Ferro, Jeffrey. Juvenile crime. II. Title.
   HV9104.F448 2010
   364.360973—dc22   2010013189

Facts On File books are available at special discounts when purchased in bulk quantities for businesses, associations, institutions, or sales promotions. Please call our Special Sales Department in New York at (212) 967-8800 or (800) 322-8755.

You can find Facts On File on the World Wide Web at http://www.factsonfile.com

Text design by Ron Monteleone
Composition by Hermitage Publishing Services
Cover printed by Art Print, Taylor, Pa.
Book printed and bound by Maple Press, York, Pa.
Date printed: August 2010
Printed in the United States of America

10 9 8 7 6 5 4 3 2 1

This book is printed on acid-free paper.

CONTENTS

PART I
OVERVIEW OF THE TOPIC

Chapter 1
Introduction to Juvenile Crime   **3**

Chapter 2
The Law of Juvenile Justice   **43**

Chapter 3
The Juvenile Justice System   **80**

Chapter 4
Chronology   **100**

Chapter 5
Biographical Listing   **112**

Chapter 6
Glossary   **122**

PART II
GUIDE TO FURTHER RESEARCH

Chapter 7
How to Research Juvenile Crime and
Juvenile Justice Issues   **139**

Chapter 8
Annotated Bibliography   **151**

Chapter 9
Organizations and Agencies   **207**

PART III
APPENDICES

Appendix A
Juvenile Crime Statistics   **223**

Appendix B
In re Gault et al.   **248**

Index   **287**

PART I

OVERVIEW OF THE TOPIC

CHAPTER 1

INTRODUCTION TO
JUVENILE CRIME

"Our youth love luxury. They have bad manners and contempt for authority. Children are now tyrants. . . ."

Those statements might be considered relevant to American youth of today, particularly juvenile offenders. In fact, the words were spoken some 2,500 years ago by the Greek philosopher Socrates. More recently, the *New York Times* observed that "the number of boy burglars, boy robbers and boy murderers is so astoundingly large as to alarm all good men." That was 150 years ago. Back then, recordkeeping was not what it is today, making it difficult to quantify the prevalence of juvenile crime in American society. Nonetheless, it is clear that concern about juvenile crime and delinquency is not a new phenomenon.

In the early 19th century in the United States, the law viewed juvenile offenders in much the same way as adults. For example, in Illinois in 1827, the legal age of criminal responsibility was 10. Given the recent example of Lionel Tate, sentenced in 2001 to life without parole for a murder he committed when he was 12 years old, it may appear to some that society has come full circle in terms of how the justice system deals with juvenile offenders, particularly the most violent.

Historically, local police have had wide discretion in the handling of juvenile offenders. For example, in Detroit, Michigan, at the beginning of the 20th century, police conducted roundups of boys for petty offenses. These roundups served as warnings not to engage in future criminal behavior. However, the juveniles were usually handled informally and were rarely referred to court. Twenty-five years later, that began to change. Youthful offenders were increasingly arrested for serious crimes. In Los Angeles, California, during the 1930s, the Los Angeles Police Department (LAPD) began to place greater emphasis on arresting juveniles for felonies than for

3

less serious offenses. Those efforts were focused particularly on minority youth and auto thieves. During the same time period, the homicide rate in the United States was rising dramatically, from a rate of about two homicides per 100,000 people in 1900 to nearly 10 per 100,000 by 1935. The increase in homicides came at a time of great industrial development that resulted in a large influx of population to northern urban centers such as New York City and Chicago, Illinois. This wave of migration included many who were new to this country, as well as many southern blacks, all of whose customs and lifestyles challenged what was then perceived as a "traditional" American value system. By the 1920s, there was a growing concern that white youth were being "seduced" by the new lifestyles of both immigrants and African Americans, all of whom found themselves living side by side in metropolitan centers. There were also the influences of movies and modern music, especially jazz, which were thought to be undermining traditional values and glamorizing dancing, sex, and drinking. With the devastating stock market crash of 1929, the country faced a major economic crisis. Prohibition of alcohol was proving to be a failure and the criminal activity of bootlegging, or smuggling and selling liquor, was thriving. In response to what was perceived as a rising crime wave (no national crime statistics were kept until 1930), President Herbert Hoover established the National Commission on Law Observance and Enforcement, commonly known as the Wickersham Commission. The commission's report, issued in 1931, included findings that turf wars were being waged in America's large cities by rival criminal groups fighting for control of bootleg liquor distribution. As a result, homicides and other violent crimes, including drive-by shootings, were on the rise.

After settling back to a rate of just under five homicides per 100,000 persons in 1960, the homicide rate again began to climb in the United States, according to Federal Bureau of Investigation (FBI) statistics. The rate peaked at 10.2 per 100,000 in 1980. That same year marked the beginning of a steady rise in the number of homicides involving teenagers, both as victims and as offenders. The trend of rising homicides and gun violence by juveniles peaked in 1993 and began a steady decline, but by then the public outcry over the rise in juvenile violence was prompting many states to enact new, tougher measures for the handling of juvenile offenders, including trying the most serious in adult criminal court.

During the 1990s, the rate of juvenile crime in the United States paralleled the rate of overall crime, peaking in 1994 and then declining by more than 50 percent by 1999, as measured by arrest rates. That overall trend continued through 2005 when the number of criminal offenses committed by persons under 18 years of age declined by 6 percent from 2001 levels, according to the FBI. However, overall arrest rates increased 1 percent from 2005 to 2006, with larger increases in some categories. Most noticeably, robbery arrest rates increased by 19 percent for all persons under 18 years of age, and by 9 percent for females under 18. On the other hand, several offense categories showed large decreases from 2005 to 2006, including rape (down 10 percent), larceny (down 8 percent), and motor vehicle theft (down 8 percent).

For some, a perceived rise in gang activity has been more troubling than the 1 percent increase in overall juvenile arrests. According to the National Youth Gang Survey, a survey of police departments across the country, the prevalence of gang problems steadily increased over the years 2001–07, with a 25.5 percent increase in reported gang members and a 7.7 percent increase in numbers of gang crimes 2002–07.[1] Yet as others note, difficulties in assessing what a gang is and who gang members are cause uncertainty in these statistics.

HISTORICAL BACKGROUND

In order to understand the history of juvenile delinquency, it is first necessary to examine the evolving role of the child in society. From ancient times to the early Christian era, the child was essentially defined by membership in a family. As such, a child was under the absolute authority of the head of the family, usually the father, who literally possessed the power of life or death over his children (although a father could be punished for using his authority in an arbitrary manner). So empowered, the head of the family was expected by society to deal with children who ran afoul of social customs. Juvenile lawbreakers generally were dealt with in the same way as adults. For example, in ancient Rome prior to the fifth century, juveniles were, like adults, subject to Roman law, codified in the Twelve Tables. Beginning in the fifth century, however, children under the age of seven became exempt from criminal responsibility under Roman law. Boys over the age of 14 and girls over the age of 12 were considered as adults for the purposes of criminal liability. Still, from ancient times through the Middle Ages, there was little if any appreciation for the "special nature" of children. In essence, the concept of childhood as understood today did not exist. The purpose of children, in general, was to further a family's economic goals, which sometimes resulted in what today would be considered brutal and even inhuman treatment of children. Although bonds of affection certainly existed between parents and their children, those relationships did not form the central focus of family life as they do today.

Around the beginning of the 16th century, ideas of childhood began to evolve and there emerged new ways of thinking about children and youth. One example of this new way of viewing the child occurred in the English colonies of North America. Under the influence of Puritanism, more attention was given to childhood and, in particular, to the process of child rearing. Puritans viewed proper child rearing as essential to an individual's eternal salvation, and they believed that without good child rearing salvation was impossible. This view arose from the belief that every human—and, therefore, every child—was innately sinful and predisposed to evil acts. Puritan thinking was that children were born with original sin and had to be taught as soon as possible to seek salvation. As a result, Puritans sought to "break" a child's natural will and force the child's subordination to parents, society, and God. In so doing, Puritans recognized and even emphasized the importance of children in and of themselves, and they thereby began to foster a new attitude about children as a distinct class of people. This new way of thinking about children eventually found its way into Puritan law. For example, under Puritan law, any male child 16 years of age or older who refused to obey his parents could be taken before local magistrates for a hearing and, if found guilty, could be punished or even sentenced to death. As such, the Puritans effectively legislated the first known "status" offense in North America: incorrigibility. (A status offense is an act that is illegal for children but not for adults.)

Beginning in the 19th century, the Puritan ideal of dogmatic, patriarchal control of children began to erode. The strict view of the child as innately sinful began to be tempered by the notion that children were also good in nature and amenable to being molded and encouraged, as opposed to subordinated through fear alone. From these changing views of children there emerged the early formulations of the concept of "juvenile delinquency" in the late 19th century. The notion that children and adults were the same under the law could not be as easily reconciled with the new ideas of childhood's special nature and the growing attention being given to the process of nurturing as part of successful child rearing.

At the same time, a process of urbanization in the United States was occurring as the result of the Industrial Revolution. From 1783 to 1790, the population of New York City increased from approximately 12,000 to 33,000. Some 35 years later, the population of New York City had reached 166,000. Urban centers such as New York City were ill prepared for such growth. Municipal services were slow to expand in areas of sanitation, clean water, and public health, resulting in depressed urban areas—slums—that were crowded with a growing underclass of poor men, women, and children. Due in part to such depressed economic and social conditions in urban America during the early 19th century, there was a rise in property crimes such as burglary among male juveniles, and a rise in the rate of prostitution among female juveniles. There also emerged a "street corner" subclass of youth who were often not in school, were unemployed, and were to some extent independent of adult supervision. The question of how to deal with such juveniles began to emerge as a new social issue. The problem of "juvenile delinquency" was born—and it was largely identified as a problem of the urban poor.

In 1904, with the publication of *Adolescence: Its Psychology and Its Relations to Physiology and Education*, American psychologist G. Stanley Hall brought psychology to bear on adolescent development. According to Hall's view, children tended to be well adjusted to their environment until the onset of adolescence at about the age of 12, which was marked by "intense states of mind" and "sudden shifts of mood." Hall believed that adolescents were overly aggressive and assertive, and "overeager for independence." Hall's ideas quickly took root among reformers and others concerned with the rise of juvenile crime in urban centers. As a result, juvenile delinquency came to be seen in terms of a stage of life, and not solely as a product of poverty or an otherwise deprived environment. One important outgrowth of the connection between juvenile delinquency and adolescence was the concept of "decriminalizing" delinquency. Delinquent acts were viewed less as criminal acts and more as a product of adolescence itself due to impulses that were not under the control of the adolescent.

The theories of delinquency formed in the early 20th century shaped the modern study of delinquency. These theories emphasized environmental factors such as urbanization and the process of adolescence as the two leading factors in the cause and rise of juvenile delinquency in the United States during the modern era. Issues of race, class, and gender in American society and the erosion of a strong, cohesive family life are also assumed to have played significant roles.

Prior to the 20th century, there was no national system in place to track juvenile offenders in the United States. In 1929, the U.S. Department of Justice began keeping a statistical measure of crime in the United States as part of the Uniform Crime Reporting Program. Published annually since 1930 by the FBI, the Uniform Crime Reports (UCR) track offenses reported to law enforcement agencies across the country. Initially, submission of data by local law enforcement agencies was voluntary. As a consequence, information on national crime trends, especially juvenile crime trends, was somewhat incomplete prior to about 1960. As of 1997, 44 states had enacted laws mandating the report of adult and juvenile crime statistics to the UCR.

The UCR collects information on the specific crimes of homicide, forcible rape, robbery, aggravated assault, burglary, larceny-theft, motor vehicle theft, and arson. The UCR also tracks arrests in more than 20 additional crime categories. Each spring, the UCR publishes preliminary findings for the previous year. For example, preliminary findings for 2008 were released in spring 2009. A detailed annual report, *Crime in the United States*, is then issued the following calendar year. In addition to crime counts and trends, *Crime in the United States* includes data on persons arrested by age, sex, and race. For homicides, the age, sex, and race of victims and offenders, as well as the victim-offender relationship, weapons used, and circumstances surrounding the homicides, are also reported.

In 1973, the U.S. Department of Justice added a second statistical measure of crime nationally. Administered by the Bureau of Justice Statistics, the National Crime Victimization Survey (NCVS) compiles information on crime incidents, victims, and trends through surveys of crime victims. Among the crimes that the NCVS tracks are rape, sexual assault, personal robbery, aggravated and simple assault, household burglary, theft, and motor vehicle theft. The NCVS cannot measure homicide, as the victim is deceased, nor does it include commercial crimes. The survey summarizes crimes suffered by individuals, whether or not they were reported to law enforcement, and provides information on the age, sex, and ethnicity of both victims and offenders.

A third measure of juvenile crime is self-reported data. These consist of surveys administered to students to measure crime victimization as well as behaviors such as alcohol and drug use.

In general, crimes fit into one of two categories: person and property. Person crimes, which include violent crimes such as murder and rape, are crimes committed against persons, whereas property crimes, such as larceny or motor vehicle theft, usually involve the taking or destruction of things—even though there may be human victims. For example, robbery is the taking of something by force or fear from a person and, as such, it is categorized as a person crime. Burglary, which broadly defined is illegal entry into a house or building with the intent to commit a crime, is categorized as a property crime because the criminal action is directed at a house or building—even though the residents or occupants may be victimized, even traumatized. For juveniles there is a third type of offense, called status offenses. These include running away and incorrigibility—actions which are against the law only for juveniles, not for adults. As such, status offenses are not actually crimes; however, they can result in arrest and adjudication in juvenile court.

VIOLENT CRIME TRENDS

Crime trends do not exist in a vacuum. Historical factors often contribute to the rise or fall of crime during a given period. For example, the dramatic rise in the rate of homicides in the United States from 1900 to the mid-1930s coincided with the migration of Americans to urban areas as an outgrowth of the Industrial Revolution. In addition, during the 1920s, the failure of Prohibition resulted in the rise of bootlegging and the sometimes violent criminal activity associated with it. By the late 1920s and early 1930s—near the peak of the rising trend in homicides—the country suffered its worst stock market crash and was plunged into an economic depression.

Because national statistics on crime were not kept until 1930, when the FBI began publishing the UCR, it is difficult to trace trends in person crimes (other than homicide) and property crimes before then. By contrast, with the advent of computers and increasingly sophisticated methods of statistical analysis, crime trends since about 1960 can be analyzed in greater detail.

The post–World War II era began with low crime rates in the United States; however, by the 1960s the crime rate began to rise for reasons not entirely clear to criminologists and social historians. One theory— that a major wave of immigration contributed to the rise in crime—appears to be discounted by statistical evidence that immigrants during that period were involved in less crime than nonimmigrants. Beginning in the 1960s, crimes by females began to increase, resulting in rising arrest rates for women for the person crimes of robbery, aggravated assault, and other assault, as well as for the property crimes of larceny, forgery, embezzlement, burglary, motor vehicle theft, stolen property, and arson.

During the 1980s and early 1990s, the availability of guns was one of the key factors associated with the rising juvenile crime rate. Statistically, the rising rate of homicides committed by 14- to 17-year-olds virtually mirrored the rise in crimes committed with firearms during that period. Similarly, since 1993, the decline in the rate of homicides by offenders between 14 and 17 years of age nearly parallels the decline in crimes committed with firearms.

According to the NCVS, in 1973 there were just under 1 million incidents of serious violent crime by juvenile offenders ages 12 to 17, as perceived by their victims. The incidence of serious violent crime by juveniles decreased somewhat and leveled off until 1981, when it rose to about 1973 levels. The following year, 1982, the rate declined again and remained more or less constant through 1987, reaching a low in 1986 of about half the 1973 rate. Then, in 1988, the trend reversed and the rate of violent juvenile offenders, as reported by their victims, rose steadily to a peak of more than 1 million offenses in 1993. That period of rapid growth was reversed beginning in 1994. By 2000, the incidence of violent serious crime by juveniles was less than the previous low point set in 1986.

NCVS historical trends were roughly paralleled by arrest trends from the FBI's UCR. Arrest trends for violent crimes committed by juvenile offenders remained fairly steady from 1980 to 1987. From 1988 to 1994, arrests of violent juvenile offenders increased by more than 60 percent. Then, in 1995, arrests for violent juvenile crimes began a sustained decline. During the 10 years from 1997 through 2006, the total number of persons arrested for violent crimes under 18 years of age decreased by nearly 20 percent, compared to a decline of 8.2 percent for persons 18 years of age and over, as reported by the FBI for the years 1998–2007. That included declines for murder and nonnegligent manslaughter (down 42 percent), forcible rape (down 31 percent), robbery (down 16 percent), and aggravated assault (down 21 percent).

Arrests of violent female juvenile offenders did not decrease as significantly during the same 10-year period. According to the FBI, from 1997 to 2006, overall arrests of violent female juvenile offenders were down by 12 percent, compared to a decrease of 22 percent of males under 18 years of age. Arrests of female juvenile offenders for aggravated assault declined by 10 percent, compared to a decrease of 24 percent for male juveniles during the same time period. For some offenses, arrest rates of females increased over the years 1997–2006 while male arrest rates decreased. This includes simple assault (19 percent increase for females, 4 percent decrease for males), weapons offenses (5 percent increase for females, 11 percent decrease for males), and disorderly conduct (33 percent increase for females, 2 percent decrease for males). Despite the fact that female arrest rates have increased *relative to male arrest rates*, it is not clear that female juveniles are more involved in actual crime than they were 10 years ago. Instead, some scholars have suggested that their behaviors have remained similar, but that due to changing notions of gender, female delinquency is less likely to be ignored now compared to years ago.[2]

Although arrest rates for serious violent offense have declined steadily since peaking in 1993, self-reported violent offenses have showed no decline.[3] While the arrest rate for serious violent crimes fell by 32 percent between 1994 and 2003, self-reported incidents of serious assault and robbery remained at the same level during that period. Trends in self-reported data provide compelling evidence that many violent offenders are never arrested for their crimes.

TRENDS FOR PROPERTY CRIMES

Juvenile arrests for property crimes began an overall decline in the early 1990s, according to the FBI. During the 10-year period from 1998 to 2007, the number of persons under 18 years of age arrested for property crimes decreased by 33 percent, compared to a decline of 19.5 percent for persons 18 years of age and older. During that period, arrests of juvenile offenders decreased across the board for burglary (down 30 percent), larceny-theft (down 32 percent), motor vehicle theft (down 49 percent), and arson (down 19 percent).

As with violent offenses, the decline of 18 percent of female juveniles arrested for property crimes was less than the 39 percent decline among males under 18 years of age. This held true for burglary and larceny-theft,

10

but not for motor vehicle theft, for which males and females saw similar declines in arrest rates (down 49 percent and 50 percent, respectively).

TRENDS FOR STATUS OFFENSES

Only juveniles may be arrested for what are called status offenses, such as running away, curfew violations, and liquor law violations (usually buying or possessing liquor under the legal age)—none of which are crimes for adults. From 1983 to 1991, arrests for running away increased by nearly 70 percent. Since then, trends reported by the FBI show sustained declines in the number of arrests of runaways. From 1998 to 2007, arrests for running away dropped by 36 percent. Declines for females (down 38.8 percent) were greater than those for males (down 33.1 percent) for running away.

While arrests for curfew and loitering violations increased during the early 1990s, the rate of arrests fell by 30 percent from 1998 to 2007. Females (down 30.5 percent) and males (down 30.1 percent) showed similar declines in arrest rates for curfew and loitering violations.

From 1998 to 2007, arrests for liquor law violations declined by 20 percent among persons under 18 years of age. The decline of 2 percent among female juveniles arrested for liquor law violations was much less than the 28 percent decline in arrests of male juveniles.

JUVENILE OFFENDERS

According to the FBI, in 2007 18.1 percent of all females arrested were juveniles, while 14 percent of all males arrested were juvenile offenders under 18 years of age. Of juveniles arrested for violent criminal offenses in 2007, 47 percent were white and 51 percent were black (including Hispanics and non-Hispanics). For property offenses, 66 percent of juveniles arrested were white, and 32 percent were black. According to the Census Bureau, in 2008 some 41.1 million African Americans composed 13.3 percent of the U.S. population. By comparison, 64.4 percent of the U.S. population in 2000 was composed of non-Hispanic whites, making the rate of arrests per population far more disproportionate for African Americans than for white Americans.

In 2007, some 28 percent of juveniles arrested for violent crimes and 31 percent for property crimes were under 15 years of age. According to the Office of Juvenile Justice and Delinquency Prevention's most recent estimate, "national data show that in 1999 police arrested about one-quarter million (230,800) youth age 12 and younger." Known as "child delinquents," these very young offenders represented about 9 percent of all juveniles arrested in 1999. About 25 percent of child delinquents in 1999 were females. It is believed that the number of child delinquents reported in 1999 is an underestimate because many jurisdictions preclude minors under the age of 12 from being referred to juvenile court, where they could be more accurately tracked.

CAUSES OF DELINQUENCY

In the late 19th century, early theories on the causes of criminal behavior and delinquency tended to focus on the physical characteristics of criminal offenders versus those of nonoffenders. A pioneer of such theories was Cesare Lombroso (1835–1909), a physician and professor of medicine at the University of Turin in Italy. In 1876, Lombroso published *The Criminal Man*, in which he described his observations of the physical characteristics of two groups of Italian men—prisoners and soldiers. Based on these observations, Lombroso concluded that criminal offenders were throwbacks to a more primitive stage of human evolution and could be distinguished from nonoffenders by certain physical characteristics, such as the shape of the head. Following Lombroso's lead, other scientists such as English physician Charles Goring (1870–1919) and physical anthropologist Earnest A. Hooton (1887–1945), who taught at Harvard University, attempted to apply scientific methodology to identify genetic traits that predisposed certain individuals to criminality from birth. This focus on the constitutional, or bodily, characteristics of criminals is known as the Positivist School.

By the beginning of the 20th century, Positivist explanations of delinquency and criminal behavior fell out of favor, as more emphasis was placed upon social and psychological factors in understanding criminal behavior. In 1904, American psychologist G. Stanley Hall published *Adolescence: Its Psychology and Its Relations to Physiology, Anthropology, Sociology, Sex, Crime, Religion and Education,* which identified adolescence as a distinct stage in life that was critical to the formation of character. At the same time, Sigmund Freud's psychoanalytic theories on the human personality were influencing thinking on criminality and its underlying causes. Freud's focus was on problems or disturbances that may have affected emotional development in childhood. Thus, because of problems that may have occurred early in life, Freud believed that certain juveniles were psychologically predisposed to engage in criminal behavior. According to Freud, these "latent delinquents" tended to seek immediate gratification, gave primary importance to satisfying their own needs, and satisfied those instinctive urges without regard for the social ramifications of their actions.

Freud's theories, although not universally accepted by delinquency researchers, spawned other psychological theories of delinquency. The conditioning theory, developed by British psychologist Hans J. Eysenck, proposed that delinquency was caused by the failure of certain juveniles to incorporate the rules of society in their minds. Eysenck believed that conscience was what made individuals behave in a socially acceptable manner and that conscience was developed through a long process of conditioning.

Another psychological theory of delinquency that developed after Freud was the frustration-aggression theory, formulated in 1939 by psychologists John Dollard and Neal Miller. According to Dollard and Miller, frustrations experienced as the result of failing to attain certain satisfactions or goals resulted in aggressive responses in certain individuals. The frustration-aggression theory helped to explain, in psychological terms, why deprivations endured by impoverished youth might result in aggressive behavior. More recently, criminologist Robert Agnew extended and reformulated this idea to consider a general strain theory that links frustration and delinquency.

During the early 20th century, the emergence of sociology within the United States and particularly the Chicago school of urban sociology also provided explanations to the problem of delinquency. Scholars such as Robert Park, Ernest Burgess, Clifford Shaw, and Henry McKay sought to explain why certain areas of the city were continually marked by high crime rates, even though the residents of these areas changed frequently. The theory that came from their insights, social disorganization, suggests that delinquency is the result of a neighborhood's inability to control its residents. Problems such as heterogeneity and mobility lead to weak connections between residents and moral cynicism, which in turn mean that neighborhoods will have high delinquency rates. By focusing entirely on communities rather than on individuals, this early sociological theory of crime drew attention to how social factors heavily influence delinquency.

The differential association theory was developed by criminologist Edwin H. Sutherland (1883–1950). Its primary assertions were that criminal behavior is learned as the result of participation with intimate personal groups, such as family or peers, and that an individual who has learned behavior inclined to favor violating the law is more likely to engage in criminal or delinquent acts. Sutherland's differential association theory gained wide acceptance among delinquency researchers and theorists; however, the theory has a significant drawback. It cannot account for individuals who respond differently to similar situations. For example, not all individuals with lawbreaking parents go on to become lawbreakers themselves, although some do.

The social bonding theory of delinquency grew out of studies of delinquents and nondelinquents in northern California conducted in the 1960s by Travis Hirschi. According to the theory, to the extent that a child fails to become attached to the control agencies of society, such as family and schools, the greater the likelihood that a child will engage in delinquent behavior. The theory identifies four types of social bonding: attachment (the emotional bond between a juvenile and others), commitment (the energy spent in pursuit of goals), involvement (engaging in law-abiding behaviors), and belief (feelings about the legitimacy of social values).

The labeling theory of delinquency, developed during the 1950s and 1960s, proposed that an individual labeled and stigmatized by society as a "delinquent" or a "criminal" is more likely to act accordingly. Proponents of the labeling theory believe that an individual's contact with the criminal justice system may have the unintended consequence of promoting further delinquent or criminal activity, not deterring it.

The rational choice theory of crime originally stems from 18th-century philosophers Cesare Beccaria and Jeremy Bentham, though it regained popularity in the 1980s. This theory suggests that crime and delinquency result from individual, rational calculations about whether the costs outweigh the benefits of any particular action. This idea is popular among the general public because it appeals to commonsense notions about individuality and morality, and it has been the driving force behind juvenile justice laws over the past few decades; these laws seek to prevent delinquency by raising punishments for arrested youth, thereby attempting to raise the actual costs of criminal behavior. Yet, since it assumes that youth understand what the costs and benefits of their actions will be and that criminal action is the result of conscious deliberation rather than impulsiveness, it is often criticized as being overly simplistic. Additionally, it ignores juveniles' life circumstances and focuses on individual-level choices as if all youth have equal ability to make informed decisions about their behaviors.

In 2000, the Office of Juvenile Justice and Delinquency Prevention released the results of a study group on the predictors of serious youth violence. Over two years, some 22 researchers reviewed 66 studies on delinquency and identified the following risk factors associated with the development of violent behavior among juvenile offenders.

- *Individual Risk Factors:* pregnancy and delivery complications; low resting heart rate; internalizing disorders; hyperactivity, concentration problems, restlessness, and risk taking; aggressiveness; early initiation of violent behavior; involvement in other forms of antisocial behavior; beliefs and attitudes favorable to deviant or antisocial behavior.
- *Family Risk Factors:* parental criminality; child maltreatment; poor family management practices; low levels of parental involvement; poor family bonding and family conflict; parental attitudes favorable to substance use and violence.
- *School Risk Factors:* academic failure; low bonding to school; truancy and dropping out of school; frequent school transitions.

- *Peer-related Risk Factors:* delinquent siblings; delinquent peers; gang membership.
- *Community and Neighborhood Risk Factors:* poverty; community disorganization; availability of drugs and firearms; neighborhood adults involved in crime; exposure to violence and racial prejudice.

SUBSTANCE ABUSE

Beginning in 1995, some 1,172 males and 658 females held in the Cook County Juvenile Temporary Detention Center in Chicago, Illinois, were assessed for alcohol, drug, and mental (ADM) disorders. Two-thirds of the study group showed one or more ADM disorders. According to Linda A. Teplin in her report "Assessing Alcohol, Drug, and Mental Disorders in Juvenile Detainees," "preliminary data suggests that, nationwide, more than 670,000 youth processed in the juvenile justice system each year would meet diagnostic criteria for one or more ADM disorders that require mental health and/or substance abuse treatment."[4] Although substance abuse does not directly cause other types of delinquent behavior, or vice versa, "the two behaviors are strongly correlated and often bring about school and family problems, involvement with negative peer groups, a lack of neighborhood social controls, and physical or sexual abuse," according to the report by the Office of Juvenile Justice and Delinquency Prevention.[5]

The UCR defines drug abuse violations as those offenses involving "the unlawful possession, sale, use, growing, and manufacturing of narcotic and non-narcotic drugs," as reported in *Drug Offense Cases in Juvenile Courts, 1989–1998.*[6] Between 1991 and 2004, the number of juvenile drug offense cases in juvenile court more than doubled.[7] Juvenile arrest rates for drug abuse between 1980 and 2000 reflect a different pattern when compared to the rates for either violent or property crimes. From 1980 to 1992, the arrest rates for juvenile drug offenders fluctuated between a low of 291.6 in 1983 and a peak of 421.3 in 1992. The next year, the rate of juveniles arrested for drug abuse began to rise significantly, from a rate of 421.3 in 1993 to 748.6 in 1997, a growth of 78 percent. Since then, the rate has fallen by about 14 percent from its peak in 1997, to a rate of 640.2 in 2000, still more than twice the 1983 rate. Despite the recent downward trend, between 1991 and 2000 the rate of juveniles arrested for drug offenses increased by 220 percent for females and 135 percent for male juvenile drug offenders. In terms of overall numbers, the UCR reported that in 2004 some 193,700 juveniles were arrested for drug abuse violations.

MARIJUANA USE

Marijuana was the drug most commonly used by both male and female juvenile detainees, as reported in the *2000 Arrestee Drug Abuse Monitoring Program Report (ADAM)*.[8] Nationwide, marijuana use among 12th graders has decreased nearly 20 percent from its peak in the mid-1990s to 2007, while decreases during the same time are over 40 percent for eighth graders and 30 percent for 10th graders, according to the *2007 Monitoring the Future* study *(MTF)*, an annual self-report survey of some 50,000 students between the eighth and 12th grades in public and private schools.[9]

Based on data from *ADAM*, the *MTF*, and the *National Household Survey on Drug Abuse*,[10] there was "a rapid increase in marijuana use during the 1990s, especially among youths," as reported in *The Rise of Marijuana as the Drug of Choice Among Youthful and Adult Arrestees*.[11] The upsurge was referred to as the New Marijuana Epidemic in order to distinguish it from the widespread use of marijuana during the 1960s and 1970s, according to Golub and Johnson. As they reported, "The doubling of marijuana use among youthful *ADAM* arrestees during the 1991 to 1996 provides some of the strongest evidence to suggest that a New Marijuana Epidemic has occurred . . . especially among youths who tend to get in trouble with the law." Since then, however, marijuana use has consistently declined.

DRUGS AND ALCOHOL

By design, the *MTF* survey excludes dropouts, institutionalized, homeless, and runaway youth. Still, the study serves as a baseline for the incidence of drug use among the entire juvenile population. The 2007 *MTF* study reported the following findings:

- Between 2006 and 2007, lifetime use of cocaine by 10th graders increased slightly from 4.8 to 5.3 percent. Lifetime use of crack cocaine increased from 2.2 to 2.3 percent.

- Lifetime heroin use among 12th graders has been either 1.5 or 1.4 percent since 2003.

- Lifetime use of hallucinogens decreased from 3.4 to 3.1 percent among eighth graders, increased from 6.1 to 6.4 percent among 10th graders, and did not change for 12th graders from 2006 to 2007.

- The use of steroids by high school seniors decreased from 2.7 percent in 2006 to 2.2 percent in 2007.

- Among eighth graders, 38.9 percent reported having tried alcohol and 17.9 percent reported that they had been drunk at least once. About one-fifth (22 percent) of eighth graders had tried cigarettes.[12]

Overall, the survey reports steadily decreasing rates of drug and alcohol use among youth. In 2007, 7.4 percent of eighth graders, 16.9 percent of 10th graders and 21.9 percent of 12th graders report using any illicit drug in the past 30 days.[13]

Juvenile arrest rates for drunkenness closely parallel the rates for juveniles arrested for driving under the influence between 1980 and 2000. In 1980, the rates for both were at their 20-year peaks. Since then, the juvenile arrest rate for both offenses has generally declined. In 2000, the juvenile arrest rates for drunkenness and for driving under the influence were both 55 percent below the rates in 1980.

CLUB DRUGS AND INHALANTS

Use of so-called club drugs, such as ecstasy (MDMA), Rohypnol (known as the "date rape" drug), GHB, and ketamine, had grown by 2001 but has declined since. In 2001, some 9 percent of 12th graders, 6.2 percent of 10th graders, and 3.5 percent of eighth graders reported that they had used ecstasy within the past year. By 2007, those figures decreased to 4.5, 3.5, and 1.5 percent, respectively.[14] Because all of these club drugs are now scheduled under the Controlled Substances Act (Title II of the Comprehensive Drug Abuse Prevention and Control Act of 1970), they are illegal and their use constitutes a criminal offense. In addition, "ecstasy is being sold with heroin and powder crack cocaine . . . and ecstasy users are also using these other illicit drugs," according to *Pulse Check: Trends in Drug Abuse, January–June, 2001.*[15] Users of ecstasy as well as the club drugs GHB, ketamine, and Rohypnol were generally between the ages of 13 and 30 and overrepresented by whites, according to the report. While users of ecstasy were evenly split between males and females, males tended to be the most common users of GHB, ketamine, and Rohypnol.

The abuse of inhalants such as aerosols and volatile solvents—also known as "huffing"—increased by 158 percent between 1990 and 1999, primarily among 12- to 17-year-olds, making inhalants the fourth most abused substance, behind alcohol, cigarettes, and marijuana, according to the *2000 National Household Survey on Drug Abuse.* Among eighth to 12th graders, more than 636,000 had tried inhalants for the first time in 1999, more than twice the rate among 18- to 25-year-olds who reported using inhalants in 1999. The *1999 Youth Risk Behavior Survey* reported that 14.6 percent of ninth to 12th grade students reported using inhalants at least once in their lifetime. Males and females were equally likely to abuse inhalants. Yet by 2007, lifetime inhalant use declined substantially to 15.6 percent for eighth graders (down from 21.6 percent in 1995), 13.6 percent for 10th graders (down from 19.3 percent in 1996), and 10.5 percent for 12th graders (down from 17.7 percent in 1994), according to the *MTF* survey.[16]

YOUTH GANGS

Though researchers' definitions of youth gangs vary considerably, most consider a youth gang to be a group involved in a pattern of criminal acts and typically composed only of juveniles, although it may also include some young adults. Youth gangs are different from prison gangs, ideological gangs, hate groups, and motorcycle gangs, all of which are usually composed of adults.[17]

It is generally believed that youth gangs first appeared in Europe or Mexico. "No one is sure when or why they emerged in the United States," according to James C. Howell in *Youth Gangs: An Overview* (1998). The first record of their appearance in the United States may have been as early as 1783, near the end of the American Revolution. Others suggest their emergence was later, around 1813, following the Mexican Revolution and the Mexican migration to the southwestern United States. According to Howell, "They may have grown out of difficulties Mexican youth encountered with social and cultural adjustment to the American way of life under extremely poor conditions." Youth gangs soon spread to the first large cities in United States—New York, Boston, and Philadelphia—during the urban migration associated with the Industrial Revolution.

Youth gangs gained a foothold in Chicago and other large urban centers and "seem to have been most visible and most violent during periods of rapid population shifts," according to Howell. There were four distinct periods of growth in youth gang activity in the United States—the late 1800s, the 1920s, the 1960s, and the 1990s. Beginning in the 1970s, youth gangs became more dangerous because of increased mobility due to the automobile and greater access to firearms. Weapons used in gang fights escalated from fists and brass knuckles to guns and drive-by shootings. By the 1980s, youth gangs increasingly began to focus on the sale and distribution of illicit drugs, especially crack cocaine. Howell points out that "some gangs seldom use drugs and alcohol, and some have close community ties." Nonetheless, gangs in the 1980s and 1990s tended to include more members with prison records or ties to prison inmates, used alcohol and drugs more extensively, and trafficked in drugs to a greater degree than ever before.

During the 1970s, about 1 percent of all U.S. cities reported having youth gang problems. By 1998, that figure had risen to 7 percent.[18] The biggest growth in gang cities occurred between the 1980s and 1990s, when they increased in numbers by 281 percent. Between 1995 and 1998, gang activity was reported in some 1,550 cities and 450 counties where it had previously gone unreported. In 1999, youth gangs were active in 100 percent of cities with populations of 250,000 or more, 47 percent of suburban counties, 27 percent of cities with populations below 25,000, and 18 percent of rural counties.[19]

From 1996 to 1998, the number of gang cities increased by 325 percent in Oregon, the highest increase in the United States, followed by 270 percent in Utah, 171.4 percent in Iowa, and 171 percent in Washington State. States reporting the most gang cities in 1998 were California, Illinois, Texas, Florida, and Ohio. In the 1970s, only eight states reported having five or more gang cities. Two decades later, all 50 states did so. From 1970 to 1998, the size of the average gang city fell from 182,000 to 34,000. By 1998, cities with populations of fewer than 25,000 comprised 57 percent of all gang cities, and cities of fewer than 10,000 comprised 32 percent of gang cities across the nation.

As gangs have spread to smaller cities across the country, they have become decentralized. In the 1970s, "gang counties were concentrated in a relatively small number of States, principally California and Texas. By 1998, gang counties were spread widely through the Nation . . . and were distributed more evenly than gang cities," reported Walter B. Miller in *The Growth of Youth Gang Problems in the United States: 1970–98*. Some 40 percent of gang cities were located in the top five gang-city states in 1998, while less than 25 percent of all gang counties were located in the top five states. In the 1970s, three of the five states ranked highest in the number of gang counties were in the Northeast—New York, New Jersey, and Pennsylvania. By 1998, they had been replaced by the southern states of Texas, Florida, and Georgia, with California and Illinois rounding out the top five states with the highest number of gang counties.

In "Gangs in Middle America," David M. Allender identified two ways in which gangs can spread. Using the "imperialist method," members of a large street gang move to a new city or neighborhood and set up a chapter of the gang. An established gang can also spread by "franchising"—recruiting new members in another city to carry on criminal activity, such as drug trafficking, with the established gang receiving a cut of the profits generated by the new gang.[20] Others, however, suggest that new gangs arise from local conditions, such as poverty, rather than from franchising or deliberate spreading of established gangs.

Since 1996, the National Youth Gang Center has conducted the National Youth Gang Survey (NYGS), an annual survey of all police and sheriff's departments serving cities and counties with populations of 25,000 or greater. In addition, the NYGS surveys a random sampling of law enforcement agencies serving rural localities with populations between 2,500 and 25,000. Respondents are asked to report information for youth gangs in their jurisdiction, excluding motorcycle gangs, hate or ideology-based groups, prison gangs, and adult gangs. In "Highlights of the 2007 National Youth Gang Survey," Arlen Egley, Jr., and Christina E. O'Donnell reported that 86 percent of law enforcement agencies in larger cities, 50 percent of agencies in suburban counties, 35 percent in smaller cities, and 15 percent in rural counties reported "experiencing youth gang problems in 2007."

According to Egley and O'Donnell, an estimated 27,000 gangs were active in the United States in 2007. This is the highest estimate since before 2000. In 2007, there were some 788,000 active gang members in the United States, according to Egley and O'Donnell. Earlier surveys suggest that most youth gang members were males (94 percent), although 39 percent of all youth gangs were reported to have female members. The racial and ethnic composition of gangs changed little over the period of 1996 to 2000, with survey respondents reporting that 47 percent of gang members were Hispanic, 31 percent were African American, 13 percent were white, and 7 percent were Asian.

GANG-RELATED HOMICIDES AND OTHER CRIMINAL OFFENSES

Gang homicides and other gang-related crimes were recently assessed in the 2007 "National Youth Gang Survey Analysis," conducted by the National Youth Gang Center. According to this survey, 13.3 percent of large cities reported at least 10 gang-related homicides per year, and 31.9 percent reported none per year; 4.5 percent of suburban areas reported more than 10 gang-related homicides per year, while 55.4 percent reported zero per year. Gang-related homicides were even less frequent in rural areas, with no rural areas reporting at least 10 per year and 79.6 percent reporting zero per year.

The National Youth Gang Center also reports that about one-third of the police agencies included in their survey report a gang problem. The percentage reporting a gang problem had decreased from 39.9 percent in 1996 to a low of 23.9 percent in 2001, but it has since increased steadily to 34.8 percent in 2007.[21]

Yet reports on gang crime can often be conflicting. For example, though the NYGS illustrates decreases through 2001 in police department–reported gang problems, other sources reported increasing problems during the same time: The *Los Angeles Times* reported that "the number of firearms deaths in Los Angeles County rose nearly 9 percent in 2000 over the previous year." In the article, Los Angeles County sheriff Lee Baca "blamed the increasing numbers [of firearms deaths] on the availability of guns, but also the use of those guns by gang members, whom he said accounted for a disproportionate number of gun-related homicides."[22] According to Baca, 46 percent of all homicides were gang related in Los Angeles in 2000, compared with 39 percent in 1999.

According to the report "Highlights of the 2000 National Youth Gang Survey," 72 percent of survey respondents identified gang members returning to the community from prison as having a negative impact on youth gang problems in their jurisdiction.[23] More recently, the 2007 Youth Gang Survey Analysis found that 41.9 percent of survey respondents reported that gang members returning from confinement significantly influenced gang-related violence.

YOUTH GANGS IN THE 21ST CENTURY

Many modern gangs still bear the names of long-established gangs, like the Los Angeles–based Bloods and Crips, or the Chicago-based Black Gangster Disciples and Vice Lords. These established gangs tend to be structured into subgroups or cliques and have developed national coalitions with other gangs, forming so-called gang nations, such as Folks and People. In recent years, new gangs have emerged that are localized and have no affiliation with any of the established gangs, even though they may share their name. Known as hybrids, these new gangs have tended to take root in communities that had no youth gang culture prior to the 1980s or 1990s. Although hybrids have existed in the United States since the 1920s as ethnically or racially mixed gangs, the modern version of hybrid gangs is more complex in the following ways:

- *Location:* Local institutions, especially schools, have increasingly become a gathering point for local gangs. Although some are neighborhood based, they occupy smaller territories such as schoolyards or shopping malls.
- *Organization:* Modern hybrid gangs tend not to be highly organized criminal enterprises like some of their well-established namesakes. Lifetime membership is not a requirement, and members may change their affiliation from one gang to another or claim multiple affiliations. Existing gangs may merge to form a new gang.
- *Less Crime-Driven:* Gangs that emerged in new localities during the 1990s were "far less likely" to be involved in violent crimes (homicide, aggravated assault, robbery, and use of firearms), property crimes, and drug-dealing than gangs formed prior to 1986.
- *Less Allegiance:* Hybrid youth gangs tend to have less allegiance to a traditional gang color, as indicated by the mixing of multiple gang symbols in hybrid gang graffiti.[24]

FEMALE GANGS

As gangs proliferated in the 1980s and 1990s, the number of gang members who were female was substantial.[25] While surveys by law enforcement agencies identified only 3.2 percent of gang members as females in the early

1990s, other surveys put the figure much higher, at 8 to 38 percent. According to the 2007 Youth Gang Survey Analysis, rural counties and smaller cities are more likely than larger cities to have gangs with female members. Like males, females are exposed to the same precursors to joining a gang, such as a maladjusted childhood or low academic achievement (discussed later in this section). However, according to the report *Female Gangs: A Focus on Research*, there is one aspect of gang life that appears to be unique to females—"the gang as a refuge for young women . . . who have experienced sexual abuse at home." According to surveys conducted in Los Angeles and Hawaii, the proportion of female gang members who had been sexually abused at home was 29 percent and 66 percent, respectively. Another common precursor to joining a female gang appears to be drug addiction.

The type of delinquency and criminality attributed to gang activity also appears to differ among female gang members when compared to their male counterparts. "In general, female gang members commit fewer violent crimes than male gang members and are more inclined to property crimes and status offenses," as reported in *Female Gangs: A Focus on Research*. Among female arrestees in Chicago in 1996, 38.5 percent had committed gang-related violent offenses, and 37.7 percent of female arrestees accounted for gang-related drug offenses, as reported by Moore and Hagedorn using data provided by the Illinois Criminal Justice Information Authority. Other gang-related offenses by female arrestees in Chicago in 1996 included prostitution (9.8 percent), weapons violations (2.8 percent), and liquor law violations (3.5 percent).

JOINING AND REMAINING IN A GANG

In the most recent large-scale study on the topic, the report "Early Precursors of Gang Membership: A Study of Seattle Youth" examined the results of the Seattle Social Development Project, which tracked 808 youths from 1985, when they were fifth-grade students from high-crime areas attending public schools in Seattle, Washington.[26] The study identified a variety of childhood predictors of joining and remaining in a gang, and assigned odds to each of them. Among those risk factors with odds of 3 to 1 or higher for joining or remaining in a gang were learning disability (3.6), availability of marijuana (3.6), low academic achievement (3.1), other neighborhood youth in trouble (3.0), and a family with one parent plus other adults residing together (3.0).

Some 46 percent of participants in the study identified themselves as European Americans, 24 percent as African Americans, 21 percent as Asian Americans, 6 percent as Native Americans, and 3 percent as other ethnicities. Of those, 21.8 percent of the males and 8.6 percent of the females (a total of 124 participants) reported that they had joined a gang between the ages of 13 and 18. African Americans comprised 26.2 percent of those who joined a gang; Asian Americans, 12.4 percent; European Americans, 10.2 percent.

Of the 124 study participants who joined a gang between 13 and 18, more than two-thirds (69 percent) joined for one year or less. Less than 1 percent who had joined a gang at 13 still belonged to a gang at age 18. Those who remained in a gang for several years "were the most behaviorally and socially maladjusted in childhood," according to the study. "In particular, youth who exhibited early signs of violent externalizing (e.g. aggression, oppositional behavior, and inattentive and hyperactive behaviors) and those who associated with antisocial peers were more than twice as likely to remain in a gang for more than one year."

During the period of their gang involvement, 64 percent of participants reported committing an assault, compared to 18 percent of non–gang participants. Marijuana use was reported by 54 percent in gangs, compared to 26 percent not in gangs. Of participants who had been arrested or who were involved in drug selling, 51 percent were gang members, compared to 14 percent and 9 percent, respectively, among non–gang members. Gang members reported committing robbery, breaking and entering, and felony theft at a rate three times higher or more than non–gang members.

Although gang membership was equated with a significantly higher incidence of criminal activity, youths may not necessarily join a gang with that intent. In "Gangs in Middle America," David M. Allender reported that "young people normally seek gang involvement for some combination of the following five reasons:

- **Structure:** Youths want to organize their lives but lack the maturity to do so on their own. The gang provides rules to live by and a code of conduct.

- **Nurturing:** Gang members frequently talk of how they love one another. This remains true even among the most hardened street gangs. These young people are trying to fill a void in their lives by substituting the gang for the traditional family.

- **Sense of Belonging:** Because humans require social structure, some young people find that the gang fulfills the need to be accepted as an important part of a group.

- **Economic Opportunity:** Gang members motivated by this consideration alone probably would become involved in criminal activity anyway.

- **Excitement:** Gangs composed of these types of individuals usually have a very fluid membership, with associates joining and leaving to be replaced by others with a passing interest."

GANGS AT SCHOOL

In 2007, 23 percent of students ages 12 through 18 reported that gangs were present at their schools. This is a small increase from 2001, when 20 percent of students reported gangs at their schools, as reported in *Indicators of School Crime and Safety: 2008.*[27] In 2001, 25 percent of public-school students reported the presence of gangs at their schools, compared to only 5 percent of students attending private schools. The incidence of gangs reported at urban schools was 36 percent, compared to 21 percent at suburban schools and 16 percent at rural schools in 2005. Black and Hispanic students were more likely than white students to report the existence of gangs at their schools.

According to the report "Gang Problems and Gang Programs in a National Sample of Schools," of the 1,279 schools surveyed, about 5 percent of principals reported that gangs were a problem at their schools.[28] Of those, principals at urban secondary schools were most likely to report gang problems at school. According to the report, about 20 percent of schools surveyed had gang intervention programs that included counseling, social work, or psychological/therapeutic intervention. Some 13 percent of the schools surveyed had classroom instruction or training that focused on gang prevention, and about 10 percent of schools had gang prevention programs in place that emphasized improving intergroup relations or relations between the school and community.

SCHOOL CRIME

During the 2006–07 school year, there were an estimated 1.7 million nonfatal crimes committed in public schools against students ages 12 to 18, as reported in *Indicators of School Crime and Safety: 2008*. Though this is indeed a large number, crimes in school—and especially violence—have been steadily decreasing since the mid-1990s. In 2007, 4.3 percent of students aged 12–18 reported being the victim of a crime in school, and 1.6 percent of students were the victims of violent crime. These numbers are half of the victimization rates from 1995 (9.6 percent overall, 3 percent for violence).[29]

There were 35 violent deaths of school-aged youth (ages five–18) in school in the United States from July 1, 2006, through June 30, 2007. Of those, 27 were homicides at school and eight were suicides. Each year since 1992, there have been at least 50 times as many murders of youth away from school than at school and at least 140 times as many suicides off school grounds than on school grounds.[30]

There was a total of two multiple-victim homicides at U.S. schools in the 1998–99 school year, compared to six such incidents during the 1997–98 academic year. With the exception of the 1993–94 school year, there was at least one multiple-victim homicide during each school year from 1992 to 2001, as reported in "School Violence: An Overview."[31] From the fall of 1997 to spring 2001, there were 10 high-profile shootings in U.S. schools, with handguns used in nine out of 10 such incidents, according to the report "Where'd They Get Their Guns? An Analysis of the Firearms Used in High-Profile Shootings, 1963–2001."[32] In eight of those shootings, the guns were legally purchased by a family member or an acquaintance of the shooter.

- *October 1, 1997:* Three were killed and seven wounded at Pearl High School in Pearl, Mississippi. The .30-30 rifle used was legally obtained.
- *December 1, 1997:* Three were killed and five wounded at Heath High School in West Paducah, Kentucky. The firearm used, a Ruger .22 pistol, was illegally obtained.
- *March 24, 1998:* Five were killed and 10 wounded at Westside Middle School in Jonesboro, Arkansas. Of the nine guns used in the shootings, all were purchased legally.
- *May 21, 1998:* Four were killed and 25 wounded at Thurston High School in Springfield, Oregon. Of the three guns used in the shootings, all were legal.
- *April 20, 1999:* Fifteen were killed and 23 wounded at Columbine High School in Littleton, Colorado. The four guns used in the shootings were procured illegally.
- *May 20, 1999:* Six were wounded at Heritage High School in Conyers, Georgia. The two guns used in the shootings were purchased legally.
- *December 6, 1999:* Four were wounded at Fort Gibson Middle School in Fort Gibson, Oklahoma. The firearm, a Taurus 9 mm pistol, was legally obtained.
- *February 29, 2000:* A six-year-old student was killed at Theo J. Buell Elementary School in Mt. Morris Township, Michigan. The Davis Industries .32 pistol used was illegally obtained.
- *May 26, 2000:* One student was killed at Lake Worth Middle School in Lake Worth, Florida. The firearm used, a Raven .25 pistol, was legally obtained.
- *March 5, 2001:* Two were killed and 13 wounded at Santee High School in Santana, California. The .22 Arminius eight-shot revolver used was legally obtained.

Since 2001, the following school shootings at the hands of students have resulted in at least one death:

- *April 24, 2003:* A 14-year-old student shot and killed the principal of Red Lion Area Junior High School in south-central Pennsylvania before killing himself.
- *September 24, 2003:* A 15-year-old student fatally shot two fellow students at Rocori High School in Cold Spring, Minnesota.
- *March 21, 2005:* A 16-year-old student shot and killed five schoolmates, a teacher, and an unarmed guard at Red Lake High School on the Red Lake Indian Reservation in Minnesota before taking his own life.
- *November 8, 2005:* A high school freshman fatally shot an assistant principal and wounded two other school administrators at Campbell County High School in eastern Tennessee.
- *September 29, 2006:* A 15-year-old student brought two guns to Weston Schools in rural Cazenovia, Wisconsin, and fatally shot his principal after the principal had given him a disciplinary warning for having tobacco on school grounds.
- *August 5, 2007:* Four young people were shot in the head at close range, three fatally, in the parking lot of the K-8 Mount Vernon School in Newark, New Jersey.
- *October 10, 2007:* A 14-year-old gunman opened fire at Success Tech Academy in Cleveland, Ohio, wounding two students and two teachers before killing himself.
- *February 12, 2008:* In Oxnard, California, a 14-year-old shot a 15-year-old classmate, who later died of his injuries.[33]

Though large-scale shootings have occurred on college campuses, including those in April 2007 at Virginia Tech and in February 2008 at Northern Illinois University, K–12 schools have not seen incidents of this magnitude in recent years.

In "The School Shooter: A Threat Assessment Perspective," Mary Ellen O'Toole, reported that "news coverage magnifies a number of widespread but wrong or unverified impressions of school shooters. Among them are: All school shooters are alike; the school shooter is always a loner; school shootings are exclusively revenge motivated; and, easy access to weapons is the most significant risk factor."[34]

O'Toole set forth a four-pronged approach in assessing "the totality of the circumstances" known about a student in four major areas: personality of the student, family dynamics, school dynamics, and social dynamics. O'Toole identified the following factors in making that assessment.

- Student appears to be "detached" from school, including other students, teachers, and school activities.

- The school does little to prevent or punish disrespectful behavior between individual students or groups of students.
- The use of discipline is inequitably applied—or has the perception of being inequitably applied by students and/or staff.
- The school's culture is static, unyielding, and insensitive to changes in society and the changing needs of newer students and staff.
- Certain groups of students are officially or unofficially given more prestige and respect than others.
- Few feel they can safely tell teachers or administrators if they are concerned about another student's behavior or attitudes. Little trust exists between students and staff.
- Unsupervised computer access.

Bullying at school may also play a factor. As reported in "School-Associated Violent Deaths in the United States, 1994–1999," students who committed homicide between 1994 and 1999 "were more than twice as likely as homicide victims to have been bullied by peers."[35]

WEAPONS AT SCHOOL

According to *Indicators of School Crime and Safety: 2008*, in 2007 almost 6 percent of students reported carrying a weapon on school grounds at least one day in the 30 days prior to the survey. Overall, male students (9 percent) were more likely than females (2.7 percent) to carry a weapon, and white students (5.3 percent) somewhat less likely than black (6 percent) or Hispanic (7.3 percent) students. Carrying a weapon varied little by grade, as the percentage of ninth graders (6 percent), 10th graders (5.8 percent), 11th graders (5.5 percent), and 12th graders (6 percent) who reported carrying a weapon were very similar. In 2003 (the most recent year for this measurement), *fewer* students in urban schools reported carrying a weapon (5.6 percent) compared to suburban (6.4 percent) and rural (6.3 percent) students. These numbers represent large decreases in weapons on school grounds. In 1993, twice as many students (11.8 percent) reported carrying a weapon in the previous 30 days—this percentage has dropped in every survey (taken every two years) since then.[36]

The percentage of secondary-school students who reported being threatened or injured at school with a weapon such as a gun, knife, or club fluctuated between 7 and 9 percent from 1993 through 2007, according to *Indicators of School Crime and Safety: 2008*. Male students were almost twice as likely as female students to report being threatened or injured with a weapon in 2007 (10.2 percent for males, 5.4 percent for females). Reported rates of threat or injury by weapon also vary by race and ethnicity, since 6.9

percent white students, 9.7 percent of black students, and 8.7 percent of Hispanic students report threats or injuries. Secondary students in lower grades were more likely than students in higher grades to be threatened or injured with a weapon at school.[37]

NONFATAL SCHOOL CRIMES

In 2006, there were an estimated 173,600 nonfatal serious violent crimes (rape, sexual assault, robbery, and aggravated assault) against students ages 12 to 18 while at school. Aggravated assault is the deliberate attempt to cause serious bodily injury, or the infliction of serious bodily injury upon another as the result of recklessness or negligence. Simple assault is the attempt to cause or the infliction of bodily injury which is less than serious. When simple assault was factored in, the number of school-related nonviolent victimizations increased significantly, to about 767,000 in 2006.

In 2007, 1.6 percent of students ages 12–18 reported being the victim of a violent crime at school during the previous six months. This is a decrease from 1995, when 3 percent of students reported violent victimization. For serious violent crimes, only 0.4 percent of students reported victimization in 2007. Theft is the most common type of nonfatal victimization at school. There were 909,500 reported thefts against students ages 12–18 in schools in 2006, and 3 percent of students ages 12–18 reported being the victim of theft at school in the past six months. According to *Indicators of School Crime and Safety: 2008*, students in grades seven to nine were more likely to report victimization than students in the 12th grade, but there were no measureable differences in victimization by sex or in the percentages of white, black, or Hispanic students who reported victimization.[38]

Teachers are also occasional crime victims at school. In the 2003–04 school year, there were 127,500 reported physical attacks on teachers and 253,100 teachers who reported being threatened with injury. Fewer teachers reported being threatened with injury (7 percent) or physically attacked (3 percent) in 2003–04 compared to the 1993–94 school year (12 percent threatened with injury and 4 percent physically attacked). Teachers in city schools were more likely to report being threatened with injury or physically attacked than teachers in suburban, town, or rural schools. In 2003–04, 10 percent of teachers in city schools reported threats of injury, compared to 6 percent in suburban schools, 5 percent in town schools, and 5 percent in rural schools. With regard to grade level, secondary school teachers were most likely to report being threatened with injury (8 percent, compared with 6 percent of elementary school teachers), but elementary school teachers were more likely to report having been physically attacked than secondary school teachers (4 percent compared with 2 percent).[39]

In 2007, about 5 percent of male students and 4 percent of females in grades nine through 12 reported that they had used alcohol on school grounds during the previous 30 days, while 5 percent of all students reported using marijuana on school property, according to *Indicators of School Crime and Safety: 2008.* Some 22 percent of students in grades nine through 12 in 2007 reported that drugs were made available to them on school property during the previous 12 months. More specifically, 26 percent of male students reported that illegal drugs were available at school, compared to 19 percent of females.[40]

FEELING SAFE AT SCHOOL

One potential consequence of school violence is that it can cause fear among students that can reduce student's readiness and ability to learn and can negatively affect the school environment. In 2007, some 5 percent of students between the ages of 12 and 18 reported fearing that they would be attacked or harmed at school, compared to more than twice that number (12 percent) in 1995. Those percentage of students reporting a fear of being attacked or harmed while traveling to and from school also declined, from 6 percent in 1999 to 4 percent in 2007. Of students surveyed, a larger percentage of blacks and Hispanics feared such attacks than did white students.

Another measure of how safe students feel at school is their avoidance of certain areas at school. In 2007, some 6 percent of students ages 12 to 18 reported that they avoided one or more places in school, compared to 9 percent of students in 1995. Students in lower grades were more likely to avoid certain areas than those in upper grades. In urban areas, some 6 percent of students reported avoiding certain areas in school, compared to 4 percent of suburban students in 2005.[41]

The perception of safety at school is also influenced by a student's exposure to hate-related words or symbols at school. In 2007, some 10 percent of students ages 12 to 18 reported that someone at school had called them a derogatory word having to do with their race, ethnicity, religion, disability, gender, or sexual orientation. Some 35 percent of students reported seeing hate-related graffiti at school. In 2005, hate-related words were most likely to be reported by students in rural schools (16 percent), and hate-related graffiti most likely at urban schools (41 percent of students). Male and female students reported similar rates of being called by a hate word. About 11 percent of black and Hispanic students reported being slurred, compared to 9 percent of white students.[42]

Finally, bullying and cyber-bullying may also substantially shape students' fears and the quality of a school's learning environment. According to *Indicators of School Crime and Safety: 2008,* in 2005–06, 24 percent of public schools reported that student bullying was a daily or weekly problem. In 2007, 32 percent of students ages 12–18 reported being the victims of bullying at school. Males (31 percent) were slightly less likely to report being bullied than females (34 percent). White students were the most likely to report being bullied at school, at 34 percent, compared to 30 percent of black students and 27 percent of Hispanic students. Of the students who reported being bullied, most incidents occurred inside school (79 percent), and the most common type of bullying incident was being made fun of, called names, or insulted.[43]

In 2001, some 32 percent of parents said they feared for their child's physical safety while at school, according to a poll by Gallup News Services. Of those, 39 percent of parents had at least one child in the sixth grade or higher, while 22 percent of parents of children in the fifth grade or below reported fearing for their child's safety at school.

JUVENILE SEX OFFENDERS

It is estimated that juvenile sex offenders account for up to 20 percent of rapes and nearly 50 percent of child molestations that occur in the United States every year, according to a report from the Institute of Law, Psychiatry, and Public Policy at the University of Virginia.[44] Adolescent males account for most such offenses, although females and prepubescent males also engage in sexually abusive behavior. Juvenile sex offenders exist within all racial and cultural groups. Some of the factors that contribute to juvenile sexual aggression include childhood abuse and exposure to aggressive role models, substance abuse, and exposure to pornography.

Juvenile male sex offenders fall primarily into two categories: those who target younger children, and those who offend against peers or adults. Those who offend against younger children generally share certain characteristics, including the following:

- Their victims are more likely to be males than are the victims of juveniles who offend against peers and adults.
- Nearly 40 percent of their victims are members of their immediate or extended family.
- They are less likely to use physical force and more likely to use bribes and threats in order to make their victims comply with the molestation.
- They often lack self-esteem and social competency.
- They often have symptoms of depression.
- They are less likely to exhibit emotional indifference than are juveniles who sexually offend against peers and adults.

By comparison, juveniles who sexually offend against peers or adults tend to share the following similarities:

- They predominantly assault females, strangers, or casual acquaintances.
- They are more likely to sexually offend while engaged in other types of criminal activity, such as burglary.
- They are more likely to have histories of delinquency.
- They are more likely to offend sexually in public areas.
- They are generally more aggressive and violent during the sexual offense.
- They are more likely to use weapons and to injure their victims.

Among both groups of juvenile sexual offenders there is often evidence of learning disabilities and academic underachievement, a history of substance abuse, the presence of a diagnosable conduct disorder, and difficulty in controlling impulse and judgment.

According to the report, effective treatment of juvenile sex offenders includes the following components:

- Establishing positive self-esteem and cultural pride.
- Promoting an understanding of healthy human sexuality.
- Improving social competency.
- Teaching impulse control and an understanding of the cycle of thoughts, feelings, and behaviors that triggers sexual acting-out.
- Training in how to manage anger and resolve interpersonal disputes.
- Promoting an awareness of the negative impact of sexual abuse on victims and their families.

PROBATION AND CONFINEMENT

According to Charles Puzzanchera and Melissa Sickmund in *Juvenile Court Statistics, 2005*, the likelihood that a delinquency case would be handled informally (without being filed in juvenile court) decreased from 1985 to 2005.[45] This means that a larger percentage of cases became eligible for court-ordered probation or confinement, or both, "reflecting the trend toward more formal processing of delinquency cases," according to Meghan C. Black in *Juvenile Delinquency Probation Caseload, 1989–1998*.[46]

Among cases that were adjudicated delinquent in juvenile court, the juvenile court equivalent of being "found guilty," the number that resulted in out-of-home placement increased 30 percent between 1985 and 2005. Out-of-home placement includes confinement but can also include options such as boot camps or other punishments outside one's home. This trend is most pronounced for drug offense cases, which saw a 139 percent increase in out-of-home placement, followed by public order offenses (94 percent) and person offenses (89 percent). Placements for property offense cases decreased 25 percent. In 2005, 140,100 delinquency cases received out-of-home placements, down from 182,800 cases at its peak in 1997. Of these cases, 32 percent were property offenses, 31 percent public order offenses, 27 percent person offenses, and 10 percent drug offenses. The likelihood of receiving an out-of-home placement varied by offense type—in 2005 it was 25 percent for person offenses, 24 percent for public order cases, 21 percent for property cases, and 19 percent for drug offense cases. It also varied somewhat by race, with 26 percent of black juveniles' cases ending in out-of-home placement, compared to 21 percent of white juveniles' cases in 2005.

Probation caseloads increased as well, going up 95 percent between 1985 and 2005. Most of this increase occurred from 1985 to 1997, since probation caseloads have been steady since then. This increase since 1985 has been fueled by a 236 percent increase in drug offense cases, a 220 percent increase in public order offenses, and a 203 percent increase in person offenses. Probation is the most common disposition given in juvenile court, as it was the result for about 60 percent of all cases adjudicated delinquent in 2005. Males are somewhat less likely to receive probation than females (59 percent for males compared to 62 percent of females' cases that are adjudicated delinquent), and white youth are somewhat more likely than black youth to receive probation if adjudicated delinquent (62 percent for white youth, 56 percent for black youth).

The number of juveniles that were detained pre-adjudication also increased, by 48 percent, from a total of 239,900 in 1985 to 354,100 cases in 2005. The largest relative increases were for person offenses (increased 144 percent), drug offense cases (increased 110 percent), and public order cases (increased 108 percent). However, though the number increased, the percentage of cases detained was the same—21 percent—in 1985 and 2005. Though black youth represented only 33 percent of the overall delinquency caseload in 2005, 42 percent of the youth who were detained were black. Males were also more likely to be detained, at 22 percent, compared with 17 percent of female cases.

Nationwide, there were 96,655 juveniles confined in residential placement facilities in 2003, according to Howard N. Snyder and Melissa Sickmund, *Juvenile Offenders and Victims: 2006 National Report*. Of these, 64,662 were held in public facilities, and 27,059 in privately run facilities.[47] This represents a decrease of 8 percent since 1997. During that time, placement rates decreased 6 percent for person offenses, including a 54 percent decrease for homicide and a 33 percent decrease for robbery. Placement rates also decreased 16 percent for property offenses, 12 percent for drug offenses, and 29 percent for status offenses, but increased 14 percent for technical violations (violations of probation or parole). Overall, then, these figures suggest that the juvenile justice system has become somewhat more punitive over the past 20 years, with rising rates of formal prosecution, out-of-home placement, and technical probation/parole violations.

JUVENILES DOING ADULT TIME

In many cases juveniles are tried as adults. As a consequence, juvenile offenders may be sentenced to prison instead of a juvenile correctional facility. Juvenile offenders may also be confined in adult jails while awaiting trial or sentencing in adult criminal court. In some cases, especially in rural districts where juvenile detention facilities are not close by, juveniles may be detained in adult jails while awaiting processing by the juvenile court. However, such detentions are usually limited to 48 hours. Though juveniles confined in adult correctional facilities must be held "out of sight and sound" of adult inmates, as mandated by the Juvenile Justice and Delinquency Prevention Act of 1974, often this does not apply when juveniles (under age 18) are defined as adults under state laws.

There were 2,364 state prisoners under the age of 18 as of June 30, 2006, as reported in "Prison and Jail Inmates at Midyear 2006."[48] Of those, 2,259 were male and 105 were female. Juveniles under the age of 18 made up less than 1 percent of state prisoners in 2001. Their overall numbers declined from 3,896 in 2000 and from a high of 5,309 in 1995.

Racial disparities were apparent among juvenile offenders incarcerated as adults, according to the report "Youth Crime/Adult Time: Is Justice Served?" by Jolanta Juszkiewicz.[49] Based on a study of some 2,584 cases in 18 jurisdictions nationwide involving a juvenile charged with at least one felony offense, Juszkiewicz reported that "minority youth, particularly African American youth, were over-represented and received disparate treatment at several stages of the process." During the study period—the first six months of 1998—82 percent of juvenile cases filed in criminal court in the 18 jurisdictions involved minority youth. Of those, 57 percent were African American and 23 percent were identified as Latino in the study. While more African Americans were charged, their rate of conviction was less than all other groups. Some 43 percent of African-American juveniles in the study were not convicted, compared to 28 percent of Latino youth and 24 percent of whites, and less than half (46 percent) of African-American juveniles prosecuted for violent offenses in adult court were convicted. However, of those convicted, 43 percent of African-American juveniles in the study received a sentence of incarceration, compared to 37 percent of Latinos and 26 percent of whites. Of violent offenders, 58 percent of African-American youth were incarcerated, compared to 46 percent of Latino juveniles and 34 percent of whites, according to Juszkiewicz. Similarly, 37 percent of African-American juvenile drug offenders received sentences of straight incarceration, compared to 33 percent of Latino juveniles and 24 percent of whites. The same pattern held for property offenses and public order offenses, although the differences between racial groups were less. Public order offenses include vagrancy, loitering, unlawful assembly, and other behaviors that undermine decency and civility.

PERCEPTIONS OF JUVENILE CRIME

What effect does the news media have on the public perception of juvenile crime? This was among the central questions in a survey of more than 100 articles on the coverage of juvenile crime in the media conducted by Building Blocks for Youth, a multiorganizational initiative on juvenile justice issues by the Youth Law Center, the American Bar Association Juvenile Justice Center, the Center on Juvenile and Criminal Justice, the Juvenile Law Center, Minorities in Law Enforcement, the National Council on Crime and Delinquency, and the Pretrial Services Resource Center. Of the articles surveyed, 65 were published in peer-reviewed journals and 45 were published by organizations and researchers without the benefit of peer review. In April 2001, the results of the survey were released in the report "Off Balance: Youth, Race & Crime in the News," prepared by Lori Dorfman and Vincent Schiraldi.[50] According to various opinion polls analyzed in the survey, in 1998 some 62 percent of Americans felt that juvenile crime was rising—despite the fact that violent juvenile crime was at its lowest point in the past 25 years, as measured by the National Crime Victimization Survey. In a *USA Today* poll, respondents were 49 percent more likely to express fear of their school in 1999 than in 1998—although school-associated deaths had declined by 40 percent during that year. A 1996 poll of Californians found that 60 percent of respondents believed that juveniles were responsible for most violent crime when, in reality, juveniles were responsible for only about 13 percent of violent crime that year. According to the report, "In an environment in which fear of youth crime and actual crime are so out of sync, policies affecting young people are bound to be influenced. For example, crime by youth fell more during the 1990s than adult crime in California, yet voters overwhelmingly passed Proposition 21 in 2000, requiring that youth as young as age 14 be automatically tried as adults for certain offenses."

One reason for such perceptions given by the report is the increase in crime coverage in the media while actual crime rates have declined. From 1992 to 1993, crime coverage doubled on network news programs, from

830 to 1,698 stories, and the coverage continued rising through 1994 and 1995, when it peaked, in large part due to coverage of the O. J. Simpson trial. Although crime news declined by 39 percent in 2000, it was still the third most frequent topic on the network news, as reported by the Center for Media and Public Affairs. At the same time, news stories on juveniles are usually connected to violence. According to the report, news images of boys "emphasized theft and violence primarily because status offenses were not included in [news] coverage. By failing to report on status offenses, which represent the more common problems facing a greater number of young people, the news picture of youth, like adults, is focused on the more unusual yet far less frequent crimes."

Studies on crime coverage in Hawaii's two major daily newspapers, *The Honolulu Star Bulletin* and *The Honolulu Advertiser*, showed a 30-fold increase in the coverage of juvenile crime from 1987 to 1996—despite the fact that juvenile crime rates were falling or stable during that time period in Hawaii. The Center for Media and Public Affairs found that of 9,678 youth-related network and local TV news stories in 2000, only nine stories singled out teenagers for their community service or educational achievement. Also of concern was the emphasis in news stories on juvenile offenders over juvenile victims of crime. According to the report, a 1998 survey of the *San Francisco Examiner* found more stories about youth perpetrators than youth victims, despite statistics by the FBI and other agencies showing that far more juveniles are victimized by crime than commit crime. "The bias toward theft and violence may be influencing legislators to enact inappropriate policy as a consequence of believing the underlying messages in the news coverage," according to the report. "Further, when youth crime receives a far larger share of all crime coverage than youths actually commit, and when youth crime coverage dramatically increases while actual youth crime is decreasing, the public that relies on media coverage as its primary source of information about youth crime is misinformed."

CAUSES AND PREVENTION OF DELINQUENCY

There are two primary developmental trajectories for the emergence of youth violence: "Early Onset" describes children who commit their first serious act of violence before puberty, and "Late Onset" applies to children who become violent during adolescence. As noted in "Youth Violence: A Report of the Surgeon General," "youths who commit most of the violent acts, who commit the most serious violent acts, and who continue their violent behavior beyond adolescence begin during childhood."[51] According to several studies cited in the report, 20 percent to 45 percent of male juveniles and 45 percent to 69 percent of females who were serious violent offenders initiated their violence in childhood. Still, this means that most male violent offenders are Late Onset and began their violent behavior during adolescence.

In addition to developmental trajectories, researchers have identified risk factors for youth violence by linking certain personal characteristics (such as low IQ) and social conditions (such as poverty and abuse) to violent acts committed at a later stage of childhood or adolescence. Although these risk factors are not causes of youth violence, they can be used as a measure of predicting the onset and escalation of violent acts committed by juveniles. As such, childhood abuse is among the most telling predictors of youth violence.

In *Preventing Delinquency Through Improved Child Protective Service*, the author reported on the results of several risk-assessment studies conducted by the National Council on Crime and Delinquency.[52] Among the findings:

- Forty-five percent of juveniles who were victims of childhood abuse went on to have an official record of delinquency.

- Juveniles abused as children self-reported a higher incidence of involvement in delinquent behaviors, with 70 percent reporting that they had committed violent offenses, compared to 56 percent of nonabused juveniles.

- The arrest rate for juveniles abused as children was 27 percent, compared to an arrest rate of 17 percent for nonabused juveniles.

- Among arrested adults, 42 percent were abused as children, compared with 33 percent of adults who reported no abuse as children.

- Adult-onset criminal behavior was reported by 31 percent of those who reported being abused as children, compared with 26 percent of adults who said they had not been abused.

Besides a higher incidence of violent behavior, some 43 percent of victims of childhood abuse reported that they used drugs during adolescence, compared to 32 percent of juveniles not abused during childhood. More than 50 percent of females abused as children reported becoming pregnant during adolescence, compared to just over 30 percent of nonabused females.

The report identified several other risk factors that contributed to substance abuse, delinquency, teenage pregnancy, dropping out of school, and violence. Those risk factors included extreme economic deprivation, a family history of problem behavior, family conflict, and friends who engage in problem behaviors.

In "Blueprint for Violence Prevention," the authors reported on a survey of some 500 programs across the county designed to reduce "adolescent violent crime, aggression, and conduct disorders."[53] Of those, 11 programs were singled out as model programs—or "Blueprints"—for their effectiveness. The following is a brief overview of each of the 11 programs, as described in the report.

Prenatal and Infancy Home Visitation by Nurses sends nurses into the homes of low-income first-time mothers to provide support on issues relating to health and parenting and to help foster the physical, cognitive, and social-emotional development of the child. The visitations begin during the mother's pregnancy and continue every one or two weeks until the child is two years old. One study reported a 79 percent decrease in the abuse and neglect of children among mothers who participated in the program. Additionally, participating mothers had 31 percent fewer subsequent births, with an average of two years between births, 69 percent fewer arrests, and 81 percent fewer criminal convictions than nonparticipating first-time, low-income mothers.

The Incredible Years Series focuses on the prevention, reduction, and treatment of conduct problems in young children through a series of training sessions. Parents are taught interactive play and reinforcement skills, nonviolent discipline techniques, and problem-solving strategies. Classes also address family risk factors such as depression, marital discord, poor coping skills, and lack of anger management.

Promoting Alternative Thinking Strategies is a school-based intervention program for children that is taught by elementary school teachers. The classes, taught three times a week for 20 minutes per session, include lessons on self-control, emotional understanding, self-esteem, problem-solving skills, and interpersonal relationships. Control-group studies have shown that children in the program show a decreased frequency of aggressive or violent solutions to problems.

The Bullying Prevention Program was developed in Norway in response to suicides among boys who were severely bullied by their peers. The program's goal is to reduce bullying among elementary and middle-school children. Students are asked to fill out anonymous questionnaires to assess the prevalence of bullying at their school, teachers are instructed on how to enforce rules against bullying, and intervention meetings are held with bullies, their victims, and their parents. Following implementation of the project from 1983 to 1985 in Norway, bullying problems decreased by 50 percent.

Big Brothers Big Sisters of America (BBBSA) began in the early 20th century in the United States. The program matches youths between six and 18 years of age with volunteer mentors who are screened and trained. A mentor is required to meet with his or her youth at least three times a month for three to five hours. An 18-month study of eight BBBSA programs found that participating youths were 46 percent less likely to start using drugs, 27 percent less likely to start drinking, and 32 percent less likely to hit someone.

Life Skills Training focuses on the psychosocial factors associated with the onset of tobacco, alcohol, and drug use among sixth and seventh graders. The three-year curriculum includes 15 sessions in areas such as problem solving, social skills, and information on drug use. Long-term studies have shown a 66 percent reduction in the use of alcohol, tobacco, and marijuana among participants, as well as a lower incidence in the use of inhalants, hallucinogens, and narcotics.

The Midwestern Prevention Project, also known as *Project Star,* focuses on decreasing the early-onset use of tobacco, alcohol, and marijuana among 10- to 15-year-olds, as well as decreasing drug use among community residents. The program consists of a school-based classes, parent education, media campaigns, community organization, and local policy changes.

Functional Family Therapy (FFT) is aimed at delinquent youth who might otherwise be removed from their homes and separated from their families. Participating youth attend 12 one-hour sessions over three months, although more difficult cases may require more time. Family members also participate in certain phases of the program. In studies, some 80 percent of families receiving FFT services completed the treatment. Of those, 19.8 percent of youth committed an offense the following year, compared to 36 percent of similarly situated juveniles who did not participate in the program. The cost of FFT is between $700 and $1,000 per family for the duration of the program, compared to $6,000 for juvenile detention and $13,500 for residential placement for a comparable period of time.

Multisystemic Therapy (MST) is designed to help parents deal with their child's behavior problems and to assist the juvenile in coping with problems that arise within the family as well as at school, among peers, and in the neighborhood. Treatment sessions are held in the home, at school, and in community settings. Therapists with low caseloads are available to families 24 hours a day, seven days a week, and provide family therapy, parenting counseling, and cognitive behavior therapies. Studies of MST have shown reductions of up to 70 percent in the rates of rearrest, and reductions of up to 64 percent in out-of-home placements.

Multidimensional Treatment Foster Care (MTFC) closely supervises foster families, trains foster parents in parenting techniques, and supervises foster youth in the home, at school, and in the community. An MFT case manager works with the foster parents on each youth's schedule of activities and behavior expectations. There are three levels of supervision, each less structured that the previous level. During a 12-month followup study, MTFC youth committed an average of 2.6 offenses, compared to 5.4 offenses among non-MTFC youth. Youth participants also spent fewer days in lockup than juveniles in other community-based programs.

Quantum Opportunities Program (QOP) serves juveniles from families on public assistance. Each QOP coordinator provides mentoring and other services to no more than 25 high-risk juveniles entering the ninth grade. The four-year program includes 250 hours of tutoring and computer-based instruction, career and college planning, and community service opportunities. In a pilot test of QOP from 1989 through 1993, 63 percent of participants graduated from high school, compared to 42 percent of similarly-situated nonparticipants, and participants were almost three times as likely to attend college than nonparticipants.

---

[1] Arlen Egley, Jr., and Christina E. O'Donnell. "Highlights of the 2007 National Youth Gang Survey." Washington, D.C.: U.S. Department of Justice, *OJJDP Fact Sheet*, Office of Juvenile Justice and Delinquency Prevention, April 2009, pp. 1–2.

[2] Lyn Mikel Brown, Meda Chesney-Lind, and Nan Stein. "Patriarchy Matters: Toward a Gendered Theory of Teen Violence and Victimization." *Violence Against Women* 13 (2007): 1,249–1,273.

[3] *Youth Violence: A Report of the Surgeon General,* Office of the Surgeon General of the United States, 2001, p. 9; Bureau of Justice Statistics, U.S. Department of Justice. *Sourcebook of Criminal Justice Statistics 2003,* table 3.43.

[4] Linda A. Teplin. "Assessing Alcohol, Drug, and Mental Disorders in Juvenile Detainees." Washington, D.C.: U.S. Department of Justice. *OJJDP Fact Sheet,* Office of Juvenile Justice and Delinquency Prevention, January 2001, pp. 1–2.

[5] Ann H. Crowe and Linda Sydney. "Developing a Policy for Controlled Substance Testing of Juveniles." *JAIBG Bulletin,* Office of Juvenile Justice and Delinquency Prevention, May 2000, p. 12.

[6] Anne L. Stahl. "Drug Offense Cases in Juvenile Courts, 1989–1998." Washington, D.C.: U.S. Department of Justice. *OJJDP Fact Sheet,* Office of Juvenile Justice and Delinquency Prevention, September 2001, p. 1.

[7] ———. "Drug Offense Cases in Juvenile Courts, 1985–2004." Washington, D.C.: U.S. Department of Justice. *OJJDP Fact Sheet,* Office of Juvenile Justice and Delinquency Prevention, February 2008, pp. 1–2.

[8] *2000 Arrestee Drug Abuse Monitoring Program Report*, National Institute of Justice, 2000, p. 17.

[9] L. D. Johnston, P. M. O'Malley, J. G. Bachman, and J. E. Schulenberg. *Monitoring the Future: National Results on Adolescent Drug Use; Overview of Key Findings, 2007*. Bethesda, Md.: National Institute on Drug Abuse, p. 12.

[10] *2000 National Household Survey on Drug Abuse*. U.S. Department of Health and Human Services, Substance Abuse and Mental Health Services. Washington, D.C.: 2001, p. 33.

[11] Andrew Golub and Bruce D. Johnson. "The Rise of Marijuana as the Drug of Choice Among Youthful and Adult Arrestees." *Research in Brief*, National Institute of Justice, June 2001, p. 2.

[12] Johnston et al. *Monitoring the Future 2007*, pp. 47–48.

[13] ———. *Monitoring the Future 2007*, pp. 38–39.

[14] ———. *Monitoring the Future 2007*, p. 27.

[15] *Pulse Check: Trends in Drug Abuse, January–June, 2001*. Washington, D.C.: Office of National Drug Control Policy, November 2001, p. 1.

[16] Johnston et al. *Monitoring the Future 2007*, pp. 47–48.

[17] James C. Howell. "Youth Gangs: An Overview." Washington, D.C.: Department of Justice, *OJJDP Juvenile Justice Bulletin*, Office of Juvenile Justice and Delinquency Prevention, August 1998, p. 8.

[18] Walter B. Miller. *The Growth of Youth Gang Problems in the United States: 1970–98*. Washington, D.C.: Office of Juvenile Justice and Delinquency Prevention, 2001, p. 6.

[19] David Starbuck, et al. "Hybrid and Other Modern Gangs." Washington, D.C.: *OJJDP Juvenile Justice Bulletin*, Office of Juvenile Justice and Delinquency Prevention, December 2001, p. 9.

[20] David M. Allender. "Gangs in Middle America." Washington, D.C.: *FBI Law Enforcement Bulletin*, December 2001, p. 3.

[21] National Youth Gang Center. "National Youth Gang Survey Analysis." Available online. URL: http://www.iir.com/nygc/nygsa/. Accessed August 17, 2009.

[22] Lee Baca, quoted in Carla Rivera. "Gang Shootings Rise." *Los Angeles Times* (12/7/01) p. B1.

[23] Arlen Egley, Jr., and Mehala Arjunan. "Highlights of the 2000 National Youth Gang Survey." Washington, D.C.: Department of Justice. *OJJDP Fact Sheet*, Office of Juvenile Justice and Delinquency Prevention, February 2002, p. 2.

[24] David Starbuck, et al. "Hybrid and Other Modern Gangs." Washington, D.C.: U.S. Department of Justice. *OJJDP Juvenile Justice Bulletin*, Office of Juvenile Justice and Delinquency Prevention, December 2001, p. 5.

[25] Joan Moore and John Hagedorn. "Female Gangs: A Focus on Research." Washington, D.C.: U.S. Department of Justice. *OJJDP Juvenile Justice Bulletin*, Office of Juvenile Justice and Delinquency Prevention, March 2001, p. 4.

[26] Karl G. Hill, et al. "Early Precursors of Gang Membership: A Study of Seattle Youth." Washington, D.C.: U.S. Department of Justice. *OJJDP Juvenile Justice Bulletin*, Office of Juvenile Justice and Delinquency Prevention, December 2001, p. 8.

[27] R. Dinkes, J. Kemp, and K. Baum. *Indicators of School Crime and Safety: 2008*. Washington, D.C.: National Center for Education Statistics, Institute of Educa-

tion Sciences, U.S. Department of Education; and Bureau of Justice Statistics, Office of Justice Programs, U.S. Department of Justice. 2009, p. 100.

28 Gary D. Gottfredson and Denise C. Gottfredson. "Gang Problems and Gang Programs in a National Sample of Schools." Ellicott City, Md.: Report, Gottfredson Associates, Inc., October 2001, p. 3.

29 Dinkes, et al. *Indicators of School Crime and Safety: 2008*, p. 81, table 3.1.

30 ———. *Indicators of School Crime and Safety: 2008*, p. 6.

31 Margaret Small and Kellie Dressler Tetrick. "School Violence: An Overview." Washington, D.C.: U.S. Department of Justice. *OJJDP Juvenile Justice Bulletin*, Office of Juvenile Justice and Delinquency Prevention, June 2001.

32 "Where'd They Get Their Guns? An Analysis of the Firearms Used in High-Profile Shootings, 1963–2001." Washington, D.C.: Violence Policy Center, 2002, p. 14.

33 "Timeline of U.S. Shootings." *U.S. News & World Report*. Available online. URL: http://www.usnews.com/articles/news/national/2008/02/15/timeline-of-school-shootings.html. Posted February 15, 2008.

34 Mary Ellen O'Toole, Ph.D. "The School Shooter: A Threat Assessment Perspective." Washington, D.C.: Report, Federal Bureau of Investigation, 1999, p. 20.

35 "School-Associated Violent Deaths in the United States, 1994–1999." Washington, D.C.: Report, Centers for Disease Control and Prevention and U.S. Department of Education, 2001, p. 6.

36 Dinkes et al. *Indicators of School Crime and Safety: 2008*, pp. 46–47.

37 ———. *Indicators of School Crime and Safety: 2008*, p. 14–15.

38 ———. *Indicators of School Crime and Safety: 2008*, pp. 80–81.

39 ———. *Indicators of School Crime and Safety: 2008*, pp. 16–17.

40 ———. *Indicators of School Crime and Safety: 2008*, pp. 48–51.

41 ———. *Indicators of School Crime and Safety: 2008*, pp. 54–58.

42 ———. *Indicators of School Crime and Safety: 2008*, pp. 32–34.

43 ———. *Indicators of School Crime and Safety: 2008*, pp. 36–39.

44 J. A. Hunter. "Understanding Juvenile Sex Offenders: Research Findings and Guidelines for Effective Management and Treatment." Charlottesville: *Juvenile Justice Fact Sheet*, Institute of Law, Psychiatry, and Public Policy, University of Virginia, 2000, p. 2.

45 Charles Puzzanchera and Melissa Sickmund. *Juvenile Court Statistics, 2005*. Pittsburgh, Pa.: National Center for Juvenile Justice, 2008.

46 Meghan C. Black. "Juvenile Delinquency Probation Caseload, 1989–1998." Washington, D.C.: U.S. Department of Justice. *OJJDP Fact Sheet*, Office of Juvenile Justice and Delinquency Prevention, January 2002, p. 1.

47 Howard N. Snyder and Melissa Sickmund. *Juvenile Offenders and Victims: 2006 National Report*. Washington, D.C.: Office of Juvenile Justice and Delinquency Prevention, U.S. Department of Justice, 2007.

48 William J. Sabol, Todd D. Minton, and Paige M. Harrison. "Prison and Jail Inmates at Midyear 2006." Washington, D.C.: U.S. Department of Justice. *Bureau of Justice Statistics Bulletin*, June 2007, p. 4.

49 Jolanta Juszkiewicz. "Youth Crime/Adult Time: Is Justice Served?" Washington, D.C.: Report, Building Blocks for Youth, October 2000, p. 2.

[50] Lori Dorfman and Vincent Schiraldi. "Off Balance: Youth, Race & Crime in the News." Washington, D.C.: Building Blocks for Youth, April 2001, p. 4.

[51] *Youth Violence: A Report of the Surgeon General.* Washington, D.C.: Office of the Surgeon General of the United States, 2001, p. 2.

[52] Richard Wiebusch. "Preventing Delinquency through Improved Child Protective Service." Washington, D.C.: U.S. Department of Justice. *OJJDP Juvenile Justice Bulletin,* Office of Juvenile Justice and Delinquency Prevention, July 2001, p. 4.

[53] Sharon Mihalic, et al. "Blueprints for Violence Prevention." Washington, D.C.: U.S. Department of Justice. *OJJDP Juvenile Justice Bulletin,* Office of Juvenile Justice and Delinquency Prevention, July 2001, p. 2.

CHAPTER 2

THE LAW OF JUVENILE JUSTICE

Like adults, juvenile offenders are governed by state laws and prosecuted in state courts. Adult criminal proceedings have always been held to the standards of due process under the law as set forth in the U.S. Constitution. Because juvenile proceedings were historically governed by the principle of *parens patriae* (the state as parent), wide discretion was given to judicial courts in the handling of juvenile offenders. As a result, many of the constitutional guarantees afforded to adult defendants—such as the right to an attorney, the right to confront adverse witnesses, and the privilege against self-incrimination—were ignored in juvenile proceedings, creating great disparity in the way justice was dispensed to adults and juveniles. Beginning in 1966, the U.S. Supreme Court issued a series of seminal decisions that helped to define and clarify juvenile rights under the law. In addition, with the passage of the Juvenile Delinquency Prevention Act of 1972, the federal government codified the handling and processing of juvenile offenders.

FEDERAL LEGISLATION

THE ILLINOIS JUVENILE COURT ACT OF 1899 AND ITS LEGACY

As a result of the Illinois Supreme Court's decision in *People ex rel. O'Connell v. Turner* (1870), Illinois courts lost jurisdiction over status offenders, and delinquents (those charged with crimes) were treated as adults within the Illinois criminal justice system. When arrested, juveniles were detained in jails with adult offenders, and juveniles found guilty in criminal court were sentenced to prison or jail. In Chicago in 1898—one year before the passage of the Illinois Juvenile Court Act—there were some 575 juveniles confined in county jail, and nearly 2,000 more incarcerated in prison, where they often were terrorized by adult inmates.

Social reformers in Chicago not only wanted to change the conditions of confinement of juvenile offenders but saw the need to create a separate

43

justice system for juvenile offenders in which rehabilitation, not punishment, was the central objective. As early as 1892, the Chicago Women's Club had proposed the idea of a special juvenile court, and by 1895 the club had sponsored a bill in the Illinois legislature for the creation of a separate juvenile court and probation system. By 1898, the movement for a juvenile court system had become strong. The following year, 1899, the Illinois Juvenile Court Act became law.

Under the Illinois Juvenile Court Act of 1899, a new judicial jurisdiction was created for both dependents and delinquents that was separate from the adult criminal justice system. Dependent or neglected children could be taken before the juvenile court to determine the necessity of state supervision, and from there could be sent into foster care or to an appropriate institution. Juvenile offenders could be placed on probation by the court or sent to a reformatory. In any case, the Juvenile Court Act strictly forbade sending any child to an institution that housed adult criminal offenders. In addition, the juvenile court was imbued with broad discretion, in keeping with the judicial doctrine of *parens patriae* (the state as parent). The juvenile court was given procedural informality, in contrast to the more formalized manner of handling adult offenders in the criminal justice system.

Key provisions of the Illinois Juvenile Court Act of 1899 included:

- Establishing a special court, or jurisdiction for an existing court, for neglected, dependent, or delinquent children under the age of 16.
- Defining a rehabilitative rather than punitive purpose for the court.
- Establishing the confidentiality of juvenile court records to minimize stigma.
- Requiring juveniles to be separated from adults when placed in the same institution.
- Banning the detention of children under the age of 12.
- Instituting informal procedures within the court.

Once established, the Illinois juvenile court became a model for other states, but it was not the only model. In 1901, Judge Ben B. Lindsey was appointed judge of the county court in Denver, Colorado. Confronted with the case of a young boy charged with larceny, Lindsey began to search for alternative ways of handling juvenile offenders under existing Colorado law. He found it in a Colorado school law that defined an incorrigible child or habitual truant as "a juvenile disorderly person." On that basis, Lindsey requested the district attorney to begin filing complaints against children under the provisions of the Colorado school law that defined them as "juvenile disorderly person[s]," and not as criminal offenders.

The Law of Juvenile Justice

Like the juvenile court under the Illinois Act of 1899, the Lindsey court was informal, with the goal of keeping juveniles out of institutions designed to serve the criminal justice system, including Colorado's state reform schools. Instead, Lindsey sought to rely on probation as the primary means of dealing with status and juvenile offenders. Lindsey established what became known as Saturday morning report sessions, in which the judge would meet with juvenile probationers and their probation officers and teachers to discuss their progress.

Using the Chicago model, and encouraged by the work of Judge Lindsey, juvenile courts began to spread across the United States. Wisconsin and New York established juvenile courts in 1901, and Ohio and Maryland followed in 1902. By 1912, some 22 states had enacted juvenile court laws, and by 1928 only Maine and Wyoming did not have a juvenile court system of some type. The last of these, Wyoming, established a juvenile court in 1945.

Although juvenile court systems were not uniform throughout the states, all of them provided for separate court hearings of juvenile offenders and encouraged the use of probation over incarceration. Most but not all states mandated the separation of juveniles from adults while in detention. For example, North Dakota did not require separate detention of juveniles until 1969, and Maine, not until 1977. There was also a lack of clarity and uniformity on how individual states chose to define delinquency and dependency, setting the stage for the creation of federal guidelines. In 1912, the U.S. Children's Bureau was formed to address matters involving the well-being of American children, including dependents and delinquents. In a study of juvenile court systems conducted in 1918, the Children's Bureau found that young offenders continued to be confined in adult correctional institutions with adult inmates, even in states where such confinement was prohibited by law.

In the 1940s, public trust in the juvenile court system began to wane due to the public perception that juvenile delinquency was on the rise. This concern was heightened in the 1950s with the release of films such as *The Wild One* in 1954 and *Rebel Without a Cause* and *The Blackboard Jungle* in 1955, with their portrayals of alienated and rebellious youth. Pressure for change in the manner of handling juvenile offenders was beginning to mount.

By the 1960s, there was increasing concern over the issue of due process within the juvenile justice system. In 1961, California passed the California Juvenile Court Act, and in 1962 the New York Family Court Act was adopted in the state of New York. The California act, implementing recommendations from a governor's special study commission on juvenile justice, created three distinct classes of juveniles: neglected children, status offenders, and juveniles who violated criminal laws. Also mandated was a two-stage judicial process consisting of an adjudicatory hearing followed by a dispositional hearing. Like the California act, the New York act created three separate categories for children—dependents, status offenders, and criminal offenders. New York also provided for a two-stage hearing process. While the California law afforded the right to counsel to juveniles in certain cases, the New York law went further and gave the right to counsel to all juveniles coming before the court, establishing a system of "law guardians" to represent delinquents as well as status offenders and dependent children.

In 1967, the President's Commission on Law Enforcement and the Administration of Justice released the report *Crime in a Free Society.* Among the report's conclusions were that the juvenile courts had neither abated the "tide of delinquency," nor had they succeeded in "bringing justice and compassion to the child offender." In the view of the commission, juvenile crime appeared resistant to the best-intentioned efforts of the juvenile court system.

Also in 1967, the U.S. Supreme Court issued its ruling in *In re Gault,* granting juvenile offenders at risk of confinement for their offenses four basic rights afforded to adult criminal defendants: Timely notice of the charges, the right to counsel, protection against self-incrimination, and the right to cross-examine witnesses under oath. Following *Gault,* in 1970 the U.S. Supreme Court ruled in *In re Winship* that the standard of proof in juvenile adjudicatory hearings must be the same as in adult criminal trials—proof beyond a reasonable doubt. These landmark decisions seemed to show a willingness by the Court to formalize juvenile court proceedings and bring them more in line with adult criminal court trials. However, in 1971, the U.S. Supreme Court appeared to take a step back by ruling in *McKeiver v. Pennsylvania* that juveniles were not entitled to jury trials in juvenile court proceedings.

These and other decisions by the U.S. Supreme Court required states to formalize juvenile court proceedings in order to incorporate the mandates imposed by high court. In an attempt to assist states and municipalities in conforming to the due process requirements set forth by the U.S. Supreme Court, Congress passed the Juvenile Justice and Delinquency Prevention Act.

In the mid-1940s, New York created a new jurisdictional category, Persons in Need of Supervision (PINS), which included runaways, truants, and other youth who had committed acts that would not be considered criminal if committed by adults. Other states followed, creating a separate category for the "status offender"—derived from the "statutory" definition of delinquency.

Many states began to formally define the purposes of their juvenile courts. These so-called purpose clauses vary considerably from state to state. Some list their goals in detail; others do so broadly. According to *Juvenile Offenders and Victims: 1999 National Report* by Howard N. Snyder and Melissa Sickmund, "several states have purpose clauses that are modeled on the one in the Standard Juvenile Court Act. The Act was originally issued in 1925, but the most influential version was prepared in 1959. The declared purpose was that 'each child coming within the jurisdiction of the court shall receive . . . the care, guidance, and control that will conduce to his welfare and the best interest of the state, and that when he is removed from the control of his parents the court shall secure for him care as nearly as possible equivalent to that which they should have given him."[1] Other states rely on the following four-step approach, according to Snyder and Sickmund: "(a) to provide for the care, protection, and wholesome mental and physical development of children involved with the juvenile court; (b) to remove from children committing delinquent acts the consequences of criminal behavior, and to substitute . . . a program of supervision, care and rehabilitation; (c) to remove a child from the home only when necessary for his welfare or in the interests of public safety; and (d) to assure all parties their constitutional and other legal rights." Some states have also added language to their juvenile purpose clauses to hold juvenile offenders more accountable for criminal behavior by imposing punishment that is consistent with the severity of the offense. (The National Center for Juvenile Justice in Pittsburgh, Pennsylvania, provides an online listing of purpose clauses for each of the 50 states and the District of Columbia at http://www.ncjj.org/stateprofiles.)

THE JUVENILE JUSTICE AND DELINQUENCY PREVENTION ACT OF 1974

The federal government's legislative role in the area of juvenile justice has largely been to set standards for the states governing the treatment of juvenile offenders. In the Juvenile Delinquency Prevention and Control Act of 1968, Congress recommended that cases involving juveniles charged with noncriminal (status) offenses, such as truancy and incorrigibility, be handled outside the juvenile court system. In 1972, the act was revised and renamed the Juvenile Delinquency Prevention Act, and it has since been amended as recently as 2002. Its stated purpose is "to assist states and local communities in providing community-based preventative services to youths in danger of becoming delinquent, to help train individuals in occupations providing such services, and to provide technical assistance in the field." The act authorized the Office of Juvenile Justice and Delinquency Prevention to carry out its mandate.

The act defines juvenile delinquency as the commission of a crime by someone under the age of 18, and it sets forth rules designed to bring states into conformity in the areas of juvenile court procedure and punishment. The following highlights of the act, as currently amended, were provided in *Juvenile Offenders and Victims: 2006 National Report* (Howard N. Snyder and Melissa Sickmund, Office of Juvenile Justice and Delinquency Prevention, March 2006). The act establishes four custody-related requirements:

1. Juveniles charged with status offenses, acts that would not be considered crimes for adults, "shall not be placed in secure detention facilities or secure correctional facilities."
2. Juveniles found to be delinquent, either as status offenders or criminal offenders, "shall not be detained or confined in any institution in which they have contact with adult inmates." This requirement—known as the "sight and sound separation" requirement—mandates that juvenile and adult inmates can neither be permitted to see each other nor to converse with each other. As amended in 1998, brief or accidental contact in nonresidential areas does not constitute a reportable violation.
3. The "jail and lockup removal" requirements, as amended in 1980, mandates that juveniles cannot be detained or confined in adult jails or lockups. Exemptions to the requirement include juveniles waived to adult court held in secure adult facilities awaiting trial on a felony or convicted of a felony. As amended in 1998, the transfer of adjudicated juveniles to adult institutions is permissible once the juvenile has reached the state's age of full criminal responsibility. There is also a six-hour "grace period" that allows adult jails and lockups to hold juveniles until other arrangements can be made. In 1998, the six-hour period was expanded to include six-hours both before and after court appearances. Under certain conditions, jails and lockups in rural areas may hold juveniles for up to 24 hours.
4. The "disproportionate minority contact" requirement, as amended in 2002, requires that states determine the extent to which minority youth have disproportionate numbers of contacts at any stage of the justice process, and demonstrate efforts to reduce the problem.

States must agree to comply with each requirement of the act to be eligible to receive formula grants funds to develop programs for juvenile offenders.

JUVENILE JUSTICE AND DELINQUENCY PREVENTION ACT OF 2002

On October 3, 2002, the U.S. Senate voted to reauthorize the Juvenile Justice and Delinquency Prevention Act. The reauthorization had been passed in the House of Representatives earlier in the year by a vote of 400 to 4.

Among the new provisions to the Juvenile Justice and Delinquency Prevention Act of 2002 is the requirement to develop mental health standards for juvenile offenders.

The 2002 legislation retains the existing prohibition on detaining status offenders in secure correctional facilities and allows runaways to be held in secure facilities pending reunification with their family members. Also, the legislation permits authorities in rural areas to extend from 24 to 48 hours the time period that a juvenile can be held in a jail or other adult correctional facility. This provision was originally created in response to the shortage of dedicated juvenile facilities in rural parts of the United States. In addition, the revised legislation requires states to implement programs aimed at reducing the disproportionate overrepresentation of minorities in the juvenile justice system.

In 2008, Congress began to consider the reauthorization of the Juvenile Justice and Delinquency Prevention Act. In 2009, a version of the reauthorization was approved by the Senate Judiciary Committee with bipartisan support. The act is expected to be approved by Congress, although this has not happened as of this writing (April 2010).

CONSEQUENCES FOR JUVENILE OFFENDERS ACT OF 2002

In 2002, Congress also passed the Consequences for Juvenile Offenders Act, originally created in 1998 to encourage state and local agencies to develop programs that promote greater personal accountability for juvenile offenders. The revised legislation expands services and treatment for juvenile offenders, including the implementation of graduated sanctions programs such as counseling, restitution, community service, and supervised probation. The 2002 legislation also expands substance abuse programs for juvenile offenders, and offers incentives to states and municipalities to develop mental health screening and treatment programs for juvenile offenders.

STATE LEGISLATION

By the 1980s, many states began to pass more punitive laws governing juvenile offenders, particularly serious offenders. Some states removed certain classes of serious offenders from juvenile court jurisdiction, requiring them to face automatic or mandatory waiver to criminal court to be tried as adults. Prosecutors in many states were given discretion to file certain juvenile cases in adult court. Mandatory sentences were legislated for juvenile offenders in some jurisdictions.

Juvenile Crime

During the 1990s, the following five key changes to juvenile laws were enacted in most states in an effort to crack down on juvenile crime:

- *Transfer provisions* made it easier to waive juvenile offenders from juvenile court to criminal court to stand trial as adults.
- *Sentencing authority* gave juvenile courts expanded sentencing options.
- *Confidentiality* laws modified or, in some cases, removed the traditional guarantee of confidentiality to protect against stigma for juvenile offenders.
- *Victims' rights* increased the role of victims of juvenile crime, particularly in the area of restorative justice, by requiring juvenile offenders to repair the harm done to victims and to communities, and to accept responsibility for their crimes.
- *Correctional programming* allowed for the development of corrections programs to deal with the increase of juvenile offenders sentenced as adults and facing longer confinement time as the result of harsher transfer and sentencing laws.

Some states have so-called "once an adult, always an adult" provisions, stating that once a juvenile offender is waived to adult court, even if acquitted, that juvenile will stand trial in adult court for any future criminal offenses.

During 2001, a number of states passed legislation in several key areas of juvenile justice. According to the National Conference of State Legislators, "A top priority for legislatures in 2001 was providing confined juveniles with the tools necessary to successfully contribute to society once they are released."

In the area of corrections and conditions of confinement, Arizona passed legislation (H2282) requiring 40 hours per week of work from juveniles in secured facilities who are not complying with educational requirements. A Louisiana act (H1638) permits juveniles in residential facilities to be held up to six months past the age of 18 in order to complete compulsory education programs. The need for vocational training of confined juvenile offenders was addressed in the legislation by Arkansas (S185), California (S768), Mississippi (H1109), and Texas (H1758) requiring some type of vocational training for juveniles during their incarceration. The Arkansas and Texas laws require appropriate vocational training for confined female juvenile offenders. In 2001, laws forbidding correctional staff employees from engaging in sexual activities were passed in Arizona (H2284), Illinois (H2088), and Virginia (H2631).

State legislation in 2001 gave judges in some states wider discretion when imposing dispositions on juvenile offenders. In Nevada, legislation was passed (A174) allowing the juvenile court to order certain juvenile offenders to visit their county morgue as a means of demonstrating the consequences of violence. New Jersey (S1515) and Oregon (S230) passed legislation in 2001 requiring psychological counseling for juveniles who commit animal abuse.

Addressing gang-related criminal activity by juveniles, Colorado passed legislation (H1187) creating a new category of offenses for the recruitment of gang members, while Florida (H695) enhanced existing penalties for crimes committed "for the purpose of benefiting, promoting, or furthering the interests of a gang." In 2001, Mississippi passed legislation (S2895) allowing law enforcement officers to confiscate at any time firearms, ammunition, and other dangerous weapons in the possession of known gang members.

Several states expanded their sex offender registries to include juveniles in 2001. Ohio (S3) extended sex offender registration to include juveniles 14 years of age or older who commit certain sexual offenses. Oklahoma legislators enacted the Juvenile Sex Offender Registration Act (S157), and Texas passed legislation (H1118) that requires the posting of photographs of certain juvenile sex offenders on state sex offender registries.

In the area of mental health and substance abuse treatment for juveniles, Texas passed legislation (H1901) in 2001 that implements programs to identify and treat juveniles with mental health problems and substance abuse disorders who are at risk of entering the juvenile justice system. Alaskan lawmakers passed legislation (H179) creating a juvenile alcohol treatment pilot program that provides for the screening and monitoring of juveniles adjudicated for offenses involving the use of drugs or alcohol.

A continuing priority for state legislators in 2001 was school safety. Arkansas (H1583) and Virginia (H2841) passed legislation authorizing law enforcement agencies to disclose to schools the name of any student who is arrested or adjudicated for a criminal offense. Similarly, legislation passed in 2001 in Colorado (H1168) mandates the juvenile court to notify school officials when a petition is filed against a juvenile for certain offenses, and South Dakota legislation (H1004) requires notification of school officials when a minor is adjudicated in juvenile court and the petition is found to be true (guilty). Louisiana legislation (H1805) passed in 2001 requires juvenile courts to release the records of juveniles whose offenses involve the use of a deadly weapon, and North Dakota enacted legislation (H1267) that permits the disclosure of court files and records of juvenile offenders deemed to present a danger to themselves or to others.

In 2001, several state legislatures set guidelines broadening access to juvenile records, including Illinois (H2088), Maryland (H453), Missouri (H236), New Jersey (S1641), Texas (H1118), and Wyoming (H100). Nevada passed legislation (A294) that prohibits the automatic sealing of juvenile records if they contain certain offenses that would constitute a crime if committed by an adult.

California passed legislation (A701) that a written notice for a juvenile to appear before a probation officer may include an order for the juvenile to be fingerprinted and photographed—which are generally allowed only at the time of booking for a criminal offense. Hawaii passed legislation (H1255) creating a procedure for including the fingerprints of juvenile offenders in the state's automated fingerprint identification system.

The criteria for waiving/transferring juveniles to adult criminal court were expanded in 2001. Montana passed legislation (H195) adding certain drug offenses to its list of offenses that allow juveniles to be waived to criminal court. South Dakota enacted legislation (H1109) that permits juveniles convicted as adults to be detained in adult correctional facilities.

Since 2001 there have been relatively few changes to states' laws. The past several years have shown a reversal of many of the prior decade's laws that sought greater punishments for juveniles and increased numbers of youth being transferred to criminal court. Some states, such as Delaware (SB 200, June 2005) and Illinois (SB 283, August 2005), limit the types of cases that are automatically transferred to criminal court, while other states, such as Indiana (HB 1122, 2008) and Virginia (HB 3007, 2007), ended their "once an adult, always an adult" clauses. Connecticut has made a more substantial change by raising the age at which juvenile court jurisdiction ends for all youth, regardless of crimes, from 16 to 18 (SB 1500/ Public Act 07-4, 2007).

U.S. SUPREME COURT CASES

KENT V. UNITED STATES
383 U.S. 541 (1966)

Background

Morris Kent was 16 and on probation from a previous juvenile offense when, on September 5, 1961, he was taken into custody for entering the apartment of a woman in Washington, D.C., taking her wallet, and raping her. After being detained and interrogated by District of Columbia police, Kent admitted that he had participated in the crime. He was arrested for residential burglary, robbery, and rape. As a minor, Kent was subject to the exclusive jurisdiction of the District of Columbia Juvenile Court. However, the juvenile court waived its jurisdiction over Kent and sent his case to the U.S. District Court for the District of Columbia, where Kent was criminally prosecuted as an adult and convicted of six counts of residential burglary and robbery. Kent was acquitted of two counts of rape by reason of insanity.

The Law of Juvenile Justice

Legal Issues

At the time the juvenile court was considering waiving the case to adult criminal court, Kent's attorney filed motions requesting a hearing on the waiver and access to the juvenile court's file on Kent from his prior juvenile offense. The juvenile court did not rule on these motions. Instead, the court waived Kent to criminal court, stating that it was within its power to do so based on current law at that time. In criminal court, Kent's attorney moved to dismiss the case on the ground that the juvenile court had acted improperly and, therefore, the adult court had no jurisdiction over Kent. The motion was overruled and the trial went forward, resulting in conviction. On appeal, Kent's attorney argued for a reversal of the conviction because, by waiving the case to adult court without a hearing, the juvenile court had deprived Kent of his right to due process—to present evidence opposing the waiver. The U.S. Court of Appeals for the District of Columbia disagreed and let Kent's conviction stand by affirming the verdict of the trial court. The case was then appealed to the U.S. Supreme Court on the same central issue—that Kent had been deprived of his right to due process, as guaranteed in the Fourth Amendment to the Constitution.

Decision

In a 5-4 decision announced on March 21, 1966, the Supreme Court reversed the ruling of the Court of Appeals. Writing for the majority, Justice Abe Fortas held that the juvenile court's order waiving the case to adult criminal court was invalid "because of the Juvenile Court's failure to grant a hearing, to give [Kent's] counsel access to the records requested, and to state reasons for its order waiving jurisdiction . . ." The case was remanded (returned) to the trial court with an order to hold a hearing on the waiver of the case from juvenile to adult court. The Supreme Court then laid out the following factors to be considered at the hearing in deciding if the case should be moved from juvenile to criminal court:

- "The seriousness of the alleged offense to the community and whether the protection of the community requires waiver (to criminal court).
- Whether the alleged offense was committed in an aggressive, violent, premeditated or willful manner.
- Whether the alleged offense was against persons or against property, greater weight being given to offenses against persons, especially if personal injury resulted.
- The prosecutive merit of the complaint of the complaint (i.e., whether there is evidence upon which a Grand Jury [would] be expected to return an indictment).

- The desirability of trial and disposition of the entire offense in one court [if] the juvenile's associates in the alleged offense are adults who will be charged with a crime in [adult court].
- The sophistication and maturity of the juvenile as determined by consideration of his home, environmental situation, emotional attitude and pattern of living.
- The record and previous history of the juvenile, including previous contacts with . . . other law enforcement agencies, juvenile courts . . . prior periods of probation . . . or prior commitments to juvenile institutions.
- The prospects for adequate protection of the public and the likelihood of reasonable rehabilitation of the juvenile (if he is found to have committed the alleged offense) by the use of procedures, services and facilities currently available to the Juvenile Court."

Impact

Although the *Kent* decision technically applied only to the District of Columbia courts, its effects were precedent setting in the area of juvenile waivers—more commonly known today as transfer provisions. The *Kent* ruling put all 50 states on notice that juveniles waived to adult court had the right to a hearing, the right to counsel, and the right of access to court and social-services records. Effectively, it gave juveniles the right to due process under the law. Prior to *Kent*, the equal protection clause of the Fourteenth Amendment was generally accepted to mean that juveniles, as a certain class of people, could receive less due process because they received the "compensating benefit" of the court's greater concern for the interests of the child's welfare and rehabilitation. This was an outgrowth of the British concept of *parens patriae* (the state as parent). *Kent* challenged the concept of *parens patriae* as the guiding principle of the juvenile courts and put juveniles facing waiver to criminal court on the same constitutional footing as adult criminal defendants in terms of their right to due process.

IN RE GAULT
387 U.S. 1 (1967)

Background

Gerald Gault, age 15, was on probation for being in the company of another boy who took a wallet from a woman's purse. On June 8, 1964, four months into his probationary period, Gault was taken into custody by the sheriff of Gila County, Arizona, for making obscene phone calls to a neighbor. He was transported to the Children's Detention Home and confined there. Neither of Gault's parents were notified of his arrest or detention. Not until that evening, after Gault's mother returned home from work and went looking for him, did she find out what had happened. The next day a hearing was held in juvenile court. The petition, or complaint, filed with the court was not served on Gault's parents prior to the hearing. No criminal charges were alleged in the petition, only the statement that "said minor is under the age of eighteen years, and is in need of the protection of this Honorable Court." The neighbor who had accused Gault of making the obscene phone calls did not attend the hearing. There was limited testimony by Gault's mother and a deputy sheriff who recalled that "Gault had admitted making the lewd remarks." The judge ordered a continuance, and Gault was returned to the Children's Detention Home, where he was confined for several more days before being returned home. At the continued hearing on June 15, the neighbor who had accused Gault of making the obscene calls once again did not appear—despite a personal request by Gault's mother. Gault was adjudicated delinquent and committed to a state reform school until he reached the age of 21—in six years. Under Arizona law at that time, the maximum sentence for an adult convicted of a comparable offense was a fine of $50 or imprisonment of not more than two months.

Legal Issues

The Fourteenth Amendment to the U.S. Constitution, Section 1, states in part, "No State shall make or enforce any law which shall abridge the privileges or immunities of citizens of the United States; nor shall any State deprive any person of life, liberty, or property, without due process of law; nor deny to any person within its jurisdiction the equal protection of the laws." Gault contended that his fundamental right to due process and equal protection had been violated in a number of areas, including the right to notice of charges, the right to counsel, the right to question witnesses, and the right of protection against self-incrimination. Because there were no court transcripts of the juvenile hearings, Gault also contended that he had been denied the right to a transcript of the proceedings. At that time, under Arizona law there was no process in place for appellate review of juvenile matters. As a recourse, a writ of habeas corpus was brought on behalf of Gault before the Arizona Supreme Court and the matter was referred to the Superior Court for a hearing. One of those called to testify was the judge who had presided at Gault's juvenile hearings. When asked under what section of the law he had found Gault to be delinquent, the judge responded, in part, "I think it amounts to disturbing the peace. I can't give you the [penal code] section." Nonetheless, the Superior Court held that Gault's Fourteenth Amendment right to due process and equal protection under the law had not been violated—and the Arizona Supreme Court later agreed. The matter was then accepted for review by the U.S. Supreme Court.

Decision

With one dissent by Justice Potter Stewart, the Supreme Court reversed the ruling by the Arizona Supreme Court. Citing *Kent v. U.S.*, the court extended the right of due process beyond the juvenile waiver to criminal court, stating that "when [juvenile] proceedings may result in incarceration in an institution of confinement, 'it would be extraordinary if our Constitution did not require the procedural regularity and exercise of care implied in the phrase *due process.*'" Writing for the majority, Justice Fortas held that in juvenile proceedings "due process requires . . . that adequate written notice be afforded the child and his parents or guardian," that "the child and his parents must be advised of their right to be represented by counsel and, if they are unable to afford counsel, counsel will be appointed to represent the child," that "the constitutional privilege against self incrimination is applicable," and that "absent a valid confession a juvenile . . . must be afforded the rights of confrontation and sworn testimony of witness available for cross-examination." In the view of the court, Gault was entitled to these protections because rather than being helped by the juvenile court he was being punished, as an adult would be punished in criminal court.

Impact

The *Gault* decision, in the wake of *Kent*, firmly established that juveniles facing incarceration were entitled to due process under the law. In guaranteeing the right of due process to juveniles, *Gault* reined in the wide discretionary powers that had been afforded to juvenile courts up to that time and rejected the doctrine of *parens patriae* (the state as parent) as the guiding principle behind juvenile justice. As Justice Fortas noted in his written decision: "Juvenile court history has again demonstrated that unbridled discretion, however benevolently motivated, is frequently a poor substitute for principle and procedure." Juvenile court judges and hearing officers would henceforth be expected to uphold the highest standards of principle and procedure guaranteed in the U.S. Constitution. Although the court in *Gault* did not rule on a juvenile's right to appellate review or to transcripts of juvenile proceedings, it encouraged states to provide those rights.

IN RE WINSHIP
397 U.S. 358 (1970)

Background

In 1967, at the age of 12, Samuel Winship was charged with entering a locker in a store and stealing $112 from a woman's purse. A store employee claimed to have witnessed Winship fleeing the scene of the theft. Others in the store at the time expressed doubt at the store employee's account of events, saying they did not believe the employee was in a position to have seen the crime. In New York family court Winship was adjudicated delinquent (guilty) of "an act that, if done by an adult, would constitute the crime of Larceny." Instead of being held to the adult standard of guilt—beyond a reasonable doubt—Winship was adjudicated delinquent based on preponderance of the evidence, a lesser standard applied at that time in juvenile and civil courts in New York State. Winship was ordered placed in a juvenile training school until his 18th birthday—a period of almost six years.

Legal Issues

At adjudication, the judge acknowledged that proof of Winship's offense—the store employee's account of seeing Winship flee that was refuted by others—did not necessarily establish guilt beyond a reasonable doubt. Winship's attorney contended that the Fourteenth Amendment's guarantees of due process and equal protection under the law required that the standard of proof in criminal court of "beyond a reasonable doubt" should equally apply in juvenile proceedings. The judge disagreed and, instead, relied on the "preponderance of evidence" standard in accordance with state law. The Appellate Division of the New York Supreme Court agreed, although it did so without issuing an opinion. The matter was then taken before the New York Court of Appeals. With Chief Judge Fuld in dissent, the Court of Appeals also affirmed the juvenile court's finding and sustained the constitutionality of the New York State statute that authorized the application of the "preponderance of evidence" standard in juvenile adjudications.

Decision

Voting 6 to 3 to reverse the ruling by the New York Court of Appeals, the U.S. Supreme Court echoed the dissent of Chief Judge Fuld: ". . . that where a 12-year-old child is charged with an act of stealing which renders him liable to confinement for as long as six years, then, as a matter of due process . . . the case against him must be proved beyond a reasonable doubt." Relying heavily on *In re Gault*, the Supreme Court took point-by-point exception with the Court of Appeals' ruling: "In effect, the Court of Appeals distinguished the proceedings [Winship's adjudication] from a criminal prosecution by use of what *Gault* called the 'civil' label of convenience which has been attached to juvenile proceedings. . . . The Court of Appeals also attempted to justify the preponderance standard on the related ground that juvenile proceedings are designed 'not to punish, but to save the child.' However, *Gault* expressly rejected this justification. . . . Finally, we reject the Court of Appeals' suggestion that there is . . . only a 'tenuous difference' between the reasonable-doubt and preponderance [of evidence] standards. In this very case, the judge's ability to distinguish between the two standards enabled him to make a finding of guilt that he conceded he might not have made under the standard of proof beyond a reasonable doubt." The Court underscored its reliance upon *Gault* by concluding that "the constitutional safeguard of proof beyond a reasonable doubt is as much required during the adjudicatory stage of a delinquency proceeding as are those constitutional safeguards applied in *Gault*—notice of charges, right to counsel, the rights of confrontation and examination, and the privilege against self-incrimination."

Impact

By requiring that criminal standard of proof beyond a reasonable doubt be applied to juvenile proceedings, the *Winship* court built upon the guarantees previously won in *Kent* and *Gault*—the requirement of due process when waiving minors to criminal court and, for juveniles facing incarceration, the rights to notice and counsel, the right to question a witness, and the right against self-incrimination. The old machinery of juvenile justice was effectively being dismantled. Even if delinquency hearings did not conform with all of the requirements of a criminal trial, with *Kent, Gault*, and now *Winship*, the Court was emphatic in saying that juveniles must be afforded the essentials of due process and fair treatment as guaranteed by the Fourteenth Amendment.

MCKEIVER ET AL. V. PENNSYLVANIA
403 U.S. 528 (1971)

Background

Joseph McKeiver, age 16, and a large group of other juveniles chased three minors and took 25 cents from them. In May 1968, McKeiver was charged with robbery, larceny, and receiving stolen goods—all felonies under Pennsylvania law at that time. McKeiver was adjudicated delinquent in the Court of Common Pleas of Philadelphia County and placed on probation. Eight months later, in January 1969, 15-year-old Edward Terry was charged with assault and battery on a police officer and conspiracy—misdemeanors under Pennsylvania law at that time. He, too, was adjudicated delinquent in the Court of Common Pleas of Philadelphia County. Because Terry had a juvenile record, he was committed to the Youth Development Center in Cornwells Heights.

Legal Issues

Although McKeiver and Terry were adjudicated in separate proceedings by different judges, each of their attorneys had moved for a trial by jury under the due process clause of the Fourteenth Amendment—and each was denied. Because the cases were taken up on appeal on the issue of whether there was a constitutional right to trial by jury in juvenile cases, the Supreme Court of Pennsylvania consolidated them. With one justice dissenting, the Court affirmed both previous juvenile court rulings that the due process right to a jury trial did not extend to juveniles. When the matter was taken up by the U.S. Supreme Court, the cases were further consolidated with a group of juvenile cases from North Carolina in which the same issued had been raised at each of the adjudications. The central issue before the Court was essentially whether the due process guarantees for juveniles that had been won in *Gault* and *Winship* had effectively laid the groundwork to bring juvenile proceedings further in line with criminal trials by extending the Sixth Amendment's guarantee of an impartial jury "in all criminal proceedings."

Decision

The Court affirmed the previous rulings in both Pennsylvania and North Carolina—that due process does not afford to juveniles the right to trial by jury. As Justice Harry Blackmun wrote, "The applicable due process standard in juvenile proceedings is fundamental fairness, as developed by *In re Gault* and *In re Winship*, which emphasized factfinding procedures, but in our legal system the jury is not a necessary component of accurate factfinding." In seeking to balance the need for due process guarantees with the benefits of the juvenile court, the Court contended that jury trials would threaten the confidentiality of juvenile proceedings and create an atmosphere more adversarial and less amenable to the needs of minors. In so ruling, the Court made clear that while certain due process guarantees had brought juvenile proceedings more in line with criminal trials, the two systems were separate. The gains in *Gault* and *Winship* were not to come at the expense of losing the unique characteristics of the juvenile court. As Justice Blackmun concluded: "If the formalities of the criminal adjudicative process are to be superimposed upon the juvenile court system, there is little need for its separate existence. Perhaps that ultimate disillusionment will come one day, but for the moment we are disinclined to give impetus to it."

Impact

While in *Gault* and *Winship* juveniles had won more due process rights, the *McKeiver* court sought to protect some of the unique features of proceedings. In particular, the Court preserved some of the latitude afforded to the juvenile court officer as the sole trier of fact and arbiter of guilt or innocence. In that sense, the Court seemed to be reaffirming the principle of *parens patriae* that it had previously refuted in *Kent* and *Gault*. Justice Blackmun wrote, "Equating the adjudicative phase of the juvenile proceeding with a criminal trial ignores the aspects of fairness, concern, sympathy, and paternal attention inherent in the juvenile court system."

BREED V. JONES
421 U.S. 519 (1975)

Background

On February 9, 1971, a petition was filed in the Juvenile Court of Los Angeles County alleging that Gary Jones, 17, had committed armed robbery. Jones was ordered detained until his hearing on March 1, 1971. At the adjudication hearing, two witnesses testified against Jones. The allegations were found to be true and the Juvenile Court sustained the petition and found Jones to be delinquent. At the March 15 disposition (sentencing) hearing, the Juvenile Court indicated its intention to find Jones "unfit" for juvenile rehabilitation and to waive his case to criminal court. A week's continuance was granted when Jones's attorney stated that he had not been informed this was going to be a fitness (waiver) hearing. At the continued disposition hearing, Jones was declared "unfit" for treatment as a juvenile and ordered to be prosecuted as an adult in criminal court, where subsequently he was found guilty of robbery.

Legal Issues

On appeal, Jones's attorney argued that the transfer of Jones to adult court after his adjudication in juvenile court had placed him in double jeopardy—being put on trial twice for the same crime—in violation of the Fifth Amendment to the U.S. Constitution. Jones's attorney contended that jeopardy—the risk of loss of liberty that is associated with criminal prosecution—had attached (become effective) at the time Jones was adjudicated delinquent in juvenile court, and that in criminal court Jones was effectively put at jeopardy for second time when he was tried for the same offense. The U.S. District Court for the Central District of California disagreed, holding in part that "even assuming jeopardy attached during the preliminary juvenile proceedings . . . it is clear that no new jeopardy arose by the juvenile proceeding sending the case to the criminal court." That decision was later reversed when the U.S. Court of Appeals for the Ninth Circuit held that the double jeopardy clause of the Fifth Amendment applied equally to criminal trials and to juvenile proceedings because of the juvenile court's power "to impose severe restrictions upon the juvenile's liberty."

Decision

In a unanimous decision, the U.S. Supreme Court affirmed the ruling by the U.S. Court of Appeals and held that Jones had been placed in double jeopardy when he was adjudicated in juvenile court and tried in criminal court for the same offense. Citing *Gault* and *Winship* in his opinion for the Court, Chief Justice Warren Burger wrote: "Although the juvenile court system had its genesis in the desire to provide a distinctive procedure and setting to deal with the problems of youth . . . our decisions in recent years have recognized that there is a gap between the originally benign conception of the system and its realities. . . . We believe it is simply too late in the day to conclude, as did the District Court in this case, that a juvenile is not put in jeopardy at a proceeding whose object is to determine whether he has committed acts that violate a criminal law and whose potential consequences include both the stigma inherent in such a determination and the deprivation of liberty for many years." The Court expressed particular concern over the inherent unfairness to a juvenile offender when a waiver proceeding is conducted after an adjudication. As Chief Justice Burger wrote, ". . . a juvenile, thought to be the beneficiary of special consideration [afforded by the juvenile court], may in fact suffer substantial disadvantages. If he appears uncooperative, he runs the risk of an adverse adjudication, as well as of an unfavorable dispositional recommendation [to criminal court]. If, on the other hand, he is cooperative, he runs the risk of prejudicing his chances in adult court if transfer is ordered. We regard a procedure that results in such a dilemma as at odds with the goal that, to the extent fundamental fairness permits, adjudicatory hearings be informal and nonadversary."

Impact

Building on its earlier decisions in *Kent*, *Gault*, and *Winship*, the court further formalized the juvenile court proceeding and refuted the concept of juvenile adjudications as preliminary hearings. Waiver hearings could no longer be conducted postadjudication or be held out as a "carrot" or "stick" to induce a juvenile offender's cooperativeness during adjudication. Henceforth, in appropriate cases, waiver hearings were mandated prior to adjudication, before jeopardy attached to the juvenile. Consequently, waiver hearings—known as "fitness hearings" in many states—have evolved into a type of proceeding unlike any other in criminal law—a kind of preliminary minitrial in which the minor is presumed guilty, but only for the purpose of determining if the minor is "fit" for juvenile court or "unfit" and transferred to criminal court.

OKLAHOMA PUBLISHING CO. V. DISTRICT COURT
430 U.S. 308 (1977)

Background

On July 29, 1976, 11-year-old Larry Donnell Brewer appeared at a detention hearing in Oklahoma City Juvenile Court on delinquency charges alleging second-degree murder for the fatal shooting of a railroad switchman three days before. News reporters were present in the courtroom during the hearing and learned Brewer's name. Afterward, while being escorted from the courthouse, Brewer was photographed by a newspaper photographer. Several articles stating Brewer's name and using his photograph were subsequently published in newspapers within the county, including three newspapers in Oklahoma City owned by Oklahoma Publishing Company. Brewer's name was also broadcast by radio stations, and television stations showed film footage of Brewer and identified him by name. On August 3, Brewer was arraigned at a closed hearing, where the judge issued an order enjoining (prohibiting) the news media from publishing Brewer's name or photograph during a pending juvenile proceeding.

Legal Issues

Oklahoma Publishing Company moved to quash (void) the judge's order on the grounds that it was a violation of freedom of the press, as guaranteed by the Fourth Amendment to the U.S. Constitution. Their motion was denied by the District Court and, later, by the Oklahoma Supreme Court, which held that in accordance with state law at that time juvenile proceedings were to be conducted in private "unless specifically ordered by the judge to be conducted in public." The court also held that juvenile records were open to public inspection "only by order of the court to persons having a legitimate interest therein." The publication of Brewer's name and photograph were viewed by both courts as violations of state laws designed to protect and safeguard the rights of juveniles and, as such, Oklahoma Publishing Company had a legal duty not to publish them.

Decision

The U.S. Supreme Court disagreed and held that the orders of the state appellate courts "abridge[d] the freedom of the press in violation of the Fourth and Fourteenth Amendments" to the U.S. Constitution. In its ruling, the Court relied on two previous decisions it had recently handed down. In *Cox Broadcasting Company v. Cohn* (1975, 420 U.S. 469), the Court ruled it was unconstitutional for a state court to impose sanctions on a newspaper for the publication of a rape victim's name that was "publicly revealed in connection with the prosecution of the crime." Similarly, in *Nebraska Press Association v. Stuart* (1976, 427 U.S. 539), the Court held as unconstitutional an order prohibiting the publication of information tending to show the guilt of a defendant as revealed at a preliminary hearing because "once a public hearing has been held, what transpired there could not be subject to prior restraint." The Oklahoma appellate courts had found *Cox Broadcasting* and *Nebraska Press* inapplicable because Oklahoma state law at that time clearly mandated that juvenile hearings were to be held in private and imposed severe restrictions on access to juvenile court records. The Supreme Court countered that *Cox Broadcasting* and *Nebraska Press* were controlling legal precedent because ". . . members of the press were in fact present at [Brewer's] hearing with the full knowledge of the presiding judge, the prosecutor, and the defense counsel. No objection was made in the presence of the press in the courtroom or the photographing the juvenile as he left the courthouse . . . [Hence] the name and picture of the juvenile were 'publicly revealed in connection with the prosecution of the crime,' much as the name of the rape victim in *Cox Broadcasting* was placed in the public domain." In essence, because the press was given unqualified access to Brewer's juvenile proceedings, without legal objection, Oklahoma Publishing Company was not duty bound under state law to protect Brewer's confidentiality and was free to report on him.

Impact

In *Oklahoma Publishing*, the Supreme Court brought juvenile proceedings another step closer to conforming with adult criminal court by ruling that the confidentiality traditionally afforded juvenile proceedings did not trump freedom of the press as guaranteed by the Fourth Amendment. Although the news media remains circumspect in reporting the identity of many juvenile offenders, *Oklahoma Publishing* freed the press to report on minors as if they were adults when their names are placed in the "public domain." Some of the most prevalent examples of this are school shootings in which the offenders are usually minors—an area specifically addressed by the Court in the next case.

FARE, ACTING CHIEF PROBATION OFFICER, V. MICHAEL C. 442 U.S. 707 (1979)

Background

On January 19, 1976, Robert Yeager was murdered during a robbery of his home in Van Nuys, California. Several weeks later, 16-year-old Michael C., a probationer since the age of 12, was taken into custody for the crime, based in part on a witness's description of him near the Yeager home shortly before the murder. After advising him of his rights under *Miranda v. Arizona*, police began their questioning of Michael C. The following exchange took place:

> *Police: Do you want to give up your right to have an attorney present here while we talk about [the Yeager murder]?*
>
> *Michael C.: Can I have my probation officer here?*
>
> *Police: Well, I can't get a hold of your probation officer right now. You have the right to an attorney.*
>
> *Michael C.: How [do] I know you guys won't pull no police officer in and tell me he's an attorney?*

Michael C. then agreed to talk to the police outside the presence of either probation officer or an attorney and proceeded to make a series of incriminating statements. A petition was filed in juvenile court alleging that Michael C. had murdered Robert Yeager.

Legal Issues

At the adjudication hearing, Michael C.'s attorney moved to suppress the incriminating statements made to the police, arguing that Michael C.'s request to see his probation officer at the onset of the questioning amounted to an invocation of his Fifth Amendment right to remain silent, just as if Michael C. had requested to see an attorney. In support of the suppression motion, Michael C.'s probation officer testified that he had instructed Michael to contact him immediately if Michael ever had "a police contact." Ruling that the facts in the case demonstrated "a clear waiver" by Michael C. of his right to remain silent, the juvenile court denied the motion. The juvenile court noted Michael C.'s previous contacts with police and that Michael C. was not "a young, naïve minor with no experience with the courts." The California Court of Appeal affirmed the juvenile court's dismissal of the motion to suppress; however, in a divided vote, the California Supreme Court reversed the ruling and held that Michael C.'s "request to see his probation officer at the commencement of interrogation negated any possible willingness on his part to discuss his case with the police [and] thereby invoked his Fifth Amendment privilege." The California Supreme Court found "that a close relationship between juveniles and their probation officers compelled the conclusion that a probation officer, for purposes of *Miranda*, was sufficiently like a lawyer to justify extension of the . . . rule."

Decision

The U.S. Supreme Court voted 5 to 4 to reverse the California Supreme Court and restored the lower courts' ruling that held that statements made by Michael C. during a police interrogation were properly obtained and admissible as evidence against the minor. Writing for the majority, Justice Blackmun drew a sharp distinction between the role of an attorney and that of a probation officer: "For where an attorney might well advise his client to remain silent in the face of interrogation by the police . . . to protect to the extent of his ability the rights of his client, a probation officer would be bound to advise his charge to cooperate with the police. . . . We thus believe it clear that the probation officer is not in a position to offer the type of legal assistance necessary to protect the Fifth Amendment rights of an accused undergoing custodial interrogation that a lawyer can offer." Justice Blackmun went on to state that "The State cannot transmute the relationship between probation officer and juvenile offender into the type of relationship between attorney and client that was essential to the holding of *Miranda* simply by legislating an amorphous 'duty to advise and care for the juvenile defendant.'" The Court also noted that Michael C. had "voluntarily and knowingly" waived his Fifth Amendment rights and had consented to allow the police interrogation to continue past the point where he had asked to see his probation officer.

Impact

While juvenile offenders, due to their age and inexperience, may be placed at a higher risk of self-incrimination than adults during an unsupervised police interrogation, *Michael C.* established that statements made can be used against them absent a specific request to see an attorney or a refusal to respond to police questioning. The holding by the court was also tempered with the caution that any decision about a juvenile's waiver of Fifth Amendment rights must to be made on "a case-by-case" basis, leaving room for fairly wide interpretation by state courts.

EDDINGS V. OKLAHOMA
455 U.S. 104 (1982)

Background

On April 4, 1977, 16-year-old Monty Lee Eddings and several younger companions went on a joyride in a car owned by Eddings's older brother. On the Oklahoma Turnpike, Eddings, who was driving, briefly lost control of the car and was ordered to pull over by Officer Crabtree of the Oklahoma Highway Patrol. Eddings complied. When Officer Crabtree approached the car, Eddings fired a loaded shotgun that he had brought along, killing Crabtree. The state successfully moved to have Eddings stand trial as an adult, and the ruling was upheld on appeal. Eddings was convicted in criminal court on a plea of nolo contendere and was sentenced to death.

Legal Issues

At the sentencing hearing, the state alleged three of the aggravating circumstances listed in the Oklahoma death penalty statute at that time—namely, "that the murder was especially heinous, atrocious, or cruel; that the crime was committed for the purpose of avoiding or preventing a lawful arrest; and that there was a probability that the defendant would commit criminal acts of violence that would constitute a continuing threat to society." In mitigation, Eddings presented evidence of his troubled youth. His supervising probation officer testified that from the age of five Eddings had lived with his divorced mother without proper supervision due to his mother's alcoholism, and that by the age of 14 Eddings could no longer be controlled and was sent to live with his father, who beat Eddings. Other witnesses testified that Eddings was emotionally disturbed at the time of the crime. A sociologist who specialized in juvenile offenders testified that Eddings "was treatable," as did a psychiatrist who stated that he did not believe Eddings would pose a future threat to society if he was given proper treatment. In his ruling to impose the death penalty, the trial judge stated, "[The] Court cannot be persuaded entirely by the fact . . . that the youth was sixteen years old when this heinous crime was committed. Nor can the Court in following the law, in my opinion, consider the fact of this young man's violent background." On appeal, the Oklahoma Court of Criminal Appeal agreed with the trial court and affirmed the death sentence.

Decision

In a 5 to 4 ruling, the U.S. Supreme Court reversed the decision "to the extent that it sustains the imposition of the death penalty," and remanded the case to Oklahoma state courts for a new sentencing hearing. The Court held that Eddings had been sentenced to death without proper consideration given to all mitigating factors as required by the Eighth and Fourteenth Amendments to the U.S. Constitution—such as "any aspect of the defendant's character or record and any of the circumstances of the offense that the defendant proffers as a basis for a sentence less than death." The Court took issue with the trial judge's refusal to consider Eddings's violent background. Writing for the majority, Justice Powell held that ". . . just as the chronological age of a minor is itself a relevant mitigating factor of great weight, so must the background and mental and emotional development of a youthful defendant be duly considered in sentencing." Justice Powell clarified that, while age was an important factor in mitigation, the court was not suggesting "an absence of legal responsibility where a crime is committed by a minor. We are concerned here only with the manner of the imposition of the ultimate penalty: the death sentence imposed for the crime of murder upon an emotionally disturbed youth with a disturbed child's immaturity."

Impact

While stopping short of deciding whether the death penalty imposed on a minor violated the Eighth Amendment's constitutional prohibition against "cruel and unusual punishment"—an issue the Court would later rule on in *Thompson v. Oklahoma* (1988) and *Stanford v. Kentucky* (1989)—*Eddings* established that juveniles facing "the ultimate penalty" in criminal court must be afforded the same measure of mitigation as adults. For juveniles, factors in mitigation were no longer limited to the minor's age but were broadened to include the minor's background as well as the minor's mental and emotional development.

SCHALL V. MARTIN
467 U.S. 253 (1984)

Background

Gregory Martin was 14 years old at the time of his arrest on December 13, 1977. Martin was charged with first-degree robbery, second-degree assault, and criminal possession, arising out of an incident in which he and two others allegedly hit a youth on the head with a loaded gun and stole the youth's jacket and sneakers. After his arrest, Martin was detained overnight pending his initial appearance hearing in New York Family Court the following day. Citing Martin's possession of a loaded gun, the false address he initially gave to police, and the fact that the incident took place at 11:30 P.M. as evidence of lack of supervision, the judge ordered Martin detained as a preventive measure because of the "serious risk" that Martin might reoffend if released. Martin remained detained for a period of 15 days prior to his adjudication, when he was found to be delinquent and placed on two years' probation.

Legal Issues

Martin challenged the fairness of the preventive detention on the grounds that it constituted a violation of the due process and equal protection clauses of the Fourteenth Amendment. The District Court rejected the equal protection argument but agreed that the pretrial detention was a violation of Martin's right to due process. The Court gave the following three reasons for its ruling:

1. Pretrial detention without a probable cause hearing was a violation of due process, per se.
2. It was impossible to reliably predict which juveniles would reoffend if released.
3. Preventive detention amounted to punishment imposed without an adjudication of guilt.

The Court then ordered the immediate release of all juveniles who were in preventive detention under New York's Family Court Act, as Martin had been. In affirming the ruling, the New York Court of Appeals held that, "the vast majority of juveniles detained under [the Family Court Act] either have their petitions dismissed before an adjudication of delinquency or are released after adjudication [as Martin was when placed on probation]. . . . [Preventive detention] is utilized principally . . . to impose punishment for unadjudicated criminal acts."

Decision

In a 6 to 3 decision, the U.S. Supreme Court reversed the appellate decisions and ruled that the state law passed constitutional muster on two key grounds: (1) By serving the legitimate objective of protecting the juvenile and society from the potential consequences of the juvenile's criminal acts, and (2) by satisfying the procedure safeguards of due process because the preventive detention was limited by the statue to 17 days. In his opinion for the majority, Justice Rehnquist wrote that by ruling as they did in this case, the appellate courts "would apparently have us strike down New York's preventive detention statute on two grounds: first, because the preventive detention of juveniles constitutes poor public policy, with the balance of harms outweighing any positive benefits either to society or to the juveniles themselves, and, second, because the statute could have been better drafted to improve the quality of the decision-making process. But it is worth recalling that we are neither a legislature charged with formulating public policy nor an American Bar Association committee charged with drafting a model statute. The Question before us today is solely whether the preventive detention system chosen by the State of New York and applied by the New York Family Court comports with constitutional standards. Given the regulatory purpose for the detention and the procedural protections that precede its imposition, we conclude that [the statute] is not invalid under the Due Process Clause of the Fourteenth Amendment."

Impact

In *Schall v. Martin*, the court appeared ready to reassert the doctrine of *parens patriae* (state as parent) that had been the guiding principle of the juvenile justice system prior to *Kent, Gault,* and *Winship*. As the Court itself noted, "There is no doubt that the Due Process Clause is applicable in juvenile proceedings. . . . But the Constitution does not mandate the elimination of all differences in the treatment of juveniles. The State has 'a *parens patriae* interest' in preserving and promoting the welfare of the child." Much as the Court had ruled in McKeiver that juveniles did not have the right to a trial by jury, the Court in *Schall v. Martin* carved out another area—preventive detention—that separates the juvenile justice system from the adult justice system.

NEW JERSEY V. T.L.O.
469 U.S. 325 (1985)

Background

On March 7, 1980, a teacher at Piscataway High School in New Jersey discovered T.L.O., a 14-year-old freshman, and another female student smoking in a rest room in violation of school rules. Both students were taken to the principal's office. T.L.O.'s companion admitted that she had been smoking, but T.L.O. denied doing so. The principal demanded to see T.L.O.'s purse, opened it, and found inside a pack of cigarettes and a package of cigarette rolling papers. Suspecting that the rolling papers were evidence of marijuana use, the principal thoroughly searched T.L.O.'s purse and found a small amount of the drug along with a pipe, plastic baggies, cash, and two letters implicating T.L.O. in dealing marijuana. The principal notified T.L.O.'s mother and summoned the police. Later, after being transported to the police station by her mother, T.L.O. confessed to selling marijuana at the high school. On the basis of her confession and the evidence seized by the principal during his search of T.L.O.'s purse, T.L.O. was adjudicated delinquent and placed on probation for one year.

Legal Issues

At her adjudication T.L.O. moved to suppress the evidence as well as her confession, both of which she claimed were tainted by an unlawful search of her purse. In denying the motion, the juvenile court held that, although the Fourth Amendment applied to searches conducted by school officials, "a school official may properly conduct a search of a student's person if the official has a reasonable suspicion that a crime has been or is in the process of being committed *or* reasonable cause to believe that the search is necessary to maintain school discipline or enforce school policies." In applying this standard to the search of T.L.O.'s purse, the juvenile court found that the principal's initial decision to open the purse was justified based on the "reasonable suspicion" that T.L.O. had violated a school rule by smoking in the lavatory, and that once the purse was open "evidence of marijuana violations was in plain view, and [the principal] was entitled to conduct a thorough search to determine the nature and extent of T.L.O.'s drug-related activities." On appeal, the Appellate Division affirmed the juvenile court's finding that there had been no Fourth Amendment violation as to the search of T.L.O.'s purse; however, the court vacated the adjudication of delinquency and remanded the case to the juvenile court to determine if T.L.O. had "knowingly and voluntarily" waived her Fifth Amendment right against self-incrimination before confessing to police. On appeal as to the constitutionality of the search of T.L.O.'s purse, the Supreme Court of New Jersey reversed the Appellate Division and held that the search of the purse was unreasonable and, therefore, unconstitutional.

Decision

The U.S. Supreme Court reversed the New Jersey court and held that, although the Fourth Amendment prohibition on unreasonable searches and seizures applied to searches conducted by school officials, school searches were distinguished in two ways. First, the Court held that school officials were not required to obtain a warrant before searching a student who was under their authority. Second, the Court eased the "probable cause" requirement that the subject of the search had violated a law and applied a lesser standard of "reasonableness" to student searches. In applying this standard to *T.L.O.*, the Court echoed the ruling of the juvenile court judge that because T.L.O. had been caught smoking, the subsequent search of her purse for cigarettes was "reasonable," and that the discovery of cigarette rolling papers "gave rise to a reasonable suspicion that [T.L.O.] was carrying marijuana . . . and this suspicion justified the further exploration that turned up more evidence of drug-related activities." In so ruling, the Court sought to strike a balance between "the efforts of school authorities to maintain order in their schools" and, at the same time, "ensure that the interests of students will be invaded no more than is necessary to achieve the legitimate end of preserving order in the schools."

Impact

By easing the standard for school searches from a "probable cause" belief that a student is engaging in unlawful conduct to the "reasonableness" standard, the Court granted wide latitude to school officials. A minor infraction or even "suspicious" behavior could henceforth give rise to a "reasonable cause" on the part of school officials to conduct a legal search of a student. As Justice Stevens wrote in his partial dissent, "The rule the Court adopts [in T.L.O.] is so open-ended that it may make the Fourth Amendment virtually meaningless in the school context."

THOMPSON V. OKLAHOMA
487 U.S. 815 (1988)

Background

On the night of January 23, 1983, in Grady County, Oklahoma, William Wayne Thompson, 15, and three older friends beat and murdered Thompson's former brother-in-law, Charles Keene. Their alleged motive was to avenge Keene's physical abuse of Thompson's younger sister. Thompson was charged with the crime and his case was waived to adult court, due in part to Thompson's past violent behavior and the brutal nature of the homicide. At Thompson's trial, the prosecutor displayed color photographs of the victim's body to support the state's argument that Thompson's crime was "especially heinous, atrocious, or cruel" in order to satisfy the statutory requirements to establish aggravating circumstances necessary to seek the death penalty. Thompson was convicted of first-degree murder and the trial judge accepted the jury's recommendation that Thompson be executed for his crime.

Legal Issues

The Oklahoma Court of Appeals affirmed Thompson's conviction and sentence. The court of appeals held that a minor fit to stand trial as an adult may be punished as an adult, and that sentencing a minor to death did not violate the cruel and unusual punishment clause of the Eighth Amendment to the U.S. Constitution. As to the gruesome photographs of the victim admitted at trial, the Court of Appeals declared that although their admission was improper, it constituted harmless error because even without the photos there was overwhelming evidence of Thompson's guilt.

Decision

Although unable to agree on a single opinion, five justices of the U.S. Supreme Court agreed that imposing the death penalty in this case constituted a violation of the cruel and unusual punishment clause of the Eighth Amendment. The Court remanded the case to the Court of Appeals with instructions to vacate Thompson's death sentence. Justice John Paul Stevens, in an opinion joined by Justices William J. Brennan, John Marshall, and Harry Blackmun, held that the execution of any person under 16 at the time of the commission of the offense "would offend civilized standards of decency . . . and the principle that less culpability should attach to crimes

71

committed by juveniles," and therefore violated the Eighth Amendment's prohibition of cruel and unusual punishment. Justice Stevens also expressed that the admission of the victim's photographs at trial was not a factor in the decision. In her concurring opinion, Justice Sandra Day O'Connor expressed the view that the "fact that 18 legislatures . . . have set the minimum age for capital punishment at 16 or above, coupled with the fact that 14 other States have rejected capital punishment completely, suggests the existence of a [national] consensus" forbidding the execution of anyone under 16 years of age. In his dissent, Justice Antonin Scalia—joined by Justices William Rehnquist and Byron White—refuted the idea of a national consensus against executing anyone under the age of 16 and warned that suggesting such a consensus may place unwarranted restraints on states when legislating laws on the use of capital punishment. (Justice Anthony Kennedy did not participate in the-decision.)

Impact

In the six years between *Eddings* (1982) and *Thompson* (1988), the Supreme Court rejected five requests to consider the constitutionality of sentencing juveniles to death. In *Thompson*, only four of the justices (Stevens, Brennan, Marshall, and Blackmun) were in agreement that imposing the death penalty upon a juvenile offender constituted cruel and unusual punishment. Justice O'Connor, while concurring, was at odds with the death penalty as applied in *Thompson* because Oklahoma had set no minimum age for the imposition of the death penalty, thereby violating the standard of "special care and deliberation" required in capital cases. As a result, the *Thompson* decision would apply only to juveniles under the age of 16 at the time of their offense. Juveniles 16 years of age or older at the time of their offense were still technically eligible for the death penalty, as would be established by the Court the following year in *Stanford v. Kentucky* and *Wilkins v. Missouri*.

STANFORD V. KENTUCKY WILKINS V. MISSOURI
492 U.S. 361 (1989) CONSOLIDATED

Background

On January 7, 1981, in Jefferson County, Kentucky, Kevin Nigel Stanford, 17, and a companion robbed a gas station of cigarettes, fuel, and cash. During and after the robbery, Stanford and his companion raped and sodomized a female employee at the gas station, then drove her to a secluded area where Stanford shot her to death. Due to Stanford's prior history of delinquency and the seriousness of the crime, Stanford was waived to adult court. He was convicted of murder, first-degree sodomy, first-degree robbery, and receiving stolen property, and was sentenced to death. In the second case, during the attempted robbery of a convenience store in Avondale, Missouri, on July 27, 1985, 16-year-old Heath Wilkins stabbed to death a 26-year-old mother of two working behind the sales counter. Wilkins was certified for trial as an adult and pleaded guilty to first-degree murder, armed criminal action, and carrying a concealed weapon. The trial court found that there were aggravating circumstances in the commission of the crimes and sentenced Wilkins to death.

Legal Issues

Both cases were reviewed by state appellate courts, but on different issues. In *Stanford*, the Kentucky Supreme Court affirmed the death sentence and rejected Stanford's contention that as a juvenile he had a right to treatment. The court held that "there was no program or treatment appropriate for [Stanford] in the juvenile justice system," and that "age and the possibility that he might be rehabilitated were mitigating factors appropriately left to the consideration of the jury that tried him." In *Wilkins*, the Missouri Supreme Court affirmed the death sentence and rejected Wilkins's argument that it violated the Eighth Amendment's prohibition of cruel and unusual punishment. The U.S. Supreme Court consolidated the cases and granted review "to decide whether the Eighth Amendment precludes the death penalty for individuals who commit crimes at 16 or 17 years of age."

Decision

In a 5 to 4 decision, the U.S. Supreme Court affirmed the rulings by the Kentucky and Missouri courts and held that imposing the death penalty on youths who were 16 or 17 years of age at the time of their crimes did not violate standards of decency and, therefore, was permissible under the Eighth Amendment. The dissenting Justices—Brennan, Marshall, Blackmun, and Stevens—were the same four who had joined in the *Thompson* decision that executions of youths under the age of 16 constituted cruel and unusual punishment. In writing for the majority, Justice Scalia held: "The punishment is either 'cruel *and* unusual' (i.e., society has set its face against it) or it is not. The audience for these arguments, in other words, is not this Court but the citizenry of the United States. It is they, not we, who must be persuaded. . . . We discern neither a historical nor a modern societal consensus forbidding the imposition of capital punishment on any person who murders at 16 or 17 years of age." In writing the dissenting opinion, Justice Brennan disagreed: "There are strong indications that the execution of juvenile offenders violates contemporary standards of decency: a majority of States decline to permit juveniles to be sentenced to death; imposition of the sentence upon minors is very unusual even in those States that permit it; and respected organizations with expertise in relevant areas regard the execution of juveniles as unacceptable, as does international opinion. These indicators serve to confirm in my view . . . that the Eighth Amendment prohibits the execution of persons for offenses they committed while below the age of 18, because the death penalty is disproportionate when applied to such young offenders and fails measurably to serve the goals of capital punishment."

Impact

As a measure of the effect of *Stanford* and *Wilkins*, the rate of juveniles sentenced to death dropped slightly in the late 1980s, as reported "Juveniles and the Death Penalty" (Lynn Cothern, Office of Juvenile Justice and Delinquency Prevention, November 2000). However, according to Cothern, in the 1990s the rate of death sentences imposed on juvenile offenders under 18 leveled out to between 2 percent and 3 percent of all sentences. Whether or not this offends "contemporary standards of decency" continues to be a matter of considerable debate among the general public as well as members of the U.S. Supreme Court. On October 3, 2002, a divided high court in a 5 to 4 vote denied review in the case *In re Stanford* (No. 01-10009), in which the petitioner, Kevin Nigel Stanford, asked that his sentence of death be overturned on the grounds that the sentence was unconstitutional because he was under the age of 18 when he committed the offense. In his dissent, Justice Stevens, joined by Justices David Souter, Ruth Bader Ginsburg, and Stephen Breyer, wrote that "offenses committed by juveniles under the age of 18 do not merit the death penalty. The practice of executing such offenders is a relic of the past and is inconsistent with evolving standards of decency in a civilized society. We should put an end to this shameful practice."

Justice Stevens cited the case of *Atkins v. Virginia* (536 U.S. 2002), in which the same Supreme Court ruled that the execution of mentally retarded person was unconstitutional. Stevens compared the inability of a mentally retarded person to understand the gravity of the offense with that of a minor. Quoting Justice Brennan in his dissent in *Stanford v. Kentucky*, in which Stevens joined, Stevens wrote, "Proportionality analysis requires that we compare 'the gravity of the offense,' understood to include not only the injury caused, but also the defendant's culpability, with the 'harshness of the penalty.' In my view, juveniles so generally lack the degree of responsibility for their crimes that is a predicate for the constitutional imposition of the death penalty that the Eighth Amendment forbids that they receive that punishment."

Stevens went on to note that "neuroscientific evidence of the last few years has revealed that adolescent brains are not fully developed, which often leads to erratic behaviors and thought processes in that age group . . . Moreover, in the last 13 years, a national consensus has developed that juvenile offenders should not be executed. No state has lowered the age of eligibility to either 16 or 17 since our decision *(Stanford v. Kentucky)* in 1989."

VERNONIA SCHOOL DISTRICT V. ACTON
515 U.S. 646 (1995)

Background

In the fall of 1989, the Vernonia, Oregon, school board approved a student athlete drug policy. Under the terms of the policy, all Vernonia students who participated in a school sports program were required to sign a consent form submitting themselves to drug testing at the start of the season for their sport, as well as random drug testing throughout the season. In the fall of 1999, seventh-grader James Acton signed up to play football for one of the district's schools. Because Acton and his parents refused to sign the student athletic drug policy's consent form, Acton was denied participation.

Legal Issues

The Actons filed suit, alleging in part that the mandatory drug testing violated the Fourth Amendment's prohibition of unreasonable search and seizure. (The U.S. Supreme Court had established legal precedents in several cases that "compelled collection and testing of urine, such as that required by the [Student Athletic Drug] Policy, constitutes a 'search' subject to the demands of the Fourth Amendment.") The United States District Court for the District of Oregon dismissed the Actons' suit. On appeal, the United States Court of Appeals for the Ninth Circuit reversed the district court's judgment and held that Vernonia student athletic drug policy violated both the Federal Constitution's prohibition of unreasonable search and seizure, as well as a similar provision in the Oregon State Constitution.

Decision

The U.S. Supreme Court, in a 6 to 3 ruling, reversed the Ninth Circuit and held that the Vernonia drug testing policy for school athletics did not violate a student's Fourth Amendment right to be free from unreasonable searches. The Court reasoned that since the Vernonia school district had implemented the drug testing policy in response to a demonstrable rise in student drug use, the drug testing policy was reasonable. Building upon its ruling in *T.L.O.* (favoring school searches), Justice Scalia in writing for the majority held that the state's power over schoolchildren "is custodial and tutelary, permitting a degree of supervision and control that could not be exercised over free adults ... [and] for many purposes school authorities act *in loco parentis*, with the power and indeed the duty to 'inculcate the habits and manners of civility'.... Fourth Amendment rights, no less than First and Fourteenth Amendment rights, are different in public schools than elsewhere.... Legitimate privacy expectations are even less with regard to student athletes."

Impact

Building upon *T.L.O.*, the Court expanded the authority of public school officials to control their school environments, particularly in the area of student drug use. The Court went so far as to say that public schools "are different" with regard to a student's right to be free of unreasonable searches as guaranteed by the Fourth Amendment, and came closer to equating the duty of the school with that of parents by giving school officials wide latitude in their ability to monitor student behavior.

ROPER V. SIMMONS
543 U.S. 551 (2005)

Background

In 1993, 17-year-old Christopher Simmons planned and committed capital murder. He led two younger friends (one of whom dropped out before the crime was committed) in a plot to murder Shirley Crook. He had convinced his friends that they could "get away with it" because they were juveniles. Simmons and his co-offender broke into Mrs. Crook's home, bound her hands and blindfolded her, drove her to a state park and threw her off a bridge. Simmons was prosecuted in criminal court and faced overwhelming evidence: He had confessed to the crime and performed a videotaped reenactment of the murder at the crime scene, and the original co-offender who dropped out of the plot testified against him. He was convicted by a jury, who also recommended a death sentence, despite sympathetic testimony from his family and the fact that he had no criminal history.

Legal Issues

Simmons's appeal to the circuit court of Jefferson County, Missouri, was denied, as were his subsequent petitions for state and federal postconviction relief. However, in light of *Atkins v. Virginia* (536 U.S. 2002), in which the Supreme Court prohibited execution of mentally retarded persons, Simmons filed a new petition for state conviction. The new petition argued that, pursuant to the Court's reasoning in *Atkins*, it was unconstitutional to execute anyone who was younger than 18 when a crime was committed. The Missouri Supreme Court agreed, overturning Simmons's death sentence and replacing it with a sentence of life in prison without possibility for parole. This decision was based on the logic that a national consensus had developed against the execution of juvenile offenders in the years since *Stanford v. Kentucky* had been decided. The decision was appealed to the U.S. Supreme Court by the State of Missouri and by the correctional facility where Simmons was held (Donald P. Roper was the facility superintendent).

Decision

In a 5-4 decision, the U.S. Supreme Court upheld the Missouri Supreme Court, finding that it was cruel and unusual to execute anyone who committed a crime while under the age of 18, based on the "evolving standards of decency" test used by the Missouri court. Justice Kennedy, who wrote for the majority (joined by Justices Stevens, Souter, Ginsburg, and Breyer), included several arguments to justify the decision: that recent social science research confirms juveniles' reduced capacity (relative to adults) to make decisions about behavior, that youth under age 18 are prohibited from other legal activities such as voting or serving on juries, and that many states had recently either abolished the death penalty for juveniles or ceased to apply it. The Court also cited the international community, noting that ". . . Only seven countries other than the United States have executed juvenile offenders since 1990: Iran, Pakistan, Saudi Arabia, Yemen, Nigeria, the Democratic Republic of Congo, and China. Since then each of these countries has either abolished capital punishment for juveniles or made public disavowal of the practice. In sum, it is fair to say that the United States now stands alone in a world that has turned its face against the juvenile death penalty." The dissenting justices—Scalia, Rehnquist, and Thomas—questioned whether a national consensus against execution of juveniles did in fact exist and whether such a question was even relevant in the Court's decision. Scalia's dissent also objected to the majority's use of foreign law in interpreting the Constitution.

Impact

Building on *Stanford* and *Atkins*, the Court further restricted capital punishment for vulnerable populations, in this case youth under age 18. The fact that it based its decision on evolving standards of decency and on social science research concerning the immaturity of youth is significant. This turn is also interesting, given that in the 1980s and 1990s almost every U.S. state increased punishments for juvenile offenders and the ability to prosecute juveniles as adults.

Juvenile Crime

SAFFORD UNIFIED SCHOOL DISTRICT #1 V. REDDING
129 U.S. 2633 (2009)

Background

On October 8, 2003, an administrative assistant at Safford Middle School in Safford, Arizona, searched eighth-grader Savanna Redding for drugs. The search took place after a classmate of Redding's, who was found with prescription strength ibuprofen, knives, lighters, and a cigarette, told the school vice principal that Redding had given her the ibuprofen. With the school nurse observing, the school employee asked Redding to remove her shoes and socks, lift up her shirt and pull out her bra band, and take off her pants and pull out the elastic of the underwear. No drugs were found, and Redding denied any knowledge of the pills.

Legal Issues

Redding and her mother brought suit against the vice principal who had requested the search, the administrative assistant who performed it, the nurse who observed it, and the school district, claiming that the strip search violated her Fourth Amendment rights protecting her against unreasonable search and seizure. The district court dismissed the case, stating that the search was permissible in its scope and justified based on the information available. On initial appeal, the U.S. Court of Appeals for the Ninth Circuit affirmed the district court's judgment. However, the case was reheard by the entire court, and the appeals court ruled that the strip search was unjustified and beyond reason given the circumstances.

Decision

The U.S. Supreme Court held in an 8-1 decision that Redding's Fourth Amendment rights were violated when school officials searched her underwear for the ibuprofen. Though the Court agreed that the school had sufficient suspicion to justify searching Redding's outer clothes and backpack, the circumstances did not warrant a strip search. Writing for the majority, Justice Souter stated that during the search, Redding ". . . exposed her breasts and pelvic area to some degree, and both subjective and reasonable societal expectations of personal privacy support treatment of such a search as categorically distinct, requiring distinct elements of justification on the part of school authorities for going beyond a search of outer clothing and belongings." However, the Court also decided that the school officials responsible for the search cannot be held liable. The lone dissenter on the decision was Justice Thomas.

The Law of Juvenile Justice

Impact

Though this decision did not create new law, it did provide limits within which the Court's prior decision allowing school searches under a "reasonableness" standard, *New Jersey v. T.L.O.*, can be applied. The Court's decision was not fully in favor of protecting students from searches, since the Court established that a search was justified and that the school employees could not be held liable, but it did offer a strongly worded rebuke against invasive strip searches.

---

[1] Howard Snyder and Melissa Sickmund. *Juvenile Offenders and Victims: 1999 National Report.* Washington, D.C.: Office of Juvenile Justice and Delinquency Prevention, 1999, p. 33.

CHAPTER 3

THE JUVENILE JUSTICE SYSTEM

Since the early 1950s, the juvenile justice system has undergone changes that have brought it more in line with the adult criminal justice system. Decisions by the U.S. Supreme Court have imbued juvenile court proceedings with a level of due process that was absent historically. Meanwhile, states have made it increasingly easier to allow certain juvenile offenders to be tried as adults. Still, the juvenile justice system of today exists as a separate entity from the criminal justice system, with its own terminology and, relative to the adult system, more of a focus on rehabilitation.

HISTORICAL BACKGROUND

Beginning in England in the early 16th century, statutes known as poor laws allowed local justices of the peace to authorize wardens and overseers to identify homeless, neglected, or delinquent minors in the community, and force them to work in workhouses or apprentice them to masters or families who trained them in agriculture, a trade, or domestic service. Their indentured servitude lasted until they reached the age of 21 and sometimes beyond. This system became the standard for dealing with poor and wayward children for some 200 years and was eventually brought from England to the American colonies. By the late 17th century, poor laws had been passed in both Virginia and Massachusetts. Delinquent minors were either forced into servitude or, for the most serious offenders, punished the same as adults. Some local jurisdictions developed almshouses or poorhouses to house children who were poor, mentally ill, sick, or vagrant—usually in crowded and unsanitary conditions.

By the early 19th century, as the United States became more urbanized and industrialized, the belief arose that urban youth were more prone to engage in disruptive behavior and thus needed to be "saved" by intervention. This became the basis of the child-saving movement and spawned the development of shelter houses for youth, along with educational and social activities, often sponsored by wealthy citizens.

The child-saving movement effectively passed control from the family to the state over certain youthful behaviors, such as drinking, vagrancy, and loitering. Courts were given broader powers to commit runaways and children deemed to be "out of control" by their parents. Institutional programs were created for the handling of these youths, such as the House of Refuge in New York. Founded in 1825, the House of Refuge accepted children sent to it by court order, usually because of vagrancy or neglect, with the purpose of protecting them by taking them off the streets and into a family-like environment. In practice, the House of Refuge operated more like a prison, with strict discipline, separation of the sexes, and harsh work and study schedules. Although a high incidence of runaways eventually forced the House of Refuge to adopt more lenient rules, the concept remained popular. At that time, minors charged with criminal offenses were tried as adults in criminal court and, if convicted, were sent to prison or even executed. Prior to 1900, at least 10 children were executed in the United States for crimes committed when they were 14 years of age or younger, according to *Death Penalty for Juveniles* by Victor Streib.[1] In reaction, juries in the early 19th century began to acquit apparently guilty juvenile defendants (jury nullification) rather than subject them to the harsh sanctions imposed by the criminal justice system. Thus, the need for alternatives to deal with juvenile offenders was filled by the House of Refuge and led to the creation of others like it.

The commingling of juvenile criminal offenders and what are known today as "status offenders" (truants and incorrigibles) led a Pennsylvania man to challenge the involuntary incarceration of his daughter in a house of refuge, claiming the incarceration was illegal. In *Ex parte Crouse* (1839), the Supreme Court of Pennsylvania not only held that the incarceration was justified but refused to examine the procedures for the commitment, the length of the incarceration, or the conditions of the minor's confinement.[2] According to law professor Robert E. Shepherd, Jr., writing in *Juvenile Justice*, "This decision is often credited with originating the use of the doctrine of "parens patriae" to justify informality and paternalism in dealing with children in the courts."[3] (The term, which literally means "father of the country," was originally used in early English equity courts to provide judicial protection for orphans, widows, and others.)

REFORMATORIES

In 1826, the Boston City Council founded the House of Reformation for juvenile offenders. More reform schools followed, by the mid-19th century, in Massachusetts, New York, Ohio, Maine, Rhode Island, and Michigan. Sometimes funded privately, they housed both youthful criminal offenders and children who were deemed to be beyond the control of their parents.

Reformatories tended to take a more punitive approach toward juveniles and eventually replaced houses of refuge.

In *The Child Savers: The Invention of Delinquency*, Anthony M. Platt wrote that reform schools were created to:

- Segregate youthful offenders from adult criminals.
- Imprison youthful offenders "for their own good" by removing them from adverse home environments.
- Provide indeterminate sentences to last until the youth was reformed.
- Be used as punishment if other less restrictive approaches failed.
- Help youthful offenders avoid idleness through military drills, physical exercise, and supervision.
- Reform youthful offenders by focusing on education, with emphasis on vocational programs and religious instruction.
- Teach sobriety, thrift, industry, and prudence.[4]

Legal challenges to the incarceration of status offenders in reformatories eventually succeeded. In the 1870 case of *People ex rel O'Connell v. Turner*, the Illinois Supreme Court ruled that it was unconstitutional to confine a youth to a reform school who had not been convicted of a criminal offense or afforded due process.[5] As a result, the reform school in question eventually closed and many of the juveniles housed there who had been convicted of crimes were sent to adult prisons.

THE JUVENILE JUSTICE AND DELINQUENCY PREVENTION ACT

Enacted in 1974 and reauthorized in 1980, 1992, 1996, and 1998, and 2002, the Juvenile Justice and Delinquency Prevention Act established federal core requirements for the treatment and handling of both status and criminal juvenile offenders. The act institutionalized a federal overseer of juvenile justice—the Coordinating Council on Juvenile Justice and Delinquency Prevention. As an independent body within the executive branch of the federal government, the council monitors the detention of juveniles and coordinates all federal programs relating to delinquency prevention as well as missing and exploited children. Chaired by the U.S. Attorney General, the council was restructured in 1992 to facilitate better coordination with state and local juvenile agencies. An outgrowth of the restructuring was the adoption of the National Juvenile Justice Action Plan, which advocates the following eight key objectives:

- Ensure immediate and appropriate sanctions and treatment services.
- Enhance public safety by prosecuting certain serious and violent juveniles in criminal court.
- Decrease youth involvement in criminal activity, including gang offenses, illegal firearms, and illicit drug use.
- Break the cycle of domestic violence, victimization, and abuse and neglect.
- Create positive opportunities for children and adolescents.
- Mobilize citizens and communities by providing information about problems and solutions within the juvenile justice system.
- Evaluate programs and practices to determine if they are making a significant difference.
- Promote public awareness of juvenile justice issues.

THE JUVENILE JUSTICE PROCESS

The processing of juvenile offenders varies by state and sometimes even by community. However, there are a common series of decision points in the administration of juvenile justice in the United States.

INTAKE

Juveniles come into contact with the police in two ways—by committing a criminal offense or by committing a status offense such as truancy, incorrigibility, or possession or use of alcohol (acts which are not criminal if committed by an adult). Contact with law enforcement may be initiated by a report from a member of the community, or it may be as the result of direct observation of inappropriate behavior by a law enforcement officer. Either way, the first critical decision in the juvenile justice process must be made at this juncture: to release the minor or to take the minor into custody. In making this decision, law enforcement officers attempt to gather as much information as possible at the scene of the alleged offense. If after questioning the minor and any witness, and after looking for possible evidence, the law enforcement officer is convinced that the minor committed no offense, then the minor is released and a report is filed stating that the incident occurred. This report is often referred to as a field interrogation, or FI report. The FI report may be kept for future reference by the law enforcement agency; however, the report is not filed with the juvenile court, nor is it made public.

On the other hand, if the law enforcement officer determines that an offense has been committed, the process becomes more formalized. In the case of a status offense or a minor criminal offense, such as misdemeanor vandalism, a citation is generally issued to the minor and to the minor's parents or guardians, and the minor is released to their custody. The citation usually requires the minor and the minor's parent or guardian to appear in juvenile court to face the specified allegations.

Generally, a juvenile is taken into custody when a law enforcement officer determines that the juvenile has committed a more serious offense, or, when a less serious offense is committed by a juvenile who is currently on probation or has a warrant outstanding for his or her arrest. On being taken into custody, the juvenile must be advised of his or her constitutional rights as mandated in the U.S. Supreme Court's 1966 ruling in *Miranda v. Arizona.* Commonly called a *Miranda* warning, the minor is advised of the right to remain silent, the right to an attorney, and that any of the minor's statements made while in custody can be used against the minor in court.

According to the FBI, in 2001 some 19 percent of juvenile offenders nationwide who were taken into custody were handled informally by the controlling law enforcement agency and released to parents or guardians. About 72 percent were formally referred to the juvenile court. The remaining juveniles were either referred to adult criminal court, referred to another police agency (often as the result of outstanding warrants or other pending cases), or referred to a welfare agency. In 2005, 56 percent of all delinquency cases were formally referred to the juvenile court.[6]

When a juvenile is referred to the juvenile court, either by citation or as the result of being taken into custody, an initial evaluation of the minor is conducted, often referred to as an intake screening. The intake screening is generally performed by a probation officer who gathers information about the incident and the minor's background. This, in effect, works as a screening process for the juvenile court. If no formal court action is deemed necessary the minor is screened out, usually by agreeing to diversion.

DIVERSION

Diversion, also commonly referred to as "informal probation," is the process of directing a juvenile offender from formal processing through the juvenile court to an alternative process that favors an informal resolution that may include seeking community-based assistance for the minor, such as youth development programs or tutoring. There are several advantages to diversion. It avoids the social stigma often associated with formal delinquency adjudication, while at the same time easing the burden on the juvenile court system by reducing caseloads and allowing more resources to be directed at serious juvenile offenders. Also, because diversion programs tend to be community based, they are often able involve the victim and other interested parties in resolving the problem.

Diversion is usually offered by the probation department or local law enforcement agency. Court-ordered diversion exists, but diversion cannot be imposed and must be agreed to by the juvenile offender. The terms of diversion may include community service, restitution (monetary or work), a letter of apology, an essay or art project about the harm caused by the offense, attending classes or support groups, and participation in community activities, mentoring programs, and tutoring programs.

Most diversion programs fall into two main categories: Alternative Dispute Resolution (ADR) or community-based programs. ADR programs often utilize a neutral facilitator to assist in discussing issues and in developing resolutions acceptable to both the juvenile offender and the victim. These types of ADR programs include victim-offender mediation. Other types of ADR programs include teen court, peer juries, and citizen hearing boards. Community-based programs may include mentoring, educational and work programs, and family-focused counseling programs. The goal of both types of diversion programs is to ensure that the juvenile offender receives close supervision and is able to take advantage of opportunities designed to facilitate better socialization and attachment to the community.

In order to ensure fair treatment to all parties involved in the process, a diversion program should fulfill the following requirements:

- Diversion as an alternative to adjudication should be authorized by state statute or court rule, and should be sanctioned by the juvenile court, prosecutor, and public defender.
- The goals and operational procedures of a diversion program should be documented and published, with guidelines on both victim and juvenile offender consent.
- A formal referral process should be in place, and it should include clearly defined eligibility requirements.
- Participation in diversion programs must be voluntary by all parties involved, including the juvenile offender, the offender's family, and the victim.
- Service providers and community volunteers involved in the diversion program should be properly trained and understand the diversion process from both a legal and operational standpoint.
- The terms of diversion should be articulated in a formal written agreement between the juvenile offender and the diversion provider.
- A formal process of review by the juvenile court and by probation should be in place in order to monitor compliance with diversion programs.

- Diversion agreements should contain written conditions that, if successfully completed, there will be no official record or finding of delinquency, and that any records kept during the diversion process will be destroyed.
- Sanctions for failure to fulfill the diversion agreement should be clearly stated and immediately enforced.

If the minor successfully complies with the conditions of so-called informal probation, the matter is dismissed and no juvenile record is created. If the minor fails to meet the conditions, the probation officer generally has two options: Give the minor another chance, or initiate formal juvenile court proceedings and refer the case for an adjudicatory hearing, just as if the initial intake decision had been to proceed formally.

DETENTION

If formal court proceedings are initiated and the minor is taken into custody, either for a status or criminal offense, the next decision point is whether to release the minor to the custody of a parent or guardian or to detain the minor pending adjudication. Usually, a detention hearing is held to determine if keeping the minor in custody is appropriate. Strict limits are placed on the amount of time a minor may be held in custody prior to a detention hearing, usually no more than 24 hours or until the next day court is in session. If that period of time is exceeded, the minor's case may be dismissed.

At a detention hearing, some of the common factors weighed are the need to protect the minor, whether the minor presents a serious danger to self or others, and the likelihood that the minor will return to court for adjudication. The minor has a right to counsel at the detention hearing, and a finding to detain the minor must be supported by factual evidence.

Juvenile detention in secure detention facilities is allowed under the following conditions:

- Detention should be as brief as possible.
- Detained juveniles must be held in a safe and humane environment, with appropriate staffing to ensure both physical and psychological safety.
- Degrees of restriction should be based on the needs of the juvenile offender, from maximum to minimum security.
- The detention of a juvenile offender is lawful in order to prevent further serious or violent delinquent behavior.
- Juveniles may be detained pending a hearing, disposition, or placement.
- Complete clinical services (medical, dental, psychological) should be available from properly credentialed providers.

In addition to traditional detention in a juvenile or adult correctional facility, there are alternative detention programs. These include home detention and supervision programs, which allow juveniles to live at home and attend school. However, home detention requires intensive supervision, often daily by a probation officer, as well as strict curfews and, in some cases, electronic monitoring. Day and evening reporting centers are another form of alternative detention. These programs require the juvenile to check in every day at a designated reporting center in order to participate in structured and closely supervised activities, or to receive counseling, tutoring, or vocational training. Residential programs are another type of detention alternative. These facilities are sometimes referred to as "shelters" where juvenile offenders can receive court-ordered services and participate in programs and activities required by the terms of probation.

In recent years, many states have put measures in place to separate status offenders and criminal offenders in detention facilities. Some states require status offenders to be placed in youth shelters rather than traditional lockups. Under the Juvenile Justice and Delinquency Prevention Act (discussed previously), states receiving federal funds for the administration of juvenile justice programs are required to remove detained juveniles from adult jails, where juveniles are often subjected to physical and sexual abuse. Still, the practice of housing juveniles and adults in the same detention facilities persists throughout the United States, most acutely in rural areas where there are often limited facilities. In "Prison and Jail Inmates at Midyear 2006," William J. Sabol et al. reported that the number of juveniles in local adult jails decreased from 7,615 at midyear 2000 to 6,104 at midyear 2006.[7]

In *Juvenile Court Statistics 2005*, Puzzanchera and Sickmund reported a 18 percent increase in the number of delinquency cases involving detention from 1985 to 2005, increasing from 239,900 to 354,100. According to Puzzanchera and Sickmund, "The largest relative increase was for person offense cases (144 percent), followed by drug offense cases (110 percent), and public order cases (108 percent)." Cases of black juveniles were more likely than those of white juveniles to involve detention, since in 2005 black youth represented 33 percent of the overall delinquency caseload but 42 percent of the detention caseload.

PLEA BARGAINING

Prior to adjudication, a minor may admit (plead guilty to) the allegations contained in the petition, or to less serious allegations, in exchange for more lenient treatment than if the minor were to proceed to adjudication and lose. When a minor makes an admission as part of a plea bargain, the juvenile court requires that the minor knows of the right to an adjudication, that the admission is made voluntarily, and that the minor understands the allegations and the consequences of the plea.

THE ADJUDICATORY HEARING

An adjudicatory hearing, or adjudication, is a trial in juvenile court. Allegations against the juvenile are brought by the prosecutor and are set forth in a petition. A juvenile court officer—usually a judge but sometimes a referee or a commissioner—weighs the evidence against the juvenile. In addition to the usual court personnel of judge, prosecutor, defense attorney, court reporter, and clerk, there may also be a court probation officer from the juvenile probation department in that jurisdiction. The job of the court probation officer is generally one of coordination, such as ensuring that probation reports are received by the court and counsel, or arranging for further detention of the minor or for the release of the minor from custody. Immediate members of the minor's family are allowed in the courtroom, as well, and often their presence is required. In general, the proceedings are closed to the public and to the press, although some states have opened certain juvenile proceedings to the media.

An adjudication is conducted in much the same way as a trial in criminal court. Evidence of guilt is presented by the prosecuting attorney, while the defense presents evidence of innocence or factors in mitigation, such as the minor's history of mental illness or physical or sexual abuse. Witnesses for each side, including experts in mental health, forensics, or other specialties relevant to the case, may be called and cross-examined, and the minor may elect to testify or not. After all of the evidence and testimony have been presented and the prosecutor and defense attorney have made their closing arguments, the judge must then find the allegations in the petition to be true (guilty) or deny the allegations (not guilty), using the standard of proof beyond a reasonable doubt. If the allegations are found to be true, the minor must face disposition (sentencing). Disposition can take place immediately and often does if the minor is placed on probation. Otherwise, a disposition hearing is set for a later date.

DISPOSITION AND TREATMENT

At disposition, a sentence is imposed on the juvenile offender based on the severity of the offense(s) as well as the juvenile's prior record and family history. Usually, the judge has broad discretionary powers as to the type of disposition imposed. At this juncture, the court has the opportunity to place controls or conditions on the minor with the goal of changing the minor's behavior. At its best, the disposition is like an individualized treatment plan for the minor. To determine the appropriate disposition, the juvenile court may consider recommendations from the probation department, from social agencies, and any psychiatric evaluations or psychological assessments.

Disposition recommendations are generally submitted by the probation department to the juvenile court, which in turn issues a disposition order. In general, three basic issues are taken into consideration in recommending and determining an appropriate disposition for a juvenile offender.

- **Public Protection:** Facts relevant to the immediate and long-term risks to the general public are examined in order to keep the community safe.
- **Accountability:** The disposition should reflect the harm caused to the victim and to the community, in an attempt to hold the juvenile offender accountable for criminal actions.
- **Rehabilitation:** An assessment is made regarding the juvenile offender's needs, and appropriate programs and services are ordered by the court based on those needs, and as allowed by local and state law.

Generally, the following dispositional alternatives are available to the court:

- **Dismissal of the Petition:** Generally, this is done when, in the opinion of the court, justice would not be served or the minor would be unfairly harmed by the imposition of any of the other dispositional alternatives.
- **Suspended Judgment:** The court may decline to enter a judgment in the case on the condition that the minor perform certain requirements, such as court-ordered counseling or community service. If the minor successfully completes the requirements, a judgment is not entered.
- **Probation:** A judgment is entered, and the minor is declared a ward of the court and is placed under the legal control of the court. The court imposes conditions such as counseling, community service, and restitution, as well as restrictions on the minor's behavior that may include a curfew or a prohibition against associating with certain individuals or groups, such as gangs. The minor is assigned a probation officer who monitors the minor's progress. Should the minor violate any of the conditions of probation, the minor may be taken into custody and a new adjudicatory process may be initiated—just as if the minor had violated the law.
- **Placement in a Community Treatment Program, Either Public or Private:** These can include group homes, military-style probation camps, or residential treatment facilities for drug abuse or mental health issues. While the minor is confined in a community treatment program, the minor's progress is monitored by a probation officer and a progress report is prepared for the court to review, usually after a period of months. Because the minor is on probation, noncompliance with any of the

conditions of a treatment program can result in a probation violation and an adjudication.

- *Commitment to a State Institution for Juvenile Offenders:* Generally, this is reserved for serious juvenile offenders or for those who have failed at less restrictive levels of disposition. Although counseling and vocational training programs are usually available, state institutions for juvenile offenders are run like prisons. After a period of confinement, the juvenile offender is paroled, just as an adult is paroled from state prison.

Many states have implemented systems of graduated sanctions for juvenile offenders that provide a range of dispositional options like those discussed above. Graduated sanctions allow juvenile courts to apply the least restrictive disposition initially, then move to more restrictive sanctions only if the minor reoffends or violates probation. Under this system, institutionalization is seen as a last resort and is imposed only after efforts at treatment and normalization have failed. The Juvenile Justice and Delinquency Prevention Act of 1974 mandated deinstitutionalization for status offenders. To date, all 50 states have complied at least in part with the mandate.

Since the 1990s a number of states have adopted so-called blended sentencing statutes allowing juvenile courts to impose some combination of juvenile and adult sanctions upon certain juvenile offenders. In *Juvenile Offenders and Victims: 1999 National Report*, authors Snyder and Sickmund identify five types of blended sentencing options that carve out a "middle ground" between juvenile and adult sanctions.

- *Juvenile-Exclusive Blend:* The juvenile court has the discretion to impose either a juvenile sanction or an adult sanction.
- *Juvenile-Inclusive Blend:* The juvenile court may impose a combination of juvenile and adult sanctions.
- *Juvenile-Contiguous Blend:* A juvenile correctional sanction may remain in force after the offender is past the age of the juvenile court's jurisdiction, at which time the offender is transferred to the adult correctional system to complete the sentence.
- *Criminal-Exclusive Blend:* The criminal court may impose a juvenile sanction or an adult sanction.
- *Criminal-Inclusive Blend:* The criminal court may impose both juvenile and adult correctional sanctions.

JUVENILE PROBATION

One of the key features of the Illinois Juvenile Court Act of 1899 was giving the primary responsibility for the handling of juvenile offenders to local probation departments and probation officers. As a result, in 1907 juvenile probation officers formed a professional association known as the National Probation Association (NPA). In 1914, the NPA published *Juvenile Courts and Probation*, which promoted probation as "an active, constructive force in the lives of children under its influence." The book also called for the professionalizing of juvenile probation officers. Consequently, state probation commissions throughout the country designated probation officers as civil service employees and, in many cases, increased their level of training.

By the mid-1960s, as the landmark U.S. Supreme Court decisions in *Kent v. United States* and *In re Gault* formalized juvenile court proceedings, the process of juvenile probation also became more formalized. The broad discretion that had previously been afforded to juvenile courts and juvenile probation officers was no longer legally possible. With these new constraints, the work of probation officers became more formalized and began to shift from a rehabilitative approach to one that was more closely aligned with law enforcement and punishment. This shift in approach continued with the escalation of serious and violent juvenile crime during the 1980s and 1990s.

As juvenile crime rates began to abate in the late 1990s, juvenile probation began to focus on a balanced approach to the treatment of young offenders. Under this approach, the goals of juvenile probation are to protect the community, hold juvenile offenders accountable for their actions, and assist juvenile offenders in developing skills needed to become law-abiding adults. The victims' rights movement also shaped the role of juvenile probation by bringing the victim and the victim's interests into what had once been a strictly offender-focused process of rehabilitation.

Research on the process of adolescent and moral development associated with delinquency has also had an impact on the role of the juvenile probation and on the training of juvenile probation officers. One example of this is the theory of moral development proposed by Lawrence Kohlberg, which identifies the following stages of moral development:

- *Power Orientation:* Doing what is right only as a response to authority or to avoid punishment.
- *Self-Benefit Orientation:* Behaving morally for pragmatic reasons, usually to get something.
- *Approval/Acceptance Orientation:* Seeking approval by being "good" in the eyes of others.
- *Social Contract Orientation:* Recognizing the rights and interests of others.
- *Universal Principles Orientation:* Acting according to ethical principles no matter what others say to the contrary.

Because probation officers often have contact with a juvenile offender at the earliest stages of the juvenile justice process, they are often in a position to identify some of the following risk factors associated with delinquency:

- Individual risk factors, including a sense of alienation and detachment, as well as poor impulse control.
- Peers who may be encouraging delinquent or antisocial behavior.
- Family dysfunction, including physical or sexual abuse, drug abuse, and parents with criminal histories who may be viewed as role models.
- School problems, such as failure of an elementary grade or a general lack of commitment toward education.
- Community risk factors such as high levels of criminal activity in the neighborhood and the availability of guns.

Increasingly, juvenile probation officers must deal with special populations of juvenile offenders. These include juveniles who are alcohol and drug involved, mentally ill, and learning disabled, as well as minorities, females, sex offenders, arsonists, and gang members.

MENTAL HEALTH TREATMENT

A growing area of study is the treatment of mentally ill juvenile offenders. According to the report "Youth with Mental Health Disorders: Issues and Emerging Responses," offenders within the juvenile justice system "experience substantially higher rates of mental health disorders than youth in the general population . . . and it is safe to estimate that at least one out of every five youth in the juvenile justice system has serious mental health problems."[8] In addition, mental illness among juvenile offenders is often exacerbated by substance abuse. One study cited in the report found that some 73 percent of adult jail detainees with serious mental health disorders had a co-occurring substance abuse disorder. According to the report, "Among the juvenile justice system population, the rates may be even higher."

Many mentally ill juvenile offenders do not receive adequate aftercare due to inadequate screening and assessment, the lack of trained correctional staff, and insufficient funding for mental health services. One way of providing better mental health treatment is to divert mentally ill juvenile offenders from the juvenile justice system. According to the report, "Given community concerns about safety, there are youth who, regardless of their mental health needs, will need to be placed in the juvenile justice system because of their serious and violent offenses. For other youth, however, their penetration into the juvenile justice system and placement into juvenile detention and correctional facilities will serve to further increase the number of mentally ill youth in the nation's juvenile facilities who are receiving inadequate mental health services."

One means of diverting mentally ill offenders was the creation of the juvenile mental health court, which handles only those juvenile offenders with diagnosed mental disorders as well as serious learning disabilities. The first such court opened in Los Angeles on October 1, 2001. In addition to a judge, attorneys, and court probation staff, the juvenile mental health court utilizes the services of mental health professionals and school representatives. Unlike traditional juvenile court, the juvenile mental health court views juvenile crime as a symptom of mental illness. Only juveniles who have committed less serious crimes are currently eligible for handling by the Los Angeles Juvenile Mental Health Court.

In addition to screening for mental health, a growing number of juvenile courts have also begun considering juveniles' competence to stand trial. These courts consider whether youth are able to participate in their defense, work appropriately with their attorneys, and understand court proceedings. Youth who are judged to be incompetent, either through immaturity or because of mental health deficits, may either be diverted from court permanently (by having their cases dismissed) or diverted temporarily to treatment before their cases resume.

CORRECTIONAL MODELS

There are four basic correctional models or theories on how best to deal with juvenile offenders in the juvenile justice system. They are the treatment model, the justice model, the crime control model, and the balanced and restorative justice model.

Parens patriae (the state as parent) forms the basis for the treatment model. Under this philosophy, the state must deal with juveniles differently than with adults by using more informal and flexible procedures. The court views delinquency as a symptom of an underlying emotional or personality problem and attempts to treat the minor as an individual, much as a parent would do. The treatment model approach to juvenile offenders was widely promoted by the so-called child savers in the early 20th century, who advocated for the formation of a juvenile court and a separate juvenile justice system, and who tended to focus more on the psychological and social conditions of delinquents than on their crimes.

The medical model, an outgrowth of the *parens patriae* philosophy, views youth crime empirically, as a problem that can be identified, isolated, and treated, much like a disease. Punishment is discouraged as ineffective and harmful to the youthful offender. Advocates of the medical model generally view delinquents as being unable to exercise free choice or to use reason.

The justice model challenges the *parens patriae* philosophy in favor of a due-process-oriented system of juvenile justice, thereby providing more constitutional safeguards for juvenile offenders. Proponents of this model believe that juveniles, like adults, are responsible for their actions and that those who violate the law should be punished in proportion to the severity of their offense. Under the justice model, juvenile courts would move toward a policy of determinate (fixed) sentencing, and correctional programming would be based on compliance with treatment and work programs. Advocates of the justice model seek to further reform the juvenile justice system by decriminalizing status offenses, and require restitution and community service sanctions to give juvenile offenders the opportunity to make amends for the harm they have caused to victims and others.

The crime control model emphasizes punishment over rehabilitation for juvenile offenders. Supporters of the crime control model view punishment as instructive and believe that it instills moral values. Proponents believe that the emphasis on rehabilitation in the juvenile justice system is misguided because most juvenile offenders are not psychologically abnormal and, therefore, require not therapy but consequences for their actions. They also believe that punishment deters juveniles from reoffending.

A fifth model—balanced and restorative justice—builds upon the justice model with the goal of reconciling the interests of the victim, the juvenile offender, and the community. Rather than simply punishing delinquents, proponents of this model advocate holding the offender responsible and encouraging restitution while at the same providing treatment and training to offset the chances of reoffending.

WAIVER OF JURISDICTION

Prior to 1899 in the United States, juvenile offenders were routinely tried as adults. With the establishment of the first juvenile court in Illinois, a separate jurisdiction was created for juveniles with emphasis on rehabilitation over punishment. Nonetheless, states still place certain serious offenses under the sole jurisdiction of the criminal courts, whether committed by a juvenile or an adult.

In general, sending a juvenile to adult court is accomplished in one of three ways. The first method, judicial transfer, is when a juvenile court judge decides to transfer the youth to adult criminal court. This requires a hearing—commonly called a waiver hearing, a transfer hearing, or a fitness hearing (to determine if the minor is "fit" or "unfit" to remain under the juvenile court's jurisdiction). A transfer hearing must take place before the adjudication, as established by the U.S. Supreme Court in the 1975 case *Breed v. Jones*. Unlike other hearings, in a transfer hearing the minor is usually presumed guilty, but only for the purpose of deciding if the minor is to remain in juvenile court or be waived to adult court. After the decision, the minor is then presumed innocent of all charges and proceeds to adjudication or trial.

Judicial transfer has been a part of juvenile court processing since the very first juvenile court opened its doors in 1899. However, in recent years, it has largely been replaced by the other two transfer mechanisms, legislative transfer and direct file, which have become more common. Legislative transfer occurs when a state's laws mandate which youth, defined by age and charged offense, are to be prosecuted directly in criminal rather than juvenile court. Direct file occurs when a prosecutor makes a decision to bypass the juvenile court and directly file an individual case in the criminal court. Neither legislative transfer or direct file requires a juvenile court hearing, unlike judicial transfer.

THE TREATMENT OF JUVENILES
IN THE CRIMINAL JUSTICE SYSTEM

In 1997, the American Bar Association (ABA) created a task force to address the increasing number of juvenile offenders being transferred to the adult court. The task force, a joint effort by the ABA's criminal justice section and juvenile justice committee, released its recommendations in 2001. Titled *Youth in the Criminal Justice System: Guidelines for Policymakers and Practitioners*, the report focused on procedures for the handling of juveniles after they have been transferred to the criminal justice system and set forth the following seven general principles on practices that should be followed at various stages of the criminal justice process:

- Youth are developmentally different from adults, and these developmental differences must be taken into account at all stages and in all aspects of the adult criminal justice system.

- Pretrial release or detention decisions regarding youth awaiting trial in adult criminal court should reflect their special characteristics.

- If detained or incarcerated, youth in the adult criminal justice system should be housed in institutions or facilities separate from adult facilities until at least their 18th birthday.

- Youth detained or incarcerated in the adult criminal justice system should be provided with programs that address their educational, treatment, health, mental health, and vocational needs.

- The right to counsel in the adult criminal justice system should not be waived by a youth without consultation with a lawyer and without a full inquiry into the youth's comprehension of the right and capacity to make the choice intelligently, voluntarily, and understandably. If the right to counsel is voluntarily waived, standby counsel should always be appointed.

- Judges in the adult criminal justice system should consider the individual characteristics of the youth during sentencing.
- The collateral consequences normally attendant to the adult criminal justice process should not necessarily apply to all youth for crimes committed before the age of 18.

JUVENILES AND THE DEATH PENALTY

In the 1989 case *Stanford v. Kentucky*, the U.S. Supreme Court held that the Eighth Amendment does not prohibit the death penalty for juvenile offenders who are 16 or older at the time of their offense. From 1973 through 2001, a total of 213 juvenile death sentences were imposed on offenders who were juveniles at the time of their crimes. Yet in the 2005 case *Roper v. Simmons*, the U.S. Supreme Court prohibited the death penalty for any youth who committed a crime while younger than 18.

A primary reason cited by the Court in its decision was the international condemnation of capital punishment for juveniles. According to law professor Victor L. Streib, in "The Juvenile Death Penalty Today: Death Sentences and Executions for Juvenile Crimes, January 1, 1973–February 28, 2008," the death penalty for juvenile offenders had become "a uniquely American practice, in that it has been abandoned legally by nations everywhere else due to the express provisions of the United Nations Convention on the Rights of the Child and of several other international treaties and agreements."[9] The United Nations Convention (Article 37(a)) states, "Neither capital punishment nor life imprisonment without possibility of release shall be imposed for offences committed by persons below eighteen years of age."

CONFIDENTIALITY

Since the Juvenile Court Act of 1899, juvenile records maintained by law enforcement and the juvenile courts have been kept confidential with the goal of preventing any social stigma for the minor. As the result of the toughening of state laws governing juvenile offenders in the 1990s, the confidentiality traditionally afforded to juveniles offenders has eroded. In many states, once-confidential juvenile records have been opened to schools, social service agencies, victims, and the press. Although access by these so-called interested parties to a juvenile's records may require a court order in many jurisdictions, it is now possible where it once was not.

Some states now require the notification of a juvenile offender's school district if the minor is a serious or violent offender. Most states allow photographing of serious juvenile offenders for the purpose of establishing a record of criminal history.

Media access to juvenile records is now permitted in most states. In some states, the media is given full access to juvenile records, and many more states allow the release of a juvenile offender's identity and photograph in certain cases, usually involving a serious crime. In a few states, the media may attend juvenile proceedings. For example, in Illinois a court order is required for access to juvenile proceedings, while in the District of Columbia juvenile hearings are presumed to be open to the public and members of the press may freely attend them, absent a court order barring media coverage.

THE JUVENILE AND CRIMINAL JUSTICE SYSTEMS

Although each state has its own distinct juvenile and criminal justice system, there are general similarities and differences between them.

KEY DIFFERENCES

- *Rehabilitation vs. Punishment:* Because juveniles are recognized as developmentally different than adults, the juvenile justice system seeks to balance rehabilitation and punishment. The criminal justice system seeks to punish adult offenders commensurate with their crimes as a means of deterring future criminal activity.
- *Confidential vs. Public:* Although the veil of confidentiality has been partially lifted in recent years by a number of states, limits are placed on public access to juvenile proceedings and records to avoid stigmatization. Adult court proceedings and criminal records are open to the public.
- *Social History vs. Legal Facts:* In juvenile proceedings, a minor's social and developmental history are weighed along with the legal facts of the case. Defendants in criminal proceedings are prosecuted largely based on the legal facts.
- *Trial by Judge vs. Jury:* Juveniles do not have a constitutional right to trial by jury. Adults do.
- *Status vs. Criminal Offenses:* Juveniles may be taken into custody for status offenses such as truancy or incorrigibility, which are not crimes for adults.

- *School Searches vs. Probable Cause:* Any juvenile can be searched at school without probable cause or a warrant. Probable cause must be established to legally search an adult who is not on probation or parole.
- *Death Penalty:* Capital punishment does not exist in the juvenile justice system, as it does in the criminal justice system.

Key Similarities

- **Miranda Warning:** On being taken into custody, the juvenile must be advised of his or her constitutional rights as mandated in the U.S. Supreme Court's 1966 ruling in *Miranda v. Arizona*, commonly called a *Miranda* warning. The minor is advised of the right to remain silent, the right to an attorney, and that any of the minor's statements made while in custody can be used against the minor in court.
- *Lineups:* Juveniles and adults are protected from prejudicial lineups.
- *Constitutional Rights:* Juveniles and adults share certain rights, such as the right to counsel, the right to confront witnesses, the privilege against self-incrimination, and the right to due process under the law.
- *Pretrial Detention:* Both juveniles and adults may be confined in detention facilities pending the outcome of their court proceedings.
- *Hearing and Appeal:* Juveniles have the same right to a hearing and to an appeal as adults.
- *Standard of Evidence:* Proof beyond a reasonable doubt is required in both juvenile and adult court proceedings.
- *Plea Bargaining:* Permitted for juveniles as well as for adults.
- *Probation:* Juveniles and adults may be placed on probation in lieu of confinement.

Recent research suggests that, although transfer from juvenile to criminal court is intended to subject youth to the practices of criminal court rather than those of juvenile court, this may not always be the case. Transfer policies often suggest that by prosecuting youth in criminal courts, they will be punished severely and judged only for their offenses and not with their developmental and social backgrounds in mind. Yet in *Judging Juveniles: Prosecuting Adolescents in Adult and Juvenile courts*, Aaron Kupchik finds that youths in adult court are still viewed as youths, not adults. They receive harsher punishment than youth in juvenile court, but they are still judged with "juvenile justice criteria" in mind, such as their school attendance, family functioning, and emotional development.[10]

Because the juvenile and adult systems of justice are separate entities, each has its own terminology.

- Juveniles commit delinquent acts; adults commit crimes.
- Juveniles face allegations contained in a petition; adults face charges contained in an indictment.
- Juveniles are held to answer at an adjudicatory hearing (or adjudication); adults stand trial.
- Juvenile petitions are found true; adults are found guilty.
- Juvenile petitions are denied; adults are found not guilty.
- Juveniles are held in a detention facility; adults are held in jail.
- Juveniles receive a disposition; adults receive a sentence.
- Juveniles receive a commitment; adults are incarcerated.
- Juveniles are released from commitment to aftercare; adults are released from incarceration to parole.

---

[1] Victor Streib. *Death Penalty for Juveniles*. Bloomington: Indiana University Press, 1987, p. 21.

[2] *Ex parte Crouse* (1839) 4 Wharton 9.

[3] Robert E. Shepherd, Jr. Washington, D.C.: U.S. Department of Justice. *Juvenile Justice*, Office of Juvenile Justice and Delinquency Prevention, December 1999, p. 4.

[4] A. M. Platt. *The Child Savers: The Invention of Delinquency*, 2d ed. Chicago: Ill.: University of Chicago Press, 1977, p. 44.

[5] *People ex rel O'Connell v. Turner* (1870) 55 Ill. 280.

[6] Charles Puzzanchera and Melissa Sickmund. *Juvenile Court Statistics, 2005*. Pittsburgh, Pa.: National Center for Juvenile Justice, 2008, p. 37. Available online. URL: http://ojjdp.ncjrs.org/ojstattbb/njcda/pdf/jcs2005.pdf.

[7] William J. Sabol, Todd D. Minton, and Paige M. Harrison. *Prison and Jail Inmates at Midyear 2006*. Washington, D.C.: Bureau of Justice Statistics, June 2007, p. 5. Available online. URL: http://www.ojp.usdoj.gov/bjs/pub/pdf/pjim06.pdf.

[8] Joseph J. Cocozza and Kathleen Skowyra, "Youth with Mental Health Disorders: Issues and Emerging Responses," *Juvenile Justice Journal*, Office of Juvenile Justice and Delinquency Prevention, vol. 7, April 2000, p. 3.

[9] Victor L. Streib. "The Juvenile Death Penalty Today: Death Sentences and Executions for Juvenile Crimes, January 1, 1973–February 28, 2005," p. 8. Available online. URL: http://www.law.onu.edu/faculty_staff/faculty_profiles/course materials/streib/juvdeath.pdf. Last updated October 7, 2005.

[10] Aaron Kupchik. *Judging Juveniles: Prosecuting Adolescents in Adult and Juvenile Courts*. New York: NYU Press, 2006, pp. 93–94.

CHAPTER 4

CHRONOLOGY

This chapter presents a chronology of significant developments in the history of juvenile justice in the United States.

A.D. 500s

- The age of seven is established under Roman law as the age under which youthful offenders would not be prosecuted for their crimes. This becomes the basis for "the age of reason" under English common law.

1535

- In Elizabethan England, the creation of "poor laws" makes it possible to compel destitute or neglected children into forced labor as servants.

1601

- Elizabethan poor laws become the model for dealing with poor or wayward children.

1642

- The first recorded execution of a juvenile offender in the United States occurs when Thomas Graunger is put to death in Plymouth Colony, Massachusetts. Graunger was hanged for the crime of bestiality, committed when he was 16 years of age.

1646

- Poor laws are passed in Virginia to force poor youth into apprenticeships.

1678

- Poor laws are passed in Connecticut and Massachusetts.

Chronology

1764

- Cesare Beccaria publishes *On Crimes and Punishment*, in which he advocates that punishment for criminal offenders be carried out swiftly and be commensurate with the underlying criminal offense. Beccaria's views continue to have influence among researchers in the areas of delinquency deterrence and accountability.

1783

- Youth gangs first appear at the end of the American Revolution, according to some gang scholars. Other researchers claim that youth gangs in the United States did not appear until 1813, as the result of difficult culture adjustments by Mexican youth who migrated with their families after the Mexican Revolution to what would later become to the southwestern United States.

1785

- Of the 20 criminal offenders executed for their crimes in London, 18 are juveniles.

1789

- The newly enacted U.S. Constitution includes a provision in Article III, Section 2 that requires a trial by jury for most crimes.
- The Judiciary Act establishes the office of the attorney general of the United States.

1791

- The First through Tenth Amendments to the U.S. Constitution are ratified, establishing freedom of speech (First), the ban against unreasonable searches and seizures (Fourth), the privilege against self-incrimination (Fifth), and the prohibition of cruel and unusual punishment (Eighth).

1816

- The New York Society for the Prevention of Pauperism is founded.

1825

- The Society for the Prevention of Juvenile Delinquency establishes the New York House of Refuge, designed to accommodate juvenile delinquents. Similar institutions are set up around the country by juvenile justice reformers known as the "child savers."

1826

■ The House of Reformation for juvenile offenders is founded by the city council of Boston, Massachusetts.

1831

■ In its ruling in *Ex parte Crouse* the Pennsylvania Supreme Court establishes the doctrine of *parens patriae* (the state as parent).

1841

■ John Augustus, a shoemaker in Boston, begins the practice of supervising wayward youth in the community instead of institutionalizing them. This practice evolved into the system of juvenile probation.

1848

■ A reform school is opened in Westboro, Massachusetts. Juveniles are subjected to harsh discipline, whippings, and isolation in an effort to correct delinquent behavior. Over the ensuing 12 years more such reform schools are founded in New York, Ohio, Maine, Rhode Island, and Michigan.

1851

■ The New York Juvenile Asylum is opened by the Child Savers to house delinquents and orphans under the age of 12 until they can be placed with rural families, who often force them to work.

1853

■ The Children's Aid Society is founded in New York City by philanthropist Charles Brace with the goal of placing neglected and delinquent juveniles in private homes where they will be cared for, not punished. This system becomes the precursor to the foster home program.

1860

■ The "placing out" system for juvenile offenders is developed in Massachusetts by reformers such as Samuel G. Howe who are troubled by the poor conditions in state reform schools. Under the "placing out" system, juvenile offenders are placed with families who are given a stipend in exchange for rearing the juvenile to adulthood.

Chronology

1868

- The Fourteenth Amendment to the U.S. Constitution is ratified, establishing due process guarantees and equal protection under the law.

1869

- Massachusetts creates a state office responsible for the supervision of children under the state's care.

1870

- The Illinois Supreme Court rules it is unconstitutional to confine a juvenile who has not been convicted of a crime to a Chicago reform school. Two years later, the school closes.

1875

- The New York Society for the Prevention of Cruelty to Children is founded.

1876

- The first U.S. reformatory for juvenile offenders opens in Elmira, New York.

1878

- The city of Boston is authorized to appoint the first paid probation officer.

1889

- Hull-House, a neighborhood-based social welfare agency, is founded in Chicago by social reformer Jane Addams. Because of her experiences working with poor youth at Hull-House, Addams later becomes a key advocate for the formation of the first juvenile court.

1895

- *Hull-House Maps and Papers* is published by social reformer Florence Kelly. Kelly's account of conditions in Chicago sweatshops and tenements was instrumental in influencing Illinois lawmakers to pass a legislation prohibiting child labor. Kelly went on to help establish the U.S. Children's Bureau in 1912.

Juvenile Crime

1899

- The passage of the Illinois Juvenile Court Act creates the first juvenile court in the United States and will be recognized as the model of the juvenile court system that develops nationwide.

1903

- Judge Ben B. Lindsey of Denver, Colorado, spearheads the passage of "An Act Concerning Delinquent Children," which sets forth guidelines for the handling of juvenile offenders similar to those in the Illinois Juvenile Court Act of 1899.

1904

- Psychologist G. Stanley Hall publishes his pioneering study, *Adolescence: Its Psychology and Its Relations to Physiology and Education.* Hall's ideas on adolescence as a critical stage of development marked by aggressive and assertive behaviors influences social reformers and others concerned with the rise of juvenile crime in urban areas.

1907

- The National Association of Probation Officers is founded. (It will be renamed the National Probation Association in 1911.)

1908

- The Bureau of Investigation—later to become the Federal Bureau of Investigation—is established within the U.S. Department of Justice.

1910

- Some 32 states have established juvenile courts and/or probation services.

1912

- Legislation establishing the U.S. Children's Bureau is signed into law by President William Howard Taft. The bureau, originally housed within the Department of Commerce and Labor, is created to "investigate and report . . . upon all matters pertaining to the welfare of children and child life among all classes of our people."

1913

- Physician Charles Goring publishes *The English Convict,* in which he promotes the theory of criminal diathesis—that criminals are mentally, morally, or physically deficient from birth, and that their criminal activity is the result of their inherent inability to deal with their environment.

1923

■ Chief August Vollmer of the Berkeley (California) Police Department establishes a youth bureau within the department to deal with juvenile offenders. The concept spreads to other police agencies.

1925

■ All but two states have established juvenile courts and/or probation services with the aim of turning delinquent youth into productive citizens through treatment, not punishment.

1927

■ Sociologist Frederic Thrasher publishes *The Gang*, in which he identifies youth gangs as training groups for members who go on to commit crimes as adults. Thrasher believed that the solution to gang violence was to address the underlying social conditions identified as precursors to gang involvement.

1929

■ The U.S. Department of Justice begins keeping a statistical measure of crime in the United States called the Uniform Crime Reporting Program. Compiled annually by the Federal Bureau of Investigation, the Uniform Crime Reports track offenses reported to law enforcement agencies nationwide.

1930

■ Sociologists Clifford R. Shaw and Henry D. McKay publish *The Jack-Roller: A Delinquent Boy's Own Story*, which is followed by other biographies of delinquents. Shaw and McKay go on to conduct pioneering research on delinquency in Chicago in which they demonstrate that rates of delinquency varied significantly in different areas of the cities and remained relatively stable over time regardless of which ethnic group formed the majority of an area's population.

1934

■ The Chicago Area Projects is founded with the goal of addressing delinquency and youth welfare at the local level because of a loss of faith in institutions such as reform schools intended to deal with those issues.

1937

- The National Council of Juvenile and Family Court Judges is founded.

1955

- Sociologist Albert K. Cohen publishes *Delinquent Boys*, in which he argues that the American class structure leads to the formation of youth gangs, and that for certain youth, delinquency is a solution to problems of adjustment for which established culture provides no satisfactory solution.

1957

- The International Juvenile Officers Association is founded to establish standards and procedures for police officers working when dealing with juvenile offenders.

1966

- In *Kent v. United States*, the U.S. Supreme Court sets in place a process for waiving juvenile offenders to adult court with certain constitutional safeguards, such as the right to a hearing, commonly known today as a transfer or waiver hearing.
- In *Miranda v. Arizona*, the U.S. Supreme Court places constitutional limitations on police interrogations of adult criminal offenders.
- The California Probation Subsidy Program is established to pay counties to provide probation services for every juvenile offender who is not committed to a state correctional institution.

1967

- *In re Gault* establishes certain constitutional rights for all minors coming under the jurisdiction of a juvenile court—the right to notice, the right to counsel, the right to cross-examination of witnesses, and the privilege against self-incrimination. By so ruling, the U.S. Supreme Court brings juvenile court proceedings more closely in line with adult criminal trials and places limits on the wide discretion historically afforded to juvenile courts under the principle of *parens patriae*.
- The President's Commission on Law Enforcement and the Administration of Justice issues a task force report, *Juvenile Delinquency and Youth Crime*, and finds a lack of effectiveness and procedural safeguards in the juvenile justice system.

1968

- The Juvenile Delinquency Prevention and Control Act recommends that cases involving juveniles charged with status offenses, such as truancy and incorrigibility, be handled outside the juvenile court system.

1969

- In his book *The Child Savers*, author Anthony M. Platt observes that the turn-of-the-century child savers, many of whom were affluent, chose to punish behaviors prevalent in or specific to children from lower socio-economic classes, such as begging and staying out late.
- In his book *Causes of Delinquency*, Travis Hirschi articulates his social bonding theory of delinquency—that delinquency is the result of a lack of social bonds such as ties to social institutions. This remains one of the most influential theories in shaping both perceptions of the causes of delinquency and policies designed to prevent it.

1970

- *In re Winship* establishes that the burden of proof in adjudicatory hearings must be "beyond a reasonable doubt." Prior to this ruling by the U.S. Supreme Court, juveniles were commonly held to the lesser standard of a "preponderance of the evidence," which is the standard of proof in most civil matters.
- Nationally, many state legislatures begin to debate lowering the age of majority in order to prosecute certain juvenile offenders as adults.

1971

- In *McKeiver v. Pennsylvania*, the U.S. Supreme Court rejects allowing jury trials in juvenile court, reaffirming the principle of *parens patriae* to the extent that it preserved the discretion of juvenile court officers as the sole triers of fact in juvenile proceedings.

1973

- The U.S. Department of Justice adds a second statistical measure of crime nationally. Administered by the Bureau of Justice Statistics, the National Crime Victimization Survey (NCVS) compiles information on crime incidents, victims, and trends through surveys of crime victims.
- The National Advisory Commission on Criminal Justice Standards and Goals recommends that probation officers be required to refer clients to community services for treatment and other support.

1974

- The Juvenile Justice and Delinquency Prevention Act sets federal standards governing the treatment of juvenile offenders. Expanded in scope and revised from the Juvenile Delinquency Prevention and Control Act of 1968, its stated purpose is "to assist states and local communities in providing community-based preventative services to youths in danger of becoming delinquent, to help train individuals in occupations providing such services, and to provide technical assistance in the field." The act establishes the Office of Juvenile Justice and Delinquency Prevention.

- In *Nelson v. Heyne*, the Seventh U.S. Circuit Court of Appeals upholds the constitutional right to treatment for institutionalized juvenile offenders under the Fourteenth Amendment and becomes the first federal appellate court to affirm a constitutional right to treatment.

1975

- *Breed v. Jones* establishes that jeopardy attaches in adjudicatory hearings. In effect, this ruling by the U.S. Supreme Court means that a minor can be tried in juvenile court or in adult court, but not in both for the same offense.

1977

- In *Oklahoma Publishing Co. v. District Court* the U.S. Supreme Court allows the publication of a juvenile's name and photograph in connection with a criminal proceeding when reporters are legally present in the courtroom and no objection is made to their presence.
- Washington State passes one of the first determinate sentencing laws for juvenile offenders, requiring "flat" sentences without the possibility of parole for certain crimes.

1979

- In *Fare v. Michael C.* the U.S. Supreme Court rules that statements made by juveniles during unsupervised police interrogations can be used against them absent the specific request to see an attorney or a refusal to respond to questioning.
- In *Smith v. Daily Mail Publishing Company*, the U.S. Supreme Court rules that the First Amendment right of a newspaper to publish the name of an alleged juvenile offender effectively trumps the protections of confidentiality afforded to minors in juvenile proceedings, as long as the information is obtained legally.

1982

- In *Eddings v. Oklahoma*, the U.S. Supreme Court holds that imposing the death penalty on a minor who was 16 at the time of the offense constitutes an unlawful violation of the Eighth Amendment's protection against "cruel and unusual punishment."

1984

- In *Schall v. Martin,* the U.S. Supreme Court rules that preventive or pretrial detention of juveniles is lawful and does not violate the due process clause of the Fourteenth Amendment.

1985

- *New Jersey v. T.L.O.* permits searches of students by school officials without a warrant. The U.S. Supreme Court also eases the standards of "probable cause" in school searches to the lesser standard of "reasonableness."

1988

- In *Thompson v. Oklahoma,* a divided U.S. Supreme Court narrowly holds that the imposition of the death penalty against minors who are under the age of 16 at the time of their offense violates the Eighth Amendment's ban on "cruel and unusual punishment."

1989

- In *Stanford v. Kentucky, Wilkins v. Missouri,* the U.S. Supreme Court, in a 5 to 4 decision, affirms rulings by Kentucky and Missouri courts that imposing the death penalty on youths 16 or 17 years of age at the time of their crimes does not violate standards of decency and, therefore, is permissible under the Eighth Amendment.

1994

- Juvenile arrest rates for the Violent Crime Index reach a peak. Since 1980, arrest rates for juveniles 15 to 17 years of age have increased by 62 percent. The number of juveniles waived to adult criminal court is 11,700, a historic high.
- The Violent Crime Control and Law Enforcement Act of 1994 authorizes harsher penalties for violent and drug trafficking crimes committed by gang members, authorizes adult prosecution of minors 13 years of age or older who are charged with certain violent crimes, and prohibits the transfer of a firearm to a juvenile.

1995

- In *Vernonia School District v. Acton,* the U.S. Supreme Court holds that a policy requiring high school students to submit to drug testing does not violate the Fourth Amendment prohibition against unreasonable searches.

- Nineteen states pass laws requiring schools to suspend or expel students for possessing weapons on school grounds.

1997

- Since 1992, 47 states have enacted laws that make their juvenile justice systems more punitive. These include broadening transfer provisions to adult court, giving courts expanded sentencing powers, modifying confidentiality laws designed to shield juvenile offenders from stigma, and increasing the role of the victim in the juvenile justice process.

1999

- *April 20:* In the worst school shooting in U.S. history, 15 are killed and 23 are wounded at Columbine High School in Littleton, Colorado.

2002

- *October 3:* The U.S. Senate votes to reauthorize the Juvenile Justice and Delinquency Prevention Act. The reauthorization was passed in the House of Representatives earlier in the year by a vote of 400 to 4.

2003

- *January 8:* University of Pittsburgh researchers release results of a study that finds delinquent children are four times as likely to have elevated concentrations of lead in their bones. Based on their findings, researchers attribute 11 to 38 percent of juvenile delinquency in Allegheny County, Pennsylvania, to lead exposure.

2005

- In *Roper v. Simmons*, the U.S. Supreme Court holds that it is unconstitutional to execute anyone for committing a crime while younger than 18. The Court's decision was based on a growing national and international consensus against capital punishment for juveniles, as well as recent research documenting the immaturity and reduced decision-making ability of juveniles.

2007

- Connecticut raises its age of adult court jurisdiction from 16 to 18, meaning that unless transferred to the criminal court, all youths younger than 18 are prosecuted as juveniles.

Chronology

- The Centers for Disease Control releases its report "Effects on Violence of Laws and Policies Facilitating the Transfer of Youth from the Juvenile to the Adult Justice System," which recommends against laws that facilitate youth being prosecuted in adult criminal court: "Available evidence indicates that transfer to the adult criminal justice system typically increases rather than decreases rates of violence among transferred youth."

2009

- The Office of Juvenile Justice and Delinquency Prevention releases the report *Juvenile Arrests, 2007*, which documents a 2 percent decrease in juvenile arrests, overall, from 2006 to 2007. In 2007, there were an estimated 2,180,500 juveniles arrested in the United States.
- In *Safford Unified School District # 1 v. Redding*, the U.S. Supreme Court puts limits on a school's ability to search students, noting that a strip search of a student must be warranted by the circumstances of the case.

CHAPTER 5

BIOGRAPHICAL LISTING

Grace Abbott, a social worker and public administrator who in 1917 became the director of the child labor division of the U.S. Children's Bureau, where she administered the Keating-Owen Act of 1916, the first federal statute that placed restrictions on the employment of juveniles (later declared unconstitutional). Abbott attempted to win public support for a constitutional amendment against child labor that was submitted to the states in 1924 but never ratified. In 1938, Abbott published her two-volume work *The Child and the State.*

Jane Addams, a social reformer who in 1889 cofounded Hull-House, a neighborhood-based social welfare agency (called a social settlement). Originally created to serve the needs of poor immigrant families in the neighborhood, Hull-House under Addams's leadership was expanded to include a day nursery, playground, and housing for needy children. Due in part to her experiences working with poor youth at Hull-House, Addams went on to become one of the key advocates for creating the first juvenile court.

Barbara Allen-Hagen, program manager for the Office of Juvenile Justice and Delinquency Prevention until 2006, who directed major studies on issues including the conditions of confinement of juvenile offenders and the handling of juveniles in custody, as well as the statistical series *The Children in Custody Census.*

John Altgeld, an attorney who in 1882 toured the House of Corrections in Chicago and discovered hundreds of children as young as eight housed in jail-like conditions with adults. Altgeld joined with Jane Addams and others in lobbying Illinois lawmakers for the creation of a juvenile court. Altgeld went on to become the governor of Illinois from 1893 to 1897.

John Augustus, a citizen who in 1841 began the community supervision of criminal offenders released to his custody, many of them juveniles. Largely due to Augustus's success and the low rate of recidivism among wards under his supervision, in 1878 the Massachusetts legislature authorized the appointment of a paid probation officer for the city of Boston, a concept that quickly spread throughout Massachusetts and to other jurisdictions.

Cesare Beccaria, author who in 1764 published *On Crimes and Punishments*, which stressed that effective punishment for criminal offenders must be done swiftly and must be proportionate to the underlying criminal offense. Beccaria's ideas continue to have an influence in the areas of delinquency deterrence and accountability.

Jeremy Bentham, prolific 18th-century author who expanded on the ideas of Cesare Beccaria. Bentham believed that because people act in a calculated manner to advance their own good, the aim of criminal law should be to fix penalties to crime in order to deter potential offenders.

Donna M. Bishop, author since the 1980s of numerous articles on the transfer of juveniles to criminal court and on juvenile reform legislation.

Harry A. Blackmun, associate justice of the U.S. Supreme Court (1970–94). Blackmun wrote the majority opinion in *McKeiver v. Pennsylvania* (1971) and *Fare v. Michael C.* (1979). In *McKeiver,* the Court rejected allowing jury trials in juvenile court, reaffirming the principle of *parens patriae* to the extent that it preserved the discretion of juvenile court officers as the sole triers of fact in juvenile proceedings. In *Fare,* the Court ruled that that statements made by juveniles during unsupervised police interrogations can be used against them absent the specific request to see an attorney or a refusal to respond to questioning.

Charles Brace, philanthropist who helped found the Children's Aid Society in 1853. Brace's idea of rescuing neglected and delinquent youth from their harsh inner-city environment and placing them in private homes across the country to be properly cared for evolved into the foster care system.

Sophonisba Preston Breckinridge, the first woman to receive a Ph.D. in political science from the University of Chicago (1901) and, later, a law degree (1904). She worked with Jane Addams at Hull-House and with the U.S. Children's Bureau to promote judicial reforms in juvenile justice. Breckinridge was the author of 12 books, including *The Delinquent Child* in 1912 and *The Family and the State* in 1934.

William J. Brennan, Jr., associate justice of the U.S. Supreme Court (1956–90). He wrote the majority opinion in *In re Winship* (1970), in which the Court established that the burden of proof in adjudicatory hearings must be "beyond a reasonable doubt." Prior to this ruling, juveniles were commonly held to the lesser standard of a "preponderance of the evidence," which is the standard of proof in most civil matters.

Warren Earl Burger, chief justice of the U.S. Supreme Court, (1969–86). He wrote the majority opinion in *Breed v. Jones* (1975) and in *Smith v. Daily Mail Publishing Co.* (1979). In *Breed,* the Court established that jeopardy attaches in adjudicatory hearings, thereby precluding a minor from being tried in both adult and juvenile court for the same criminal offense. In *Smith*, the Court ruled that the First Amendment right of a newspaper to publish the name of an alleged juvenile offender effectively trumps the protections of confidentiality afforded to minors in juvenile proceedings, as long as the information released is obtained legally.

Jeffrey A. Butts, researcher and author of numerous reports on crime and delinquency for the Office of Juvenile Justice and Delinquency Prevention. In 2009, he became the executive vice president for research at Public/Private Ventures, a nonprofit research and advocacy organization.

Meda Chesney-Lind, sociologist who has been a pioneer since the 1970s in research on female delinquency and the experiences of girls in the juvenile justice system.

Albert K. Cohen, sociologist and author of *Delinquent Boys* (1955), in which he posited that the nature of American culture leads to the formation of youth gangs. Cohen believed that for certain youths, delinquency was seen as a solution to problems of adjustment for which the established culture provided no satisfactory solution, and that delinquency was a gang member's response to achieving status and self-respect.

Dewey Cornell, clinical psychologist and researcher in the areas of juvenile homicide, psychological characteristics of violent youth, school violence, and youth gangs. Cornell has written widely on his forensic experience working with juvenile violent offenders.

Delbert S. Elliott, director of a series of longitudinal studies conducted since the 1960s, including the National Youth Survey and the San Diego Delinquency and Dropout Study. A longitudinal study is concerned with the development of persons or groups over time, usually years.

Jeffrey Fagan, researcher of juvenile crime and justice issues, including gun use and violent crimes by adolescents, and author of *Firearms and Youth Violence* (1997) and *The Comparative Impacts of Juvenile and Criminal Court Sanctions for Adolescent Felony Offenders* (1996).

Mathea Falco, author of *The Making of a Drug-Free America: Programs That Work* (1994) and a national speaker and commentator on issues of juvenile crime and substance abuse.

David Farrington, researcher at Cambridge University's Institute of Criminology since 1969 and director of the Cambridge Study in Delinquent Development. He has conducted many studies of risk factors for delinquency.

Barry C. Feld, author of books and articles since the 1970s on juvenile justice administration, including waiver policy and the sentencing of serious young offenders as juveniles and as adults. Feld served on the Juvenile Justice Task Force, which rewrote the Minnesota juvenile code.

Lucy Louisa Coues Flower, a noted welfare worker who in the 1890s helped to promote the then-faltering campaign for the establishment of a juvenile court system in Chicago. Working with Jane Addams and Julia Clifford Lathrop, Flower organized support for the idea and help to draft the Illinois Juvenile Court Act of 1899 that eventually resulted in the creation of the first juvenile court in the United States. Flower also founded the Juvenile Court Committee to raise money to pay salaries for probation officers.

David Fogel, author and advocate in the 1970s of the justice model philosophy, which holds that juvenile offenders are volitional and responsible human beings who deserve to be punished if they break the law.

Abe Fortas, associate justice of the U.S. Supreme Court (1965–69). Fortas wrote the majority opinions in *Kent v. United States* (1966) and *In re Gault* (1967). In *Kent*, the Court set in place a process for waiving juvenile offenders to adult court with certain constitutional safeguards, such as the right to a hearing, commonly known today as a transfer or waiver hearing. In *Gault*, the Court established certain constitutional rights for all minors coming under the jurisdiction of a juvenile court—the right to notice, the right to counsel, the right to cross-examination of witnesses, and the privilege against self-incrimination.

James Alan Fox, criminologist and author of books and articles on issues including juvenile crime and school violence. Fox served on President Clinton's advisory committee on school shootings and on the U.S. Department of Education Expert Panel on Safe, Disciplined and Drug-Free Schools.

Sigmund Freud, psychoanalyst whose concepts on understanding human behavior at the start of the 20th century helped shape modern thinking on how delinquent acts reflect personal pathology or mental problems.

Charles Goring, physician and author who in 1913 published *The English Convict*, which promoted the theory of "criminal diathesis"—that criminals are mentally, morally, or physically deficient from birth and that their criminal activity was the result of their inherent inability to deal with their environment.

Thomas Grisso, director of the law-psychiatry program at the University of Massachusetts Medical School. His research interests include developmental issues in juvenile law and the mental health needs of youths in the juvenile justice system.

G. Stanley Hall, psychologist whose publication in 1904 of *Adolescence: Its Psychology and Its Relations to Physiology, Anthropology, Sociology, Sex, Crime, Religion and Education* helped to reshape popular ideas about youth. Hall identified the period of adolescence as a crucial phase in the development, and he suggested that the period of adolescence presented an opportunity for molding and shaping a person's character.

Juvenile Crime

Adele Harrell, researcher on substance abuse among juvenile offenders. Harrell has conducted numerous evaluations since the early 1990s of drug testing programs at various stages of the juvenile justice process, and developed a drug-prevention program for young juveniles 11 to 13 years of age.

J. David Hawkins, developer of the social development model, a theoretical model for the prevention of delinquency and drug abuse, and the Preparing for Drug (Free) Years prevention program, which focuses on strengthening family bonds to minimize risk factors associated with drug abuse.

Travis Hirschi, author of *Causes of Delinquency* (1969) and proponent of the social bonding theory of delinquency—that to the extent that a young person fails to become attached to the control agencies of society, such as family and school, the greater the chance of engaging in delinquent behavior.

Eric Holder, attorney general (since 2009) of the United States and head of the Department of Justice, which includes the FBI and the Bureau of Justice Programs, the agencies that publish the Uniform Crime Reports and the National Crime Victimization Survey, respectively.

James C. Howell (Buddy Howell), senior research associate with the National Youth Gang Center in Tallahassee, Florida. Howell worked at the federal Office of Juvenile Justice and Delinquency Prevention (OJJDP) in the U.S. Department of Justice for 21 years, mostly as Director of Research and Program Development. He also was also director of the National Institute of Juvenile Justice and Delinquency Prevention and deputy administrator of OJJDP.

Karen Hunt, cofounder of InsideOUT Writers Program, which uses volunteers to teach creative writing to juveniles confined at Los Angeles County Juvenile Hall. In 1998, Hall published *What We See: Poems and Essays from Inside Juvenile Hall.*

Sarah Ingersoll, author of *How Communities Can Bring Up Youth Free from Fear and Violence* (1995). Ingersoll has developed community-based violence prevention projects in cities nationwide.

Lonnie Jackson, founder of the nationally recognized Minority Youth Concerns Program, which provides support systems and resources for minority juvenile offenders during their transition from confinement to their return to the community.

Florence Kelly, social reformer and a graduate of Northwestern University Law School in 1894. Kelly's chronicle of conditions in sweatshops and tenements in *Hull-House Maps and Papers* (1895) contributed to the passage of an Illinois law that prohibited child labor. Kelly helped to establish the U.S. Children's Bureau in 1912.

R. Gil Kerlikowske, director since 2009 of the White House Office of National Drug Control Policy, established by the Anti-Drug Abuse Act of 1988 to reduce illicit drug use, manufacturing, and trafficking of drugs, as well as drug-related crime and violence.

Lawrence Kohlberg, proponent in 1958 of the theory of moral development, which links delinquency to moral viewpoints that are immature in regard to ideas of justice and fairness.

Barry Krisberg, president of the National Council on Crime and Delinquency, a nonprofit organization whose goals include reform of the juvenile justice system, particularly in the area of race and justice since 1983.

Julia Clifford Lathrop, a social worker who in 1912 was appointed by President William Howard Taft to head the newly created U.S. Children's Bureau, becoming the first woman to head a statutory federal bureau. Working with a small budget, she funded studies on juvenile delinquency and illegitimacy.

Ben B. Lindsey, judge. Lindsey spearheaded the passage in the early 1920s of "An Act Concerning Delinquent Children" in Colorado, which set forth guidelines for the handling of juvenile offenders similar to those in the Illinois Juvenile Court Act of 1899.

Cesare Lombroso, physician and author who in 1876 published *The Criminal Man,* which posited that criminals had distinct physical characteristics, including facial and body abnormalities, and that criminals were "born," not shaped through their life experiences.

Edward Loughran (Ned Loughran), executive director of the Council for Juvenile Correctional Administrators and former Commissioner of the Massachusetts Department of Youth Services (1985–93).

Bart Lubow, director since 2002 of the programs for high-risk youth and their families at the Annie E. Casey Foundation.

Gordon A. Martin, Jr., associate justice of the Massachusetts Trial Court for 20 years. Judge Martin chaired the discussion of model legislation concerning the transfer of juveniles to adult court, which was cosponsored by the National Council of Juvenile and Family Court Judges and the National Consortium for Alternatives in Sentencing. He also chaired the Advisory Committee on the Effectiveness of Juvenile Offender Prevention and Treatment Programs sponsored by the National Center for Juvenile Justice.

David Matza, sociologist who wrote *Delinquency and Drift* (1964), a landmark study in causes of and responses to delinquency.

Joan McCord, criminologist and first female president of the American Society of Criminology (in 1989), who evaluated crime prevention programs.

Jerome G. Miller, cofounder in 1977 of the National Center on Institutions and Alternatives and clinical director of the Augustus Institute for Mental Health in Virginia. While serving as commissioner of the Massachusetts Department of Youth Services (1969–73), Dr. Miller closed all

Massachusetts reform schools and replaced them with community-based programs. He was later appointed director of the Illinois Department of Children and Family Services and commissioner of Children and Youth for the Commonwealth of Pennsylvania.

Jody Miller, criminologist and author of *Getting Played: African American Girls, Urban Inequality, and Gendered Violence* (2008) and *One of the Guys: Girls Gangs and Gender* (2000).

Robert S. Mueller, III, director of the FBI since 2001. The FBI publishes the annual Uniform Crime Reports as well as other publications on the incidence of crime in the United States, including juvenile crime.

Sandra Day O'Connor, associate justice of the U.S. Supreme Court (1981–2006). O'Connor's concurring opinion in *Thompson v. Oklahoma* (1988) allowed a divided court to rule that the imposition of the death penalty against minors who are under the age of 16 at the time of their offense violates the Eighth Amendment's ban on "cruel and unusual punishment."

Anthony Platt, author of *The Child Savers* (1969). The book is critical of the late 19th-century "child savers," many of whom were affluent, who chose to punish chiefly behaviors prevalent among and specific to children from lower socioeconomic classes, such as begging and staying out late.

Lewis F. Powell, Jr., associate justice of the U.S. Supreme Court (1972–87). Powell wrote the majority opinion in *Eddings v. Oklahoma* (1982), in which the Court held that imposing the death penalty on a minor who was 16 at the time of the offense constituted an unlawful violation of the Eighth Amendment's protection against "cruel and unusual punishment."

William H. Rehnquist, chief justice of the U.S. Supreme Court (1972–2005, total tenure; 1986–2005, chief justice). Rehnquist wrote the majority opinion in *Schall v. Martin* (1984), in which the Court held that that preventive or pretrial detention of juveniles is lawful and does not violate the due process clause of the Fourteenth Amendment.

Marsha Renwanz, former chief policy adviser to the U.S. Senate Juvenile Justice Subcommittee on the 1992 reauthorization of the Juvenile Justice and Delinquency Prevention Act.

Laurie O. Robinson, former assistant attorney general for the Office of Justice Programs, U.S. Department of Justice and founder of the American Bar Association's Juvenile Justice Center in 1982.

Liz Ryan, founder of campaign for youth justice, an organization dedicated to ending the practice of trying, sentencing, and incarcerating youth under the age of 18 in the adult criminal justice system.

David Satcher, 16th Surgeon General of the United States (1998–2002). During Satcher's tenure, the Office of the Surgeon General released the report *Youth Violence: A Report of the Surgeon General.*

Biographical Listing

Antonin Scalia, associate justice of the U.S. Supreme Court (1986 to present). Scalia wrote the majority opinion in *Vernonia School District v. Acton* (1995), in which the Court held that a policy requiring high school students to submit to drug testing did not violate the Fourth Amendment prohibition against unreasonable searches.

Vincent Schiraldi, director of Washington, D.C.'s, Department of Youth Rehabilitation Services and founder in 2002 of the Center on Juvenile and Criminal Justice, is the author of numerous studies on such topics as juvenile homicides, race and incarceration, and alternative sentencing of juvenile offenders.

Robert G. Schwartz, cofounder of the Juvenile Justice Law Center, a public interest law firm that works to reform state systems that serve children, including state systems of juvenile justice in 1975.

Clifford R. Shaw and Henry D. McKay, sociologists who in 1930 jointly published *The Jack-Roller: A Delinquent Boy's Own Story,* followed by other biographies of delinquents. Shaw and McKay's pioneering research on delinquency in Chicago demonstrated that rates of delinquency varied significantly in different parts of the city, and that those rates remained relatively stable over time, regardless of which ethnic group comprised the majority of an area's population.

Melissa Sickmund, statistical researcher for the National Center for Juvenile Justice since 1986. The center's primary publication series, *Juvenile Offenders and Victims,* is a collection of reference documents on delinquency and the juvenile justice system that is designed to be accessible to the general public.

Jeff Slowikowski, designated the acting administrator of the Office of Juvenile Justice and Delinquency Prevention (OJJDP) on January 20, 2009. The OJJDP was created by the Juvenile Justice and Delinquency Prevention Act of 1974 to promote issues and fund projects in juvenile justice.

Howard Snyder, researcher on issues of juvenile crime and author of numerous publications available through the Office of Juvenile Justice and Delinquency Prevention, including the report "Juvenile Arrests, 2006."

Mark Soler, former attorney and president of the Youth Law Center until 2006, when he became the executive director of the Center for Children's Law and Policy. Soler was lead attorney in major class action suits involving juveniles and their rights in the juvenile justice system, and has advocated on behalf of juvenile justice and children's rights nationwide.

Benjamin Spock, physician and educator who helped to shape ideas on child rearing in the 20th century. Spock promoted the idea that that the key to successful child rearing was the recognition of individual differences in children, and he fostered the idea that democratic, nonauthoritarian family life produces psychologically healthy children.

Lawrence Steinberg, former director (1997–2008) of the John D. and Catherine T. MacArthur Foundation Research Network on Adolescent Development and Juvenile Justice. Professor Steinberg conducts research on adolescent development and juvenile justice.

John Paul Stevens, associate justice of the U.S. Supreme Court (1975 to 2010). Stevens wrote the opinion in *Thompson v. Oklahoma* (1988), with only three other justices joining, in which a divided court narrowly held (with a concurring opinion by Justice Sandra Day O'Connor) that the imposition of the death penalty against minors who are under the age of 16 at the time of their offense violates the Eighth Amendment's ban on "cruel and unusual punishment."

Edwin H. Sutherland, sociologist and author whose differential association theory of criminal behavior (1939) posits that criminal behavior is learned, and that the criminal learning process includes not only techniques for committing crimes but also the shaping of motives, drives, rationalizations, and attitudes about criminal behavior.

William Howard Taft, president of the United States (1908–12). Taft signed legislation in 1912 establishing the U.S. Children's Bureau to "investigate and report . . . upon all matters pertaining to the welfare of children and child life among all classes of our people."

Terence P. Thornberry, author and editor of numerous articles and books on delinquency and crime, including *Taking Stock of Delinquency: An Overview of Findings from Contemporary Longitudinal Studies* (2003). Thornberry directed the Rochester Youth Development Study, which examined the correlation between serious delinquency and substance abuse.

Frederic Thrasher, sociologist who in 1927 published *The Gang*, which described juvenile gangs as training groups for adult crime. Thrasher believed that the solution to gang violence was not to break up gangs, but to address the underlying social conditions identified as precursors to gang involvement.

Robert D. Vinter, social worker and member of the President's Committee on Juvenile Delinquency and Youth Crime in 1962. Vinter's research included the National Assessment of Juvenile Corrections, conducted from 1971 to 1976, which documented the problems of juvenile justice and juvenile corrections nationwide.

August Vollmer, chief of the Berkeley (California) Police Department (1909–32). Vollmer created the first youth bureau within a police department for the handling of juvenile offenders. Vollmer believed that creating such a unit would enhance the department's juvenile crime prevention efforts.

Byron Raymond White, associate justice of the U.S. Supreme Court (1962–93). White wrote the majority opinion in *New Jersey v. T.L.O.* (1985), in which the Court held that searches of students by school officials without a warrant were permissible, and that the standards of "probable cause" in school searches should be eased to the lesser standard of "reasonableness."

John J. Wilson, served as senior legal counsel and later as deputy administrator of the Office of Juvenile Justice and Delinquency Prevention (OJJDP) under President William Jefferson Clinton. Wilson was coauthor of the OJJDP publication *Comprehensive Strategy for Serious, Violent, and Chronic Juvenile Offenders* and served as editor of *A Sourcebook: Serious, Violent and Chronic Offenders.*

Franklin E. Zimring, criminologist who has written several books on criminal and juvenile justice issues, including *American Juvenile Justice* (2005) and *American Youth Violence* (1998).

CHAPTER 6

GLOSSARY

This chapter presents a glossary of terms as they apply to the areas of juvenile crime and the juvenile justice system.

absconder   Juvenile offender whose whereabouts are unknown as a result of failing to report for probation or parole supervision, or leaving the juvenile court jurisdiction without permission of the supervising authority.

adjudicate   To hear and decide a case against a minor who is alleged to have committed delinquent acts, as determined by state law.

adjudication   Process of rendering a judicial decision as to whether the facts alleged in a juvenile petition are true (guilty) or denied (not guilty).

adjudicatory hearing   A court proceeding to determine if the facts support the allegations contained in a juvenile petition (complaint), using the standard of proof of beyond a reasonable doubt. The hearing is similar to a trial in adult court with two significant exceptions: There is no jury, and the proceedings are generally closed to the public.

affirm   To find, in a higher (appellate) court, that a lower court's ruling was justified.

aftercare   Parole in the juvenile justice system. See **parole**.

aftercare officer   The equivalent of a parole officer in the juvenile justice system. Such an officer monitors a juvenile offender upon release from a correctional institution for juvenile offenders.

age of majority   The age at which a person is legally considered to be an adult according to state law.

age of onset   The beginning of law-violating behavior by a juvenile offender.

aggravated assault   The deliberate attempt to cause serious bodily injury, or the infliction of serious bodily injury upon another as the result of negligence or recklessness.

aggravating factors (aggravating circumstances)   Factors that increase the seriousness of an underlying allegation and may be considered by the court in determining the level of disposition. For example, if the underlying allegation is robbery, aggravating factors could include use of a weapon or serious injury to the victim during the commission of the robbery.

allegation A criminal offense or accusation against a juvenile offender that is listed in a juvenile court petition.

appeal A higher court's review of a case to determine if a ruling by the lower court was justified in whole or in part, based on constitutionality, state law, and legal precedent (previous cases dealing with similar issues).

arraignment (initial hearing) A juvenile offender's first appearance before the juvenile court in a given case, during which the state must offer some proof that an offense was committed by the minor, a date is set for a future hearing, and the minor is provided with legal counsel.

arrest To take a person suspected of a crime into custody, thereby depriving the person of the opportunity to leave and requiring that the person be advised of certain rights, commonly known as a *Miranda* warning. Juvenile offenders are usually said to be taken into custody rather than arrested.

arson The intentional or negligent burning of a home, structure, or vehicle for criminal purposes such as profit, revenge, fraud, or crime concealment.

assault An attempt to physically harm another person in a manner that makes that person feel threatened or in imminent danger. No physical contact is required.

balanced and restorative justice A model of juvenile justice that focuses on victim restoration, providing treatment to the offender, and protecting the public.

battery Any intentional and unlawful physical contact inflicted upon a person without that person's consent.

beyond a reasonable doubt The burden of proof used in adult criminal cases that was applied to all juvenile proceedings by the U.S. Supreme Court in *In re Winship* (1970). Prior to *Winship*, the lesser standard of proof "by a preponderance of the evidence" was routinely used in juvenile courts throughout the United States.

blended sentencing The practice of giving a sentence that spans the juvenile and criminal justice systems. Blended sentencing often means that youth are sentenced to juvenile punishments until they turn a certain age (often 18), at which point they are transferred to the adult criminal justice system.

booking The formal processing by the police of an arrest, which often includes fingerprinting and photographing the person taken into custody. An administrative record is created, listing particulars such as the offender's name, date of birth, and physical description, as well as the name of the arresting officer.

burden of proof The obligation to prove every charge or complaint in a court of law. In juvenile proceedings, the burden of proof is beyond a reasonable doubt, and burden falls upon the prosecutor.

burglary The breaking and entering of any building with the intent to commit a felony.

capital offense A crime punishable by death.

certiorari An order (writ) from a higher court to a lower court to turn over a case for review.

child savers Late-19th-century reformers in the United States who developed programs for delinquent youth and advocated for the formation of a juvenile court and a juvenile justice system.

chronic offender As defined by state law, a repeat juvenile offender with a minimum number of offenses within a proscribed period of time; for example, three or more violent offenses within one year.

classical theory The theory that offenders freely choose to engage in criminal behavior, usually for reasons of greed or personal need, and that crime can be controlled by the fear of punishment.

commissioner A finder of fact in juvenile court with the same powers as a judge.

commitment Dispositional status of minors placed by the juvenile court under the care, custody, or control of an agency or correctional institution as the result of being adjudicated delinquent.

community service Specified period of supervised work or service ordered by a court or parole agency to be performed by the offender within a specified period of time. Also called "symbolic restitution" and "uncompensated public service."

competency development Goal that juvenile offenders leave the juvenile justice system with the skills necessary to be law-abiding and productive citizens.

comprehensive assessment The evaluation of a juvenile offender's physical, psychological, educational and social condition, and family environment, in order to assess the minor's need for services, such as counseling or out-of-home placement.

comprehensive juvenile justice A model advocating preventative and community programs for juveniles and behavior control programs for aggressive juvenile offenders.

concurring opinion A written opinion by one or more Supreme Court justices that agrees with the Court's ruling in a case but gives different reasons or legal justifications for doing so.

confession An admission of wrongdoing made by a person accused of a crime, usually to the police.

confidentiality The closure of most juvenile proceedings to the public and often to the press as well in order to protect the minor from stigma arising from the allegations. Criminal court trials are open to the public and press.

conflict of interest   Situation or circumstance with the potential to cause a private interest to interfere with the exercise of a public duty.

conspiracy   An agreement between two or more persons to commit a crime, followed by an act done in the furtherance of that crime.

cooperative supervision   Supervision by a correctional agency of one jurisdiction of a person placed on probation or parole in another jurisdiction.

corrections officer   An officer responsible for the direct supervision and control of inmates in prison, jail, halfway houses, or confined to an institution for juvenile offenders.

criminal court   A court that hears offenses committed by criminal defendants who are legally adults, as determined by each state's age of majority and juvenile waiver provisions.

criminal justice process   The system by which government enforces the law as it relates to adult criminal offenders, from arrest to sentencing. Although there are many similarities, the criminal justice process is distinct from the juvenile justice process.

criminal offense   A crime, as defined by state law, whether committed by an adult or a juvenile.

cruel and unusual punishment   Punishment that violates society's "evolving standards of decency," as interpreted by the U.S. Supreme Court, and that is banned by the Eighth Amendment to the U.S. Constitution.

curfew   An ordinance that prohibits certain persons (usually juveniles) from engaging in unsupervised activity during designated hours within a city or county.

custody   Being under the control of an official agency, such as law enforcement. In the juvenile justice system, being taken into custody is the equivalent of being arrested in the criminal justice system.

DARE (Drug Abuse Resistance Education)   A national school-based antidrug program first implemented in Los Angeles.

deferred prosecution   Also known as "deferred entry of judgment." After an admission or an allegation is found to be true, the court withholds entering a formal judgment for a period of time (commonly six months). If during that time the minor successfully completes all court-ordered sanctions and abides by the conditions of probation, a formal judgment is not entered and no juvenile record is created.

delinquent act   An act committed by a juvenile that, if committed by an adult, would constitute a criminal offense.

delinquent juvenile   A minor adjudicated (judged to be) delinquent in a juvenile court.

dependent Juvenile in need of the services or intervention of the state as the result of parental abandonment, neglect, abuse, or failure or inability to control the juvenile.

detention Custody and confinement in a secure or nonsecure facility, or at home, while awaiting adjudication, disposition, or placement.

detention center A facility, usually secured, for the confinement of detained juveniles.

detention hearing A formal hearing to determine if a juvenile offender should be held in a detention facility due to the seriousness of the allegations or because the minor is at risk of reoffending or harming self or others.

developmental perspective An approach to understanding juvenile violence that focuses on the interaction of juveniles with their environment at particular times in their lives.

differential association theory The concept that criminality is directly related to an offender's exposure to antisocial attitudes and values.

direct file The process by which a prosecutor chooses which cases should be prosecuted in adult criminal court rather than juvenile court and directly files these cases in criminal court without a hearing.

dismissal The release of a case with no further sanctions or consequences to the minor.

disposition The equivalent of sentencing in adult court, except that disposition has historically been aimed at rehabilitation rather than punishment of the juvenile offender. Possible dispositions in juvenile court include dismissal of the case, "informal" and formal probation, residential placement, or commitment to an institution for juvenile offenders.

disposition hearing A formal proceeding in juvenile court, conducted after adjudication, to determine the type and level of sanctions to be imposed upon a juvenile offender who has been adjudicated delinquent.

diversion The process by which a juvenile offender is channeled away (diverted) from processing in the juvenile justice system and, instead, is directed to community-based social service agencies.

due process The constitutional safeguards against arbitrary or unfair procedures in state or federal court proceedings, as guaranteed by the Fifth and Fourteenth Amendments. Due process requirements include timely notice of a hearing to inform the accused of the charges, the opportunity to confront accusers and present evidence, the presumption of innocence, the right to be advised of constitutional rights at the earliest stage of the criminal process (usually arrest), the protection against self-incrimination, the right to legal counsel, and the prohibition against being tried for the same crime twice (double jeopardy).

early-onset trajectory A pattern of violent behavior that emerges prior to the onset of adolescence and usually persists over time.

Glossary

Eighth Amendment Amendment to the U.S. Constitution, part of the Bill of Rights, that prohibits "cruel and unusual punishment" of adult and juvenile offenders.

electronic monitoring The use of electronic equipment, often an ankle bracelet, attached to a juvenile offender on probation to monitor the juvenile's activities.

emancipation The point at which an individual is no longer under the legal control of parents or guardians, usually occurring at the age of majority but sometimes earlier if granted by a court of law.

equal protection The right of all persons and of certain classes of persons (such as juveniles) to equal treatment under the law, as guaranteed by the Fourteenth Amendment to the U.S. Constitution.

escalation The increase in the number and frequency of offenses by an offender.

fact finder In juvenile proceedings, the judge or court officer—not a jury—who hears the evidence and determines if the allegations are true.

federal courts The system of courts with federal jurisdiction, administered by the U.S. government, that includes district (trial) courts, circuit (appellate) courts, and the U.S. Supreme Court.

felony A serious criminal offense that, if committed by an adult, is punishable by prison sentence of more than one year.

foster home A family residence where a minor is temporarily placed by the court or by a local welfare department when the minor cannot receive appropriate care or supervision at home.

foster parent The adult given responsibility for the care and supervision (including room and board) of a minor who has been removed from parental custody.

graduated sanctions Penalties for criminal behavior or disobeying a court order imposed upon a juvenile offender serially, beginning with the least restrictive and moving to more restrictive with each subsequent offense.

group home Usually a state-licensed home for dependency wards and for juvenile offenders who, based on their offense and behavior, do not require a higher level of confinement in a secured facility.

guardian An adult with the legal authority to provide care and supervision for a minor.

hate crime A crime committed against a person, or a person's property, because of the person's perceived race, ethnicity, religion, ancestry, national origin, disability, gender, or sexual orientation.

hearing In juvenile matters, a formal court proceeding that requires notice and affords the juvenile offender the right to present argument and evidence.

homicide The killing of another human being that is criminal, noncriminal (such as accidental), or negligent.

house arrest   Court-ordered alternative to secure detention in a correctional facility, usually with the requirement to remain at home or with other restrictions of individual liberty.

Illinois Juvenile Court Act of 1899   State legislation that established the first separate jurisdiction in the United States for the handling of juvenile offenders. The model was eventually adopted in whole or in part in all jurisdictions throughout the country.

incorrigible minor   A minor who is habitually truant, runs away from home, disobeys curfew laws, or for some other reason is beyond the control of a parent or guardian.

index crimes   Eight serious crimes, the incidence of which is annually reported in the FBI's Uniform Crime Reports—murder, rape, assault, robbery, burglary, arson, larceny, and motor vehicle theft.

intake   The initial screening of status and criminal offenders in the juvenile justice system to determine what action should be taken to best serve the juvenile and the community. Usually made by a probation officer, the decision may be to refer the case for formal proceedings in juvenile court or to handle the case "informally" by referring the juvenile to social service or community-based agencies.

Interstate Compact on Juveniles   Formal agreement among states authorizing the supervision of adjudicated juvenile offenders and status offenders on probation or parole, or the return of juvenile runaways, escapees, and absconders who have crossed state lines.

interstate transfer   Transfer of an adjudicated juvenile offender or status offender from one state to another, under authority of the Interstate Compact on Juveniles.

jail   A place of short-term secured confinement for adults awaiting trial or sentencing or serving terms for misdemeanor offenses. Jails are used to house persons under the age of majority who are accused of crimes for which they can be tried in adult criminal court, according to state law.

judicial transfer   The process by which a juvenile court judge decides that a case should be transferred to the adult criminal court. As set forth by the U.S. Supreme Court in *Kent v. U.S.* (1966), juveniles have a right to a hearing before judicial transfer occurs.

jury   A group of citizens empaneled by a court to be the triers of fact in a criminal or civil proceeding. Juvenile offenders are not eligible for jury trials, as set forth by the U.S. Supreme Court in *McKeiver v. Pennsylvania* (1971).

juvenile   A minor under the age of majority (as determined by state law) who cannot be held accountable as an adult for either criminal or civil liability.

juvenile court   A court, or jurisdiction, established to hear matters involving minors charged with criminal or status offenses.

Glossary

juvenile delinquency Illegal behavior by a person under the age of majority.

juvenile hall A secured facility where certain juvenile offenders are confined while awaiting adjudication, disposition, or placement.

Juvenile Justice and Delinquency Prevention Act of 1974 Federal legislation, since amended, that set forth guidelines for the handling of juvenile status and criminal offenders, and established the Office of Juvenile Justice and Delinquency Prevention to conduct research on juvenile justice issues and to fund grants to state and local agencies aimed toward improving the care and treatment of juvenile offenders.

juvenile justice process The handling of juvenile offenders from intake through disposition. Under the *parens patriae* philosophy upon which the first juvenile court was founded, juvenile procedures were informal and nonadversarial, as opposed to trials in criminal court. However, the process has become more formalized and aligned more closely with adult proceedings in the wake of rulings by the U.S. Supreme Court, beginning with *Kent v. United States* in 1966 and *In re Gault* in 1967.

juvenile justice system The system of governmental and nongovernmental institutions and agencies that deal with juvenile criminal and status offenders.

kidnapping The unlawful seizure of a person for ransom or reward.

late-onset trajectory A pattern of violent behavior in juveniles that emerges after the onset of adolescence, according to the developmental perspective.

malice Ill will or intent to cause harm.

manslaughter The unlawful killing of a human being without malice or premeditation.

mentoring Programs designed to place juvenile offenders or at-risk youth in regular, one-to-one contact with an adult role model.

minor A person under the age of majority (adulthood), as established by state law.

Miranda **warning** As the result of the U.S. Supreme Court decisions in *Escobedo v. Illinois* (1964) and *Miranda v. Arizona* (1966), law enforcement officers must inform anyone in their custody of their constitutional right to remain silent, to have an attorney present, and that any statements made by the person in custody can be used against them in court.

misdemeanor A criminal offense that, if committed by an adult, is punishable by a fine and/or a sentence of one year or less.

mitigating factors Factors considered in the adjudicatory process that tend to lessen the seriousness of the offense.

motion Oral or written request made to the court for a specific judgment, order, or finding.

motive The reason or factors that compel an individual to commit a criminal offense.

murder The unlawful killing of a person with malice aforethought.

National Crime Victimization Survey Compiled by the Department of Justice, the reports on crime statistics gathered from the victims of certain crimes.

nolo contendere A plea in a criminal case indicating that the accused will not contest the charges or allegations but is not admitting guilt or denying guilt.

nonpetitioned case The informal handling of a juvenile offender when no petition is filed in juvenile court. Often, the juvenile is referred to a social service agency or agrees to some type of counseling or community service.

nonsecure detention Temporary care of a juvenile in a facility in which restriction of the minor's movement or activity is imposed only by staff members, and not by physical barriers such as cells or locked gates.

offender Any person convicted or adjudicated for the commission of a criminal offense.

offense A felony, misdemeanor, or status offense. Felonies and misdemeanors are crimes; status offenses are not crimes.

Office of Juvenile Justice and Delinquency Prevention A component of the U.S. Department of Justice responsible for supporting and implementing programs in the furtherance of juvenile justice.

officer of the court Person holding an office of public trust, with the power and duty to perform functions prescribed by the court (such as a prosecutor or a defense attorney).

parens patriae The philosophy of the state as parent, which historically governed the handling of juvenile offenders until it was eroded by a series of Supreme Court decisions beginning in 1966. These brought juvenile court proceedings more in line with proceedings in adult criminal court.

parental responsibility laws Statutes that hold parents responsible, usually monetarily, for delinquent acts committed by their children.

parole A convicted criminal offender's release from prison before completing the full term of the sentence. Juveniles confined to state-run correctional facilities for juvenile offenders are often paroled in much the same way as adults.

parole officer Agent or officer responsible for the community supervision of criminal or juvenile offenders paroled from correctional institutions.

person offense A criminal act directed toward a human victim, such as assault or battery.

petition The equivalent of the "complaint" or "indictment" in criminal court, this document contains each charge or allegation being brought against a juvenile offender in juvenile court.

Glossary

petitioned case   A case that is formally handled by the juvenile court, beginning with the filing of a petition containing allegations of delinquency against a minor.

placement   As ordered by a juvenile court, the removal of a juvenile offender from home so that the juvenile may reside in a secured or nonsecured residential facility.

plea   In a juvenile court, an admission by the juvenile offender to the allegation(s) contained in the petition, usually in exchange for a recommendation to the court by the prosecutor for a more favorable disposition.

plea bargain   An agreement, usually negotiated by attorneys for the defense and for the prosecution, in which the offender agrees to plead guilty to a one or more specified allegations, usually in exchange for a more lenient disposition.

poor laws   Seventeenth-century English laws that allowed vagrant or abandoned children to be placed into indentured servitude.

predisposition investigation   Court-ordered background investigation of a juvenile offender performed by a probation officer, which is taken into consideration by the court at the time of disposition.

preponderance of evidence   The standard of proof used in civil trials by which the prevailing party must provide the greater weight of evidence. This standard of proof was commonly used in juvenile courts throughout the country until the U.S. Supreme Court ruled in *In re Winship* (1970) that juvenile offenders must be held to the same standard as adult criminal defendants—proof beyond a reasonable doubt.

presumptive transfer   A system for transferring youth from juvenile court to the adult criminal court. Presumptive transfer shifts burden to the defense, in that cases are presumed to be eligible for transfer unless the defendant can convince a judge otherwise.

preventative detention   The holding of a juvenile or adult based on the substantiated belief that the detainee might commit a crime or could harm self or others.

probable cause   A reasonable belief, acquired through personal knowledge or reliable sources, that a person has committed a criminal offense. Also, the standard necessary to sustain a legal search or seizure, except in the case of school searches, where the standard was lowered to "reasonableness" by the U.S. Supreme Court in *New Jersey v. T.L.O.* (1985).

probation   Court-ordered legal status that permits an adjudicated offender to remain in the community, subject to supervision by a probation officer, with conditions and restrictions imposed by the court, or treatment prescribed by the court. Juvenile probation is known as "community control" in Florida and as "conditions release" in New Hampshire.

probation officer   Agent or officer responsible for the court-ordered investigation and community supervision of criminal or juvenile offenders and, in some jurisdictions, for status offenders.

property offense   A criminal act not directed at a person, such as burglary, larceny, or arson.

prosecutor   The government's attorney in a criminal case responsible for proving the charges or allegations beyond a reasonable doubt.

protective factors   The three factors in a juvenile's life that reduce or ameliorate the impact of risk factors attributed to delinquency. They are personal characteristics, positive adult relationships, and clear standards of conduct.

public defender   An attorney paid by the county of jurisdiction to defend criminal offenders who cannot afford to hire an attorney. In most jurisdictions, juvenile offenders automatically qualify to be represented by public defenders or court-appointed counsel.

rational choice theory   The theory that delinquent behavior is a rational choice made by an offender who thinks that the potential gains of the criminal activity outweigh the risk of punishment.

reasonableness   The standard that requires a search or seizure to be reasonable but does not necessarily require probable cause (as in the case of school searches).

recidivism   Involvement in continued criminal activity, following court involvement or punishment.

referee   A finder of fact in juvenile court with the same powers as a judge.

rehabilitation   The process of changing or reforming a juvenile offender into a law-abiding individual.

residential placement   The placement of a juvenile offender in nonsecured facility such as a foster home or drug treatment center, or in a secured private or government-operated facility.

restitution   Money paid or services rendered by a juvenile as direct compensation for damage done to the victim of the offense.

restorative justice   Process by which all interested parties collectively determine how to deal with the aftermath of a criminal offense, including the imposition of sanctions on the criminal or juvenile offender. This approach involves the collaboration among victims, offenders, and others from the community, and focuses on the well-being of both the victim and the offender—in contrast to retributive justice, which deals with lawbreakers in a strictly punitive way.

revocation   Termination of probation or parole following a hearing and the finding of a violation of probation or parole by the offender, usually resulting in a more restrictive disposition or sentence, including confinement.

Glossary

revocation hearing Judicial or administrative process to determine if an offender's probation or parole status should be terminated as the result of the offender's alleged violation of the conditions of probation or parole. The standard of proof is usually preponderance of the evidence.

right to treatment The philosophy that juvenile and adult offenders have a legal right to treatment. However, a federal constitutional right to treatment has not been established.

risk factors Problem behaviors, negative relationships, or unhealthy environment that may contribute to later delinquency.

robbery The unlawful taking of property from a person by force or threat of force.

runaway Nondelinquent minor who has left the home of parents or guardians without permission, and who has failed to return within a reasonable period of time.

sanction The penalty for violating a law or court order.

school search The legal search of a juvenile's person, possessions, or areas of use (such as school lockers) without a search warrant or probable cause, as established by the U.S. Supreme Court in *New Jersey v. T.L.O.* (1985).

sealing of juvenile record The permanent closure of a minor's juvenile court record, usually requiring a court order or upon the court's own motion.

self-control theory The theory that delinquency is caused by impulsive behavior by minors who may feel disengaged from society.

self-defense The right to defend oneself with force that is reasonable and in proportion to the perceived threat of force.

self-incrimination Supplying evidence, making statements, or answering questions about oneself that would tend to show personal involvement in a criminal offense.

self-report studies Research surveys that ask individuals questions about their personal behavior, such as drug use or criminal victimization.

shelter care The care of a child in a physically unrestricted facility, often as a means of temporary housing or to provide closer supervision of juvenile and status offenders.

simple assault The deliberate attempt to cause bodily injury, or the infliction of bodily injury upon another as the result of negligence or recklessness.

specialization offenses Offenses that demonstrate the tendency of a criminal offender to repeat one type of crime.

standard of proof The level of proof required at various stages of the justice system. Probable cause is the standard of proof for an arrest. Beyond a reasonable doubt is the standard of proof for trials and adjudicatory hearings.

status offender   A minor adjudicated for conduct that would not constitute an offense if committed by an adult. Status offenses include running
away, truancy, and drinking or possessing alcoholic beverages.

status offenses   Acts that are noncriminal for adults but illegal if committed by a juvenile, such as truancy or possession of alcohol or cigarettes.

statute   A law enacted by a legislature.

statute of limitations   The legally defined period of time following the
commission of a crime after which an individual cannot be prosecuted
for that crime.

statutory rape   Sexual intercourse with a minor, regardless of whether the
minor consents to the sexual act.

statutory transfer   The automatic transfer of a juvenile from the juvenile
court to the adult criminal court, as set forth by state law for specific age
and offense categories.

stop and frisk   A "pat down," or superficial search, by law enforcement
of a person believed to be acting suspiciously or carrying a weapon or
contraband.

subpoena   Written order issued by a court clerk or judicial officer requiring a person to appear at a designated place and time in court.

supervision   Oversight of offenders by probation or parole officers in
order to monitor activities and behavior while living in the community.

tagger   An offender, often juvenile, who defaces property with graffiti or
other markings, often denoting gang affiliation.

technical violation   An act by a probationer or parolee that is in violation
of the conditions of probation or parole, but does not rise to the level of
a criminal offense.

transcript   The verbatim written record of a court proceeding, kept by
the court reporter.

transfer hearing (waiver hearing)   A formal court hearing that determines if a juvenile offender is suitable to remain under the jurisdiction of
the juvenile court or should be prosecuted as an adult in criminal court.
The transfer or waiver hearing is conducted prior to the adjudicatory
hearing and does not determine guilt or innocence. See also **judicial
transfer, presumptive transfer, statutory transfer.**

treatment   The rehabilitative approach to juvenile offenders through
therapy and educational or vocational programs.

truant   A minor absent from school without permission or a compelling
reason.

Uniform Crime Reports (UCR)   Compiled annually by the FBI, a statistical analysis of arrests and crimes reported to the FBI by local law
enforcement agencies throughout the United States.

vandalism   The malicious defacing, damaging, or destroying of private
property.

Glossary

victim An individual, business, organization, or unit of government that suffers injury or economic loss as the result of someone's illegal conduct.

victimization The result of an act that causes physical or psychological harm to a person.

violation An offense designated by statute, ordinance, or regulation for which the punishment is a fine, forfeiture, or other civil remedy—but not loss of liberty. Also known as an infraction.

violation of parole Conduct that is prohibited according to the conditions of parole, or failing to perform an action required by the conditions of parole.

violation of probation Conduct that is prohibited according to the conditions of probation, or failing to perform an action required by the conditions of probation. The standard of proof for a finding of violation of probation is usually preponderance of evidence.

violent crime Serious person offenses such as rape, robbery, assault, or murder.

violent offender A juvenile offender charged with a violent offense, including murder, nonnegligent manslaughter, kidnapping, violent sexual assault, robbery, and aggravated assault.

ward In juvenile court, a juvenile offender placed under the legal authority of the court, even though the minor may still reside with a parent or guardian.

waiver hearing *See* transfer hearing.

youth gang A group of juveniles and young adults who associate for social or criminal purposes.

PART II

GUIDE TO FURTHER RESEARCH

CHAPTER 7

HOW TO RESEARCH JUVENILE CRIME AND JUVENILE JUSTICE ISSUES

Myriad resources are available to the researcher on the issues of juvenile crime and juvenile justice. This chapter discusses resources that are generally accessible to the public. Thus, while a broad range of resources are presented, other research tools are available—for example, databases that charge a subscription fee, or those available at a local library or college. In addition, much of the information available through the various research tools presented here is national or statewide in scope. For information on crime and justice issues at the community level, readers are directed to their local newspaper or law enforcement agency.

SPECIFIC JUVENILE CRIME AND JUSTICE WEB SITES

The Office of Juvenile Justice and Delinquency Prevention (OJJDP) and the National Criminal Justice Reference Service (NCJRS) are the best starting points for research on juvenile crime and justice. Both are federal agencies that offer public access to extensive collections of publications on juvenile crime, all facets of the juvenile justice system, and delinquency prevention—usually free of charge.

More detailed information on state transfer provisions is available from the National Criminal Justice Reference Service (Office of Justice Programs, U.S. Department of Justice), available online at http://www.ncjrs.gov, and also from the National Center for Juvenile Justice, available at http://www.ncjj.org.

OJJDP PUBLICATIONS

Publications by the Office of Juvenile Justice and Delinquency Prevention are available online at http://www.ojjdp.ncjrs.org. They are downloadable and printable. Hard copies are also available by email at puborder@ncjrs. org, by telephone at 800-851-3420, or by U.S. mail through the NCJRS at P.O. Box 6000, Rockville, MD 20849-6000. For online access, by clicking on the "Publications" link the researcher will be directed to a page offering links to OJJDP publications as well as juvenile justice publications world-wide. The OJJDP also provides a publications list (available online), in which publications are listed by subject area.

OJJDP offers the following types of publications on issues of juvenile crime and juvenile justice:

- *Fact Sheets:* Each two-page summary provides an overview of an OJJDP research topic and often includes a link to a full publication on that topic.
- *Bulletins:* Ranging from four to 32 pages in length, these documents summarize research and statistical data on juvenile crime and justice issues.
- *Reports:* These provide detailed information on research and case studies on issues of juvenile crime and justice, and may be national, regional, or local in scope.
- *Summaries:* Generally 30 to 90 pages in length, they describe research findings or provide training manuals for juvenile justice professionals. Appendices and listings of additional readings are usually provided, as well.
- *Newsletter:* Published bimonthly, *OJJDP News @ a Glance* provides information on recent publications as well as notices of upcoming events, including conferences.
- *Juvenile Justice Journal:* Publishes two or three times annually; each issue generally contains up to three articles on a focus topic, such as school violence or gangs.
- *Portable Guides to Investigating Child Abuse:* Each guide is between 16 and 36 pages long and provides information on critical aspects of investigations involving child abuse, neglect, and exploitation.
- *Teleconference Videotapes:* Videotapes of OJJDP's satellite conferences are available for purchase through the NCJRS (see below).

All publications on the OJJDP's website are accessible either by topic or alphabetically by title. The topical list is divided as follows: All, Child Protection, Core Resources, Corrections/Detention, Courts, Delinquency

Prevention, Gender/Race/Ethnicity, Health, Law Enforcement/Offenses/ Offenders, Schools, Statistics, Victims. Both the topical and alphabetical lists provide links to download the entire publication or a summary of the publication.

THE NCJRS

The National Criminal Justice Reference Service is basically a clearing-house for publications from a variety of federal agencies, including the OJJDP. Some of the other federal agencies for which the NCJRS offers full-text publications include the Bureau of Justice Statistics, the Bureau of Justice Assistance, the Office for Victims of Crime, and the Office of National Drug Control Policy. These and other federal agencies publish hundreds of reports annually on crime and criminal justice that are made available through the NCJRS.

Publications from the NCJRS are available online at http://www.ncjrs. org. They may also be ordered by telephone at 800-851-3420, by fax at 301-519-5212, or by U.S. mail at P.O. Box 6000, Rockville, MD 20849-6000.

When accessing the NCJRS online, publications are offered by category. The categories include corrections, courts, drugs and crime, international, juvenile justice, law enforcement, victims of crime, and statistics. Each of these categories is subdivided with greater specificity. For example, the category of juvenile justice contains the following subcategories, each with its own additional subcategories.

- child protection/health
- corrections/detention
- delinquency prevention
- gender/race/ethnicity
- juvenile courts
- juvenile delinquency
- schools
- victims

These categories are not only helpful in locating information with some specificity but also as search terms when searching the World Wide Web, library catalogs, and databases. Searches can be performed within the NCJRS library in one of three ways:

- ***Boolean Search:*** Finds exactly the words typed and allows combinations of terms with *and, or,* and *not* as well as parentheses. For example, if searching for information on HIV/AIDS in correctional facilities, one could enter: *(AIDS or HIV) and (correctional or prison or jail)*.

- **Concept Search:** Looks for the words and phrases as typed plus related concepts.
- **Pattern Search:** Looks for the words as typed plus words with a similar spelling. This is useful when uncertain of the proper spelling of a word or a person's name.

In addition to more than 2,000 titles on crime and justice issues, the NCJRS also offers an extensive database of abstracts—brief summaries of books, reports, and articles. Searches of NCJRS abstracts may be performed in any of the three ways described above and can be further narrowed by subject area, title of the publication, author, and the NCJ number assigned to each publication offered by the NCJRS. The NCJ number is included in each abstract listing, as is the date of publication of the abstracted book, report or article. For example, in a subject search for "drugs," the first five abstracts appeared as follows:

1. "Hazswat Changed?: Combining Hazmat and SWAT Training for Tactical Operations," NCJ Number: 227061, Author: Michelle Perin, Journal: *Law Enforcement Technology* Volume: 36 Issue: 5 Dated: May 2009 Pages: 20,22,25, Publication Date: May 2009.
2. *Indicators of School Crime and Safety: 2008*, NCJ Number: 226343, Authors: Rachel Dinkes; Jana Kemp; Katrina Baum; Thomas D. Snyder, Publication Date: April 2009.
3. *ADAM II 2008 Annual Report: Arrestee Drug Abuse Monitoring Program II*, NCJ Number: 226971, Publication Date: April 2009.
4. "Exploration of Treatment and Supervision Intensity among Drug Court and Non-Drug Court Participants," NCJ Number: 227009, Authors: Christine H. Lindquist; Christopher P. Krebs; Tara D. Warner; Pamela K. Lattimore, Journal: *Journal of Offender Rehabilitation* Volume: 48 Issue: 3 Dated: April 2009 Pages:167–193, Publication Date: April 2009.
5. *Sex Offender Registration and Notification: Research Finds Limited Effects in New Jersey*, NCJ Number: 225402, Authors: Kristen Zgoba Ph.D.; Karen Bachar, Publication Date: April 2009.

Also, when searching the NCJRS abstracts library, a start date and end date can be specified, which can be helpful when trying to locate materials published within a certain time period—for instance, within the past year, or during the 1970s.

RESEARCHING JUVENILE CRIME AND JUSTICE ON THE INTERNET

As the Internet continues to expand so, too, do the number of sites offering information on juvenile crime and juvenile justice. These can include government-sponsored sites, like the OJJDP and the NCJRS, or sites sponsored by educational institutions, nonprofit advocacy groups, research foundations ("think tanks"), or by individuals with some interest or expertise in a particular area relating to juvenile crime or juvenile justice. Evaluating the legitimacy of an Internet site, and by extension the quality of its information, is largely in the hands of the researcher.

The most common way to search the Internet is by using a search engine. Search engines are driven by the user typing in a keyword and launching a search of the World Wide Web based on that term or phrase.

SEARCH ENGINES

Search engines perform keyword searches of a database. Variables such as the size of the database, the frequency of updating the database, the search capability, and speed of the search engine will affect the results.

Metasearch sites (also known as "metacrawlers") search multiple search engines. Some of the most popular metasearch sites include Dogpile (http://www.dogpile.com/index.gsp), Mamma (http://www.mamma.com), Metacrawler (http://www.metacrawler.com/index.html), and Info.com http://www.info.com.

On one day, a search of the World Wide Web using Dogpile and the keywords "juvenile crime" resulted in multiple links from the search engines Google, Yahoo!, and Ask. Dogpile also provided links to the following categories:

- Juvenile Crime Statistics
- Juvenile Justice
- Juvenile Punishments
- Juvenile Justice
- Causes of Juvenile Delinquency
- Statistics about Juvenile Delinquency
- Juvenile Crime Causes
- Juvenile Delinquency
- Juvenile Statistics

Metasearch engines can be a powerful tool for the researcher, especially when searching for obscure information. On the other hand, the results produced by metasearches on broader issues such as juvenile crime and justice can result in multiple hits for the same site and produce an excess of information to sort through.

Basic search engines are often more efficient for exploring broader topics. Some of the most popular search engines are Yahoo! (http://www.yahoo.com), Bing (www.bing.com, and Ask (http://www.ask.com). These are just a few of the many search engines available.

Search engines offer the choice of basic and advanced searches. The basic search is limited to the keyword or phrase that is used, while the advanced search offers a number of variables designed to refine the search term(s). For example, in a Google advanced search it is possible to tell the search engine to search for *all* of the words in a keyword phrase, for the *exact phrase*, or for *at least one* word in the keyword phrase. It is also possible to further limit in a number of ways, including by language, file format, and date. It is even possible to limit the search to a specific web site to locate specific information within that website. This is done by entering the keyword or phrase followed by "site:" and the domain name. For example, to search the National Criminal Justice Reference Center (NCJRS) for publications on gangs, the following was entry was typed in the Google search window: gangs site:www.ncjrs.org.

This search produced more than 100 publications on gangs available online from the NCJRS, including *Youth Gangs in Schools* (2000), *Youth Gangs: An Overview* (1998), and *Female Gangs* (2001).

Using the keywords "juvenile crime," a typical basic Google search produced approximately 1.5 million hits, the first five of which were as follows:

- *Juvenile Crime and Issues.* Juveniles are generally treated differently in the criminal justice system, but sometimes they are treated as adults. crime. about.com/od/juvenile/Juvenile_Crime_and_Issues.htm.

- *Juvenile Crime > Statistics > Violent, Sexual, Drug/Alcohol Crimes.* A juvenile crime can include any offense that can be committed by an adult, as well as status offenses, which can include curfew violation, running away . . . www.lawyershop.com/practice-areas/criminal-law/. . ./crimes/.

- *Juvenile Crime: Outlook for California.* How Prevalent Is Juvenile Crime in California? What Happens to Juvenile Offenders? It also discusses (a) reforming the division of juvenile justice and (a) . . . www.lao.ca.gov/laokktoc.html.

- *Statistical Briefing Book.* Law Enforcement & Juvenile Crime · Juveniles in Court · Juveniles on Probation · Juveniles in Corrections · Juvenile Reentry & Aftercare . . . www.ojjdp.ncjrs.gov/ojstatbb/default.asp.

- *Juvenile Crime, Juvenile Justice.* Patterns and Trends in Juvenile Crime and Juvenile Justice (25–65) . . . JUVENILE CRIME THE NATIONAL ACADEMIES National Academy of Sciences National Academy . . . www.nap.edu/books/0309068428/html/.

From these five results, it is possible to see the wide range of information produced by a basic search for "juvenile crime." For example, one of the sites had information from 1995, while another had information from 2007. Using an advanced search would make it possible to look for information on juvenile crime within the past year or even the past three months.

LIBRARY CATALOGS

Access to the Library of Congress, with the largest library catalog in the world, is available at http://catalog.loc.gov. From this page it is possible to conduct a basic search by title, author, subject, call number, keywords, and by LCCN, ISSN, or ISBN publishing numbers. A more advanced guided search is also possible and its search parameters are explained on the web page.

A basic search of "juvenile delinquency" produced a listing of subject headings with links to thousands of publications on delinquency in the United States, delinquency in foreign countries, studies of delinquency, and statistics on delinquency. A basic search of "juvenile justice" produced a similar array of subject headings.

Increasingly, catalogs for local, regional and college libraries are accessible online. The Web site http://worldcat.org allows one to search for items in libraries across the world. The local library can be an excellent starting point for research and information on juvenile crime and justice. Many libraries, including the Library of Congress, offer assistance by email from a professional librarian, which can be an invaluable timesaver.

BIBLIOGRAPHIES

Bibliographies are another way to locate books, articles, and other materials on juvenile crime and justice. Often, the best starting point for bibliographic information is a local library, where books found on the topics of juvenile crime and justice may also contain bibliography and reference sections for further reading on the topic. Other libraries with more extensive collections—like the Library of Congress or university libraries—can be excellent sources of bibliographies, as well.

Another source, as discussed earlier in this chapter, is the extensive collection of abstracts offered by the National Criminal Justice Reference

Service (NCJRS). For example, in a simple search under "annotated bibliography," the first four publications appeared as follows:

- *Annotated Bibliography on Clandestine Methamphetamine Labs*, NCJ 222922, Deanna Breslin, May 2008 (29 pages).
- *Annotated Bibliography on Women Offenders: Prisons, Jails, Community Corrections, and Juvenile Justice: Web-Accessible Items from 2001 through March 2006*, NCJ 214259, Peggy Ritchie, March 2006 (28 pages).
- *Annotated Bibliography: How Narcotics Trafficking Organizations Operate as Businesses*, NCJ 203832, John N. Gibbs, September 2002 (11 pages).
- *Annotated Bibliography of Government Documents Related to the Threat of Terrorism and the Attacks of September 11, 2001*, NCJ 201402, April 17, 2002 (98 pages).

BOOKSELLER CATALOGS

Another convenient and useful source of bibliographic information is online booksellers. For example, a simple search for "juvenile crime" under "books" at Amazon.com turned up 11,916 titles. Among the first 10 were the following:

Hard Time: A Real Life Look at Juvenile Crime and Violence (Laurel-Leaf Books), by Janet Bode and Stanley Mach, 1997.
Juvenile Crime (Library in a Book), by Jeffrey Ferro, 2003.
Juvenile Crime, Juvenile Justice, by the Treatment and Control Panel on Juvenile Crime: Prevention, Committee on Law and Justice, Youth, and Families Board on Children, and National Research Council, 2001.

FREE PERIODICAL INDEXES

InfoTrac is a widely available database that indexes articles from general-interest magazines and newspapers as well as somewhat specialized periodicals. Many public libraries subscribe to InfoTrac and, increasingly, it is often accessible via the library's web site to patrons with library cards. InfoTrac presented the following selection of databases along with a description of each one.

Academic OneFile

A comprehensive database of more than 8,000 journals covering the physical sciences, technology, medicine, social sciences, the arts, theology, literature, and other subjects. Most of the journals are in full text, available in HTML and PDF formats. Content includes hundreds of podcasts and transcripts from NPR, CNN, and the CBC, as well as full-text New York Times *articles from 1995 to the present.*

Computer Database

Provides indexing and abstracting of high-tech publications in the areas of computer science, electronics, telecommunications, and microcomputer applications. The full text of many articles is available.

Expanded Academic ASAP Plus

Provides indexing and abstracting of over 3,000 scholarly and general interest periodicals, with the full text of articles from many of these periodicals available, as well as indexing of the most current six months of the New York Times. *The database integrates core titles in every major academic concentration; area- and issue-specific journals; academic journals with application in the professions; and publications with national news coverage and commentary.*

General Business File ASAP

Provides indexing and abstracting of more than 900 periodicals and full text for 460 titles. It is an excellent source of information on management theories, business law, key industries, mergers, acquisitions and joint ventures, international trade, new technologies, small and emerging companies, marketing and advertising, job-hunting strategies, and banking. It includes indexing of the current year of the Wall Street Journal *and the financial section of the* New York Times *and the current six months of the* Asian Wall Street Journal.

General OneFile

Includes some 3,000 full-text periodicals covering a wide range of topics: business, computers, current events, economics, education, environmental issues, health care, hobbies, humanities, law, literature and art, politics, science, social sciences, sports, technology, and many general interest topics. Has the full text of New York Times *articles from 1995 to the present as well as audio files and transcripts of National Public Radio (NPR) programs from 1990 to the present. Also has a large set of more than 20 reference sources. There are currently over 11,000 titles in InfoTrac OneFile, with most of the content in full text and without embargos. The database also includes the periodical content from the other Gale Resource Center databases, i.e., Biography Resource Center, Business and Company Resource Center, and Literature Resource Center.*

Health Reference Center Academic

Health and wellness research designed especially for the layperson. It contains indexing to medical journals and consumer health magazines. In addition, the full text of more than 500 health pamphlets, six medical reference books, and articles from more than 1,500 general interest magazines is available.

Juvenile Crime

Using the General OneFile, a basic search using the keyword "delinquency" resulted in 3,265 hits for books, news stories, magazine articles, academic journals, and multimedia sources. One can narrow the search results by subject, with a list that includes the following:

Juvenile delinquency	1,042 entries
Crime	138 entries
Juvenile offenders	92 entries
Youth	77 entries
Administration of justice	65 entries

Databases such as InfoTrac gather information from a wide range of publications and periodicals. Increasingly, individual Web sites are available for many newspapers and magazines. These Web sites often provide a searchable database of articles for that particular publication. This can be especially useful for research that is confined to a specific geographic area. For example, a good starting point for information on gang violence in Los Angeles would be the *Los Angeles Times*, at http://www.latimes.com. Web sites for individual publications are also useful when researching technical areas. For example, for information on the role of social workers in the areas of delinquency and juvenile justice, two good starting points might be the journals *Social Work*, at http://www.naswpress.org/publications/journals/sw.html, and *Social Work Research*, at http://www.naswpress.org/publications/journals/swr.html.

Another useful source of information from periodicals that is available free of charge online is FindArticles (URL: www.findarticles.com). FindArticles is an archive of articles published in magazines and journals from 1997 onward. Searches in FindArticles can be done by subject or by publication.

For a search by subject, the following search categories are available on a drop-down menu: Arts, Autos, Business, Health, Home & Garden, News, Reference, Sports, and Technology. It is also possible to search articles from "all magazines" archived by FindArticles. A search under the category "News" using the search word "delinquency" produced 1,768 articles from publications including *The FBI Law Enforcement Bulletin*, *Australian and New Zealand Journal of Criminology*, and *Crime Control Digest*. Using the keyword "delinquency" under the category "Reference" produced 812 articles from publications such as *Social Forces*, *Juvenile Justice Digest*, and *Education*.

A search by publication is also possible by clicking on the category link provided on the home page of FindArticles. For example, the category "News" includes publications such as *American Journal of Economics and Sociology*, *The FBI Law Enforcement Bulletin*, *Social Justice*, and *USA Today*. A link is provided for each publication which leads to a brief description of the publication. For example, the link for *The FBI Law Enforcement Bulletin* provided the following description: "A collection of criminal justice stories, reports and project findings." Additionally, with each description a link is provided to that publication's Web site. So, for example, when articles from *The FBI Law Enforcement Bulletin* were referenced in the results of a subject search of the term *delinquency* under "News," it was possible to locate that publication under the "News" link and go directly to *The FBI Law Enforcement Bulletin* Web site for further research—without having to perform an additional search via an outside search engine.

LEGAL RESEARCH

Researching laws and legislation can be somewhat daunting and frustrating even for a practiced researcher. However, with a basic understanding of how to use legal citations and with some help from the Internet, legal research can be both efficient and productive.

FINDING LEGISLATION

When legislation is passed it becomes part of a code. For example, federal legislation becomes part of the United States Code (U.S.C.), where it is organized into sections called titles. The U.S.C. is divided into 50 titles. Each title is further divided by chapters, subchapters, and sections. For example, the Juvenile Justice and Delinquency Prevention Act of 1974 is located in Title 42, Chapter 72, Subchapter, Section 5601 of the U.S.C. That is its formal citation. Like an address, the citation serves as the locator for each piece of legislation. However, when searching a legal database, only the title and section numbers are used. Thus, the citation 42 U.S.C. 5601 is used for the Juvenile Justice and Delinquency Prevention Act of 1974.

The Legal Information Institute at Cornell University School of Law (http://www.law.cornell.edu) provides a free online searchable database of federal legislation as well as Supreme Court decisions. By clicking on the link "Constitutions and Codes," and then "U.S. Code" one is directed to a search page that also provides a listing (with links) of all U.S.C. titles. Simply enter the title and section numbers where indicated to be directed to the appropriate legislation.

If the formal citation is not known, it is possible to perform a search of the Legal Information Institute's databases according to the informal title of the legislation. However, it is often more efficient to perform the title search through a search engine such as Google. A Google search for "Juvenile Justice and Delinquency Prevention Act of 1974" produced the full citation with a link to the Legal Information Institute.

For state legislation, the best source is often the web site for that state. Usually there are links to "Justice" and sometimes to "Juvenile," as well.

FINDING LAWS

An excellent resource available to the public for laws at both the state and federal level is FindLaw, at http://www.findlaw.com/casecode/index.html. Links are provided to U.S. federal laws and to U.S. state laws. Under the heading "US Court of Appeals—Opinions & Resources" there was a link for "United States Supreme Court." Clicking that link led to a search page, where searches can be performed by citation or by party name. In the "party name" search box, simply tying the word "Gault" produced a link to the case "In re Gault" 387 U.S. 1 (1967). By following that link, the full text of the opinion was presented.

State laws may also be researched in a similar fashion on FindLaw. However, when the party names and case citations are unknown, an excellent source is the National Center for Juvenile Justice (NCJJ), at http://www.ncjj.org. The link "State Profiles" leads to a pull-down menu where it is possible to select the District of Columbia or any state in the United States for information on that state's juvenile laws and how they govern the handling of juvenile offenders. For example, one check on New York produced extensive information contained under the following headings:

Delinquency Services Summary
Court(s) with Delinquency Jurisdiction
Highlights
Detention
Delinquency Intake Screening
Diversion
Predisposition Investigation
Victim Rights and Services
Probation Supervision
Juvenile Probation Officer Qualifications, Certification, and Training
Juvenile Corrections Continuum
Commitment to State
Direct Placement
Release
Aftercare/Re-entry
State Laws
   Legal Resources
   Purpose Clause
   Delinquency Jurisdiction
   Juvenile Transfer Laws
   Juvenile Justice Leadership
Resources/Contacts

CHAPTER 8

ANNOTATED BIBLIOGRAPHY

This chapter provides an extensive bibliography for juvenile crime and juvenile justice issues. The works presented range from articles found in daily newspapers and weekly newsmagazines to reports by experts in the fields of juvenile crime and justice. Whenever possible, Internet links are provided for more scholarly publications that might not be carried by one's local library. As this bibliography suggests, an abundance of material on juvenile crime and juvenile justice can be downloaded directly from the World Wide Web.

The bibliography is divided into the following five sections:

- Juvenile crime (includes general information on juvenile crime, including arrest statistics and types of juvenile offenders)
- Youth gangs
- School violence
- Substance abuse (as it relates to delinquency and juvenile crime)
- Juvenile justice (includes juvenile court statistics, dispositions, and other topics such as mental health among juvenile offenders and juvenile law)

Each of these five sections is subdivided as follows:

- Books
- Articles and papers
- Web documents
- Audiovisual

JUVENILE CRIME

BOOKS

Arthur, R. *Family Life and Youth Offending: Home Is Where the Hurt Is.* New York: Routledge, 2007. Analysis of how family factors are related to youth offending. An emphasis is placed on early prevention, based on the understanding that multiple risk factors need to be considered, including family problems, social inequality, and economic deprivation.

Asquith, S., ed. *Children and Young People in Conflict with the Law*. Bristol, Pa.: Jessica Kingsley Publishers, 1996. Addresses a number of specific areas related to juvenile crime in western Europe and the United States.

Chesney-Lind, M., and R. G. Shelden. *Girls, Delinquency and Juvenile Justice*, 3rd ed. Pacific Grove, Calif.: Brooks/Cole Publishing Company, 2003. Analysis of female juvenile delinquency, with focus on the nature and causes of female delinquency. Presents data supporting the theory that female delinquents and status offenders have different needs from those of male offenders.

Chesney-Lind, M., and K. Irwin. *Beyond Bad Girls: Gender, Violence and Hype*. New York: Routledge, 2008. Sociological analysis of media images and constructions of girls' aggression and violence, compared to actual trends in girls' delinquency and violent behavior. The authors argue that popular images of female defiance have social consequences for public negative perceptions about girlhood.

Empey, L. T. *American Delinquency: Its Meaning and Construction*. Homewood, Ill.: Dorsey Press, 1982. Examines the causes and scientific explanations of delinquency in the United States; was one of the first delinquency textbooks to explore the historical context of how society views children.

Farrington, D. P., and B. C. Welsh. *Saving Children from a Life of Crime: Early Risk Factors and Effective Interventions*. New York: Oxford University Press, 2007. This study draws on extensive research and literature reviews to set forth a strategy for preventing juvenile delinquency through early intervention. Early intervention is characterized by (a) measures implemented in the early years of a child's life, sometimes from prior to birth to early adolescence; (b) intervention with children and youth, before the onset of delinquency, which involves the whole community; and (c) interventions targeted at children who are at risk of offending.

Finkelhor, D. *Childhood Victimization: Violence, Crime, and Abuse in the Lives of Young People*. New York: Oxford University Press, 2008. Discusses the prevention and treatment of juvenile victims of crime, violence, and abuse. The author creates a framework for viewing the social agencies that respond to help the child victim and provides proposals for the prevention and intervention of child victimization.

Hendrix, Elaine Hallisey, et al., eds. *Atlas of Crime: Mapping the Criminal Landscape*. Phoenix, Ariz.: Oryx Press, 2000. Discusses the geographic distribution of crime in schools and examines such topics as the role of weapons in juvenile delinquency.

Howell, J. C., J. D. Hawkins, and J. Wilson, eds. *Sourcebook on Serious, Violent, and Chronic Offenders*. Thousand Oaks, Calif.: Sage Publications,

1995. Discusses responses to serious, violent, and chronic delinquency. Consists of chapters written by an array of prominent researchers and is still one of the most comprehensive sources of research on the topic.

Jones, M. A., and B. Krisberg. *Images and Reality: Juvenile Crime, Youth Violence, and Public Policy*. San Francisco, Calif.: National Council on Crime and Delinquency, 1994. A widely cited and influential text that presents findings that the most important factor related to youth violence and juvenile homicide is the availability of firearms.

Lotz, R. *Youth Crime in America: A Modern Synthesis*. Upper Saddle River, N.J.: Pearson Prentice Hall, 2004. This text examines the latest developments in youth crime, delinquency, theory, and research. Topics examined include making youth crime into a social issue, data on youth crime, theories of delinquency, and official responses to delinquency.

McCord, Joan, Cathy Spatz Widom, and Nancy A. Crowell, eds. *Juvenile Crime, Juvenile Justice*. Washington, D.C.: National Academy Press, 2001. The Committee on Law and Justice and Board on Children, Youth, and Families presents the findings of a National Research Council panel established to review research from 1980 to 2000 to determine what is known about juvenile delinquency and its prevention, treatment, and control.

Miller, Jody. *Getting Played: African American Girls' Urban Inequality and Gendered Violence* New York: New York University Press, 2008. This study examines the victimization of African-American girls living in disadvantaged neighborhoods in St. Louis, Missouri. The intersection of gender, race, class, and place at the center of the girls' lives and victimization experiences is explored as the brutal circumstances of the girls lives are described.

Roleff, Tamara L. *Crime and Criminals*. Opposing Viewpoints Series. San Diego, Calif.: Greenhaven Press, 2000. Young Adult. Offers opposing points of view on how society should address crime and handle criminal offenders. Includes a chapter on how society should treat juvenile offenders.

Siegel, Larry J. *Juvenile Delinquency: The Core*, 3rd ed. Belmont, Calif.: Wadsworth Publishing Company, 2007. Textbook designed to help college students understand the nature of juvenile delinquency, its causes and correlates, as well as the current strategies being used to control juvenile crime.

Tonry, Michael, and Mark H. Moore. *Youth Violence*. Chicago, Ill.: University of Chicago Press, 1998. This collection of essays written by prominent criminologists examines youth violence in schools, violent juvenile offenders, the causes of youth violence, and violence prevention.

Watts, Meredith W., ed. *Cross-Cultural Perspectives on Youth and Violence*. Stamford, Conn.: Jai Press, 1998. Examines youth and violence from the standpoints of diverse cultural and interdisciplinary perspectives. Includes comparisons on youth violence in the United States and Brazil, Germany, and Japan.

Juvenile Crime

Zimring, Franklin E. *American Youth Violence.* New York: Oxford University Press, 1998. Presents findings of a study commissioned by the John D. and Catherine T. MacArthur Foundation on the perceptions and the reality of violence by juveniles in the United States.

ARTICLES AND PAPERS

Agnew, R., S. K. Matthews, and J. Bucher. "Socioeconomic Status, Economic Problems, and Delinquency." *Youth & Society* 40 (2008): 159–181. Considers the link between socioeconomic status (SES) and delinquency. The authors argue that theories about this link do not predict that SES in and of itself causes delinquency, but rather that the economic problems associated with SES cause delinquency.

Baron, S. W., and D. R. Forde. "Street Youth Crime: A Test of Control Balance Theory." *Justice Quarterly* 24 (2007): 335–350. Describes a study testing whether street youths' sense of control over their poverty, shelter, hunger, and other living conditions influences their participation in crime. Analyses also explore how a variety of factors affect levels of crime participation, including perceptions of risk and thrill, deviant values, self-control, deviant histories, and peer supports.

Bjerk, D. "Measuring the Relationship Between Youth Criminal Participation and Household Economic Resources." *Journal of Quantitative Criminology* 23 (2007): 23–39. Assesses the empirical relationship between household economic resources and youth criminal participation and finds a strong relationship once measurement issues are addressed.

Bouffard, J. A., and K. J. Bergseth. "The Impact of Reentry Services on Juvenile Offenders' Recidivism." *Youth Violence and Juvenile Justice* 6 (2008): 295–318. Assesses the effect on future crime of aftercare and/or reentry programs for youth who are released from correctional facilities. Results suggest that programs that are delivered as intended have modest effects in reducing future crime among youth.

Brigham, John. "Serious and Violent Juvenile Offenders: Why Should You Pay Attention?" *The Prosecutor* 35 (September/October 2001): 40–48. Examines the serious and violent juvenile offender (SVJO) and discusses what is known about the SVJO, a comparatively small part of the juvenile offender population responsible for a disproportionate percentage of juvenile crime. Includes factors used to predict future SVJOs.

Bush, Connee A., Ronald L. Mullis, and Ann K. Mullis. "Differences in Empathy Between Offender and Non-Offender Youth." *Journal of Youth and Adolescence* 29 (August 2000): 467. Examines study findings on ability of juvenile offenders to feel empathy for others, as compared to juveniles who did not offend.

Annotated Bibliography

"The 8% Solution." *Office of Juvenile Justice and Delinquency Prevention Fact Sheet*, November 2001. Available online. URL: www.ncjrs.gov/pdffiles1/ojjdp/fs200139.pdf. Explains that serious juvenile delinquency could be reduced significantly by identifying and treating the 8 percent of juveniles at risk of becoming chronic offenders when they first come into contact with the juvenile justice system.

"Exploratory and Confirmatory Spatial Data Analysis Approaches to Studying the Correlates of Juvenile Violent Crimes, Volume II Final Report." Report, Caliber Associates, 2001. Discusses findings of a study of juvenile violent crimes in Virginia, with emphasis on determining whether counties with high juvenile violent crime rates tended to cluster together. Identifies risk factors that were the primary determinants of juvenile violent crime at the county level.

Halperin, Samuel, et al. "Less Hype, More Help: Reducing Juvenile Crime, What Works—and What Doesn't." Report, The American Youth Policy Forum, June 2001. Discusses the failures of trying juveniles as adults and presents alternatives aimed at the prevention of juvenile crime.

Hay, C., E. N. Fortson, and D. R. Hollist. "The Impact of Community Disadvantage on the Relationship Between the Family and Juvenile Crime." *Journal of Research in Crime and Delinquency* 43 (2006): 326–356. An analysis of a national sample of adolescents to examine how family characteristics interact with community disadvantage to affect crime.

Hemphill, S. A., T. I. Herrenkohl, and A. N. LaFazia. "Comparison of the Structure of Adolescent Problem Behavior in the United States and Australia." *Crime & Delinquency* 53 (2007): 303–321. Examines international differences in problem behavior. The results indicate considerable similarities, especially in regard to the relationship between substance use and delinquency.

Kempf-Leonard, Kimberly, Paul E. Tracy, and James C. Howell. "Serious, Violent, and Chronic Juvenile Offenders: The Relationship of Delinquency Career Types to Adult Criminality." *Justice Quarterly* 18 (September 2001): 449–478. Examines Philadelphia study on the relationship between serious, violent, and chronic juvenile delinquency and adult criminality. Study tracked 13,160 males and 14,000 females from ages 10 to 18 until they were 26 years old who were at risk for juvenile delinquency and young adult crime.

King, Elizabeth. "Juvenile Crime Highest After School." *Corrections Today* 61 (December 1999): 16. Discusses statistical findings that most juvenile crime occurs during a three-hour period beginning when the school day ends.

Laskey, J. A. "Gang Migration: The Familial Gang Transplant Phenomenon." *Journal of Gang Research* 3 (winter 1996): 1–15. Data from Illinois, Georgia, and Wisconsin studies are used to examine the hypothesis that gang migration is partly due to the movement of families with children at risk for gang membership to new neighborhoods.

Ludwig, Jens, Greg J. Duncan, Paul Hirschfield. "Urban Poverty and Juvenile Crime: Evidence From a Randomized Housing-Mobility Experiment." *Quarterly Journal of Economics* 116 (May 2001): 655–679. Examines Baltimore study on the effects on juvenile crime of relocating families from high-poverty to low-poverty neighborhoods. Suggests that the spatial concentration of poverty in America may influence the overall volume of violent crime.

McCarthy, B., D. Felmlee, and J. Hagan. "Girl Friends Are Better: Gender, Friends, and Crime among School and Street Youth." *Criminology* 42 (2004): 805–835. A study of Toronto teens examines the effects of friendship on property crime. The results of the study indicate more females in a social network reduce property crime, while a male-dominated social network has the opposite effect.

McCord, Joan, and Kevin P. Conway. "Patterns of Juvenile Delinquency and Co-offending." Research Report, National Institute of Justice, 2001. Examines study using longitudinal data from Philadelphia focusing on juvenile offenders at the age of first arrest.

Ness, Carin M. "Perspectives on Sexually Reactive Youth." *Reclaiming Children and Youth* 10 (winter 2002): 201. A discussion of juvenile sex offenders and the psychological characteristics that distinguish this subset of juvenile offenders.

Parker, K. F., and A. Reckdenwald. "Concentrated Disadvantage, Traditional Male Role Models, and African-American Juvenile Violence." *Criminology* 46 (2008): 711–735. This study assesses the influence of male role models (older, employed black males) and the concentration of urban disadvantages on black juvenile arrests for violence. Findings suggest that the presence of traditional male role models reduces the rates of African-American youth violence.

Petrosino, Anthony J. "How Can We Respond Effectively to Juvenile Crime?" *Pediatrics* 105 (March 2000): 635. Argues that policies for prevention of juvenile crime should be based on scientific data and not created in reaction to high-profile crimes.

"Reducing Youth Gun Violence: An Overview of Programs and Initiatives." Report, Office of Juvenile Justice and Delinquency Prevention, 1996. Includes a summary of federal and state legislation to reduce youth gun violence and describes prevention and intervention programs. Includes a directory of programs, organizations, and research aimed at reducing gun violence.

Rigsby, Deborah. "Curbing Youth Violence: Doing What Works." *Nation's Cities Weekly* 20 (July 28, 1997): 9. Discusses findings presented at a U.S.

Justice Department symposium in June 1997 on measures to control of youth violence and crime.

Silverman, J. R., and R. M. Caldwell. "Peer Relationships and Violence Among Female Juvenile Offenders: An Exploration of Differences Among Four Racial/ethnic Populations." *Criminal Justice and Behavior* 35 (2008): 333–343. Analyses find that high levels of peer association and extrinsic rewards from peer relationships best predicted violence among all groups.

Sontheimer, Henry G. "Trends in Juvenile Crime and Juvenile Justice." *Criminal Justice Research Reports* 2 (July/August 2001): 89–91. Examines trends in juvenile crime and juvenile justice in the 1990s, with special focus on school violence, juvenile gangs, waiver of juveniles to adult court, and effective prevention and intervention approaches.

Toby, J. "Affluence and Adolescent Crime." In Louise I. Shelley, ed., *Readings in Comparative Criminology*, pp. 18–43. Carbondale: Southern Illinois University Press, 1981. The relationship between affluence and adolescent crime in developed countries is explored, with an emphasis on youths' rising expectations, lack of parental control, and the impact of education on juvenile crime.

Welsh, B. C. "Public Health and the Prevention of Juvenile Criminal Violence." *Youth Violence and Juvenile Justice* 3 (2005): 23–40. This article reviews the role that public health currently plays in preventing juvenile criminal violence and explores how an increasingly punitive response to juvenile criminal violence in the United States represents an unsustainable approach to the problem. A public health approach views violence as a threat to community health rather than community order, and adheres to scientific principles.

Wilkinson, D. L., M. S. McBryde, and B. Williams. "Peers and Gun Use among Urban Adolescent Males: An Examination of Social Embeddedness." *Journal of Contemporary Criminal Justice* 25 (2009): 20–44. Using interview data with 416 violent male offenders from two disadvantaged New York City neighborhoods, this article examines the roles that peer contexts play in explaining the nuanced patterns of respondent gun-related behaviors.

WEB DOCUMENTS

Baker, M. L., J. N. Sigmon, and M. E. Nugent. "Truancy Reduction: Keeping Students in School." *Office of Juvenile Justice and Delinquency Prevention Bulletin*, September 2001. Available online. URL: www.ncjrs. gov/pdffiles1/ojjdp/188947.pdf. Presents major research findings regarding the link between chronic truancy and serious delinquency, including substance abuse, gang activity, burglary, auto theft, and vandalism.

Juvenile Crime

"California's After-School Choice: Juvenile Crime or Safe Learning Time." Fight Crime: Invest in Kids California. Available online. URL: http://www.fightcrime.org/reports/ca-as.pdf. Downloaded July 31, 2009. Examines California's after-school programs, with emphasis on youth at risk and key components of quality after-school programs.

Catalano, R. F., R. Loeber, and K. C. McKinney. "School and Community Interventions to Prevent Serious and Violent Offending." *Office of Juvenile Justice and Delinquency Prevention Bulletin*, October 1999. Available online. URL: www.ncjrs.gov/pdffiles1/ojjdp/177624.pdf. Describes school and community interventions shown to reduce risk factors for drug abuse and serious and violent juvenile (SVJ) offending.

Chaiken, M. R. "Violent Neighborhoods, Violent Kids." *Office of Juvenile Justice and Delinquency Prevention Bulletin*, March 2000. Available online. URL: www.ncjrs.gov/pdffiles1/ojjdp/178248.pdf. Presents findings of research on types of delinquent behavior found among boys living in the three most violent neighborhoods in Washington, D.C., and the role of families, schools, churches, and youth-serving organizations in the boys' lives.

"Challenging the Myths." *Office of Juvenile Justice and Delinquency Prevention Bulletin*, February 2000. Available online. URL: www.ncjrs.gov/pdffiles1/ojjdp/178993.pdf. Examines the "superpredator" theory that a new breed of violent juveniles was emerged in the early 1990s. Concludes that recent data do not support the superpredator theory and offers alternative explanations of trends in juvenile crime.

Cronin, R., et al. "Lessons Learned from Safe Kids/Safe Streets." *OJJDP Juvenile Justice Bulletin*, November 2006. Office of Juvenile Justice and Delinquency Prevention. Available online. URL: http://www.ncjrs.gov/pdffiles1/ojjdp/213682.pdf. Evaluation of a multi-year, five-city program designed to reduce child abuse and neglect and its effects, including delinquency.

Decker, Scott, and Susan Pennell. "Arrestees and Guns: Monitoring the Illegal Firearms Market." Available online. URL: http://www.ncjrs.gov/pdffiles/arrest.pdf. Report, National Institute of Justice, 1995. Discusses findings of research study based on interviews with more than 4,000 arrestees in 11 cities to assess the illegal firearms market. Included in the research sample were 753 juvenile males and 103 juvenile females in the District of Columbia and the cities of Atlanta, Denver, Detroit, Indianapolis, New Orleans, Los Angeles, Miami, Phoenix, San Diego, and St. Louis. Findings included a strong association between carrying a gun and gang membership and between carrying a gun and illicit drug selling.

Ericson, N. "The YMCA's Teen Action Agenda." *Office of Juvenile Justice and Delinquency Prevention Fact Sheet*, May 2001. Available online. URL: http://www.ncjrs.gov/pdffiles1/ojjdp/fs200114.pdf. Presents survey findings that teens unsupervised during the after-school hours of 3 P.M. to 6 P.M. are more likely to engage in delinquent behaviors. Also describes local YMCA programs for teens during after-school hours.

"Facts About Gang Life in America Today: A National Study of Over 4,000 Gang Members." *Report,* National Gang Crime Research Center, 1997. Available online. URL: http://www.ngcrc.com/ngcrc/page9.htm. Comprehensive analysis of a survey of attitudes, behaviors, and social relationships of 10,160 juveniles and adults confined in 85 facilities in 17 states, of whom 4,140 self-reported as being gang members. Analyzes in detail the female gang member, the juvenile as compared to adult gang member, and the gang as a social organization.

Finkelhor, D., and R. Ormrod. "Reporting Crimes Against Juveniles." *Office of Juvenile Justice and Delinquency Prevention Bulletin,* 1999. Available online. URL: www.ncjrs.gov/pdffiles1/ojjdp/178887.pdf. Presents an analysis of National Crime Victimization Survey (NCVS) data on reports of crimes against juveniles to police and other authorities, such as school officials. Focus is on the categories of violent crime (rape and sexual assault, robbery, and assault) and theft included in NCVS data.

Hawkins, D. F., et al. "Race, Ethnicity, and Serious and Violent Juvenile Offending." *Office of Juvenile Justice and Delinquency Prevention Bulletin,* June 2000. Available online. URL: www.ncjrs.gov/pdffiles1/ojjdp/181202. pdf. Discusses racial and ethnic differences in the rates of serious and violent offending among juveniles and summarizes statistics on national trends in juvenile offending by race and ethnicity.

Hawkins, J. D., et al. "Predictors of Youth Violence." *Office of Juvenile Justice and Delinquency Prevention Bulletin,* April 2000. Available online. URL: www.ncjrs.gov/pdffiles1/ojjdp/179065.pdf. Presents findings of two-year study on serious and violent juvenile offenders. Describes risk factors for youth violence, including family, school, peer-related, community/neighborhood, and situational factors.

Hawkins, S. R., et al. "Resilient Girls—Factors That Protect against Delinquency." *Girls Study Group Series Bulletin,* Office of Juvenile Justice and Delinquency Prevention. Available online. URL: http://www.ncjrs.gov/pdffiles1/ojjdp/220124.pdf. Compares male and female adolescent offending and considers risk and protective factors for female delinquency.

Hockenberry, S. "Person Offense Cases in Juvenile Court, 2005." *Office of Juvenile Justice and Delinquency Prevention Fact Sheet,* June 2009. Available online. URL: http://www.ncjrs.gov/pdffiles1/ojjdp/224537.pdf. Presents statistics on person offense cases processed by juvenile courts in 2005.

Huizinga, D., et al. "Co-occurrence of Delinquency and Other Problem Behaviors." *Youth Development Series Bulletin,* January 2009. Office of Juvenile Justice and Delinquency Prevention, November 2000. Available online. URL: www.ncjrs.gov/pdffiles1/ojjdp/182211.pdf. Examines the co-occurrence of serious delinquency with specific problem areas: school behavior, drug use, and mental health.

"Kids and Guns." *Office of Juvenile Justice and Delinquency Prevention Bulletin,* March 2000. Available online. URL: www.ncjrs.gov/pdffiles1/ojjdp/178994.pdf. Presents an overview of statistics on the impact of gun availability on the lives of youth. Examines data on gun use in homicides committed by and against juveniles, weapons arrest rates, relationship of handgun carrying to other problem behaviors, and firearm-related suicide.

Levitt, Steven D., and Lance Lochner. "Determinants of Juvenile Crime." Report, University of Chicago and American Bar Foundation, 2002. Available online. URL: http://web.econ.rochester.edu/lochner/levitt-lochner.pdf. Considers the social costs of youth crime and the personal risks and costs borne by delinquent youth. Presents evidence that juvenile crime is responsive to punishment.

Lizotte, A., and D. Sheppard. "Gun Use by Male Juveniles: Research and Prevention." *Office of Juvenile Justice and Delinquency Prevention Bulletin,* July 2001. Available online. URL: http://www.ncjrs.gov/pdffiles1/ojjdp/188992.pdf. Examines patterns of gun ownership and gun carrying among adolescents. Also examines the relationship between gangs and guns and describes prevention programs.

Loeber, R., D. P. Farrington, and D. Petechuk. "Child Delinquency: Early Intervention and Prevention." *Child Delinquency,* May 2003. Office of Juvenile Justice and Delinquency Prevention. Available online. URL: http://www.ncjrs.gov/pdffiles1/ojjdp/186162.pdf. Presents information on the nature of child delinquency and describes early intervention and prevention programs that effectively reduce delinquent behavior.

Loeber, R., L. Kalb, and D. Huizinga. "Juvenile Delinquency and Serious Injury Victimization." *Office of Juvenile Justice and Delinquency Prevention Bulletin,* August 2001. Available online. URL: www.ncjrs.gov/pdffiles1/ojjdp/188676.pdf. Examines data from two OJJDP longitudinal studies on the causes of delinquency and the relationship between delinquency and victimization. Findings show that many victims engaged in illegal activities, associate with delinquent peers, and victimize other delinquents.

Males, Mike, and Dan Macallair. "Dispelling the Myth: An Analysis of Youth and Adult Crime Patterns in California over the Past 20 Years." Report, The Center of Juvenile and Criminal Justice, 2000. Available online. URL: http://www.cjcj.org/files/dispelling.pdf. Examines the theory of growing criminality among youth. Focuses on youth and adult crime rates in California between 1978 and 1998.

McCurley, C. "Burglary Cases in Juvenile Court, 1989–1998." *Office of Juvenile Justice and Delinquency Prevention Fact Sheet,* May 2002. Available online. URL: www.ncjrs.gov/pdffiles1/ojjdp/fs200208.pdf. Discusses the burglary caseload handled by juvenile courts between 1989 and 1998, including trends in the number of such cases for male and female juvenile offenders.

Menard, Scott. "Short- and Long-Term Consequences of Adolescent Victimization." *Youth Violence Research Series Bulletin,* Office of Juvenile Justice and Delinquency Prevention, February 2002. Available online. URL: www.ncjrs.gov/pdffiles1/ojjdp/191210.pdf. Describes findings of National Youth Survey data that being a victim of crime during adolescence increases the likelihood of certain negative outcomes in adulthood, including violent and property offending and victimization, domestic violence perpetration and victimization, drug use, and mental health problems.

Nessel, P. A. "Youth for Justice." *Office of Juvenile Justice and Delinquency Prevention Bulletin,* April 2001. Available online. URL: www.ncjrs.gov/html/ojjdp/jjbul2001_4_l/contents.html. Describes the Youth for Justice Program and its role in preventing juvenile crime.

Newman, Sanford A., James A. Fox, Edward A. Flynn, and William Christeson. "America's After-School Choice: The Prime Time for Juvenile Crime, or Youth Enrichment and Achievement." Available online. URL: http://www.fightcrime.org/reports/as2000.pdf. Downloaded July 31, 2009. Discuses after-school programs that cut crime. Emphasis on the hours after school when students are released without adult supervision or constructive activities and are most prone to criminal behavior or victimization.

"OJJDP Publications List." Office of Juvenile Justice and Delinquency Prevention. Available online. URL: www.ncjrs.gov/publications/PubResults.asp. Provides a detailed listing of OJJDP publications by year, for the following subject areas: corrections and detention, courts, delinquency prevention, gangs, general, missing and exploited children, restitution, status offenders, substance abuse, violence and victimization, and youth in action.

"OJJDP Research: Making a Difference for Juveniles." *Office of Juvenile Justice and Delinquency Prevention Report,* 1999. Available online. URL: http://www.ncjrs.gov/pdffiles1/177602.pdf. Reviews research findings on the causes of juvenile delinquency and other topics, including very young offenders, school violence, and females in the juvenile justice system.

Oldenettel, D., and M. Wordes. "Community Assessment Centers." *Office of Juvenile Justice and Delinquency Prevention Fact Sheet,* June 1999. Available online. URL: http://www.ncjrs.gov/pdffiles1/fs99111.pdf. Describes Community Assessment Centers, where juveniles who are at risk of becoming serious, violent, and chronic offenders receive comprehensive assessments and followup.

"Promising Strategies to Reduce Gun Violence." *Office of Juvenile Justice and Delinquency Prevention Report*, 1999. Available online. URL: www.ojjdp. ncjrs.org/pubs/gun_violence/173950.pdf. Presents profiles of 60 demonstrated or promising programs and strategies that address the problem of gun violence and examines the nature of the problem from a national perspective.

Puzzanchera, C. M. "The Youngest Offenders." *Office of Juvenile Justice and Delinquency Prevention Fact Sheet*, November 1998. Available online. URL: www.ncjrs.gov/pdffiles/fs-9887.pdf. Summarizes the arrest profile of youth under age 15 and discusses comparisons with older juvenile offenders.

———. "Self-Reported Delinquency by 12-Year-Olds." *Office of Juvenile Justice and Delinquency Prevention Fact Sheet*, March 2000. Available online. URL: www.ncjrs.gov/pdffiles1/ojjdp/fs200003.pdf. Presents data from the National Longitudinal Survey of Youth 1997, in which some 9,000 juveniles aged 12 to 16 were asked to report if they had engaged in delinquent behaviors.

———. "Juvenile Arrests 2007." *OJJDP Juvenile Justice Bulletin*. Office of Juvenile Justice and Delinquency Prevention, April 2009. Available online. URL: http://www.ncjrs.gov/pdffiles1/ojjdp/225344.pdf. Summarizes 2007 juvenile crime and arrest data reported by local law enforcement agencies across the country and cited in the FBI report *Crime in the United States 2007*.

———. "Person Offenses in Juvenile Court, 1990–1999." *OJJDP Fact Sheet*. Office of Juvenile Justice and Delinquency Prevention, September 2003. Available online. URL: http://www.ncjrs.gov/pdffiles1/ojjdp/fs200303.pdf. Presents statistics on person offenses (assault, robbery, rape, and homicide) handled by juvenile courts between 1990 and 1999.

Righthand, S., and C. Welch. "Juveniles Who Have Sexually Offended: A Review of the Professional Literature." *Office of Juvenile Justice and Delinquency Prevention Report*, March 2001. Available online. URL: www. ncjrs. gov/pdffiles1/ojjdp/184739.pdf. Review of research on juvenile sex offenders and treatment approaches for such offenders.

Rumsey, E., C. A. Kerr, and B. Allen-Hagen. "Serious and Violent Juvenile Offenders." *Office of Juvenile Justice and Delinquency Prevention Juvenile Justice Bulletin*, May 1998. Available online. URL: http://ncjrs.gov/pdffiles/170027.pdf. A examination of the serious and violent juvenile (SVJ), including key differences between the SVJ and the typical juvenile offender.

Sheppard, David. "Strategies to Reduce Gun Violence." *Office of Juvenile Justice and Delinquency Prevention Fact Sheet*, February 1999. Available online. URL: http://www.ncjrs.gov/pdffiles1/fs9993.pdf. Presents an overview of the findings from a national survey of more than 400 local programs designed to address gun violence.

Sheppard, D., et al. "Fighting Juvenile Gun Violence." *Office of Juvenile Justice and Delinquency Prevention Bulletin,* September 2000. Available online. URL: www.ncjrs.gov/pdffiles1/ojjdp/182679.pdf. Describes programs to reduce juvenile gun violence in Louisiana, California, and New York.

Shure, M. B. "Preventing Violence the Problem-Solving Way." *Office of Juvenile Justice and Delinquency Prevention Bulletin,* April 1999. Available online. URL: www.ncjrs.gov/pdffiles1/172847.pdf. Examines 20 years of research on interpersonal problem-solving skills related to high-risk behaviors that may develop into serious problems such as violence and substance abuse.

Sickmund, M. "Delinquency Cases in Juvenile Court, 2005." *OJJDP Fact Sheet.* Office of Juvenile Justice and Delinquency Prevention. June 2009. Available online. URL: http://www.ncjrs.gov/pdffiles1/ojjdp/224538.pdf. Presents statistics on delinquency cases handled in U.S. juvenile courts between 1985 and 2005.

Snyder, Howard N. "Law Enforcement and Juvenile Crime." *Office of Juvenile Justice and Delinquency Prevention Bulletin,* 2001. Available online. URL: http://www.ncjrs.gov/pdffiles1/ojjdp/191031.pdf. Provides general information on the function of law enforcement within the juvenile justice system.

Snyder, H. N., and M. Sickmund. *Juvenile Offenders and Victims: 2006 National Report,* Office of Juvenile Justice and Delinquency Prevention, 2006. Available online. URL: http://ojjpd.ncjrs.gov/ojstatbb/nr2006/downloads/nrc2006.pdf. Presents comprehensive information on juvenile crime, violence, and victimization and on the juvenile justice system. Includes numerous tables, graphs, and maps, accompanied by analyses in clear, nontechnical language. The report provides baseline information on juvenile population trends; patterns of juvenile victimization, including homicide, suicide, and maltreatment; the nature and extent of juvenile offending, including data on arrest rates, antisocial behavior, and juveniles in custody; and the structure, procedures, and activities of the juvenile justice system, including law enforcement agencies, courts, and corrections.

Stahl, A. L. "Drug Offense Cases in Juvenile Courts, 1985–2004." *OJJDP Fact Sheet.* Office of Juvenile Justice and Delinquency Prevention. February 2008. Available online. URL: http://www.ncjrs.gov/pdffiles1/ojjdp/fs200803.pdf. Provides data on delinquency cases involving drug offenses between 1985 and 2004 by nearly 1,900 juvenile courts across the United States. Between 1991 and 2004, the number of juvenile drug offense cases in juvenile courts more than doubled.

Stern, K. R. "A Treatment Study of Children with Attention Deficit Hyperactivity Disorder." *Office of Juvenile Justice and Delinquency Prevention Fact*

Sheet, May 2001. Available online. URL: www.ncjrs.gov/pdffiles1/ojjdp/fs200120.pdf. Discusses the core symptoms of attention deficit hyperactivity disorder and its potential links to juvenile delinquency.

Thornberry, T. P., et al. "Family Disruption and Delinquency." *Office of Juvenile Justice and Delinquency Prevention Bulletin,* October 1999. Available online. URL: www.ncjrs.gov/pdffiles1/ojjdp/178285.pdf. Examines the impact of changes in family structure on the risk of serious problem behavior among juveniles. Draws on data from interviews of some 4,000 juveniles.

————. "Teenage Fatherhood and Delinquent Behavior." *Youth Development Series Bulletin,* Office of Juvenile Justice and Delinquency Prevention, January 2000. Available online. URL: www.ncjrs.gov/pdffiles1/ojjdp/178899.pdf. Presents findings from two studies on the role of delinquency in early fatherhood. Both studies concluded that early delinquency is a highly significant risk factor for becoming a teen father.

"Violence After School." *Office of Juvenile Justice and Delinquency Prevention Bulletin,* November 1999. Available online. URL: www.ncjrs.gov/pdffiles1/ojjdp/178992.pdf. Examines data on temporal patterns, including time of day and school vs. nonschool days, of violent crimes committed by and against juveniles. Presents findings that serious violent juvenile crime peaks in the hours immediately after school, and discusses implications of the data for community strategies to reduce violent juvenile crime.

Wasserman, G. A., et al. "Risk and Protective Factors of Child Delinquency." *Child Delinquency Bulletin.* Office of Juvenile Justice and Delinquency Prevention. April 2003. Available online. URL: http://www.ncjrs.gov/pdffiles1/ojjdp/193409.pdf. Focuses on four types of risk and protective factors: individual, family, peer, and school and community.

Wasserman, G. A., L. S. Miller, and L. Cothern. "Prevention of Serious and Violent Juvenile Offending," April 2000. Available online. URL: http://www.ncjrs.gov/pdffiles1/ojjdp/178898.pdf. Describes developmental precursors to serious and violent juvenile offending and discusses prevention of such offending.

Wiebush, R., R. Freitag, and C. Baird. "Preventing Delinquency Through Improved Child Protection Services." *Office of Juvenile Justice and Delinquency Prevention Bulletin,* July 2001. Available online. URL: www.ncjrs.gov/pdffiles1/ojjdp/187759.pdf. Reviews research on the link between childhood maltreatment and juvenile and adult offending and the role that child protective services prevention efforts can play in the prevention of delinquency.

Wyrick, P. A. "Law Enforcement Referral of At-Risk Youth: The SHIELD Program." *Office of Juvenile Justice and Delinquency Prevention Bulletin,* November 2000. Available online. URL: www.ncjrs.gov/pdffiles1/ojjdp/184579.pdf. Examines a program that facilitates early identification and treatment of at-risk youth.

Annotated Bibliography

Zahn, M. A., et al. "Violence by Teenage Girls: Trends and Contexts." *Girls Study Group Series Bulletin.* May 2008. Office of Juvenile Justice and Delinquency Prevention. Available online. URL: http://www.ncjrs.gov/pdffiles1/ojjdp/218905.pdf. Examines the involvement of girls in violent activity (including whether such activity has increased relative to the increase for boys) and the contexts in which girls engage in violent behavior.

AUDIOVISUAL MATERIALS

Bully Girls. DVD, 20 min., Meridian, 2006. This documentary describes the extent of bullying by girls, why it happens, and how it occurs. It attempts to alert audiences to the fact that bullying is a problem among girls as well as boys and to educate on warning signs and helpful responses to the problem.

It's Not Only Murder: Discovering the Violence in Your Life. DVD, 12 min., Hazelden Educational Materials, 2001. URL: http://www.hazelden.org. Video and accompanying 38-page manual explore the causes and effects of a wide range of violent behavior among youth.

"Mentoring Matters Videoconference: OJJDP Teleconference Series." February 2003. Office of Juvenile Justice and Delinquency Prevention. Highlights the importance of mentoring as an effective approach to delinquency prevention; examines mentoring in community, faith-based, school, and work settings; and shares strategies for recruiting mentors effectively.

"Reducing Youth Violence: A Comprehensive Approach." CD-ROM, Office of Juvenile Justice and Delinquency Prevention, 1999. Interactive disk describes a broad array of publications and other resources on prevention and intervention programs for at-risk juveniles and those involved in the juvenile justice system.

YOUTH GANGS

BOOKS

Esbensen, F., S. G. Tibbetts, and L. Gaines. *American Youth Gangs at the Millennium.* Long Grove, Ill.: Waveland, 2004. A collection of essays arranged in four sections attempting to explain the connection between youth gangs and violence.

Fremon, Celeste. *G-dog and the Homeboys: Father Greg Boyle and the Gangs of East Los Angeles.* Albuquerque, N.M.: University of New Mexico Press, 2004. Young Latino gang members narrate their experiences of criminal activities on the streets of East Los Angeles and their redemption from criminality through the efforts of the Jesuit priest Greg Boyle.

Grennan, Sean, Marjie T. Britz, Jeffrey Rush, and Thomas Barker. *Gangs: An International Approach.* Upper Saddle River, N.J.: Prentice-Hall, 2000. College textbook profiles gangs throughout the world, including their history, territory, and economics. Includes general information on gangs in history, the definition of a gang, gang structure and organization, and descriptions of specific types of gangs.

Kelly, Robert J. *Encyclopedia of Organized Crime in the United States: From Capone's Chicago to the New Urban Underworld.* Westport, Conn.: Greenwood Publishing Group, 2000. Reference volume describes the many new ethnic and racial criminal organizations and gangs in American society. Includes timeline, bibliography, and index.

Kontos, Luis, David Brotherton, and Luis Barrios. *Gangs and Society: Alternative Perspectives.* New York: Columbia University Press, 2003. Anthology of previously unpublished articles about gangs and the communities in which they are found. Chapters focus on theory about gangs and methods for studying them, gangs and politics, gangs and at-risk youth, women and gangs, and controlling gangs.

Mendoza-Denton, N. *Homegirls: Language and Cultural Practice among Latina Youth Gangs.* Malden, Mass.: Blackwell, 2008. Ethnographic study explores the linguistic and ethnographic patterns and interrelationships among Mexican-American high school girls in northern California who are members of girl gangs.

Padilla, F. M. *Gang as an American Enterprise.* Piscataway, N.J.: Rutgers University Press, 1992. Recounts the story of a Puerto Rican youth gang in Chicago. Issues include neighborhood and school experience of gang members, relations with police, the process of initiation into the gang, drug dealing, and the consequences of gang participation.

Short, J. F., and L. A. Hughes. *Studying Youth Gangs.* Lanham, Md.: AltaMira, 2006. This anthology of previously published and unpublished papers examines the structure and dynamics of urban gangs in the United States.

Spergel, I. *The Youth Gang Problem: A Community Approach.* New York: Oxford University Press, 1995. Seminal study that describes the scope and seriousness of the gang problem, the relationship between gang members and drug activity, the structure of gangs and the demographics of gang members, the process of gang life, and other aspects of youth gangs.

Whitman, J. L., and R. C. Davis. *Snitches Get Stitches: Youth, Gangs, and Witness Intimidation in Massachusetts.* Washington, D.C.: National Center for Victims of Crime, 2007. This study explores factors that influence youths' decisions to cooperate with the criminal justice process and the extent and nature of intimidation within their communities after crimes occur.

Annotated Bibliography

ARTICLES AND PAPERS

Brandt, Gerri-Ann, and Brenda Russell. "Differentiating Factors in Gang and Drug Related Homicide." *Gang Research* 9 (winter 2002): 23–40. Discussion of study investigating factors involved with gang- and drug-related homicide utilizing data from 372 homicides in the St. Louis area. Findings suggest a strong drug use pattern among offenders in gang-related homicides.

Brownfield, David, and Kevin Thompson. "Distinguishing the Effects of Peer Delinquency and Gang Membership on Self-Reported Delinquency." *Journal of Gang Research* 9 (winter 2002): 1–10. Examines the distinction between peer delinquency and gang membership and counters past assumptions that linked peer delinquency and gang membership.

Decker, S. H., C. M. Katz, and V. J. Webb. "Understanding the Black Box of Gang Organization: Implications for Involvement in Violent Crime, Drug Sales, and Violent Victimization." *Crime & Delinquency* 54 (2008): 153–172. Using interview data from juvenile detention facilities in three Arizona sites, this article examines the relationship between gang organizational structure and involvement in violent crime, drug sales, victimization, and arrest.

Esbensen, F., and F. M. Weerman. "Youth Gangs and Troublesome Youth Groups in the United States and the Netherlands: A Cross-National Comparison." *European Journal of Criminology,* 2 (2005): 5–37. Examines characteristics of American and Dutch gangs and gang members in one of the few comparative perspectives on gangs.

Garot, R. "'Where You From!': Gang Identity as Performance." *Journal of Contemporary Ethnography* 36 (2007): 50–84. Investigates how young people in an inner-city ecology invoke the relevance of gangs. Rather than conceptualizing young people as gang members and gangs as a static group, this analysis shows how the way youths understand their gang membership and interact with other members is strategic and context sensitive.

Gelzinis, Peter. "Gang Cop." *Boston Magazine* 91 (May 1999): 46. Discusses the pioneering work of a Boston police lieutenant in tracking street gangs and redirecting juvenile gang members to more productive lives.

Gottfredson, Gary D., and Denise C. Gottfredson. "Gang Problems and Gang Programs in a National Sample of Schools." Report, Gottfredson Associates, 2001. Study of gang prevention and intervention in a national sample of schools and the activities undertaken to prevent problem behavior and to promote safe school environments.

Green, S. L. "Youth Gangs of Rural Texas: College Students Speak Out." *Journal of Gang Research* 12 (2005): 19–40. This study compares youth activities in urban and rural areas of Texas. Gangs were found to exist in rural areas of Texas, though it is not clear how urban and rural environments are conducive to gang creation and development.

Hope, Trina L., and Kelly R. Damphousse. "Applying Self-Control Theory to Gang Membership in a Non-Urban Setting." *Journal of Gang Research* 9 (winter 2002): 41–61. Discussion of a study attempting to explore the characteristics of gang members in a nonurban setting, in contrast to prior research on gang membership and its relationship to delinquency that focused on populations of urban, racially heterogeneous participants.

Horowitz, R., and G. Schwartz. "Honor, Normative Ambiguity and Gang Violence." *American Sociological Review* 39 (April 1974): 238–251. Examines gang violence in a Mexican-American community.

Hughes, L. A., and J. F. Short. "Disputes Involving Youth Street Gang Members: Micro-social Contexts." *Criminology* 43 (2005): 43–76. This study examines how gang members interact during violent and nonviolent dispute-related incidents involving gang members. Disputes tend to relate to norm violations, attacks on one's identity, and retaliation.

Hunt, G., K. Joe-Laidler, and K. MacKenzie. "Moving into Motherhood: Gang Girls and Controlled Risk." *Youth & Society* 36 (2005): 333–373. Focuses on a group of girls and young women who were pregnant or mothers and who were engaged in a risky lifestyle through their heavy involvement in gangs, partying, and drinking. The authors consider the extent to which different stages of motherhood influence a homegirl's overall alcohol consumption and drinking practices both within and outside of the gang.

Joe, K. "Chinese Gangs and Tongs: An Exploratory Look at the Connection on the West Coast." Washington, D.C.: National Institute on Drug Abuse, 1992. Explores connection between Chinese youth gangs and organized crime groups in Chinese communities in the United States and in Asia.

Know, George W. "Responding to Gangs in the 21st Century: A Research and Policy View." *Journal of Gang Research*, vol. 9, pp. 63–74, winter 2002. A review of several issues of research and policy as they relate to dealing with gangs, including the initiatives that the National Gang Crime Research Center (NGCRC) will undertake within the next five years.

McFeely, Richard A. "Enterprise Theory of Investigation." *FBI Law Enforcement Bulletin*, vol. 70, pp. 19–25, May 2001. Describes the Enterprise Theory of Investigation (ETI), the standard investigative model that the FBI uses in conducting investigations into criminal organizations and gangs.

"National Conference on Youth Gangs and Violent Juvenile Crime, October 7–9, 1991, Reno, Nevada: A Summary of the Proceedings." National Institute of Justice, 1991. Report on conference highlights, including speeches and panel presentations and discussions of the relationship between youth gangs and violent crimes.

Quinn, J. F., and B. Downs. "Predictors of Gang Violence: The Impact of Drugs and Guns on Police Perceptions in Nine States." *Journal of Gang Research* 2 (spring 1995): 15–27. A survey of municipal police departments in nine states explores the frequency of two types of gang violence: internecine violence within gangs and violence directed at non-gang-members.

Rogers, Joseph. "Confronting Transnational Gangs in the Americas." *Journal of Gang Research* 10 (2003): 33–44. Examines the nature of transnational youth gangs, policies that tend to exacerbate the situation, and some approaches that are used to minimize the influence of gangs in certain countries of the Western Hemisphere. The most effective antigang programs focus on local communities where the youth are influenced by the presence and images of gang culture.

Saccente, D. D. "RAP to Street Gang Activity." *Police Chief* 60 (February 1993): 28–31. Examines the use of the Racketeer Influenced and Corrupt Organizations Act (RICO) and asset forfeiture laws to prosecute gang members and weaken the street gang structure.

St. Cyr, Jenna L. "The Folk Devil Reacts: Gangs and Moral Panic." *Criminal Justice Review* 28 (2003): 26–46. Examines the extent to which a moral panic over gangs has infiltrated gang-impacted communities. The analysis compares gang and nongang youths' perceptions of the gang problem within St. Louis, Missouri, with those of juvenile detectives and gang task force members.

Schneider, Jacqueline L. "Niche Crime: The Columbus Gangs Study." *American Journal of Criminal Justice* 26 (fall 2001): 93–106. Examines the types of criminal activities in which gang leaders participate. Also includes information on the structure of gangs that suggests that gangs no longer fit the stereotype of semiorganized groups of juveniles and young men.

Sirpal, Suman Kakar. "Familial Criminality, Familial Drug Use, and Gang Membership: Youth Criminality, Drug Use, and Gang Membership—What Are the Connections?" *Journal of Gang Research* 9 (winter 2002): 11–22. Examines the effects of familial criminality and parental drug and alcohol use on children's behavior in their decision to use alcohol and drugs or get involved in gangs and delinquent behavior.

Strosnider, Kim. "Anti-Gang Ordinances After *City of Chicago v. Morales:* The Intersection of Race, Vagueness Doctrine, and Equal Protection in the Criminal Law." *American Criminal Law Review* 39 (winter 2002): 101–146. Examines the influence of the *City of Chicago v. Morales* decision, a 1999 U.S. Supreme Court case that struck down Chicago's antigang loitering ordinance for vagueness under the due process clause of the 14th Amendment. Includes a survey of antigang ordinances nationwide and the impact that the decision in *Morales* had on those laws.

Sullivan, M. L. "Maybe We Shouldn't Study 'Gangs': Does Reification Obscure Youth Violence?" *Journal of Contemporary Criminal Justice* 21 (2005): 170–190. Discusses the extensive study of youth gangs over the years despite the absence of commonly accepted definition of what youth gangs are. The author suggests a broader focus on youth violence and youthful collective behavior.

Taylor, T. J., D. Peterson, and F. Esbensen. "Gang Membership as a Risk Factor for Adolescent Violent Victimization." *Journal of Research in Crime and Delinquency* 44 (2007): 351–380. Examines the link between gang membership and violent victimization. The results suggest that gang membership increases the likelihood of violent victimization.

Tita, G. E., J. Cohen, and J. Engberg. "An Ecological Study of the Location of Gang 'Set Space'" *Social Problems* 52 (2005): 272–299. This ecological study of violent urban youth gangs in Pittsburgh examines the social, economic, and physical organization of places where gangs congregate. Diminished social control, in the absence of capable guardians and physical abandonment of place, and underclass features increased the likelihood of observing violent youth gangs hanging out in a particular area.

Valdez, A. "In the Hood: The Highways and Byways of Crime." *Police* 23 (February 1999): 44–46. Examines the use of America's roadways to spread criminal activity. Discusses some of the unique relationships between West Coast and East Coast gangs in the development of formal east-west drug transportation corridors or land drug routes.

Zhang, L., S. F. Messner, Z. Lu, and X. Deng. "Gang Crime and Its Punishment in China." *Journal of Criminal Justice* 25 (1997): 289–302. Examines characteristics of youth gangs, gang crime, and official punishment in contemporary China and compares gangs in China to those in the United States.

WEB DOCUMENTS

Battin-Pearson, S. R., et al. "Gang Membership, Delinquent Peers, and Delinquent Behavior." *Office of Juvenile Justice and Delinquency Prevention Bulletin,* October 1998. Available online. URL: www.ncjrs.org/pdf-files/171119.pdf. Describes the findings of OJJDP-funded longitudinal research on the link between gang membership and a higher incidence of delinquency.

Burch, J., and C. Kane. "Implementing the OJJDP Comprehensive Gang Model." *Office of Juvenile Justice and Delinquency Prevention Fact Sheet,* July 1999. Available online. URL: www.ncjrs.org/pdffiles1/fs99112.pdf. Describes gang intervention projects in five U.S. cities and strategies for dealing with gang-involved youth.

Annotated Bibliography

Cahill, M., et al. "Community Collaboratives Addressing Youth Gangs: Interim Findings from the Gang Reduction Program," May 2008. Urban Institute. Available online. URL: http://www.urban.org/UploadedPDF/411692_communitycollaborativcs.pdf. This 523-page report presents interim findings of the Urban Institute's evaluation of the Gang Reduction Program (GRP). The GRP is a multiyear initiative to reduce youth street gangs in Los Angeles, California; Milwaukee, Wisconsin; North Miami Beach, Florida; and Richmond, Virginia.

Curry, G. D., C. L. Maxson, and J. C. Howell. "Youth Gang Homicides in the 1990's." *Office of Juvenile Justice and Delinquency Prevention Fact Sheet*, March 2001. Available online. URL: www.ncjrs.org/pdffiles1/ojjdp/fs200103.pdf. Discusses the results of a study of youth gang homicides in U.S. cities in the 1990s conducted by the Office of Juvenile Justice and Delinquency Prevention's National Youth Gang Center. Summarizes gang homicide trends in the early to mid-1990s and in the late 1990s.

Egley, A. "National Youth Gang Survey Trends From 1996 to 2000." *Office of Juvenile Justice and Delinquency Prevention Fact Sheet*, February 2002. Available online. URL: www.ncjrs.org/pdffiles1/ojjdp/fs200203.pdf. Presents key findings from five National Youth Gang Surveys conducted annually since 1996 by the National Youth Gang Center. Topics include patterns of gang activity, numbers of gangs and gang members, gang-related homicides, and demographics of gangs and gang members.

Egley, A., and C. E. O'Donnell. "Highlights of the 2007 National Youth Gang Survey." *OJJDP Fact Sheet*, April 2009. Office of Juvenile Justice and Delinquency Prevention. Available online. URL: http://www.ncjrs.gov/pdffiles1/ojjdp/225185.pdf. Reports findings from the 2007 National Youth Gang Survey. Based on survey results, it is estimated that nearly 3,550 jurisdictions across the United States experienced gang activity in 2007.

Esbensen, F. "Preventing Adolescent Gang Involvement." *Youth Gang Series Bulletin*, Office of Juvenile Justice and Delinquency Prevention, September 2000. Available online. URL: www.ncjrs.org/pdffiles1/ojjdp/182210.pdf. Provides an overview on the history of American youth gangs and current knowledge about gangs. Also examines risk factors associated with gang membership.

Greene, J., and K. Pranis. "Gang Wars: The Failure of Enforcement Tactics and the Need for Effective Public Safety Strategies," July 2007. Justice Policy Institute. Available online. URL: http://www.justicepolicy.org/images/upload/07-07_REP_GangWars_GC-PS-AC-JJ.pdf. This report examines gangs and antigang strategies and compares these strategies to evidence-based interventions. These comparisons highlight common misconceptions about gangs and gang violence that influence antigang laws and police enforcement.

Howell, James C. *Youth Gang Programs and Strategies.* Summary, Office of Juvenile Justice and Delinquency Prevention, August 2000. Available online. URL: www.ncjrs.org/pdffiles1/ojjdp/171154.pdf. Describes programs to disrupt gangs and divert youth from gang life and discusses the effectiveness of such programs.

Howell, J. C., Arlene Egley, and Debra K. Gleason. "Modern-Day Youth Gangs." *Office of Juvenile Justice and Delinquency Prevention Bulletin,* August 2002. Available online. URL: http://www.ncjrs.gov/pdffiles1/ojjdp/191524.pdf. Discusses the recent proliferation of gangs into smaller cities, towns, suburbs, and rural communities and how these gangs differ from more traditional urban-based youth gangs. Draws on data from the 1996 and 1998 National Youth Gang Surveys.

Howell, J. C., and J. P. Lynch. "Youth Gangs in Schools." *Youth Gang Series Bulletin,* Office of Juvenile Justice and Delinquency Prevention, August 2000. Available online. URL: www.ncjrs.org/pdffiles1/ojjdp/183015.pdf. Examines characteristics of gangs in schools, reasons for greater gang prevalence in some schools, and the impact of gangs on victimization at school.

Howell, J. C., and S. H. Decker. "The Youth Gangs, Drugs, and Violence Connection." *Office of Juvenile Justice and Delinquency Prevention Bulletin,* January 1999. Available online. URL: www.ncjrs.org/pdffiles1/93920.pdf. Describes the relationship among youth gangs, drugs, and violence. Reviews studies that refute the popular image of youth gangs as violence-prone interstate drug traffickers.

Major, A. K., et al. "Youth Gangs in Indian Country," *OJJDP Juvenile Justice Bulletin: Youth Gang Series Report,* March 2004. Office of Juvenile Justice and Delinquency Prevention. Available online. URL: http://www.ncjrs.gov/pdffiles1/ojjdp/202714.pdf. Describes the nature and makeup of youth gangs in Indian Country, compares these results to information about gangs in other communities, and discusses programs that respond to the problem of gangs in Indian Country.

Miller, W. B. *The Growth of Youth Gang Problems in the United States: 1970–98.* Report, Office of Juvenile Justice and Delinquency Prevention, April 2001. Available online. URL: www.ncjrs.org/html/ojjdp/ojjdprpt_yth_gng_prob_2001. Presents findings from a study of the growth of youth gang problems in the United States from 1970 to 1998, offers possible explanations for the growth of youth gang problems, and uses trend and rate analyses to project future growth in gangs.

Moore, J., and J. Hagedorn. "Female Gangs: A Focus on Research." *Youth Gang Series Bulletin,* Office of Juvenile Justice and Delinquency Prevention, March 2001. Available online. URL: www.ncjrs.org/pdffiles1/ojjdp/186159.pdf. Summary of research on female gangs and the increased public recognition of female gang involvement as a significant social problem. Topics include motivations for female gang membership, delinquency and criminal activity of female gang members, and the long-term consequences of gang membership.

National Youth Gang Center. "Best Practices to Address Community Gang Problems: OJJDP's Comprehensive Gang Model." Office of Juvenile Justice and Delinquency Prevention, June 2008. Available online. URL: http://www.ncjrs.gov/pdffiles1/ojjdp/222799.pdf. Guides communities responding to a gang problem by implementing OJJDP's Comprehensive Gang Model. Describes best practices learned from practitioners experienced in planning and implementing the model and notes findings from evaluations of programs demonstrating the model.

Seymour, Anne, and Morna Murray, eds. "Victims of Gang Violence." Research Report, 2000 National Victim Assistance Academy, April 2001. Available online. URL: http://www.ojp.usdoj.gov/ovc/assist/nvaa2000/academy/V-22-3GN.htm. Presents statistics on gang-related violence and reviews victim assistance programs for victims of gang violence.

Starbuck, D., J. C. Howell, and D. Lindquist. "Hybrid and Other Modern Gangs." *Youth Gang Series Bulletin*, Office of Juvenile Justice and Delinquency Prevention, December 2001. Available online. URL: www.ncjrs.org/pdffiles1/ojjdp/189916.pdf. Describes the nature of modern youth gangs, in particular, hybrid gangs characterized by mixed racial and ethnic membership and vague codes of conduct.

Wyrick, P. A. "Vietnamese Youth Gang Involvement." *Office of Juvenile Justice and Delinquency Prevention Fact Sheet*, February 2000. Available online. URL: www.ncjrs.org/pdffiles1/ojjdp/fs200001.pdf. Summarizes findings from a study examining factors related to gang involvement by Vietnamese-American youth.

AUDIOVISUAL MATERIALS

18 with a Bullet: El Salvador's American-Style Gangs. DVD, 57 minutes, Wide Angle Reports, 2006. Documents the transnational gang known as "18," which is believed to have been brought from Los Angeles to San Salvador. Video also focuses on U.S. antigang efforts, particularly with regard to immigrants.

Neustra Familia, Our Family—Educator's Edition. DVD, 59 minutes (plus 56 minutes of bonus material), Center for Investigative Reporting, 2006. Explores life in Salinas, California, amid a war between two Latino gangs: Neustra Familia and the Mexican Mafia. Uses interviews of gang members and law enforcement officers to explore the formation and structure of Neustra Familia.

Real Life Teens: Teens and Gangs. DVD, 17 min., Films on Demand, 2007. Video and accompanying instructor's guide discuss why teens might turn to gangs and what problems teens might have once they join gangs.

Teenagers and Gangs: A Lethal Combination. DVD, 19 min., Meridian, 2000. Grades nine to 12. Former gang members and gang experts talk about gang life, acknowledging its attractions but exposing its dangers and disappointments.

SCHOOL VIOLENCE

BOOKS

Benbenishty, R., and R. A. Astor. *School Violence in Context: Culture, Neighborhood, Family, School, and Gender.* New York: Oxford University Press, 2005. Examines factors that associate school violence and victimization in Israel between 1998 and 2000 before comparing the results with California schools.

Cornell, Dewey. *School Violence: Fears Versus Facts.* Mahwah, N.J.: Lawrence Erlbaum, 2006. Illustrated with numerous case studies, this text identifies myths and misconceptions about youth violence, from ordinary bullying to rampage shootings. The text demonstrates how fear of school violence has resulted in misguided, counterproductive educational policies and practices.

Denmark, F., H. H. Krauss, and R. W. Wesner. *Violence in Schools: Cross-national and Cross-cultural Perspectives.* New York: Springer, 2005. This anthology of previously unpublished papers by academics in various disciplines examines violence in schools from cross-national and cross-cultural perspectives. A general discussion on school violence is followed by specific descriptions of such violence in the United States, Japan, the Philippines, the Arab world, and Australia. Strategies and interventions to prevent school violence are offered.

Elliott, D. S., et al., eds. *Violence in American Schools: A New Perspective.* New York: Cambridge University Press, 1998. A collection including essays from prominent criminologists. The writers describe an overview of violence in American schools, link this violence to adolescent behaviors outside of school, and evaluate school and community-based interventions to prevent violence.

Grapes, Bryan J., ed. *School Violence.* San Diego, Calif.: Greenhaven Press, 2000. Presents seven papers on the nature of school violence, the causes of school violence, personal narratives of school violence, and the prevention of school violence.

Hamburg, Al, et al., eds. *Violence in American Schools: A New Perspective.* New York: Cambridge University Press, 1998. Presents research on various aspects of school violence, including juvenile delinquency, school security, child development, sexual assaults at school, the causes of violence, and programs aimed at preventing school violence.

Annotated Bibliography

Lawrence, Richard. *School Crime and Juvenile Justice*, 2nd ed. New York: Oxford University Press, 2006. Examines the nature, extent, and causes of school crime and disruptive behavior, offering a comprehensive overview.

Newman, K. S. *Rampage: The Social Roots of School Shootings.* New York: Basic Books, 2004. Presents a new theory on the motives behind school shootings, the importance of motives in school shootings, and the manner by which close-knit communities can inadvertently produce school shootings.

Sullivan, Mercer L., Rob T. Guerette, and William DeJong. *Deadly Lessons: Understanding Lethal School Violence.* Washington, D.C.: The National Academies Press, 2003. Analyzes the findings of the 2001 Committee to Study Youth Violence in Schools. The results indicate significant and long-lasting harm in each community that results from school violence, although there are different responses to the violence depending on where the community is located.

Thomas, R. M. *Violence in America's Schools: Understanding, Prevention, and Responses.* Westport, Conn.: Praeger, 2003. A textbook that discusses school violence, prevention, and treatment for offenders and victims.

Webber, Julie A. *Failure to Hold: The Politics of School Violence.* Lanham, Md.: Rowman & Littlefield, 2003. Studies the dynamics of conflict in schools and argues that addressing school violence through surveillance and containment only impairs students' development of the basic skills needed for their functioning in a democratic society.

ARTICLES AND PAPERS

Addington, Lynn A. "Students' Fear after Columbine: Findings from a Randomized Experiment." *Journal of Quantitative Criminology* 19 (2003): 367–387. Analyzes student reports of fear to find that the Columbine event produces only a small increase in fear at school, in terms of both the population affected and the change in frequency reported.

Agron, Joe. "Lessons Learned." *American School & University* 71 (July 1999): 10. A discussion of crisis management and the implementation of security measures in the wake of high-profile school shootings in the United States.

Bernier, Shaun E. "School Safety: The Efforts of States and School Programs to Make Schools Safe." *Policy and Practice* (1999): 1–12. Profiles incidences of school violence in Kentucky, Tennessee, and Mississippi and presents approaches to school safety.

Bridges, Dennis. "Safeguarding Our Schools." *FBI Law Enforcement Bulletin* 68 (September 1999): 22–25. A discussion of security measures undertaken by school officials and local law enforcement agencies in response to highly publicized incidents of school violence.

Burrow, J. D., and R. Apel. "Youth Behavior, School Structure, and Student Risk of Victimization." *Justice Quarterly* 25 (2008): 349–380. Examines how student activities and school characteristics shape young people's risk for victimization at school.

Bynum, Timothy S., et al. "Reducing School Violence in Detroit: An Evaluation of an Alternative Conflict Resolution Intervention." Research Report, Michigan State University School of Criminal Justice, 1999. Examines pilot program of conflict resolution implemented in several Detroit middle schools and discusses results of the program.

Cao, L., Y. Zhang, and N. He. "Carrying Weapons to School for Protection: An Analysis of the 2001 School Crime Supplement Data." *Journal of Criminal Justice* 36 (2008): 154–164. Examines the reasons why adolescents bring guns to schools. In particular, the authors argue that the rationale for carrying weapons other than guns to school is different from that for carrying guns for protection.

Carney, Dan. "Colorado Rampage Impels a Search for New Methods to Combat Juvenile Crime." *Congressional Quarterly Weekly* 57 (April 24, 1999): 959. Discusses the need to identify juveniles at risk of violent offending and presents alternatives to the traditional handling of such offenders.

Chen, G. "Communities, Students, Schools, and School Crime: A Confirmatory Study of Crime in U.S. High Schools." *Urban Education* 43 (2008): 301–318. Investigates how community characteristics, student background, school climate, and zero-tolerance policies interact to affect school crime. Larger schools and schools with higher student transience and misbehavior have higher levels of criminal incidents. Tough-on-crime policies are associated with higher level of school crime, controlling for community and school variables.

Eitle, David, and Tamela M. Eitle. "Segregation and School Violence." *Social Forces* 82 (2003): 589–615. Examining data from 740 schools in 40 countries, the authors find that lower levels of school district segregation correspond to higher levels of violent crime in the schools. The problem is amplified under conditions of greater racial inequality.

Ferguson, Harv. "Looking Beyond the School Shooter Profile: Developing a Comprehensive Protocol for School Violence Prevention." *Police Chief* 68 (May 2001): 48–52. Available online. URL: http://www.theiacp.org. Considers the personality of the potential school shooter, stressful events experienced by the potential shooter, and the setting of the shooting in order to develop a violence prevention strategy for schools.

Finley, L. L. "Examining School Searches as Systemic Violence." *Critical Criminology* 14 (2006): 117–135. The author considers three types of school searches—metal detectors, drug tests, and strip searches—as forms of violence against students. In addition to being an ineffective means of preventing and addressing school violence and student drug use, these measures harm students, teachers, and society at large.

Furlong, Michael, et al. "Using Student Risk Factors in School Violence Surveillance Reports: Illustrative Examples for Enhanced Policy Formation, Implementation, and Evaluation." *Law & Policy* 23 (July 2001): 271–295. Presents information about the incidence of school violence, drawing upon data from the Centers for Disease Control's Youth Risk Behavior Surveillance surveys and the California Student Survey.

Harper, Frederick D., and Farah A. Ibrahim. "Violence and Schools in the USA: Implications for Counseling." *International Journal for the Advancement of Counseling* 21 (1999): 349–366. Reviews the causes and consequences of school violence, prevention efforts, and counseling for perpetrators and victims, and provides international comparisons.

Henry, Stuart. "What Is School Violence?: An Integrated Definition." *Annals of the American Academy of Political and Social Science* 567 (January 2000): 16–29. Analysis of school violence as a complex problem that defies simplistic explanations.

Herda-Rapp, Ann. "The Social Construction of Local School Violence Threats by the News Media and Professional Organizations." *Sociological Inquiry* 73 (2003): 545–574. Considers the effect of claims by the news media and professional organizations about school violence: Once constructed as an urban problem, school violence, was relocated and reconstructed as both a national and a rural or suburban phenomenon.

Hoang, Francis Q. "Addressing School Violence: Prevention, Planning, and Practice." *FBI Law Enforcement Bulletin* 70 (August 2001): 18–23. Examines the steps communities should take to address school violence.

Holmes, Shirley R. "Homicide in School: A Preliminary Discussion." *Journal of Gang Research* 7 (summer 2000): 29–36. Discussion of seven school shootings from 1997 to 1999 in the United States, including the shooting at Columbine High School in Littleton, Colorado. Includes a listing of profile factors common to the shooters involved at the seven sites.

Kellam, Sheppard G., Ron Prinz, and Joseph F. Sheley. "Preventing School Violence: Plenary Papers of the 1999 Conference on Criminal Justice Research and Evaluation—Enhancing Policy and Practice Through Research, Volume 2." Research Report, U.S. Department of Justice, 2000. Presents three research papers on the prevention of school violence, plus an overview of the federal government's response to school violence.

Kerbs, J. J., and J. M. Jolley. "The Joy of Violence: What about Violence Is Fun in Middle School." *American Journal of Criminal Justice* 32 (2007): 12–29. Examines how middle school students view violence. Approximately 70 percent of interview respondents reported violence to be an enjoyable experience to some degree.

Klein, J. "An Invisible Problem: Everyday Violence against Girls in Schools." *Theoretical Criminology* 10 (2006): 147–177. A media analysis examining the role of masculinity in violence against juvenile girls, including school shootings, dating violence, and sexual harassment. The results indicate that masculinity plays a key role in these crimes but is ignored in the media narrative.

Lipman, Lisa R., ed., "Growing Use of School Suspensions Raises Concerns." *Juvenile Justice Update* 7 (December 2001/January 2002): 1–12. Discusses the rising use of school suspensions at a time when school-related crime is declining.

Maeroff, Gene I. "Symbiosis of Sorts: School Violence and the Media." Research Report, Columbia University Teachers College, 2000. Analysis of the relationship between violence at schools and media coverage of school violence.

Menifield, Charles E., et al. "Media's Portrayal of Urban and Rural School Violence: A Preliminary Analysis." *Deviant Behavior* 22 (September–October 2001): 447–464. Examines newspapers' portrayal of urban and rural school violence, and the public perceptions about school violence and juvenile crime fostered by media coverage.

Nicholson, Jane. "Reconciliations: Prevention of and Recovery from School Violence." *Annals of the American Academy of Political and Social Science* 567 (January 2000): 186–197. Presents the author's self-designed recovery process after her husband was murdered in his university office by a distressed graduate student.

Nicoletti, John, Kelly Zinna, and Sally Spencer-Thomas. "Dynamics of 'Schoolplace' Violence." *Police Chief* 66 (October 1999): 74–92. Explores the similarities between school shootings and workplace violence, including the profile of perpetrators as "loners" with poor social skills who are often obsessed with violence and weapons.

Pagliocca, Pauline M., and Amanda B. Nickerson. "Legislating School Crisis Responses: Good Policy or Just Good Politics?" *Law & Policy* 23 (July 2001): 373–407. Presents an overview of crisis-response initiatives implemented by school districts following incidents of school violence and examines the political and legislative measures aimed at curbing school violence.

Payne, A. A. "A Multilevel Analysis of the Relationships among Communal School Organization, Student Bonding, and Delinquency." *Journal of Research in Crime and Delinquency* 45 (2008): 429–455. Analyzes data on students' involvement in delinquency. Results find that students who attend more communally organized schools are more likely to be bonded to school and less likely to engage in delinquency.

Peterson, Reece, et al. "Preventing School Violence: A Practical Guide to Comprehensive Planning." Research Report, Indiana Education Policy Center, 2001. Available online. URL: http://www.indiana.edu/~iepc/.

Presents an overview of school violence prevention and examines programs on conflict resolution and violence prevention, peer mediation, improved classroom behavior management, and bullying prevention.

"Preventing School Violence: Voices of Junior and Senior High School Students." Research Report. New Jersey City University, 2001. Available online. URL: http://www.njcu.edu. Reports on the findings of a survey of some 300 junior and senior high school students who participated in a forum on the effects of school violence and ways to eliminate it.

"Preventing Youth Violence." Research Report, U.S. Department of Health and Human Services and the Centers for Disease Control and Prevention, 2000. Presents guidelines for parents, students, and school officials on preventing school violence.

Redding, Richard E., and Sarah M. Shalf. "Legal Context of School Violence: The Effectiveness of Federal, State, and Local Law Enforcement Efforts to Reduce Gun Violence in Schools." *Law & Policy* 23 (July 2001): 297–343. Examines the patterns of school violence in the United States, gun acquisition by juveniles, and the effectiveness of various laws and law enforcement measures aimed at curbing school violence.

Rigoni, David, and David X. Swenson. "Beyond Scripted Blame: A Systems Approach for Understanding School Violence." *Systemic Practice and Action* 13 (2000): 279–296. Examines an alternative to common analyses of school violence by describing the underlying nature of violence, including membership in deviant peer groups, social alienation, and emotional disturbances due to early trauma, genetic predisposition, dysfunctional family systems, and a violent cultural context.

Rosen, Barry, and Diane Dobry. "Examining School Violence." *Teachers College Reports* 3 (winter 2001): 1–8. Reports on what the Columbia University Teachers College is doing through research and conferences to help counter violence in schools.

Sandhu, Dava Singh, and Cheryl Blalock, eds. "Violence in American Schools: A Practical Guide for Counselors." Research Report, American Counseling Association, 2000. School violence reduction efforts implemented at Wilson High School in Long Beach, California, are described as a process model for other schools.

"School Violence Prevention Task Force, Final Report." Research Report, Texas Office of the Attorney General, 2000. URL: http://www.oag.state.tx.us. Report of the Texas attorney general's School Violence Prevention Task Force emphasizes programs for preventing school violence.

Tebo, Margaret G. "Zero Tolerance, Zero Sense." *American Bar Association Journal* 86 (April 2000): 40–113. An analysis of strict, inflexible policies to prevent school violence, such as all-or-nothing punishment, reveals that they may alienate students and punish behaviors that do not compromise school security.

Thompkins, Douglas E. "School Violence: Gangs and a Culture of Fear." *Annals of the American Academy of Political and Social Science* 567 (January 2000): 54–71. Discusses the theory that measures to prevent school violence, such as the presence of security officers, metal detectors, and security cameras, may deter some students from committing acts of violence, while at the same time cause heightened fear among students and teachers and increase the power of some gangs and the perceived need of some students to join gangs.

Wallace, Lisa Hutchinson. "Reports from Rural Mississippi: A Look at School Violence." *Journal of Security Administration* 24 (December 2001): 15–32. Presents findings of a study testing two alternative theories of school violence.

Welsh, W. N. "Individual and Institutional Predictors of School Disorder." *Youth Violence and Juvenile Justice* 1 (2003): 346–368. Based on survey data, this article examines how school climate and student characteristics affect school disorder. While student characteristics explain a great deal about the variance in offending, school climate (such as, clarity of rules and fairness) explains much of the variance in minor misconduct.

Zinna, Kelly. "Violent Students: Six Warning Signs." *Campus Safety* 10 (2002): 14–15. Available online. URL: http://www.campusjournal.com. Presents six early warning signs of students prone to violence and outlines a three-step approach to dealing with threats of violence at school.

WEB DOCUMENTS

"Annual Report on School Safety." Report, U.S. Department of Education and U.S. Department of Justice, 2002. Available online. URL: www.ncjrs.gov/pdffiles1/ojjpd/193163.pdf. Describes the type and extent of crime and violence in U.S. schools. Examines data on homicides and suicides at school, injuries at school, crimes against students, crimes against teachers, weapons at school, and student perceptions of school safety.

Brooks, Kim, Vincent Schiraldi, and Jason Ziedenberg. "School House Hype: Two Years Later." Research Report, The Justice Policy Institute, 2000. Available online. URL: http://www.justicepolicy.org-images/upload/00-04_REP_SchoolHouseHype2_JJ.pdf. Analysis of data on school crime and judicial decisions on school violence concludes that the actual risks that students experience in schools differ substantially from the image presented in opinion polls and reported by the media. Presents an inventory of federal school violence prevention activities and programs.

Catalano, R. F., R. Loeber, and K. C. McKinney. "School and Community Interventions to Prevent Serious and Violent Offending." *Office of Juvenile Justice and Delinquency Prevention Bulletin*, 1999. Available online. URL: www.ncjrs.org/pdffiles1/ojjdp/177624.pdf. Describes school and community interventions shown to reduce risk factors for drug abuse and serious and violent juvenile offending.

Coleman, Peter T., and Morton Deutsch, "Cooperation, Conflict Resolution, and School Violence: A Systems Approach." Research Report, Columbia Teachers College, 2000. Available online. URL: http://www. parentsassociation.com/health/conflict_resolution.html. Examines school-based violence prevention programs that are founded on cooperation and conflict resolution and describes specific program components that schools can implement.

Decker, S. H. "Increasing School Safety Through Juvenile Accountability Programs. *Office of Juvenile Justice and Delinquency Prevention Bulletin,* December 2000. Available online. URL: www.ncjrs.org/pdffiles1/ ojjdp/179283.pdf. Describes common features and key elements of effective school safety programs that emphasize student accountability.

Dinkes, R., J. Kemp, and K. Baum. *Indicators of School Crime and Safety: 2008,* April 2009. National Center for Education Statistics and Bureau of Justice Statistics. Available online. URL: http://nces.ed.gov/pubs2009/2009022. pdf. Uses national survey of students to describe victimization, discipline, and social climate in schools.

Ericson, N. "Addressing the Problem of Juvenile Bullying." *Office of Juvenile Justice and Delinquency Prevention Fact Sheet,* June 2001. Available online. URL: www.ncjrs.org/pdffiles1/ojjdp/fs200127.pdf. Discusses juvenile bullying as a form of violence among children and summarizes findings of a report by the National Institute of Child Health and Human on the long- and short-term effects of bullying.

Finkelhor, D., and R. Ormrod. "Homicides of Children and Youth." *Office of Juvenile Justice and Delinquency Prevention Bulletin,* October 2001. Available online. URL: www.ncjrs.org/pdffiles1/ojjdp/187239.pdf. Presents statistics on juvenile homicide and discusses certain types of juvenile homicide, including school homicides.

Kadel, Stephanie, Jim Watkins, Joseph Follman, and Cathy Hammond. "Reducing School Violence: Building a Framework for School Safety." Report, Serve Publications, 2001. Available online. URL: http://www. serve.org/downloads/publication.rsu.pdf. Topics include gang violence in schools and measures to prevent school violence.

Kramen, Alissa J., Kelly R. Massey, and Howard W. Timm. "Guide for Preventing and Responding to School Violence." Report by the International Association of Chiefs of Police, 2000. Available online. URL: http://www.theiacp.org/PublicationsGuides/contentbyTopic/tabid/216/ default.aspx?id=88&v=l. Presents strategies and approaches for creating safer learning environments in schools.

Mihalic, S., et al. "Blueprints for Violence Prevention." *Office of Juvenile Justice and Delinquency Prevention Bulletin,* July 2001. Available online.

URL: http://www.ncjrs.org/pdffiles1/ojjdp/187079.pdf. Provides information on violence prevention and intervention programs that are effective in reducing adolescent violent crime, delinquency, and substance abuse, and aggression and conduct disorders.

Naumann, Kurt. "Briefing Paper: Bullying." Research Report, School Violence Resources Center, 2001. Available online. URL: http://www.svrc. net/files/bullying.pdf. Examines bullying, the most pervasive form of school violence, and describes successful antibullying programs. Provides Internet links to antibullying organizations.

Neiman, S., J. F. DeVoe, and K. Chandler. "Crime, Violence, Discipline, and Safety in U.S. Public Schools: Findings from the School Survey on Crime and Safety: 2007–2008." National Center for Education Statistics, May 2009. Available online. URL: http://nces.ed.gov/pubs2009/2009326. pdf. Reports the results of a nationwide survey on school crime and violence as well as schools' efforts to prevent crime.

"Reporting School Violence." Research Report, National Center for Victims of Crime, 2002. Available online. URL: http://www.ojp.usdoj.gov/ ovc/publications/bulletins/legalseries/bulletin2/ncj189191.pdf. Presents an overview of recently enacted state laws addressing violence in U.S. schools, particularly those laws concerning the collection of data and the reporting of school violence incidents and current issues related to the reporting of school violence.

"School Violence: An Overview." *Juvenile Justice Journal*, vol. 8, June 2001, pp. 1–40. Available online. URL: http://www.ncjrs.org/pdffiles1/ojjdp/188158. pdf. Issue features three articles that examine the extent and nature of school violence and review promising approaches to creating safe schools and resolving conflicts peacefully.

Vossekuil, Bryan, et al. "Final Report and Findings of the Safe School Initiative: Implications for the Prevention of School Attacks in the United States." Research Report, United States Department of Education, 2002. Available online. http://www.ed.gov/admins/lead/safety/prevent ingattacksreport.pdf. Findings of the Safe School Initiative, a cooperative effort between the U.S. Department of Education and the U.S. Secret Service begun in response to the Columbine High School shootings in 1999. The initiative studied 37 school shootings between 1974 and 2000 in order to identify a profile of pre-attack behaviors and prevention strategies.

"Want to Resolve a Dispute? Try Mediation." *Office of Juvenile Justice and Delinquency Prevention Bulletin*, March 2000. Available online. URL: www.ncjrs.org/pdffiles1/ojjdp/178999.pdf. Discusses the process of mediation as a tool to reduce violence in schools and neighborhoods, including peer mediation, in which students are recruited and trained to act as mediators for classmates involved in a dispute.

Annotated Bibliography

AUDIOVISUAL MATERIALS

"Community Responses to Truancy: Engaging Students in School Video-conference: OJJDP Teleconference Series." Streaming video, 90 min., Office of Juvenile Justice and Delinquency Prevention, 2003. Available online. URL: http://www.juvenilenet.org/jjtap/trvancy/view.html. Reviews the collaborative process and provides examples of programs and communities that use the process in preventing or intervening in delinquency, violence, substance abuse, and other problems.

"Comprehensive Framework for School Violence Prevention." VHS video, 90 min., Hamilton Fish Institute (for the Office of Juvenile Justice and Delinquency Prevention Teleconference Series), 2000. Presents the proceedings of October 2000 conference on the prevention of school violence using six approaches—administrative, school security, schoolwide education in violence prevention, counseling, alternative education, and community involvement.

"Managing School Violence: In Higher Schools." VHS video, 35 min., KidSafety of America, 2000. URL: www.kidsafetystore.com. Provides instruction in how higher schools can prevent and respond to violent incidents on school grounds.

"Managing School Violence: The Mental Health Issues." VHS video, 35 min., KidSafety of America, 2000. URL: www.kidsafetystore.com. Identifies mental health issues that contribute to school violence, with emphasis on prevention.

"Managing School Violence in Preschools and Elementary Schools." VHS video, 15 min., KidSafety of America, 2001. URL: http://www.kidsafety store.com. Presents guidelines for a school safety plan and a crisis response plan to respond to violence in preschools and elementary schools.

"Managing School Violence: Students Talk." VHS video, 12 min., KidSafety of America, 2000. URL: www.kidsafetystore.com. Includes dramatizations and actual conversations by high school students that focus on what students can do to help prevent violent behavior at school by other students.

"Preventing School Violence & Delinquency." CD-ROM, National Center on Education, Disability, and Juvenile Justice, 2001. URL: http://www.edjj.org. Developed for the 2001 Preventing School Violence and Delinquency Conference. Provides resources for further research on the prevention of youth violence.

"School-wide Education for Violence Prevention: OJJDP Teleconference Series." VHS, Office of Juvenile Justice and Delinquency Prevention, 2002. Highlights elements of schoolwide strategies deemed effective for violence prevention, including anger management, conflict resolution, social skills training, communications skills, and use of mediation, law enforcement, and legal services.

Teen Truth: An Inside Look at Bullying and School Violence. DVD, 24 min., Human Relations Media, 2006. Explores the relationship between bullying and school violence through fictional illustrations as well as interviews with experts and students.

SUBSTANCE ABUSE

BOOKS

Babbit, Nikki. *Adolescent Drug and Alcohol Abuse: How to Spot It, Stop It, and Get Help for Your Family.* Sebastopol, Calif.: O'Reilly & Associates, 2000. A primer on use, abuse, and dependency issues. Provides information specific drugs and their effects, as well as resources for recovery and drug-education programs.

Prichard, J., and J. Payne. *Alcohol, Drugs and Crime: A Study of Juveniles in Detention.* Canberra, Australia: Australian Institute of Criminology, 2005. Examines the drug and alcohol use and criminal behaviors of a sample of juvenile detainees in Australia. The evidence suggests that substance use exacerbates criminal offending.

Sanders, B. *Drugs, Clubs and Young People: Sociological and Public Health Perspectives.* Burlington, Vt.: Ashgate, 2006. This edited collection offers insights on drug use among youths by exploring behaviors common at raves and nightclubs.

Walker, Samuel. *Sense and Nonsense About Drugs and Crime: A Policy Guide.* Belmont, Calif.: Wadsworth Publishing, 2000. Evaluates conservative and liberal views on crime control proposals, guns and crimes, drug policies, the war on drugs, and the legalization of drugs.

ARTICLES AND PAPERS

Belenko, Steven, and Richard Dembo. "Treating Adolescent Substance Abuse Problems in the Juvenile Drug Court." *International Journal of Law and Psychiatry* 26 (2003): 87–110. This essay and review provides an overview of juvenile drug courts. A key distinguishing factor of a drug court is the collaboration among criminal justice agencies, courts, treatment agencies, and community organizations. Existing studies suggest that juvenile drug courts have a positive impact on youth.

Belenko, Steven, Jane B. Sprott, and Courtney Petersen. "Drug and Alcohol Involvement among Minority and Female Juvenile Offenders: Treatment and Policy Issues." *Criminal Justice Policy Review* 15 (2004): 3–36. Reports on the impact of drug and alcohol use on the juvenile case processing of girls and minorities in the United States. Instead of viewing substance abuse as secondary to punishment and control, adopting a more problem-solving, public health–oriented approach would spur the juvenile justice system to focus on the need to create more individualized treatment and prevention programs that are gender and culturally specific.

Braithwaite, Ronald L., Rhonda C. Conerly, and Alyssa G. Robillard. "Alcohol and Other Drug Use Among Adolescent Detainees." *Journal of Substance Abuse* 8 (2003): 126–131. Describes alcohol and other drug use among adolescent detainees at two state juvenile justice facilities, based on interviews with over 2,000 male and female detainees ages 11 to 18. Results show that high-risk adolescents engage in considerably more substance use than the general U.S. adolescent population.

Brown, Victoria L., Isaac D. Montoya, and Cheryl A. Dayton-Shotts "Trends of Criminal Activity and Substance Use in a Sample of Welfare Recipients." *Crime & Delinquency* 50 (2004): 6–23. This longitudinal study explores the interplay among welfare reform, criminal behavior, and substance use.

Doherty, E. E., K. M. Green, and M. E. Ensminger. "Investigating the Long-Term Influence of Adolescent Delinquency on Drug Use Initiation." *Drug and Alcohol Dependence* 93 (2008): 72–84. Investigates the long-term relationship between serious adolescent delinquency and the onset of marijuana and cocaine use. Overall, serious adolescent delinquency has at least some causal influence on drug use initiation that extends into midlife.

Ford, J. A. "Nonmedical Prescription Drug Use among Adolescents: The Influence of Bonds to Family and School." *Youth & Society* 40 (2009): 336–352. Examines the impact of social bonds to family and school on nonmedical prescription drug use among adolescents. The findings provide support for social control theory. Adolescents with strong bonds to family and school are less likely to report nonmedical prescription drug use. Important implications and future research needs are discussed.

Gilmore, A. S., N. Rodriguez, and V. J. Webb. "Substance Abuse and Drug Courts: The Role of Social Bonds in Juvenile Drug Courts." *Youth Violence and Juvenile Justice* 3 (2005): 287–315. Examines the effect of juvenile drug court treatment on curbing delinquent behavior. Results indicate social bonds (such as, parents' substance abuse, siblings' substance abuse, peers' substance abuse, and gang membership) play a significant role in curbing delinquent behavior and promoting program completion.

Gottfredson, D. C., and D. A. Soulé. "The Timing of Property Crime, Violent Crime, and Substance Use among Juveniles." *Journal of Research in Crime and Delinquency* 42 (2005): 110–120. Examines the timing of juvenile delinquent behavior by crime type. Results suggest that timing of drug crimes and other crimes may vary, since violence rates are higher during after-school hours but property and drug crime rates are not.

Neff, J. L., and D. E. Waite. "Male versus Female Substance Abuse Patterns among Incarcerated Juvenile Offenders: Comparing Strain and Social Learning Variables." *Justice Quarterly* 24 (2007): 106–132. Explores gender differences in substance use among a juvenile correctional population. The extent of substance use and abuse appears to be quite similar among males and females.

Parsai, M., S. Voisine, and F. F. Marsiglia. "The Protective and Risk Effects of Parents and Peers on Substance Use, Attitudes, and Behaviors of Mexican and Mexican American Female and Male Adolescents." *Youth & Society* 40 (2009): 353–376. Explores the extent to which parental and peer behaviors and norms may affect substance use, personal antidrug norms, and intentions to use drugs in a group of preadolescents of Mexican heritage.

Strunin, Lee, and Serkalem Demissie. "Cultural Identification and Alcohol Use Among 'Black' Adolescents." *Substance Use & Abuse* 36 (2001): 2,025–2,041. Three hundred Haitian and non-Haitian black students in the ninth to 12th grades in three inner-city public schools were interviewed in a study to test the relationship between cultural identification and alcohol use.

WEB DOCUMENTS

Dickinson, T., and A. Crowe. "Capacity Building for Juvenile Substance Abuse Treatment." *Juvenile Justice Bulletin*, December 1997. Available online. URL: http://www.ncjrs.gov/pdffiles/167251.pdf. Presents an overview of juvenile delinquency and substance abuse, discusses drug testing in the juvenile justice system, and reviews substance abuse services within juvenile justice systems nationwide.

Johnston, L. D., P. M. O'Malley, J. G. Bachman, and E. J. Schulenberg. "Monitoring the Future National Results on Adolescent Drug Use: Overview of Key Findings, 2008." Bethesda, Md.: National Institute on Drug Abuse, 2009. Available online. URL: http://www.monitoringthe future.org/pubs/monographs/overview2008.pdf. Presents overview of findings from a large, nationally representative annual study on adolescents' self-reported rates of drug use.

McClelland, G. M., L. A. Teplin, and K. M. Abram. "Detection and Prevalence of Substance Use Among Juvenile Detainees." *OJJDP Juvenile Justice Bulletin*, June 2004. Office of Juvenile Justice and Delinquency Prevention. Available online. URL: http://www.ncjrs.gov/pdffiles1/ojjdp/203934.pdf. Presents background information on the effects of substance use and abuse on adolescent development and delinquency, and presents empirical findings from the Northwestern Juvenile Project on the prevalence of illicit substance use among detained juveniles by age, gender, race/ethnicity, and type of substance.

Stahl, Anne L. "Drug Offense Cases in Juvenile Courts, 1989–1998." *Office of Juvenile Justice and Delinquency Prevention Bulletin*, 2001. Available online. URL: http://www.ncjrs.org/pdffiles1/ojjdp/fs200136.pdf. Provides statistics on drug offense cases in juvenile courts from 1989 to 1998 in the United States. The number of juvenile court cases involving drug offenses more than doubled between 1993 and 1998.

AUDIOVISUAL MATERIALS

Combating Underage Drinking. VHS video, 150 min., Eastern Kentucky University, Juvenile Justice Telecommunications Project, 2000. Contains the proceedings of a live national satellite broadcast sponsored by the Office of Juvenile Justice and Delinquency Prevention in September 2000 to address ways of preventing underage drinking.

Let's Help Youth Stay Drug Free, Part V, Social Problems & Substance Abuse: Organizing for Effective Solutions. VHS video, 120 min., produced by the National Clearinghouse for Alcohol and Drug Information, 1999. Presents a panel discussion of issues facing youth, including violence, AIDS, and drug abuse, and examines the relationship between these issues and youth crime.

JUVENILE JUSTICE

BOOKS

Bartollas, Clemens, and Stuart J. Miller. *Juvenile Justice in America*, 5th ed. Saddleback, N.J.: Prentice Hall Publishing, 2007. Examines and defines the significant components of and debates over juvenile justice in the United States.

Bazemore, Gordon, and Lode Walgrave, eds. *Restorative Juvenile Justice: Repairing the Harm of Youth Crime.* Monsey, N.Y.: Criminal Justice Press/ Willow Tree Press, 1999. Focuses on the impact of restorative juvenile justice on the lives of crime victims. Examines the claims of restorative justice advocates and the implications for programs, policy, and research in the field of restorative justice in the United States as well as Canada, New Zealand, Australia, and the United Kingdom. Includes a review of research in restorative justice.

Binder, Arnold, Gilbert Geis, and Dickson D. Bruce, Jr. *Juvenile Delinquency: Historical, Cultural and Legal Perspectives.* 3rd ed. Cincinnati, Ohio: Anderson Publishing, 2001. Delinquency is discussed in a historical framework that traces the evolution of the Western perception of the child and the juvenile justice system. Presents classical, psychological, sociological and critical theories of criminological thought on the causes of delinquency.

Boesky, Lisa M. *Juvenile Offenders with Mental Health Disorders: Who Are They and What Do We Do with Them?* Lanham, Md.: American Correctional Association, 2002. This guide is intended to assist professionals who supervise, treat, or manage juvenile offenders with mental health disorders housed in residential facilities or under community supervision.

Champion, D. J., and G. L. Mays. *Transferring Juveniles to Criminal Courts: Trends and Implications for Criminal Justice.* New York: Praeger Publishers, 1991. Describes the process of transferring juveniles to criminal courts and discusses the outcomes that characterize most transfers.

Cicourel, A. V. *Social Organization of Juvenile Justice,* 2nd ed. Piscataway, N.J.: Transaction Publishers, 1995. This seminal study focuses on juvenile justice in two California cities and discusses the theory that agencies such as police and probation may generate juvenile delinquency by their routine encounters with youth.

Del Carmen, Rolando V., Mary Parker, and Frances P. Reddington. *Briefs of Leading Cases in Juvenile Justice.* Cincinnati, Ohio: Anderson Publishing, 1998. Briefs major cases on juvenile justice from the U.S. Supreme Court, U.S. Courts of Appeals, and U.S. District Courts, as well as state cases of relevance. A list of cases with their principles of law are provided.

Emerson, R. *Judging Delinquents: Context and Process in Juvenile Court,* 2nd ed. Piscataway, N.J.: Transaction Publishers, 2007. Classic study, originally published in 1969, of how juvenile courts are organized and how court actors understand youth and their delinquent acts. Describes how agencies work together to actively create norms and standard practices that help them make decisions on youths' cases.

Fagan, J. A., and F. E. Zimring. *The Changing Borders of Juvenile Justice: Transfer of Adolescents to the Criminal Court.* John D. and Catherine T. MacArthur Foundation Series on Mental Health and Development. Chicago, Ill.: University of Chicago Press, 2000. A collection of essays written by the most prominent scholars in the field on transferring youth from juvenile to criminal court, which challenges the widespread use of the practice.

Feld, B. C. *Bad Kids: Race and the Transformation of the Juvenile Court.* New York: Oxford University Press, 1999. Comprehensive study that analyzes the beginnings of the juvenile court and traces changes in how youth are prosecuted. Offers a critical analysis of contemporary juvenile justice policies.

Grisso, T., and R. G. Schwartz, eds. *Youth on Trial: A Developmental Perspective on Juvenile Justice.* John D. and Catherine T. MacArthur Foundation

Annotated Bibliography

Series on Mental Health and Development. Chicago, Ill.: University of Chicago Press, 2003. Edited collection that considers adolescent development and juvenile justice policy.

Hawkins, D. F., and K. Kempf-Leonard, eds. *Our Children, Their Children: Confronting Racial and Ethnic Differences in American Juvenile Justice.* John D. and Catherine T. MacArthur Foundation Series on Mental Health and Development. Chicago, Ill.: The University of Chicago Press, 2005. A collection of essays dealing with ethnic and racial disparities in the juvenile justice system with an emphasis on the offending and processing of juveniles.

Krisberg, B., and J. F. Austin. *Reinventing Juvenile Justice.* Newbury Park, Calif.: Sage Publications, 1993. Questions the survival of the juvenile court as it exists. Explores the social forces on youth and their families that are related to violent juvenile crime. Other topics include juvenile justice laws and court procedures, and the influences of gender and race on detention.

Kupchik, A. *Judging Juveniles: Prosecuting Adolescents in Adult and Juvenile Courts.* New York: NYU Press, 2006. Compares the prosecution of adolescents in juvenile court and in criminal (adult courts) and considers policies to prosecute more youth in adult courts.

Manfredi, Christopher P. *The Supreme Court and Juvenile Justice.* Lawrence, Kan.: The University Press of Kansas, 1997. Review of significant decisions by the U.S. Supreme Court in the area of juvenile justice. Briefs key decisions such as *In re Gault* and discusses the impact of such landmark rulings on juvenile courts throughout the United States.

Muraskin, Roslyn, and Albert R. Roberts, eds. *Visions for Change: Crime and Justice in the Twenty-first Century,* 5th ed. Upper Saddle River, N.J.: Prentice Hall Publishing, 2008. Looks at significant criminal justice issues, including juvenile justice and gangs, in the past and projects their trends into the 21st century.

Palacios, Wilson R., Paul F. Cromwell, and Roger G. Dunham. *Crime & Justice in America: Present Realities and Future Prospects,* 2nd ed. Saddle River, N.J.: Prentice-Hall, 2002. Topics includes the juvenile justice system, juvenile justice reform, and juvenile restitution.

Schlossman, S. L. *Love and the American Delinquent: The Theory and Practice of "Progressive" Juvenile Justice, 1885–1920.* Chicago: University of Chicago Press, 1977. Seminal study that examines the origins of correctional reform movements in the United States from the perspective of legal, intellectual, and social history.

Shoemaker, Donald J., ed. *International Handbook on Juvenile Justice.* Westport, Conn.: Greenwood Publishing Company, 1996. Reviews the development of the juvenile justice system in the United States and in other countries and discusses possible reforms.

Sulton, A. T., ed. *African-American Perspectives on Crime Causation, Criminal Justice Administration and Crime Prevention.* Woburn, Mass.: Butterworth-Heinemann, 1996. Collection of 14 essays by African-American criminologists on crime causes and prevention and criminal justice administration. Includes chapters on drugs and violence in gangs and an explanation of delinquency among black juvenile offenders.

Tanenhaus, David S. *Juvenile Justice in the Making.* New York: Oxford University Press, 2004. This narrative history of the rise and workings of America's first juvenile court explores the fundamental and enduring question of how the law should treat the young. The text describes the great variation in juvenile courts of the early 20th century and how histories of the juvenile court should consider this complexity.

Tonry, M., ed. *Handbook of Crime and Punishment.* New York. Oxford University Press, 1998. This book on crime and punishment treats crime as a significant political issue in contemporary American society and provides a comprehensive overview of criminal justice and juvenile justice, including information on youth gangs.

Whitehead, John T., and Steven P. Lab. *Juvenile Justice: An Introduction,* 5th ed. Cincinnati, Ohio: Anderson Publishing, 2006. Provides a comprehensive analysis of all aspects of the juvenile justice system, including history, movements toward diversion and deinstitutionalization, police interaction, court process, due process, and community intervention. Also examines female delinquency, gang delinquency, the use of the death penalty for youths, and the correct philosophical approach to juvenile justice.

Winterdyk, J. A., ed. *Juvenile Justice Systems: International Perspectives.* Toronto, Ontario: Canadian Scholars Press, 1997. A comparison of juvenile justice systems in 11 countries, including the United States, Canada, Australia, England, Italy, Japan, Russia, and the Netherlands.

ARTICLES AND PAPERS

Applegate, B. K., R. K. Davis, and F. T. Cullen. "Reconsidering Child Saving: The Extent and Correlates of Public Support for Excluding Youths From the Juvenile Court." *Crime & Delinquency* 55 (2009): 51–77. Assesses how public views of excluding youth from juvenile court are related to multiple factors, including offense and offender characteristics, views on the appropriate aims of juvenile sentencing, perceptions of juvenile maturity, and expectations about the results of transferring juvenile cases to the adult criminal justice system.

Benekos, P. J., and A. V. Merlo. "Juvenile Justice: The Legacy of Punitive Policy." *Youth Violence and Juvenile Justice* 6 (2008): 28–46. Reviews and analyzes the impact of juvenile justice policies from the 1990s. Despite declining juvenile crime rates, the adultification of youth continues to include punitive sanctions, such as incarceration and transfer to criminal court.

Cameron, Lance, and Tom Strattman. "The No-Coddle Approach to Juvenile Rehabilitation." *American Legion* 148 (June 2000): 10. A discussion of the effectiveness of boot camps in reforming delinquent, with focus on a boot camp in Manatee County, Florida, whose program includes prayer and counseling.

Cellini, Henry R. "Mental Health Concerns of Adjudicated Adolescents." *Offender Programs Report* 4 (July/August 2000): 17–26. Presents findings of a national study of mental health disorders among juvenile detainees at 95 public and private juvenile facilities.

Cusac, Anne-Marie. "Arrest My Kid." *Progressive* 65 (July 2001): 22. Describes the frustration of parents of mentally ill adolescents who refuse or cannot get mental health treatment, and how delinquent behavior that leads to arrest is often viewed by such parents as the only means of getting their child the necessary mental health treatment.

Daly, K., and B. Bouhours. "Judicial Censure and Moral Communication to Youth Sex Offenders." *Justice Quarterly* 25 (2008): 496–522. This study examines the ways in which judges interact with youths and censure offenses and what (if any) normative guidance they give concerning gender, sexuality, and violence.

Dembo, R., W. Walters, and K. Meyers. "A Practice/Research Collaborative: An Innovative Approach to Identifying and Responding to Psychosocial Functioning Problems and Recidivism Risk Among Juvenile Arrestees." *Journal of Offender Rehabilitation* 41 (2005): 39–66. Discusses the process leading to the development of a youth diagnostic protocol and reviews in detail its component instruments and decision-making activities.

Engen, Rodney L., Sara Steen, and George S. Bridges. "Racial Disparities in the Punishment of Youth: A Theoretical and Empirical Assessment of the Literature." *Social Problems* 49 (May 2002): 49. Presents research findings on racial disparities in the juvenile justice system and concludes that the causes of such disparity are unclear.

Fallon, Theodore, et al. "Recommendations for Juvenile Justice Reform." Research Report, American Academy of Child and Adolescent Psychiatry, 2001. Available online. URL: http://www.aacap.org. Monograph prepared by the Task Force on Juvenile Justice Reform discusses areas within the juvenile justice system in need of reform, including health care, the treatment of female juvenile offenders, and the disproportionate representation of minority juvenile offenders. Also includes a history of the juvenile justice system in the United States.

Fass, Simon M., and Chung-Ron Pi. "Cost-Benefit Analysis of Dispositions in the Juvenile Justice System, Final Progress Report." Report, University of Texas at Dallas, 2002. Describes the use of cost-benefit analysis in weighing the benefits of alternative juvenile dispositions and their effectiveness in reducing reoffenses against the higher costs associated with institutional confinement.

Feld, B. C. "Violent Girls or Relabeled Status Offenders? An Alternative Interpretation of the Data." *Crime & Delinquency* 55 (2009): 241–265. Examines the recent trend of increases in arrests of girls for simple and aggravated assault. The author contends that the social construction of girls' violence may reflect changes in juvenile justice policy, especially in the way that minor offenses (such as running away or truancy) are dealt with.

Gray, Doug, et al. "Utah Youth Suicide Study, Phase I: Government Agency Contact Before Death." *Child & Adolescent Psychiatry* 41 (April 2002): 427–434. Available online. URL: http://www.jaacap.com. Examines the connection between contact with the juvenile justice system and youths who commit suicide. Presents findings that nearly two-thirds of Utah youth who committed suicide between 1996 and 1999 had previous contact with the juvenile justice system.

"Handle with Care: Serving the Mental Health Needs of Young Offenders." Research Report, Coalition for Juvenile Justice, 2000. Presents findings from a year-long investigation into the scope of mental health problems among delinquents and the availability of mental health services in the juvenile justice system. Includes a glossary and bibliography.

Harris, A. "Diverting and Abdicating Judicial Discretion: Cultural, Political, and Procedural Dynamics in California Juvenile Justice." *Law and Society Review* 41 (2007): 387–427. Explores how punitive policies toward juveniles impact the ways that juvenile courts process juvenile defendants. Results illustrate how juvenile courts have become more like criminal courts by adopting more of an offense-oriented approach to cases rather than an offender-oriented, rehabilitative approach.

Jackson, Yo. "Mentoring for Delinquent Children: An Outcome Study with Young Adolescent Children." *Journal of Youth and Adolescence* 31 (April 2002): 115. Discusses the results of a study of mentoring programs for adolescent youth at risk for delinquency.

Jones, Bridgett E. "Suffer the Little Children." *Children's Legal Rights* 21 (winter 2001): 25–35. Examines the history of efforts in the United States to deal with children who get into trouble. Concludes that youth who break laws should be subject to a different system of justice than adult criminals.

Kalbeitzer, R., and N. E. Sevin Goldstein. "Assessing the 'Evolving Standards of Decency': Perceptions of Capital Punishment for Juveniles." *Behavioral Sciences and the Law* 24 (2006): 157–178. This study examines whether public opinion parallels recent judicial and statutory changes limiting the applicability of capital sentences to offenders younger than 18.

Annotated Bibliography

Kelly, W. R., T. S. Macy, and D. P. Mears. "Juvenile Referrals in Texas: An Assessment of Criminogenic Needs and the Gap Between Needs and Services." *Prison Journal* 85 (2005): 467–489. Estimates the prevalence of mental health, substance abuse, educational, and family-related needs for youths referred to seven juvenile probation departments in Texas.

Kempf, K., E. S. L. Peterson, and L. L. Sample. "Gender and Juvenile Justice in Missouri." Research Report, University of Missouri, St. Louis, 1997. Discusses the processing of female juvenile offenders and the differences between female and male offenders by offense types.

Kempf-Leonard, K. "Minority Youths and Juvenile Justice: Disproportionate Minority Contact after Nearly 20 Years of Reform Efforts." *Youth Violence and Juvenile Justice* 5 (2007): 71–87. This article describes the current status of minority youths in juvenile justice systems. Although progress is evident, the achievements of the Disproportionate Minority Contact (DMC) initiative have made it clear that the questions are more complicated than initially appeared.

Kessler, Carol. "Need for Attention to Mental Health of Young Offenders." *Lancet* 359 (June 8, 2002): 1,956. Discusses findings of a longitudinal study on the need for mental health services among male juvenile offenders confined for serious or persistent offending. High rates of substance abuse, depression, and anxiety disorders were identified in the study group.

Kinnon, Joy Bennett. "Why Children Are Killing Children." *Ebony* 54 (January 1999): 126. Discusses findings that, despite a decrease in juvenile crime rates between 1996 and 1998, African-American youth were disproportionately charged and detained for criminal offenses.

Krisberg, B. "Impact of the Justice System on Serious, Violent, and Chronic Juvenile Offenders." Oakland, Calif.: National Council on Crime and Delinquency, 1997. Examines research and statistical data on the criminal justice system's response to serious, violent, and chronic juvenile offenders.

Kupchik, A. "The Correctional Experiences of Youth in Adult and Juvenile Prisons." *Justice Quarterly* 24 (2007): 247–270. Compares the correctional experiences of young adult males incarcerated in juvenile prisons and adult prisons. Relative to one another, inmates in juvenile prisons report better relations with staff, though inmates in adult facilities report better access to education and treatment services.

———. "Prosecuting Adolescents in Criminal Courts: Criminal or Juvenile Justice?" *Social Problems* 50 (2003): 439–460. Considers what happens when adolescents are prosecuted in criminal rather than juvenile courts. Findings reveal a hybrid form of justice that borrows from processes usually used in both juvenile courts and adult criminal courts.

Kurlychek, M. C., and B. D. Johnson. "The Juvenile Penalty: A Comparison of Juvenile and Young Adult Sentencing Outcomes in Criminal

Court." *Criminology* 42 (2004): 485–517. Compares the severity of punishment given to juveniles who are prosecuted in adult criminal courts to the punishment of young adults. Results suggest that juveniles who are transferred to criminal court receive even more severe punishments than do young adults punished in the same courts for similar offenses.

Leiber, M. J., and J. D. Johnson. "Being Young and Black: What Are Their Effects on Juvenile Justice Decision Making?" *Crime & Delinquency* 54 (2008): 560–581. Examines the extent to which race and age individually and jointly determined juvenile justice case outcomes at intake and judicial disposition among males.

Logalbo, Anthony P., and Charlene M. Callahan. "Evaluation of Teen Court as a Juvenile Crime Diversion Program." *Juvenile and Family Court Journal* 52 (spring 2001): 1–11. Reports on the findings of an evaluation of a teen court program in which juveniles are tried and sentenced by a jury of their peers.

Martinez, Orlando L. "Building a Juvenile Correctional Mental Health System." *Juvenile Correctional Mental Health* 1 (September/October 2001): 81–94. Examines the creation of a juvenile correctional mental health system by the Georgia Department of Juvenile Justice.

McCormick, Patrick T. "Fit to Be Tried?" *America* 186 (February 11, 2002): 15. A review of legislation making it easier for states to try and punish juvenile offenders as adults.

Mears, D. P. "Exploring State-Level Variation in Juvenile Incarceration Rates: Symbolic Threats and Competing Explanations." *Prison Journal* 86 (2006): 470–490. Discusses competing explanations for why states vary in their juvenile incarceration rates. The article focuses specifically on how some states react more strongly than others to "symbolic threats" in that they incarcerate greater numbers of youth during times of perceived social disorder.

Mears, D. P., C. Hay, and M. Gertz. "Public Opinion and the Foundation of the Juvenile Court." *Criminology* 45 (2007): 223–257. Examines public views about abolishing the juvenile court and about the proper minimum age at which society should prosecute children for criminal offenses. Findings suggest support for the idea of rehabilitating youth in a separate juvenile justice system.

O'Neill, Brian F. "Influences on Detention Decisions in the Juvenile Justice System." *Juvenile and Family Court Journal* 53 (winter 2002). A study of 642 juvenile probationers examines the relationship between race and pretrial detention.

Pope, C. E., and W. Feyerherm. "Minorities and the Juvenile Justice System." Research Summary, Office of Juvenile Justice and Delinquency Prevention, 1993. Summarizes findings of OJJDP's study of the disproportionate representation of minorities in the juvenile justice system.

Annotated Bibliography

Redding, R. E., and E. J. Fuller. "What Do Juvenile Offenders Know about Being Tried as Adults? Implications for Deterrance." *Juvenile and Family Court Journal* 55 (2004): 35–44. Examines juveniles' knowledge and perceptions of transfer laws and criminal sanctions. Findings indicate that juveniles are unaware of transfer laws and view adult consequences for juvenile crimes as unfair.

Redding, Richard E. "The Effects of Adjudicating and Sentencing Juveniles as Adults: Research and Policy Implications." *Youth Violence and Juvenile Justice* 1 (2003): 128–155. Part of a special issue of *Youth Violence and Juvenile Justice*, this article examines issues surrounding the adjudication of juveniles in adult courts through the review of relevant literature and studies on the subject.

Rubin, Ted. "Peacemaking: From Conflict to Harmony in the Navaho Tradition." *Juvenile Justice Update* 7 (February/March 2001): 1–16. Examines how juvenile crime is addressed within the Navajo Nation and how the nation is incorporating traditional ways, such as "peacemaking," into its juvenile justice services.

Ryals, J. S. "Restorative Justice: New Horizons in Juvenile Offender Counseling." *Journal of Addictions & Offender Counseling* 25 (2004): 18–25. This essay and review discusses the principles and practices of restorative justice and its parallel constructs with counseling philosophy, with a focus on juvenile offenders.

Sanborn, Joseph B. "Victims' Rights in Juvenile Court: Has the Pendulum Swung Too Far?" *Judicature* 85 (November–December 2001): 140–146. Traces the evolution of the involvement of victims in the proceedings of the juvenile court and identifies problems that have arisen from certain types of victim participation, such as the power to obstruct court decisions intended to serve the juvenile offender's best interests.

Schaffner, Laurie, Shelley Shick, and Nancy Stein. "Changing Policy in San Francisco: Girls in the Juvenile Justice System." *Social Justice* 24 (winter 1997): 187–210. Describes study on the characteristics of girls in San Francisco's juvenile justice system, the nature of their offenses, and the effectiveness of the juvenile justice system's responses to female offenders.

Southerland, Lisa G. "Extended Jurisdiction Juvenile Prosecution in Illinois: An Unfulfilled Promise." *Children's Legal Rights Journal* 21 (fall 2001): 2–7. Examines the blended sentencing option known as Extended Jurisdiction Juvenile Prosecution in Illinois, explores its strengths and weaknesses, and examines states with longer extended jurisdiction juvenile prosecution experiences.

Steinberg, Laurence. "Should Juvenile Offenders Be Tried as Adults?" *USA Today Magazine* 129 (January 2001): 34. A discussion of punishment versus rehabilitation in the treatment of juvenile offenders.

Steiner, B., C. Hemmens, and V. Bell. "Legislative Waiver Reconsidered: General Deterrent Effects of Statutory Exclusion Laws Enacted Post-1979." *Justice Quarterly* 23 (2006): 34–59. Examines whether laws that exclude certain categories of youth from juvenile court (to be prosecuted as adults in criminal court) deter crime. Results find that only one of 22 states analyzed show decreases in crime following passage of these laws.

Steiner, B., and E. Wright. "Assessing the Relative Effects of State Direct File Waiver Laws in Violent Juvenile Crime: Deterrence or Irrelevance?" *Journal of Criminal Law and Criminology* 96 (2006): 1,451–1,477. Examines the effectiveness of direct file transfer laws in 14 states. The authors found that the laws were not a significant deterrent for violent juvenile crime or the cause of a decline in juvenile arrest rates.

Teplin, L. A., K. S. Elkington, and G. M. McClelland. "Major Mental Disorders, Substance Use Disorders, Comorbidity, and HIV-AIDS Risk Behaviors in Juvenile Detainees." *Psychiatric Services* 56 (2005): 823–828. This study examines the prevalence of 20 HIV-AIDS risk behaviors within four groups of juvenile detainees: those with major mental disorders alone, those with substance use disorders alone, those with comorbid mental and substance use disorders, and those without any major mental or substance use disorder.

Tracy, P. E., K. Kempf-Leonard, and S. Abramoske-James. "Gender Differences in Delinquency and Juvenile Justice Processing: Evidence From National Data." *Crime & Delinquency* 55 (2009): 171–215. This article traces the historical coverage of the gender issue in the criminological literature. It also provides contemporary empirical evidence about differences and similarities between girls and boys with respect to juvenile crime, and to processing by the juvenile justice system.

Trulson, C. R. "Determinants of Disruption: Institutional Misconduct among State-Committed Delinquents." *Youth Violence and Juvenile Justice* 5 (2007): 7–34. Considers the factors that are associated with misconduct among incarcerated youth. Results find several individual risk factors, such as gang affiliation and more extensive delinquent histories.

Umbreit, M., and H. Zehr. "Family Group Conferences: Differing Models and Guidelines for Practice." *Federal Probation* 60 (September 1996): 24–29. Evaluates family group conferences as a part of the restorative justice approach to juvenile justice.

Van Vleet, Russell K. "The Attack on Juvenile Justice." *Annals of the American Academy of Political and Social Science* 564 (July 1999): 203. Discusses the lack of effectiveness of get-tough reforms in the juvenile justice system in response to rising juvenile crime in the mid-1990s.

Viljoen, J. L., P. A. Zapf, and R. Roesch. "Adjudicative Competence and Comprehension of Miranda Rights in Adolescent Defendants: A Comparison of Legal Standards." *Behavioral Sciences and the Law* 25 (2007):

1–19. This study examines legal standards pertaining to juveniles' comprehension of Miranda rights and their adjudicative competence.

Walicki, Florian, Carol Hole, Julie Chavez-Navarros, and Irene Drewnicky. "Planning & Designing Comprehensive Special Juvenile Facilities." *Corrections Today* 64 (April 2002): 114–177. Discusses the need for, and the designing of, specialized juvenile detention centers geared toward serving the mental health needs of juvenile offenders.

WEB DOCUMENTS

"1998 Report to Congress: Juvenile Mentoring Program." Program Report, Office of Juvenile Justice and Delinquency Prevention, 1998. Available online. URL: www.ncjrs.gov/html/ojjdp/173424. Discusses the success of youth mentoring programs in juvenile crime prevention.

Adams, B., and S. Addie. "Delinquency Cases Waived to Criminal Court, 2005." *OJJDP Fact Sheet*, June 2009. Office of Juvenile Justice and Delinquency Prevention. Available online. URL: http://www.ncjrs.gov/pdffiles1/ojjdp/224539.pdf. Presents statistics on petitioned delinquency cases waived to criminal court between 1985 and 2005. In 2005, U.S. juvenile courts received 1.7 million delinquency cases; less than 1 percent resulted in judicial waiver to criminal court.

Altschuler, D. M., T. L. Armstrong, and D. L. MacKenzie. "Reintegration, Supervised Release, and Intensive Aftercare." *Office of Juvenile Justice and Delinquency Prevention Bulletin*, August 1999. Available online. URL: www.ncjrs.org/pdffiles1/175715.pdf. Discusses effective and ineffective programs to reintegrate juvenile offenders in the community after institutional release.

Bazemore, G., and M. Umbreit. "A Comparison of Four Restorative Conferencing Models." *Office of Juvenile Justice and Delinquency Prevention Bulletin*, February 2001. Available online. URL: http://www.ncjrs.org/pdffiles1/ojjdp/184738.pdf. Discusses four types of restorative justice conferencing: victim-offender mediation, community reparative boards, family group conferencing, and circle sentencing. Unlike retributive justice, which is primarily concerned with punishing crime, restorative justice focuses on repairing the injury that crime inflicts on victims and to the community.

Black, M. C. "Juvenile Delinquency Probation Caseload, 1989–1998." *Office of Juvenile Justice and Delinquency Prevention Fact Sheet*, September 2001. Available online. URL: www.ncjrs.org/pdffiles1/ojjdp/fs200134.pdf. Presents statistics on the 38 percent of delinquency cases placed on probation between 1989 and 1998.

Brown, David, Sarah Maxwell, Edward DeJesus, and Vincent Schiraldi. "Barriers and Promising Approaches to Workforce and Youth Development for

Young Offenders." 2002. Available online. URL: http://www.aecf.org/upload/publicationfiles.barriers%20and%20promising.pdf. Discussion of barriers and promising approaches to employment and development programs for court-involved youth.

Burrell, S., and L. Warboys. "Special Education and the Juvenile Justice System." *Office of Juvenile Justice and Delinquency Prevention Bulletin*, 2000. Available online. URL: www.ncjrs.org/pdffiles1/ojjdp/179359.pdf. Summarizes the provisions of the Individuals with Disabilities Education Act as they relate to the juvenile justice process. Presents findings that youth in the juvenile justice system are much more likely than youth in the general population to have both identified and undiscovered disabilities.

Butts, Jeffrey A. "Can We Do Without Juvenile Justice?" *Criminal Justice Magazine*, vol. 15, pp. 109, spring 2000. Available online. URL: http://www.abanet.org/crimjust/cjmag/15-1/butts.html. Examines trends in the processing of juveniles charged with crimes and suggests that the traditional dichotomy between the juvenile justice and criminal justice systems might not be effective for the future. Discusses the emergence of specialized courts within the adult system presenting an opportunity to create a new youth justice system.

Butts, J. A., and J. Buck. "Teen Courts: A Focus on Research." *Office of Juvenile Justice and Delinquency Prevention Bulletin*, October 2000. Available online. URL: www.ncjrs.org/pdffiles1/ojjdp/183472.pdf. Discusses results of a national survey of teen courts and their success as an alternative to the traditional juvenile court system for younger and less serious juvenile offenders.

"Childhood on Trial: The Failure of Trying & Sentencing Youth in Adult Criminal Court." Washington, D.C.: Coalition for Juvenile Justice, 2005. Available online. URL: http://www.juvjustice.org/media/resources/resource_115.pdf. Examines the adjudication and sentencing of youth offenders in adult courts. Suggests a change in state policy that will reduce the amount of juveniles in adult courts.

Connelly, H. "Children Exposed to Violence: Criminal Justice Resources." Bulletin, Office for Victims of Crime, 1999. Available online. URL: http://www.ojp.usdoj.gov/ovc/publications/factshts/pdftxt/cevcjr.pdf. Provides an overview of issues relating to children who are victims or witnesses of violence and describes private-sector and public-sector resources to help improve the response of the criminal and juvenile justice systems and other agencies to child victims and witnesses of violence.

Cooper, C. S. "Juvenile Drug Court Programs." *Office of Juvenile Justice and Delinquency Prevention Bulletin*, May 2001. Available online. URL: http://www.ncjrs.gov/pdffiles1/ojjdp/184744.pdf. Describes key elements of a juvenile drug court program and the potential impact on the juvenile justice system.

Annotated Bibliography

"The Costs of Confinement: Why Good Juvenile Justice Policies Make Good Fiscal Sense." May 2009. Justice Policy Institute. Available online. URL: http://www.justicepolicy.org/images/upload/09_05_REP_Costs OfConfinement_JJ_PS.pdf. Analyzes the costs of juvenile corrections and evidence for less expensive, more effective strategies, such as community-based alternatives. The article offers suggestions intended to reduce crime and save money.

Devine, P., K. Coolbaugh, and S. Jenkins. "Disproportionate Minority Confinement: Lessons Learned from Five States." *Office of Juvenile Justice and Delinquency Prevention Bulletin*, December 1998. Available online. URL: http://njcrs.gov/94612.pdf. Describes how five states (Arizona, Florida, Iowa, North Carolina, and Oregon) assessed the extent to which minority juveniles were disproportionately confined by their juvenile justice systems and implemented reforms to address the disparity.

"Employment and Training for Court-Involved Youth." *Office of Juvenile Justice and Delinquency Prevention Bulletin*, 2000. Available online. URL: http://www.ncjrs.org/pdffiles1/ojjdp/182787.pdf. Discusses promising strategies for connecting court-involved youth to the labor market.

Friel, Charles M., ed. "Criminal Justice 2000, Volume 2: Boundary Changes in Criminal Justice Organizations." Research Report, National Institute of Justice, 2000. Available online. URL: http://www.ncjrs.gov/criminal_justice2000/vol2_2000.html. Eight papers review the state of knowledge about the origins and consequences of changes in the criminal justice system over the 20th century, including the blurring of the line between juvenile and adult justice.

Garry, E. M. "A Compendium of Programs That Work for Youth." *Office of Juvenile Justice and Delinquency Prevention Fact Sheet*, November 1999. Available online. URL: www.ncjrs.org/pdffiles1/ojjdp/fs99121.pdf. Discussion of programs that effectively address a variety of concerns related to youth, including delinquent behavior.

Godwin, T. M., D. J. Steinhart, and B. A. Fulton. "Peer Justice and Youth Empowerment: An Implementation Guide for Teen Court Programs." Research Report, Council of State Governments. Available online. URL: http://ojjdp.ncjrs.org/publications/peerjustice.html. Accessed December 16, 2009. Provides an overview of the teen court concept and a discussion of how juvenile justice agencies can develop, implement, and improve teen court programs in the United States.

Griffin, P., P. Torbet, and L. Szymanski. "Trying Juveniles as Adults in Criminal Court: An Analysis of State Transfer Provisions." *Office of Juvenile Justice and Delinquency Prevention Report*, 1998. Available online. URL: www.ncjrs.org/pdffiles/172836.pdf. Analyzes the statutory mechanisms and criteria by which juveniles are transferred to the adult criminal justice system for serious and violent crimes. Topics include direct filing, statutory exclusion, "once an adult, always an adult" provisions, and reverse-waiver provisions.

Hamilton, R., and K. McKinney. "Job Training for Juveniles: Project CRAFT." *Office of Juvenile Justice and Delinquency Prevention Fact Sheet*, August 1999. Available online. URL: www.ncjrs.org/pdffiles1/ojjdp/ fs99116.pdf. Describes training and job placement in the home building industry and related occupations for adjudicated youth referred by their state departments of juvenile justice to the Community Restitution and Apprenticeship Focused Training program (Project CRAFT), sponsored by the Home Builders Institute.

Harms, P. "Detention in Delinquency Cases, 1990–1999." *OJJDP Fact Sheet*, September 2003. Office of Juvenile Justice and Delinquency Prevention. Available online. URL: http://www.ncjrs.gov/pdffiles1/ojjdp/ fs200307.pdf. Presents statistics on the use of detention in delinquency caseloads handled by juvenile courts between 1990 and 1999. Results show that the number of delinquent juveniles that were detained increased 11 percent from 1990 to 1999.

Harris, Philip W., Wayne N. Welsh, and Frank Butler. "Century of Juvenile Justice." In Gary LaFree, ed. *The Nature of Crime: Continuity and Change in Criminal Justice 2000*, vol. 1, 2000, pp. 359–425. Also available online. URL: http://www.ncjrs.org/criminal_justice2000/vol_1/02h.pdf. Examines forces that have shaped juvenile justice during the 20th century and discusses implications for the 21st century.

"Juvenile Justice: A Century of Change." *Office of Juvenile Justice and Delinquency Prevention Bulletin*, 1999. Available online. URL: http://www.ncjrs. gov/pdffiles1/ojjdp/178995.pdf. Reviews developments in juvenile justice system structure and process, beginning with the establishment of the nation's first juvenile court in 1899. Presents an overview of the history of juvenile justice, discusses significant Supreme Court decisions, compares juvenile and adult justice systems, and summarizes changes states have made with regard to transfer provisions, sentencing, and confidentiality.

"Juvenile Justice Clearinghouse." *Office of Juvenile Justice and Delinquency Prevention*. Available online. URL: ojjdp.ncjrs.org/programs/Prog Summary.asp?pi=2. Describes the Office of Juvenile Justice and Delinquency Prevention's Juvenile Justice Clearinghouse, which provides easy access to a comprehensive collection of information and resources on juvenile justice topics.

Lipsey, M. W., D. B. Wilson, and L. Cothern. "Effective Intervention for Serious Juvenile Offenders." *Office of Juvenile Justice and Delinquency Prevention Bulletin*, April 2000. Available online. URL: http://www.ncjrs. org/pdffiles1/ojjdp/181201.pdf. Presents results of a study examining whether intervention programs reduce recidivism rates among serious delinquents and, if so, what types of programs are most effective.

Livsey, S. "Juvenile Delinquency Probation Caseload, 2005." *OJJDP Fact Sheet*, June 2009. Office of Juvenile Justice and Delinquency Prevention. Available online. URL: http://www.ncjrs.gov/pdffiles1/ojjdp/224536.pdf. Presents statistics on delinquency cases resulting in probation in 2005. One-third of all delinquency cases that ended with a disposition (sentence) in juvenile court in 2005 received a sentence of probation.

Lubow, B., and D. Barron. "Resources for Juvenile Detention Reform." *Office of Juvenile Justice and Delinquency Prevention Fact Sheet*, November 2000. Available online. URL: www.ncjrs.org/pdffiles1/ojjdp/fs200018.pdf. Examines overcrowding and minority overrepresentation in juvenile detention facilities and discusses detention alternatives. Also highlights 12 monographs on detention reform published by the Annie E. Casey Foundation.

McGarrell, Edmund F. "Restorative Justice Conferences as an Early Response to Young Offenders." *Office of Juvenile Justice and Delinquency Prevention Bulletin*, August 2001. Available online. URL: www.ncjrs.org/pdffiles1/ojjdp/187769.pdf. Evaluates restorative justice conferences as an early response to young offenders. Discusses rate of recidivism among young juvenile offenders who completed restorative justice programs.

McKinney, K. "OJJDP Mental Health Initiatives." *Office of Juvenile Justice and Delinquency Prevention Fact Sheet*, August 2001. Available online. URL: www.ncjrs.org/pdffiles1/ojjdp/fs200130.pdf. Describes OJJDP's initiatives to address mental health problems of youth involved in the juvenile justice system.

Mendel, Richard A. "Less Cost, More Safety: Guiding Lights for Reform in Juvenile Justice." Research Report, American Youth Policy Forum, 2000. Available online. URL: http://www.aypf.org. Identifies eight challenges facing juvenile justice in America and describes how existing programs are being used successfully to meet the challenges at the state and local levels.

"Minorities in the Juvenile Justice System." *Office of Juvenile Justice and Delinquency Prevention Bulletin*, December 1999. Available online. URL: www.ncjrs.org/pdffiles/minor.pdf. Presents information on overrepresentation of minority youth in the juvenile justice system in comparison to their proportion in the general population, with focus on disproportionate confinement of minorities.

Mondoro, D. M., T. Wight, and J. A. Tuell. "Expansion of OJJDP's Comprehensive Strategy." *Office of Juvenile Justice and Delinquency Prevention Fact Sheet*, May 2001. Available online. URL: http://www.ncjrs.gov/pdffiles1/ojjdp/fs200118.pdf. Describes the Office of Juvenile Justice and Delinquency Prevention's Comprehensive Strategy for Serious, Violent, and Chronic Juvenile Offenders, an initiative aimed at reducing juvenile delinquency, improving juvenile justice systems, and controlling the small group of serious, violent, and chronic juvenile offenders.

Moone, J. "Innovative Information on Juvenile Residential Facilities." *Office of Juvenile Justice and Delinquency Prevention Fact Sheet*, September 2000. Available online. URL: www.ncjrs.org/pdffiles1/ojjdp/fs200011.pdf. Describes the first Juvenile Residential Facility Census, designed to collect information about the facilities in which juvenile offenders are held, including information on the health care, education, substance abuse treatment, and mental health treatment provided in these facilities.

O'Sullivan, K., N. Rose, and T. Murphy. "PEPNet: Connecting Juvenile Offenders to Education and Employment." *Office of Juvenile Justice and Delinquency Prevention Fact Sheet*, July 2001. Available online. URL: www.ncjrs.org/pdffiles1/ojjdp/fs200129.pdf. Discusses efforts to help youth involved in the juvenile justice system prepare for economic self-sufficiency through effective youth development and employment programs.

Puzzanchera, C. "Delinquency Cases Waived to Criminal Court, 1989–1998." *Office of Juvenile Justice and Delinquency Prevention Fact Sheet*, September 2001. Available online. URL: www.ncjrs.org/pdffiles1/ojjdp/fs200135.pdf. Presents statistics on the number of cases transferred from juvenile court to criminal court through the judicial waiver mechanism during the decade from 1989 and 1998.

———. "Juvenile Court Placement of Adjudicated Youth, 1989–1998." *Office of Juvenile Justice and Delinquency Prevention Fact Sheet*, February 2002. Available online. URL: www.ncjrs.org/pdffiles1/ojjdp/fs200202.pdf. Presents data on juvenile delinquency cases that resulted in out-of-home placement between 1989 and 1998. Includes the numbers of such cases and percentages of change for each type of delinquency offense and compares statistics for white youth, black youth, and youth of other races.

Puzzanchera, C., et al. "Juvenile Court Statistics 1997." *Office of Juvenile Justice and Delinquency Prevention Report*, June 2000. Available online. URL: www.ncjrs.org/pdffiles1/ojjdp/180864.pdf. Profiles some 1.7 million delinquency cases and 158,000 status offense cases handled by the juvenile courts in 1997. Detailed information is provided on offenses, detention, and case disposition.

———. "Delinquency Cases Waived to Criminal Court, 1990–1999." *OJJDP Fact Sheet*, September 2003. Office of Juvenile Justice and Delinquency Prevention. Available online. URL: http://www.ncjrs.gov/pdffiles1/ojjdp/fs200304.pdf. Presents estimates of the number of cases transferred from juvenile court to criminal court through the judicial waiver mechanism between 1990 and 1999 in the most recent examination of rates of judicial waiver over time.

———. "Juvenile Court Placement of Adjudicated Youth, 1990–1999." *OJJDP Fact Sheet*, September 2003. Office of Juvenile Justice and Delinquency Prevention. Available online. URL: http://www.ncjrs.gov/pdffiles1/ojjdp/fs200305.pdf. Presents the most recent data on juvenile delinquency cases that resulted in out-of-home placement over time. This report considers cases between 1990 and 1999.

———. "Juvenile Delinquency Probation Caseload, 1990–1999." *OJJDP Fact Sheet*, September 2003. Office of Juvenile Justice and Delinquency Prevention. Available online. URL: http://www.ncjrs.gov/pdffiles1/ojjdp/fs200306.pdf. Provides information on the number of delinquency cases placed on probation between 1990 and 1999, offering a rare view of trends over time.

Redding, R. "Juvenile Transfer Laws: An Effective Deterrent to Delinquency?" *OJJDP Juvenile Justice Bulletin*, August 2008. Office of Juvenile Justice and Delinquency Prevention. Available online. URL: http://www.ncjrs.gov/pdffiles1/ojjdp/220595.pdf. Assesses evidence on the effects of juvenile transfer laws and concludes that they are not an effective deterrent to delinquency.

Scahill, M. C. "Female Delinquency Cases, 1997." *Office of Juvenile Justice and Delinquency Prevention Fact Sheet*, November 2000. Available online. URL: www.ncjrs.org/pdffiles1/ojjdp/fs200016.pdf. Describes the types of offenses committed by juvenile female offenders and provides additional data on detention, intake decisions, waiver to criminal court, and adjudication and disposition.

Scales, B., and J. Baker. "Seattle's Effective Strategy for Prosecuting Juvenile Firearm Offenders." *Office of Juvenile Justice and Delinquency Prevention Bulletin*, March 2000. Available online. URL: http://www.ncjrs.gov/pdffiles1/ojjdp/178901.pdf. Describes the creation of a database to track juvenile firearm offenders and presents statistics on the trends and characteristics of juvenile firearm offenses in King County, Washington.

Schiraldi, Vincent, and Jason Ziedenberg. "Florida Experiment: An Analysis of the Impact of Granting Prosecutors Discretion to Try Juveniles as Adults." Report, The Center of Juvenile and Criminal Justice, 1999. Available online. URL: http://www.justicepolicy.org/images/upload/99-07_RF_8_FLExperiment_JJ_.pdf. Examines the impact of a Florida law that circumvents the juvenile court and gives prosecutors sole discretion to decide whether arrested youth should be transferred to the adult criminal justice system.

"Second Chances: Giving Kids a Chance to Make a Better Choice." *Office of Juvenile Justice and Delinquency Prevention Bulletin*, May 2000. Available online. URL: www.ncjrs.org/pdffiles1/ojjdp/181680.pdf. Presents 12 profiles of individuals petitioned into juvenile court as delinquents and discusses how the juvenile justice system helped them turn their lives around. They include Olympic athlete Bob Beamon and former senator Alan Simpson.

Shelden, R. G. "Detention Diversion Advocacy: An Evaluation." *Office of Juvenile Justice and Delinquency Prevention Bulletin*, September 1999.

Available online. URL: www.ncjrs.org/pdffiles1/ojjdp/171155.pdf. Presents an overview of diversion programs to reduce the number of juveniles in court-ordered detention and provide community-based services and supervision. Findings show that recidivism was lower among juveniles referred to detention diversion programs than for detained juveniles.

Sheppard, David, and Patricia Kelly. "Juvenile Gun Courts: Promoting Accountability and Providing Treatment." *Office of Juvenile Justice and Delinquency Prevention Bulletin*, August 2002. Available online. URL: http://ncjrs. org/pdffiles1/ojjpd/187078.pdf. Describes the concept of the juvenile gun court, a specialty court charged with the handling of juveniles charged with gun offenses. Reviews the Jefferson County, Alabama, Juvenile Gun Court.

Sickmund, Melissa, "Juvenile Offenders in Residential Placement, 1997 to 1999." *Office of Juvenile Justice and Delinquency Prevention Report*, 2002. Available online. URL: www.ncjrs.org/pdffiles1/ojjdp/fs200207.pdf. Presents data from the 1997 to 1999 Census of Juveniles in Residential Placement. Includes information on juvenile offenders in residential placement including age, race, sex, and offense.

———. "Offenders in Juvenile Court, 1997." *Office of Juvenile Justice and Delinquency Prevention Bulletin*, October 2000. Available online. URL: www.ncjrs.org/pdffiles1/ojjdp/181204.pdf. Focuses on the disposition of delinquency cases and formally processed status offense cases in juvenile courts nationwide in 1997.

———. "State Custody Rates 1997." *Office of Juvenile Justice and Delinquency Prevention Bulletin*, December 2000. Available online. URL: www.ncjrs. org/pdffiles1/ojjdp/183108.pdf. Presents detailed state-by-state statistics on custody rates for delinquents and status offenders held in public and private facilities.

———. "Juveniles in Corrections." *Juvenile Offenders and Victims National Report Series Bulletin*, June 2004. Office of Juvenile Justice and Delinquency Prevention. Available online. URL: http://www.ncjrs.gov/pdffiles1/ ojjdp/202885.pdf. Presents the latest available national and state-level data from the Census of Juveniles in Residential Placement (CJRP). Analysis show that two-thirds of residential facilities are privately run and that only 20 percent of incarcerated youth were confined due to a violent offense.

Snyder, H., M. Sickmund, and E. Poe-Yamagata. "Juvenile Transfers to Criminal Court in the 1990's: Lessons Learned from Four Studies." Summary, Office of Juvenile Justice and Delinquency Prevention, August 2000. Available online. URL: http://www.ncjrs.gov/pdffiles1/ojjdp/181301. pdf. Presents findings of studies in Pennsylvania, South Carolina, and Utah on juvenile transfers to adult criminal court.

Stahl, A. L. "National Juvenile Court Data Archive Web Site." *Office of Juvenile Justice and Delinquency Prevention Fact Sheet*, December 2001.

Available online. URL: www.ncjrs.org/pdffiles1/ojjdp/fs200140.pdf. Describes the use of the National Juvenile Court Data Archives web site in order to access detailed information on the nation's juvenile courts.

Streib, Victor L. "Juvenile Death Penalty Today: Death Sentences and Executions for Juvenile Crimes, January 1, 1973–April 30, 2004." Available online. URL: http://www.internationaljusticeproject.org/pdfs/JuvDeath April2004pdf. A compilation of data and information on the death penalty for juvenile offenders, including death sentences and executions for juvenile crimes from January 1973 to April 2004. Also includes the historical background of juvenile executions, the legal context of the American juvenile death penalty, the juvenile death penalty in other countries, current death row inmates under juvenile death sentences, and the rationale for the death penalty for juveniles.

Strom, K. J., and S. K. Smith. "Juvenile Felony Defendants in Criminal Courts: State Court Processing Statistics, 1990–94." *Office of Juvenile Justice and Delinquency Prevention Report*, 1998. Available online. URL: www.ojp.usdoj.gov/bjs/pub/pdf/jfdcc.pdf. Presents juvenile court data collected by the National Center for Juvenile Justice on juvenile felony defendants tried as adults compared with juvenile defendants processed in juvenile courts.

Torbet, P., et al. "Juveniles Facing Criminal Sanctions: Three States That Changed the Rules." *Office of Juvenile Justice and Delinquency Prevention Report*, April 2000. Available online. URL: www.ncjrs.org/pdffiles1/ ojjdp/181203.pdf. Examines recent state laws targeting serious juvenile crime by expanding eligibility for waiver to adult criminal and reducing confidentiality protections. Focuses on the exclusion of 17-year-olds from juvenile court jurisdictions in several states.

"Understanding the Effects of Maltreatment on Early Brain Development." Research Report, Child Welfare Information Gateway, 2001. Available online. URL: http://www.childwelfare.gov/pubs/focus/earlybrain/early-brain.pdf. Examines the effects of maltreatment on early brain development in children, and discusses the implications of this brain research as it relates to delinquency and the juvenile justice system.

Wiebush, R. G., B. McNulty, and T. Le. "Implementation of the Intensive Community-Based Aftercare Program." *Office of Juvenile Justice and Delinquency Prevention Bulletin*, July 2000. Available online. URL: www. ncjrs.org/pdffiles1/ojjdp/181464.pdf. Provides an overview of the Intensive Aftercare Program designed to provides followup services and supervision for serious, chronic juvenile offenders after institutional release.

Wiebush, R. G., et al. "Implementation and Outcome Evaluation of the Intensive Aftercare Program: Final Report." National Council of Crime and Delinquency. March 2005. Available online. URL: http://www.ncjrs.gov/ pdffiles1/ojjdp/206177.pdf. Presents the findings from a five-year, multisite evaluation of the implementation and outcomes of OJJDP's Intensive Aftercare Program.

AUDIOVISUAL MATERIALS

Brother 2 Brother: Positive Personal Change for At-Risk Youths. DVD, 41 min., Films Media Group, 2004. Documentary presents a mentoring program for at-risk young black men, led by older black men, that seeks positive personal change. The program emphasizes group bonds and opportunities beyond street life.

Going Home: Teens Reentering Society. DVD, 44 min., Cambridge Educational Production, 2008. Two-part video that explores the challenges teenagers face in adjusting to life outside prison and makes suggestions for how these challenges can be reduced. Focuses on Rikers Island Academy, a GED-level school housed inside New York City's Rikers Island.

Helping Victims: Victims Services Division, California Youth Authority. VHS, 27 min., produced by the California Youth Authority in association with California State University, Sacramento, 1999. A presentation of education and training programs offered by the California Youth Authority, including a program for offenders to learn about the impact of their crimes on victims, their families, and communities.

How Shall We Respond to the Dreams of Youth? VHS, 120 min., Juvenile Justice Telecommunications Project, Eastern Kentucky University, 2000. Panel discussions on topics including community-based programs to care for neglected, abused, and delinquent youth, alternatives to incarceration of juvenile offenders such as community-based treatment, and providing humane confinement for serious juvenile offenders.

Juvenile Correction Facilities. DVD, 39 minutes, ABC News, 2005. Documents six months in the lives of inmates ages 12 to 17, showing the youths engaging in self-discovery and self-improvement despite sometimes violent surroundings.

When Kids Get Life. DVD, 90 minutes, PBS Frontline, 2007. In-depth look at how juveniles can be sentenced to life in prison without possibility of parole in the United States, unlike most other countries. Documentary profiles five young men sentenced to life without parole in Colorado to explore their crimes and punishments.

CHAPTER 9

ORGANIZATIONS AND AGENCIES

The following organizations provide information on juvenile crime and juvenile justice on a national and state level. Those that are national in scope are divided into two sections: government agencies and educational/non-profit/private organizations. Following that is a state-by-state listing of Statistical Analysis Centers (SACs), state agencies that collect, analyze, and disseminate justice data. Each of the SACs listed provide statewide statistics on juvenile crime.

GOVERNMENT AGENCIES

Bureau of the Census
URL: http://www.census.gov
U.S. Census Bureau
4600 Silver Hill Road
Suitland, MD 20746
Phone: (301) 763-4636
Provides statistics and trends on the U.S. population and its various subgroups, including juveniles.

Bureau of Justice Statistics
URL: http://www.ojp.usdoj.
   gov/bjs
810 Seventh Street NW
Washington, DC 20531
Phone: (202) 307-0765
Provides current government statistics on a variety of justice-related topics, including juvenile crime, juvenile corrections, courts and sentencing, and law enforcement.

Federal Bureau of Investigation
URL: http://www.fbi.gov
J. Edgar Hoover Building
935 Pennsylvania Avenue NW
Washington, DC 20535-0001
Phone: (202) 324-3000
Publishes the Uniform Crime Reports (available online) and other special reports on crime in the United States.

**Justice Research and Statistics
   Association**
URL: http://www.jrsa.org

**777 North Capitol Street NE
Suite 801
Washington, DC 20002
Phone: (202) 842-9330**
Conducts and publishes research on justice issues and provides extensive statistical information on juvenile crime and justice on state and national levels.

**National Center for Education
  Statistics (NCES)**
URL: http://nces.ed.gov/
**1990 K Street NW
Washington, DC 20006
Phone: (202) 502-7300**
Collects and analyzes data related to education, including school violence and school discipline. The NCES conducts surveys of students and school administrators nationally and produces the annual report *Indicators of School Crime and Safety.*

**National Criminal Justice
  Reference Service (NCJRS)**
URL: http://www.ncjrs.org
**P.O. Box 6000
Rockville, MD 20849-6000
Phone: (800) 851-3420**
Offers a wide range of resources on juvenile crime and justice, including statistics and publications (which may be downloaded or ordered by mail from the NCJRS). The NCJRS provides links to related web sites plus a large database of abstracts of research literature relating to juvenile crime and ju-

venile justice. The NCJRS also serves as a conduit for information from various branches of the U.S. Department of Justice, including the Office of Juvenile Justice and Delinquency Prevention, the Office for Victims of Crime, and the National Institute of Justice.

**National Institute on Drug
  Abuse**
URL: http://www.drugabuse.
  gov/NIDAHome.html
**6001 Executive Boulevard
Room 5213
Bethesda, MD 20892-9561
Phone: (301) 443-1124**
Provides extensive information on substance abuse in the United States. Cosponsor with the University of Michigan's Institute for Social Research of the Monitoring the Future Survey on drug, alcohol, and tobacco use among eighth to 12th graders.

**Office of Juvenile Justice and
  Delinquency Prevention**
URL: http://ojjdp.ncjrs.org
**810 Seventh Street NW
Washington, DC 20531
Phone: (202) 307-5911**
Provides extensive information on all aspects of juvenile crime and juvenile justice through fact sheets, bulletins, and reports. Funds research on juvenile crime and justice issues, as well as programs at the state and local levels aimed at improving the quality of juvenile justice in the United States.

EDUCATIONAL, NONPROFIT, AND PRIVATE ORGANIZATIONS

**American Bar Association
  Juvenile Justice Committee**
URL: http://www.abanet.org/
  crimjust/juvjus/
740 15th Street NW
10th floor
Washington, DC 20005
Phone: (202) 662-1500
Provides information on court decisions of note and offers a wide range of publications relating to juvenile justice and juvenile law.

**American Civil Liberties Union
  (ACLU)**
URL: http://www.aclu.org
125 Broad Street
18th floor
New York, NY 10004
National organization dedicated to defending civil rights, including those of juveniles and juvenile offenders. Offers a wide range of publications.

**American Correctional
  Association (ACA)**
URL: http://www.aca.org
206 N. Washington Street
Alexandria, VA 22314
Phone: (703) 224-0000
Provides training and certification for correctional staff and conducts and publishes research on corrections, including juvenile corrections. The ACA publishes *Corrections Today* magazine and the journal *Correctional Compendium*.

Campaign for Youth Justice
URL: http://www.campaignfor
  youthjustice.org
1012 14th Street NW
Suite 610
Washington, DC 20005
Phone: (202) 558-3580
National organization dedicated to ending the practice of trying, sentencing, and incarcerating youth under 18 in the adult criminal justice system. Campaign for Youth Justice advocates for juvenile justice reform through providing support to federal, state, and local campaigns; coordinating outreach to parents, youth, and families; fostering national coalition-building; encouraging media relations; conducting research; and publishing reports and advocacy materials.

**Center for Research on Youth
  and Social Policy**
**University of Pennsylvania
  School of Social Policy and
  Practice**
URL: http://www.sp2.upenn.
  edu/crysp/index.html
3815 Walnut Street
Philadelphia, PA 19104-6179
Phone: (215) 898-2229
Studies issues relating to juvenile crime and juvenile justice and offers a variety of publications.

Center for the Prevention of School Violence
URL: http://www.ncdjjdp.org/cpsv
4112 Pleasant Valley Road
Suite 214
Raleigh, NC 27612
Phone: (800) 299-6054
Provides publications and other resources on school violence, with focus on prevention.

Center on Juvenile and Criminal Justice
URL: http://www.cjcj.org/
440 9th Street
San Francisco, CA 94103
Phone: (415) 621-5661
Private nonprofit organization whose mission is to reduce society's reliance on the use of incarceration as a solution to social problems.

Children of the Night
URL: http://www.childrenofthe night.org
14530 Sylvan Street
Van Nuys, CA 91411
Phone: (818) 908-4474
Provides counseling and other services to homeless youth often involved in prostitution, drug trafficking, or other criminal activities.

Committee for Children
URL: http://www.cfchildren.org
568 First Avenue South
Suite 600
Seattle, WA 98104
Phone: (800) 634-4449
International organization that offers publications, videos, and classroom instructional materials aimed

at the prevention of youth violence and child abuse.

Common Sense About Kids and Guns
URL: http://www.kidsandguns. org/
1225 I Street NW
Suite 1100
Washington, DC 20005
Phone: (877) 955-5437
Nonprofit organization that promotes gun safety and provides information on youth gun violence in the United States.

Council of Juvenile Correctional Administrators
URL: http://cjca.net/default.aspx
170 Forbes Road
Suite 106
Braintree, MA 02184
Phone: (781) 843-2663
Provides information on juvenile corrections and, under the auspices of the OJJDP, develops performance-based standards for juvenile corrections and detention facilities.

Educational Fund to End Handgun Violence
URL: http://www.csgv.org
1424 L Street NW
Suite 2-1
Washington, DC 20005
Phone: (202) 408-0061
Offers publications and educational materials on handgun violence and its effects on youth, including *Kids and Guns: A National Disgrace*.

Organizations and Agencies

FindLaw
http://www.findlaw.com/
 casecode/supreme.html
610 Opperman Drive
Eagin, MN 55123
Phone: (651) 687-7000
Legal research web site that provides information on U.S. Supreme
Court decisions.

Gangs or Us
URL: http://www.gangsorus.com
Email: info@gangsorus.com
Phone: (803) 345-2600
Provides extensive information
on youth gangs, including female
gangs, antigang statutes, court decisions, and links to research on youth
gangs.

Hamilton Fish Institute
URL: http://www.hamfish.org
2121 K Street NW
Suite 200
Washington, DC 20037-1830
Phone: (202) 496-2200
Conducts research and provides
publications on the effectiveness of
school violence prevention methods.

Juvenile Law Center
URL: http://www.jlc.org
The Philadelphia Building
1315 Walnut Street
4th floor
Philadelphia, PA 19107
Phone: (215) 625-0551
National legal advocacy organization provides updates on court cases
involving juvenile offenders and offers a range of publications relating
to juvenile law.

The Koch Crime Institute
URL: http://www.kci.org
1001 Forum Place
Suite P-2
West Palm Beach, FL 33401
Phone: (561) 616-2278
Private institute provides a wide
range of information on juvenile
offenders, with focus on the handling and treatment of youth in
the juvenile and criminal justice
systems.

National Archive of Criminal
 Justice Data
URL: http://www.icpsr.umich.
 edu/NACJD
P.O. Box 1248
Ann Arbor, MI 48106
Phone: (800) 999-0960
Provides downloadable access to a
vast library of criminal justice data
collections free of charge.

National Association of Youth
 Courts
URL: http://www.youthcourt.net
345 North Charles Street
2nd floor
Baltimore, MD 21201
Phone: (410) 528-0143
Information clearinghouse for state
youth court programs in the United
States. Youth courts (also known
as teen courts and peer courts) are
juvenile justice programs in which
youth are sentenced by their peers.

National Center for Juvenile
 Justice (NCJJ)
URL: http://ncjj.servehttp.com/
 ncjjwebsite/main.html

3700 South Water Street
Suite 200
Pittsburgh, PA 15203
Phone: (412) 227-6950
Provides statistical data on juvenile justice and the law, including a state-by-state listing of transfer provisions and purpose clauses.

National Center on Institutions and Alternatives (NCIA)
URL: http://www.ncianet.org
7222 Ambassador Road
Baltimore, MD 21244
Phone: (410) 265-1490
Advocates less restrictive forms of juvenile detention and opposes the sentencing of juveniles as adults. Offers related publications, including *Youth Homicide: Keeping Perspective on How Many Children Kill.*

National Clearinghouse for Alcohol and Drug Information
URL: http://www.health.org
Phone: (800) 729-6686
Information service of the Center for Substance Abuse Prevention of the Substance Abuse and Mental Health Services Administration, U.S. Department of Health & Human Services. Provides current statistics and a wide range of other materials concerning substance abuse.

National Council of Juvenile and Family Court Judges
University of Nevada, Reno
URL: http://www.ncjfcj.org
P.O. Box 8970
Reno, NV 89507
Phone: (775) 784-6012
Council is composed of juvenile and family court judges as well as other juvenile justice professionals with the aim of improving juvenile court practices.

National Council on Crime and Delinquency (NCCD)
URL: http://www.nccd-crc.org
1970 Broadway
Suite 500
Oakland, CA 94612
Phone: (510) 208-0500
Organization of corrections professionals and others working in the juvenile justice system that promotes community-based treatment of juvenile offenders as opposed to incarceration. Publishes the quarterly journal *Crime and Delinquency.*

National Crime Prevention Council
URL: http://www.ncpc.org
2345 Crystal Drive
Suite 500
Arlington, VA 22202
Phone: (202) 466-6272
Offers training programs on the prevention of juvenile crime and provides a variety of publications related to juvenile crime and justice issues.

National Gang Crime Research Center
URL: http://www.ngcrc.com
P.O. Box 990
Peotone, IL 60468-0990
Phone: (708) 258-9111
Nonprofit agency that conducts research on gangs and gang members, disseminates information

through publications and reports, and provides training and consulting services.

National Resource Center for Safe School (NRCSS)
URL: http://www.safetyzone.org
101 Southwest Main
Suite 500
Portland, OR 97204
Phone: (800) 268-2275
Provides a wide range of information on school crime and safety, including an annual report on school safety.

National School Safety Center
URL: http://www.nssc1.org
141 Duesenberg Drive
Suite 11
Westlake Village, CA 91362
Phone: (805) 373-9977
National research organization that studies school crime and violence. Publishes the newsletter *School Safety Update,* as well as other publications on issues related to school violence.

National Youth Gang Center
URL: http://www.iir.com/nygc
P.O. Box 12729
Tallahassee, FL 32317
Phone: (850) 385-0600
Collects and publishes statistics on youth gangs, reviews research literature related to youth gangs, and coordinates the activities of the OJJDP-sponsored Youth Gang Consortium, a collaboration of federal, state, and local agencies with

the aim of reducing crime associated with youth gangs.

National Youth Violence Prevention Resource Center (NYVPRC)
URL: http://www.safeyouth.org/scripts/index.asp
P.O. Box 6003
Rockville, MD 20849-6003
Phone: (866) 723-3968
Clearinghouse for information on prevention and intervention programs, publications, research, and statistics on violence committed by and against juveniles. The NYVPRC is a collaboration between the Centers for Disease Control and Prevention and other federal agencies.

The Rand Corporation
Criminal Justice Center
http://www.rand.org/ise/centers/cjc
1700 Main Street
P.O. Box 2138
Santa Monica, CA 90407-2138
Phone: (310) 451-6915
Research organization that provides reports and statistical data on violence prevention, substance abuse, and other topics related to criminal justice.

School Violence Resource Center
URL: http://www.svrc.net
Criminal Justice Institute
University of Arkansas System
7723 Colonel Glenn Road
Little Rock, AR 72204
Phone: (501) 570-8000

Provides fact sheet, articles, and other publications on school crime and violence.

The Sentencing Project
http://www.sentencingproject.org
514–10th Street NW
Suite 1000
Washington, DC 20004
Phone: (202) 628-0871
Nonprofit organization that advocates humane incarceration and alternatives to incarceration of adult and juvenile offenders.

Youth Crime Watch of America
URL: http://www.ycwa.org
9300 S. Dadeland Boulevard
Suite 417
Miami, FL 33156
Phone: (305) 670-2409
Seeks to reduce crime and drug use among youth through counseling and other school- and community-based programs. Offers the publication *Talking to Youth About Crime Prevention* and the video *Put an End to School Violence Today*, among other resources.

STATISTICAL ANALYSIS CENTERS

ALABAMA

Alabama Criminal Justice Information Center
URL: http://acjic.al.us
201 South Union Street
Suite 300
Montgomery, AL 36130-0660

ALASKA

University of Alaska Anchorage Justice Center
URL: http://www.jrsainfo.org/sac/ak.htm
3211 Providence Drive
Anchorage, AK 99508

ARIZONA

Arizona Criminal Justice Commission
URL: http://acjc.state.az.us/index.asp
1110 West Washington

Suite 230
Phoenix, AZ 85007

ARKANSAS

Arkansas Crime Information Center
URL: http://www.acic.org
One Capitol Mall
Little Rock, AR 72201

CALIFORNIA

Criminal Justice Statistics Center
URL: http://ag.ca.gov/cjsc
P.O. Box 903427
Sacramento, CA 94203-4270

COLORADO

Division of Criminal Justice
URL: http://dcj.state.co.us
Colorado Department of Public Safety

700 Kipling Street
Suite 1000
Denver, CO 80215

CONNECTICUT

Office of Policy and Management
URL: http://www.opm.state.
ct.us/pdpd1/justice/sac.htm
450 Capitol Avenue
Hartford, CT 06106-1379

DELAWARE

Delaware Criminal Justice
Council
URL: http://www.state.de.us/
cjc/index.html
820 North French Street
10th floor
Wilmington, DE 19801

DISTRICT OF COLUMBIA

Criminal Justice Coordinating
Council
URL: http://cjcc.dc.gov/cjcc/
site/default.asp
441 4th Street NW
Suite 727N
Washington, DC 20001

FLORIDA

Statistical Analysis Center
Florida Department of Law
Enforcement
URL: http://www.fdle.state.fl.us/
FSAC/index.asp
P.O. Box 1489
Tallahassee, FL 32302-1489

GEORGIA

Statistical Analysis Center
Criminal Justice Coordinating
Council
URL: http://cjcc.ga.gov/
researchdetails.aspx?id=184
104 Marietta Street
Suite 440
Atlanta, GA 30303-2743

HAWAII

Crime Prevention & Justice
Assistance Division
URL: http://hawaii.gov/ag/cpja
235 South Beretania Street
Suite 401
Honolulu, HI 96813

IDAHO

Idaho Department of Law
Enforcement
URL: http://www.isp.state.id.us
700 South Stratford Drive
Meridian, ID 83642

ILLINOIS

Illinois Criminal Justice
Information Authority
URL: http://www.icjia.org/
public/index.cfm
300 West Adams Street
Suite 700
Chicago, IL 60606-3997

INDIANA

Indiana Criminal Justice
Institute
URL: http://www.in.gov/cji
101 West Washington Street

Suite 1170, East Tower
Indianapolis, IN 46204

IOWA

Statistical Analysis Center
Iowa Criminal & Juvenile
  Justice Planning
URL: http://www.state.ia.us/
  government/dhr/cjjp/index.
  html
Lucas State Office Building
321 East 12th Street
Des Moines, IA 50319

KANSAS

Kansas Criminal Justice
  Coordinating Council
URL: http://www.governor.
  ks.gov/grants/kcjcc.htm
300 Southwest 10th Avenue
Room 2125
Topeka, KS 66612

KENTUCKY

Kentucky Justice and Public
  Safety Cabinet
URL: http://justice.ky.gov
Office of the Secretary
125 Holmes Street
Frankfort, KY 40601-2108

LOUISIANA

Louisiana Commission on
  Law Enforcement and
  Administration of Criminal
  Justice
URL: http://www.cole.state.la.us
1885 Wooddale Boulevard
Suite 1230
Baton Rouge, LA 70806-1511

MAINE

Maine Justice Policy Center
Edmund S. Muskie School of
  Public Service
University of Southern Maine
URL: http://www.muskie.usm.
  maine.edu/justiceresearch
P.O. Box 9300
Portland, ME 04104-9300

MARYLAND

Maryland Justice Analysis Center
University of Maryland
URL: http://www.mjac.umd.edu
1139 Taliaferro Hall
College Park, MD 20742

MASSACHUSETTS

Massachusetts Executive Office
  of Public Safety
URL: http://www.mass.gov/
  ?pageID=eopshomepage&L=
  1&LO=Home&sid=Eeops
1 Ashburton Place
Room 1301
Boston, MA 02108

MICHIGAN

Michigan Justice Statistics Center
Michigan State University
School of Criminal Justice
URL: http://www.cj.msu.edu
560 Baker Hall
East Lansing, MI 48824

MINNESOTA

Office of Justice Programs
URL: http://www.ojp.state.
  mn.us.index.htm

658 Bremer Tower
Suite 2300
St. Paul, MN 55101

MISSISSIPPI

Department of Criminal Justice
University of Southern
  Mississippi
URL: http://www.usm.edu/
  mssac
USM BOX 5127
Hattiesburg, MS 39406-5127

MISSOURI

Statistical Analysis Center
Missouri State Highway Patrol
URL: http://www.mshp.dps.
  missouri.gov/mshpweb/sac/
  index.html
1510 East Elm Street
P.O. Box 568
Jefferson City, MO 65102

MONTANA

Statistical Analysis Center
Montana Board of Crime Control
URL: http://mbcc.mt.gov/data/
  sac/aboutsac.asp
3075 North Montana Avenue
P.O. Box 201408
Helena, MT 59620-1408

NEBRASKA

Nebraska Commission on Law
  Enforcement and Criminal
  Justice
URL: http://www.ncc.state.ne.us
P.O. Box 94946
Lincoln, NE 68509-4946

NEW HAMPSHIRE

Department of Justice
Office of the Attorney General
URL: http://www.state.nh.us/
  nhdoj/coveraog.html
State House Annex
33 Capitol Street
Concord, NH 03301-6397

NEW JERSEY

Department of Law and Public
  Safety
URL: http://www.state.nj.us/lps
25 Market Street
CN-085
Trenton, NJ 08625

NEW MEXICO

Statistical Analysis Center
Institute for Social Research
URL: http://www.isrunm.net/
  centers/nmsac
2808 Central Avenue SE
MSC04 2520
Albuquerque, NM 87106

NEW YORK

Bureau of Statistical Services
New York State Division of
  Criminal Justice Services
URL: http://criminaljustice.
  state.ny.us
4 Tower Place
Albany, NY 12203-3764

NORTH CAROLINA

Governor's Crime Commission
URL: http://www.gcc.state.
  nc.us/cjac.htm

4701 Mail Service Center
Raleigh, NC 27699-4701

NORTH DAKOTA

Bureau of Criminal
  Investigation
URL: http://www.ag.nd.gov/bci/
  bci.htm
P.O. Box 1054
Bismarck, ND 58502

OHIO

Ohio Office of Criminal Justice
  Services
URL: http://publicsafety.ohio.
  gov/odps_ocjs/index.stm
1970 West Broad Street
Columbus, OH 43223

OKLAHOMA

Oklahoma Statistical Analysis
  Center
URL: http://www.ocjrc.net/
  sachome.asp
3812 North Santa Fe Avenue
Suite 290
Oklahoma City, OK 73118-8500

OREGON

Statistical Analysis Center
Oregon Criminal Justice
  Commission
URL: http://www.oregon.gov/
  cjc/index.shtml
885 Summer Street NE
Salem, OR 97301

PENNSYLVANIA

Commission on Crime and
  Delinquency

URL: http://www.pccd.state.
  pa.us/pccd/site/default.asp
P.O. Box 1167
Harrisburg, PA 17108-1167

RHODE ISLAND

Rhode Island Justice
  Commission
URL: http://www.rijustice.ri.
  gov
One Capitol Hill
Providence, RI 02908

SOUTH CAROLINA

Planning and Research Division
South Carolina Department of
  Public Safety
URL: http://www.scdps.org/ojp/
  statistics.asp
P.O. Box 1993
Blythewood, SC 29016

SOUTH DAKOTA

South Dakota Statistical Analysis
  Center
Division of Criminal Investigation
URL: http://dci.sd.gov/
  administration/sac
3444 East Highway 34
c/o 500 East Capitol
Pierre, SD 57501-5070

TENNESSEE

Statistical Analysis Center
Tennessee Bureau of
  Investigation
Crime Statistics Unit
URL: http://www.tbi.state.tn.us.
  divisions/isd_csu_sac.htm

901 R. S. Gass Boulevard
Nashville, TN 37216-2639

TEXAS

Texas Department of Criminal
  Justice
URL: http://www.tdcj.state.tx.us
P.O. Box 13084
Austin, TX 78711

UTAH

Utah Commission on Criminal
  and Juvenile Justice
URL: http://www.justice.state.
  ut.us
Utah Capitol Complex
East Office Building
Suite E330
Salt Lake City, UT 84114

VERMONT

Vermont Center for Justice
  Research
URL: http://www.vcjr.org
(802) 485-4250

VIRGINIA

Department of Criminal Justice
  Services
http://www.dcjs.state.va.us/
  research
1100 Bank Street
Richmond, VA 23219

WASHINGTON

Statistical Analysis Center
Office of Financial
  Management
URL: http://www.ofm.wa.gov/
  sac/default.asp
P.O. Box 43113
Olympia, WA 98504-3113

WEST VIRGINIA

Statistical Analysis Center
URL: http://www.wvdcjs.com/
  statsanalysis/index.html
1204 Kanawha Boulevard East
Charleston, WV 25301

WISCONSIN

Office of Justice Assistance
URL: http://oja.state.wi.us
1 South Pinckney Street
Suite 600
Madison, WI 53702

WYOMING

Wyoming Survey and Analysis
  Center
University of Wyoming
URL: http://www.uwyo.edu/
  wysac
1000 E. University Avenue
Laramie, WY 82070

PART III

APPENDICES

APPENDIX A

JUVENILE CRIME STATISTICS

ARRESTS OF PERSONS UNDER 15, 18, 21, AND 25 YEARS OF AGE, 2007
(11,936 agencies; 2007 estimated population 225,518,634)

Offense charged	Total all ages	Number of persons arrested				Percent of total all ages			
		Under 15	Under 18	Under 21	Under 25	Under 15	Under 18	Under 21	Under 25
TOTAL	10,698,310	461,937	1,649,977	3,159,716	4,753,345	4.3	15.4	29.5	44.4
Murder and nonnegligent manslaughter	10,082	103	1,011	3,027	5,084	1.0	10.0	30.0	50.4
Forcible rape	17,132	914	2,633	4,988	7,433	5.3	15.4	29.1	43.4
Robbery	96,720	5,601	26,324	47,770	62,542	5.8	27.2	49.4	64.7
Aggravated assault	327,137	13,662	43,459	80,724	129,264	4.2	13.3	24.7	39.5
Burglary	228,846	18,589	61,695	103,648	134,198	8.1	27.0	45.3	58.6
Larceny-theft	897,626	71,314	229,837	370,731	478,160	7.9	25.6	41.3	53.3
Motor vehicle theft	89,022	4,917	22,266	37,083	50,174	5.5	25.0	41.7	56.4
Arson	11,451	3,204	5,427	6,676	7,614	28.0	47.4	58.3	66.5
Violent crime[1]	451,071	20,280	73,427	136,509	204,323	4.5	16.3	30.3	45.3
Property crime[2]	1,226,945	98,024	319,225	518,138	670,146	8.0	26.0	42.2	54.6
Other assaults	983,964	70,038	181,378	278,521	413,165	7.1	18.4	28.3	42.0
Forgery and counterfeiting	78,005	294	2,353	11,760	24,739	0.4	3.0	15.1	31.7
Fraud	185,229	886	5,690	22,358	47,593	0.5	3.1	12.1	25.7
Embezzlement	17,015	49	1,288	4,745	7,871	0.3	7.6	27.9	46.3
Stolen property; buying, receiving, possessing	92,215	4,136	16,889	32,394	46,285	4.5	18.3	35.1	50.2

Vandalism	221,040	34,342	84,744	119,283	148,140	15.5	38.3	54.0	67.0
Weapons; carrying, possessing, etc.	142,745	10,577	33,187	58,664	83,152	7.4	23.2	41.1	58.3
Prostitution and commercialized vice	59,390	147	1,160	7,615	16,180	0.2	2.0	12.8	27.2
Sex offenses (except forcible rape and prostitution)	62,756	5,574	11,575	18,399	25,403	8.9	18.4	29.3	40.5
Drug abuse violations	1,386,394	21,506	147,382	392,486	636,465	1.6	10.6	28.3	45.9
Gambling	9,152	226	1,584	3,510	5,013	2.5	17.3	38.4	54.8
Offenses against the family and children	88,887	1,237	4,205	10,005	20,422	1.4	4.7	11.3	23.0
Driving under the influence	1,055,981	398	13,497	107,733	311,920	*	1.3	10.2	29.5
Liquor laws	473,671	9,592	106,537	340,122	373,174	2.0	22.3	71.1	78.0
Drunkenness	451,055	1,400	12,966	54,066	128,759	0.3	2.9	12.0	28.5
Disorderly conduct	540,270	57,602	153,293	219,327	300,984	10.7	28.4	40.6	55.7
Vagrancy	25,631	904	2,924	5,775	8,296	3.5	11.4	22.5	32.4
All other offenses (except traffic)	2,948,031	69,448	284,096	625,448	1,088,202	2.4	9.6	21.2	36.9
Suspicion	1,589	78	303	584	839	4.9	19.1	36.8	52.8
Curfew and loitering law violations	109,815	28,949	109,815	109,815	109,815	26.4	100.0	100.0	100.0
Runaways	82,459	26,250	82,459	82,459	82,459	31.8	100.0	100.0	100.0

[1] Violent crimes are offenses of murder and nonnegligent manslaughter, forcible rape, robbery, and aggravated assault.

[2] Property crimes are offenses of burglary, larceny-theft, motor vehicle theft, and arson.

* Less than one-tenth of 1 percent.

Source: Crime in the United States, 2007, Federal Bureau of Investigation (2008), table 41.

ARRESTS, BY AGE, 2007
(11,936 agencies; 2007 estimated population 225,518,634)

Offense charged	Total all ages	Ages under 15	Ages under 18	Ages 18 and over	Under 10	10-12	13-14	15	16	17	18	19	20
TOTAL	10,698,310	461,937	1,649,977	9,048,333	13,357	93,571	355,009	326,311	405,753	455,976	509,517	518,623	481,599
Total percent distribution[1]	100.0	4.3	15.4	84.6	0.1	0.9	3.3	3.1	3.8	4.3	4.8	4.8	4.5
Murder and nonnegligent manslaughter	10,082	103	1,011	9,071	1	6	96	131	294	483	736	687	593
Forcible rape	17,132	914	2,633	14,499	8	235	671	447	576	696	829	790	736
Robbery	96,720	5,601	26,324	70,396	72	784	4,745	5,353	7,229	8,141	8,590	7,236	5,620
Aggravated assault	327,137	13,662	43,459	283,678	460	3,320	9,882	8,146	10,231	11,420	12,448	12,564	12,253
Burglary	228,846	18,589	61,695	167,151	631	3,939	14,019	12,580	14,498	16,028	17,104	13,729	11,120
Larceny-theft	897,626	71,314	229,837	667,789	1,804	15,542	53,968	45,808	54,513	58,202	57,221	46,250	37,423
Motor vehicle theft	89,022	4,917	22,266	66,756	33	512	4,372	5,181	6,143	6,025	5,874	4,873	4,070
Arson	11,451	3,204	5,427	6,024	349	1,013	1,842	926	720	577	517	420	312
Violent crime[2]	451,071	20,280	73,427	377,644	541	4,345	15,394	14,077	18,330	20,740	22,603	21,277	19,202
Violent crime percent distribution[1]	100.0	4.5	16.3	83.7	0.1	1.0	3.4	3.1	4.1	4.6	5.0	4.7	4.3
Property crime[2]	1,226,945	98,024	319,225	907,720	2,817	21,006	74,201	64,495	75,874	80,832	80,716	65,272	52,925
Property crime percent distribution[1]	100.0	8.0	26.0	74.0	0.2	1.7	6.0	5.3	6.2	6.6	6.6	5.3	4.3
Other assaults	983,964	70,038	181,378	802,586	2,194	17,638	50,206	35,952	39,029	36,359	32,356	32,319	32,468
Forgery and counterfeiting	78,005	294	2,353	75,652	26	56	212	281	599	1,179	2,538	3,476	3,393
Fraud	185,229	886	5,690	179,539	56	132	698	867	1,464	2,473	4,473	5,865	6,330

Embezzlement	17,015	49	1,288	15,727	6	12	31	58	396	785	1,200	1,192	1,065
Stolen property; buying, receiving, possessing	92,215	4,136	16,889	75,326	79	667	3,390	3,509	4,366	4,878	5,773	5,251	4,481
Vandalism	221,040	34,342	84,744	136,296	1,668	8,647	24,027	16,723	17,187	16,492	13,852	11,560	9,127
Weapons; carrying, possessing, etc.	142,745	10,577	33,187	109,558	438	2,524	7,615	6,251	7,604	8,755	9,517	8,640	7,320
Prostitution and commercialized vice	59,390	147	1,160	58,230	16	14	117	184	315	514	1,890	2,327	2,238
Sex offenses (except forcible rape and prostitution)	62,756	5,574	11,575	51,181	264	1,525	3,785	2,057	1,983	1,981	2,437	2,331	2,056
Drug abuse violations	1,386,394	21,506	147,382	1,239,012	273	2,207	19,026	25,053	40,562	60,261	84,597	84,102	76,405
Gambling	9,152	226	1,584	7,568	7	12	207	283	428	647	705	664	557
Offenses against the family and children	88,887	1,237	4,205	84,682	112	234	891	804	1,026	1,138	1,796	1,909	2,095
Driving under the influence	1,055,981	398	13,497	1,042,484	193	16	186	537	3,169	9,393	23,954	33,125	37,157
Liquor laws	478,671	9,592	106,537	372,134	115	619	8,858	16,210	30,465	50,270	80,215	84,253	69,117
Drunkenness	451,055	1,400	12,936	438,089	75	82	1,243	2,119	3,118	6,329	12,727	14,163	14,210
Disorderly conduct	540,270	57,602	153,293	366,977	1,147	13,136	43,319	31,964	33,452	30,275	24,582	21,580	19,872
Vagrancy	25,631	904	2,924	22,707	15	142	747	766	859	395	1,143	938	770
All other offenses (except traffic)	2,948,031	69,448	284,096	2,663,935	2,244	12,002	55,202	57,709	72,163	84,776	102,335	118,273	120,744
Suspicion	1,589	78	303	1,286	0	15	63	55	104	66	108	106	67
Curfew and loitering law violations	109,815	28,949	109,815	-	456	4,751	23,742	25,435	30,467	24,964	-	-	-
Runaways	82,459	26,250	82,459	-	612	3,789	21,849	20,942	22,793	12,474	-	-	-

(continues)

227

ARRESTS, BY AGE, 2007 (CONTINUED)

Offense charged	21	22	23	24	25-29	30-34	35-39	40-44	45-49	50-54	55-59	60-64	65 and over
TOTAL	442,744	410,646	377,997	362,242	1,505,619	1,047,448	972,661	908,080	735,287	424,442	200,498	86,194	64,736
Total percent distribution[1]	4.1	3.8	3.5	3.4	14.1	9.8	9.1	8.5	6.9	4.0	1.9	0.8	0.6
Murder and nonnegligent manslaughter	583	545	473	456	1,758	940	680	558	432	295	175	77	83
Forcible rape	766	590	552	537	2,311	1,883	1,780	1,463	1,047	585	326	151	153
Robbery	4,579	3,881	3,311	3,001	11,175	6,860	5,871	4,865	3,219	1,403	503	178	104
Aggravated assault	12,949	12,208	11,755	11,628	50,759	36,293	32,552	29,840	23,163	13,291	6,317	2,974	2,684
Burglary	9,217	7,870	7,003	6,460	26,124	17,772	16,918	15,073	10,830	5,106	1,855	636	334
Larceny-theft	31,665	27,813	24,783	23,168	98,117	71,066	72,005	68,379	53,626	30,598	14,432	6,128	5,115
Motor vehicle theft	3,674	3,409	3,041	2,967	12,091	8,096	7,217	5,659	3,440	1,471	551	199	124
Arson	282	248	224	184	884	659	606	569	518	290	160	86	65
Violent crime[2]	18,877	17,224	16,091	15,622	66,003	45,976	40,883	36,726	27,861	15,574	7,321	3,380	3,024
Violent crime percent distribution[1]	4.2	3.8	3.6	3.5	14.6	10.2	9.1	8.1	6.2	3.5	1.6	0.7	0.7
Property crime[2]	44,838	39,340	35,051	32,779	137,216	97,593	96,746	89,680	68,414	37,465	16,998	7,049	5,638
Property crime percent distribution[1]	3.7	3.2	2.9	2.7	11.2	8.0	7.9	7.3	5.6	3.1	1.4	0.6	0.5
Other assaults	34,893	34,615	32,942	32,194	142,955	105,901	98,265	88,188	67,702	36,491	16,866	7,634	6,797
Forgery and counterfeiting	3,204	3,182	3,296	3,297	15,085	11,365	9,795	7,708	5,052	2,552	1,079	401	229
Fraud	6,217	6,325	6,217	6,476	31,504	27,390	25,795	21,084	15,204	8,838	4,327	2,074	1,420
Embezzlement	944	875	682	625	2,393	1,721	1,653	1,356	1,037	550	278	101	55

Stolen property; buying, receiving, possessing	3,929	3,599	3,270	3,093	13,060	9,157	8,076	6,909	4,785	2,357	929	390	267
Vandalism	8,739	7,606	6,486	6,026	22,524	13,942	11,605	10,071	7,568	3,890	1,815	774	711
Weapons; carrying, possessing, etc.	7,085	6,514	5,610	5,279	20,033	11,322	8,482	7,015	5,603	3,471	1,911	929	827
Prostitution and commercialized vice	2,309	2,178	2,123	1,955	9,108	7,880	8,597	7,906	5,202	2,528	1,062	462	465
Sex offenses (except forcible rape and prostitution)	1,980	1,817	1,614	1,593	6,935	5,618	6,033	5,821	4,903	3,270	2,024	1,313	1,436
Drug abuse violations	69,504	63,115	57,285	54,075	217,485	136,643	119,766	110,704	88,743	47,922	19,260	6,390	3,016
Gambling	447	415	332	309	1,071	625	489	479	429	329	297	202	218
Offenses against the family and children	2,405	2,430	2,619	2,963	15,258	14,098	13,837	11,516	7,614	3,701	1,421	603	417
Driving under the influence	53,215	52,475	50,092	48,405	190,447	126,294	111,407	104,808	91,814	58,702	32,610	15,920	12,059
Liquor laws	12,190	8,635	5,551	5,676	20,861	14,151	14,771	17,123	17,226	11,407	5,851	2,462	1,645
Drunkenness	21,096	19,512	17,445	16,640	65,982	46,290	46,582	52,731	50,967	33,497	15,716	6,437	3,994
Disorderly conduct	24,730	21,372	18,595	16,980	63,268	39,713	36,852	36,016	30,578	17,797	8,519	3,753	2,990
Vagrancy	800	589	575	557	2,450	2,071	2,662	3,237	3,206	2,060	1,011	412	226
All other offenses (except traffic)	125,274	118,755	111,059	107,666	461,776	329,556	310,342	288,901	231,296	131,986	61,178	25,502	19,292
Suspicion	68	73	62	52	205	142	123	101	83	55	25	6	10
Curfew and loitering law violations	-	-	-	-	-	-	-	-	-	-	-	-	-
Runaways	-	-	-	-	-	-	-	-	-	-	-	-	-

1 Because of rounding, the percentages may not add to 100.0.

2 Violent crimes are offenses of murder and nonnegligent manslaughter, forcible rape, robbery, and aggravated assault. Property crimes are offenses of burglary, larceny-theft, motor vehicle theft, and arson.

Source: Crime in the United States, 2007, Federal Bureau of Investigation (2008), table 38.

ARRESTS OF FEMALES, BY AGE, 2007
(11,936 agencies; 2007 estimated population 225,518,634)

Offense charged	Total all ages	Ages under 15	Ages under 18	Ages 18 and over	Under 10	10-12	13-14	15	16	17	18	19	20
TOTAL	2,587,284	142,718	485,309	2,101,975	2,565	24,670	115,483	104,190	119,987	118,414	119,022	120,648	110,581
Total percent distribution[1]	100.0	5.5	18.8	81.2	0.1	1.0	4.5	4.0	4.6	4.6	4.6	4.7	4.3
Murder and nonnegligent manslaughter	1,031	9	76	955	0	0	9	14	17	36	47	42	44
Forcible rape	186	28	49	137	0	3	25	7	7	7	9	7	11
Robbery	11,176	635	2,564	8,612	7	79	549	538	672	719	760	719	584
Aggravated assault	69,569	3,306	10,029	59,540	47	634	2,625	2,074	2,370	2,279	2,454	2,531	2,611
Burglary	33,296	2,235	7,138	26,158	76	476	1,683	1,532	1,584	1,787	1,919	1,812	1,574
Larceny-theft	358,704	29,247	99,298	259,406	475	5,724	23,048	20,258	24,352	25,441	23,817	18,981	15,652
Motor vehicle theft	15,781	936	3,668	12,113	3	97	836	900	973	859	795	760	676
Arson	1,806	363	645	1,161	25	103	235	116	104	62	58	40	42
Violent crime[2]	81,962	3,978	12,718	69,244	54	716	3,208	2,633	3,066	3,041	3,270	3,299	3,250
Violent crime percent distribution[1]	100.0	4.9	15.5	84.5	0.1	0.9	3.9	3.2	3.7	3.7	4.0	4.0	4.0
Property crime[2]	409,587	32,781	110,749	298,838	579	6,400	25,802	22,806	27,013	28,149	26,589	21,593	17,944
Property crime percent distribution[1]	100.0	8.0	27.0	73.0	0.1	1.6	6.3	5.6	6.6	6.9	6.5	5.3	4.4
Other assaults	248,386	23,129	60,959	187,427	377	4,819	17,933	13,025	13,357	11,448	9,326	9,001	8,824
Forgery and counterfeiting	29,785	81	741	29,044	8	18	55	85	206	369	908	1,345	1,229
Fraud	81,608	332	2,023	79,585	21	62	249	291	502	898	1,693	2,345	2,576
Embezzlement	8,759	18	541	8,218	3	4	11	15	167	341	599	613	566

Stolen property; buying, receiving, possessing	18,786	879	3,073	15,713	13	168	698	690	732	772	933	993	896
Vandalism	37,534	4,730	11,298	26,236	196	1,154	3,380	2,081	2,252	2,235	1,941	1,868	1,487
Weapons; carrying, possessing, etc.	11,063	1,263	3,234	7,829	39	279	945	658	697	616	532	481	405
Prostitution and commercialized vice	40,450	110	909	39,541	10	4	96	154	255	390	1,610	1,959	1,784
Sex offenses (except forcible rape and prostitution)	5,543	503	1,125	4,418	32	141	330	228	224	170	286	281	227
Drug abuse violations	261,256	4,337	23,181	238,075	50	435	3,852	4,316	6,095	8,433	12,247	12,908	11,797
Gambling	820	6	31	789	3	0	3	5	14	6	30	41	56
Offenses against the family and children	22,520	486	1,596	20,924	46	73	367	345	391	374	513	607	690
Driving under the influence	219,310	99	3,264	216,046	43	4	52	151	844	2,170	5,154	7,031	7,697
Liquor laws	132,963	4,749	39,861	93,102	35	313	4,401	7,105	11,499	16,508	24,328	23,914	18,687
Drunkenness	72,182	512	3,289	68,893	11	30	471	649	813	1,315	2,352	2,460	2,298
Disorderly conduct	142,067	20,231	50,922	91,145	224	3,978	16,029	11,490	10,799	8,402	6,072	5,333	4,836
Vagrancy	5,688	308	852	4,836	3	47	258	238	230	76	208	181	179
All other offenses (except traffic)	675,629	19,956	74,816	601,813	498	2,920	16,538	16,801	8,953	19,106	20,410	24,375	25,146
Suspicion	331	19	72	259	0	2	17	14	26	13	21	20	7
Curfew and loitering law violations	33,790	9,762	33,790	-	112	1,392	8,258	8,345	8,930	6,753	-	-	-
Runaways	46,265	14,449	46,265	-	208	1,711	12,530	12,065	12,922	6,829	-	-	-

(continues)

231

ARRESTS OF FEMALES, BY AGE, 2007 (CONTINUED)

Offense charged	21	22	23	24	25-29	30-34	35-39	40-44	45-49	50-54	55-59	60-64	65 and over
TOTAL	98,600	91,510	84,771	82,160	345,986	254,075	250,383	229,773	169,366	84,453	35,006	14,581	11,060
Total percent distribution[1]	3.8	3.5	3.3	3.2	13.4	9.8	9.7	8.9	6.5	3.3	1.4	0.6	0.4
Murder and nonnegligent manslaughter	43	51	51	46	168	125	90	105	74	36	19	5	9
Forcible rape	9	4	4	4	22	26	10	13	10	2	4	1	1
Robbery	500	422	374	398	1,508	1,025	889	728	444	167	62	20	12
Aggravated assault	2,630	2,555	2,450	2,450	10,405	7,829	7,391	6,913	5,026	2,509	1,031	400	355
Burglary	1,383	1,150	1,109	1,086	4,441	3,257	3,030	2,501	1,660	776	283	109	68
Larceny-theft	12,871	11,419	10,110	9,602	40,218	28,453	26,889	23,738	18,052	10,226	5,022	2,331	2,025
Motor vehicle theft	670	638	561	573	2,407	1,598	1,461	1,064	585	228	61	20	16
Arson	49	47	37	38	173	143	148	134	123	64	39	16	10
Violent crime[2]	3,182	3,032	2,879	2,898	12,103	9,005	8,380	7,759	5,554	2,714	1,116	426	377
Violent crime percent distribution[1]	3.9	3.7	3.5	3.5	14.8	11.0	10.2	9.5	6.8	3.3	1.4	0.5	0.5
Property crime[2]	14,973	13,254	11,817	11,299	47,239	33,451	31,528	27,437	20,420	11,294	5,405	2,476	2,119
Property crime percent distribution[1]	3.7	3.2	2.9	2.8	11.5	8.2	7.7	6.7	5.0	2.8	1.3	0.6	0.5
Other assaults	9,168	8,632	7,984	7,639	32,260	23,690	22,940	20,470	14,588	7,231	3,113	1,397	1,164
Forgery and counterfeiting	1,214	1,146	1,213	1,234	5,932	4,567	4,077	3,101	1,808	781	321	108	60
Fraud	2,742	2,700	2,731	2,983	14,675	13,272	12,066	9,233	6,235	3,464	1,580	749	541
Embezzlement	498	432	348	339	1,296	924	886	686	541	284	137	47	22
Stolen property; buying, receiving, possessing	819	784	734	684	2,961	2,096	1,829	1,450	921	394	131	56	32

Vandalism	1,522	1,436	1,194	1,155	4,507	3,014	2,676	2,367	1,639	801	372	146	121
Weapons; carrying, possessing, etc.	444	373	337	326	1,421	925	826	747	522	288	122	49	31
Prostitution and commercialized vice	1,769	1,613	1,485	1,318	6,092	5,173	5,998	5,621	3,399	1,304	323	49	44
Sex offenses (except forcible rape and prostitution)	199	191	167	185	683	484	571	492	368	189	57	22	16
Drug abuse violations	11,531	10,575	9,875	9,636	39,832	27,389	25,983	28,600	20,921	9,081	2,941	830	328
Gambling	15	21	15	14	49	58	84	90	95	78	65	38	40
Offenses against the family and children	747	795	889	943	4,455	3,518	3,200	2,252	1,291	585	238	116	85
Driving under the influence	11,873	11,445	10,372	9,629	36,544	23,897	23,813	25,190	21,790	11,984	5,508	2,462	1,657
Liquor laws	2,436	1,681	1,218	1,044	4,138	2,891	3,279	3,697	3,032	1,627	611	308	211
Drunkenness	3,221	2,612	2,506	2,321	9,622	7,201	8,623	10,117	8,645	4,301	1,623	532	259
Disorderly conduct	5,445	4,578	4,010	3,858	14,538	10,111	9,881	9,378	7,018	3,435	1,436	670	546
Vagrancy	163	13	126	137	564	554	750	787	609	324	88	35	18
All other offenses (except traffic)	26,622	25,798	24,860	24,510	107,021	81,321	79,965	70,279	49,956	24,284	9,815	4,065	3,386
Suspicion	17	9	10	8	54	34	28	20	14	10	4	0	3
Curfew and loitering law violations	-	-	-	-	-	-	-	-	-	-	-	-	-
Runaways	-	-	-	-	-	-	-	-	-	-	-	-	-

[1] Because of rounding, the percentages may not add to 100.0.

[2] Violent crimes are offenses of murder and nonnegligent manslaughter, forcible rape, robbery, and aggravated assault. Property crimes are offenses of burglary, larceny-theft, motor vehicle theft, and arson.

Source: *Crime in the United States, 2007*, Federal Bureau of Investigation (2008), table 40.

ARRESTS OF MALES, BY AGE, 2007
(11,936 agencies; 2007 estimated population 225,518,634)

Offense charged	Total all ages	Ages under 15	Ages under 18	Ages 18 and over	Under 10	10-12	13-14	15	16	17	18	19	20
TOTAL	8,111,026	319,219	1,164,668	6,946,358	10,792	68,901	239,526	222,121	285,766	337,562	390,495	397,975	371,018
Total percent distribution[1]	100.0	3.9	14.4	85.6	0.1	0.8	3.0	2.7	3.5	4.2	4.8	4.9	4.6
Murder and nonnegligent manslaughter	9,051	94	935	8,116	1	6	87	117	277	447	689	645	549
Forcible rape	16,946	886	2,584	14,362	8	232	646	440	569	689	820	783	725
Robbery	85,544	4,966	23,760	61,784	65	705	4,196	4,815	6,557	7,422	7,830	6,517	5,036
Aggravated assault	257,568	10,356	33,430	224,138	413	2,686	7,257	6,072	7,861	9,141	9,994	10,033	9,642
Burglary	195,550	16,354	54,557	140,993	555	3,463	12,336	11,048	12,914	14,241	15,185	11,917	9,546
Larceny-theft	538,922	42,067	130,539	408,383	1,329	9,818	30,920	25,550	30,161	32,761	33,404	27,269	21,771
Motor vehicle theft	73,241	3,981	18,598	54,643	30	415	3,536	4,281	5,170	5,166	5,079	4,113	3,394
Arson	9,645	2,841	4,782	4,863	324	910	1,607	810	616	515	459	380	270
Violent crime[2]	369,109	16,302	60,709	308,400	487	3,629	12,186	11,444	15,264	17,699	19,333	17,978	15,952
Violent crime percent distribution[1]	100.0	4.4	16.4	83.6	0.1	1.0	3.3	3.1	4.1	4.8	5.2	4.9	4.3
Property crime[2]	817,358	65,243	208,476	608,882	2,238	14,606	48,399	41,689	48,861	52,683	54,127	43,679	34,981
Property crime percent distribution[1]	100.0	8.0	25.5	74.5	0.3	1.8	5.9	5.1	6.0	6.4	6.6	5.3	4.3
Other assaults	735,578	46,909	120,419	615,159	1,817	12,819	32,273	22,927	25,672	24,911	23,030	23,318	23,644
Forgery and counterfeiting	48,220	213	1,612	46,608	18	38	157	196	393	810	1,630	2,131	2,164
Fraud	103,621	554	3,667	99,954	35	70	449	576	962	1,575	2,780	3,520	3,754

Embezzlement	8,256	31	747	7,509	3	8	20	43	229	444	601	579	499
Stolen property; buying, receiving, possessing	73,429	3,257	13,816	59,613	66	499	2,632	2,819	3,634	4,106	4,840	4,258	3,585
Vandalism	183,506	29,612	73,446	110,060	1,472	7,493	20,647	14,642	14,935	14,257	11,911	9,692	7,640
Weapons; carrying, possessing, etc.	131,682	9,314	29,953	101,729	399	2,245	6,570	5,533	6,907	8,139	8,985	8,159	6,915
Prostitution and commercialized vice	18,940	37	251	18,689	6	10	21	30	60	124	280	368	454
Sex offenses (except forcible rape and prostitution)	57,213	5,071	10,450	46,763	232	1,384	3,455	1,806	1,759	1,811	2,151	2,050	1,829
Drug abuse violations	1,125,138	17,169	124,201	1,000,937	223	1,772	15,174	20,737	34,467	51,828	72,350	71,194	64,608
Gambling	3,332	220	1,553	1,779	2	12	204	278	414	641	675	623	501
Offenses against the family and children	66,367	751	2,609	63,758	66	161	524	459	635	764	1,283	1,302	1,405
Driving under the influence	836,571	299	10,233	826,438	153	12	34	586	2,325	7,223	18,800	26,094	29,460
Liquor laws	345,708	4,843	66,676	279,032	80	306	4,457	9,105	18,966	33,762	55,887	60,339	50,430
Drunkenness	378,873	888	9,677	369,196	64	52	772	1,470	2,305	5,014	10,375	11,703	11,912
Disorderly conduct	388,203	37,371	102,371	295,832	923	9,158	27,290	20,474	22,653	21,873	18,510	16,247	15,036
Vagrancy	19,943	595	2,072	17,871	12	95	489	528	629	319	935	757	591
All other offenses (except traffic)	2,271,402	49,492	209,280	2,062,122	1,746	9,082	38,564	40,903	53,210	65,670	81,925	93,898	95,598
Suspicion	1,258	59	231	1,027	0	13	46	41	78	53	87	86	60
Curfew and loitering law violations	76,025	19,187	76,025	-	344	3,359	15,484	17,090	21,537	18,211	-	-	-
Runaways	36,194	11,801	36,194	-	404	2,078	9,319	8,377	9,871	5,645	-	-	-

(continues)

ARRESTS OF MALES, BY AGE, 2007 (CONTINUED)

Offense charged	21	22	23	24	25-29	30-34	35-39	40-44	45-49	50-54	55-59	60-64	65 and over
TOTAL	344,144	319,136	293,226	280,082	1,159,633	793,373	722,278	678,307	565,921	339,989	165,492	71,613	53,676
Total percent distribution[1]	4.2	3.9	3.6	3.5	14.3	9.8	8.9	8.4	7.0	4.2	2.0	0.9	0.7
Murder and nonnegligent manslaughter	540	494	422	410	1,590	815	590	453	358	259	156	72	74
Forcible rape	757	586	548	533	2,289	1,857	1,770	1,450	1,037	583	322	150	152
Robbery	4,079	3,459	2,937	2,603	9,667	5,835	4,982	4,137	2,775	1,236	441	158	92
Aggravated assault	10,319	9,653	9,305	9,178	40,354	28,464	25,161	22,927	18,137	10,782	5,286	2,574	2,329
Burglary	7,834	6,720	5,894	5,374	21,683	14,515	13,888	12,572	9,170	4,330	1,572	527	266
Larceny-theft	18,794	16,394	14,673	13,566	57,899	42,613	45,116	44,641	35,574	20,372	9,410	3,797	3,090
Motor vehicle theft	3,004	2,771	2,480	2,394	9,684	6,498	5,756	4,595	2,855	1,243	490	179	108
Arson	233	201	187	146	711	516	458	435	395	226	121	70	55
Violent crime[2]	15,695	14,192	13,212	12,724	53,900	36,971	32,503	28,967	22,307	12,860	6,205	2,954	2,647
Violent crime percent distribution[1]	4.3	3.8	3.6	3.4	14.6	10.0	8.8	7.8	6.0	3.5	1.7	0.8	0.7
Property crime[2]	29,865	26,086	23,234	21,480	89,977	64,142	65,218	62,243	47,994	26,171	11,593	4,573	3,519
Property crime percent distribution[1]	3.7	3.2	2.8	2.6	11.0	7.8	8.0	7.6	5.9	3.2	1.4	0.6	0.4
Other assaults	25,725	25,983	24,958	24,555	110,695	82,211	75,325	67,718	53,114	29,260	13,753	6,237	5,633
Forgery and counterfeiting	1,990	2,036	2,083	2,063	9,153	6,798	5,718	4,607	3,244	1,771	758	293	169
Fraud	3,475	3,625	3,486	3,493	16,829	14,118	13,729	11,851	8,969	5,374	2,747	1,325	879
Embezzlement	446	443	334	286	1,097	797	767	670	496	266	141	54	33
Stolen property; buying, receiving, possessing	3,110	2,815	2,536	2,409	10,099	7,061	6,247	5,459	3,864	1,963	798	334	235

Vandalism	7,217	6,180	5,292	4,871	18,017	10,928	8,929	7,704	5,929	3,089	1,443	628	590
Weapons; carrying, possessing, etc.	6,641	6,141	5,273	4,953	18,612	10,397	7,656	6,268	5,081	3,183	1,789	880	796
Prostitution and commercialized vice	540	565	638	637	3,016	2,707	2,599	2,285	1,803	1,224	739	413	421
Sex offenses (except forcible rape and prostitution)	1,781	1,626	1,447	1,408	6,252	5,134	5,462	5,329	4,535	3,081	1,967	1,291	1,420
Drug abuse violations	57,973	52,440	47,409	44,439	177,653	103,754	90,783	82,104	67,822	38,841	16,319	5,560	2,688
Gambling	432	394	317	295	1,022	567	405	389	334	251	232	164	178
Offenses against the family and children	1,658	1,635	1,730	2,020	10,803	10,580	10,637	9,264	6,323	3,116	1,183	487	332
Driving under the influence	41,342	41,030	39,720	38,776	153,903	102,397	87,594	79,618	70,024	46,718	27,102	13,458	10,402
Liquor laws	9,754	6,854	5,333	4,632	16,723	11,260	11,492	13,426	14,194	9,780	5,240	2,154	1,434
Drunkenness	17,875	13,700	14,539	14,319	56,360	39,089	38,059	42,614	42,322	29,196	14,093	5,905	3,735
Disorderly conduct	19,285	16,794	14,585	13,102	48,730	29,602	26,771	26,638	23,560	14,362	7,083	3,083	2,444
Vagrancy	637	476	449	420	1,886	1,517	1,912	2,450	2,597	1,736	923	377	208
All other offenses (except traffic)	98,652	82,957	86,199	83,156	354,755	248,235	230,377	218,622	181,340	107,702	51,363	21,437	15,906
Suspicion	51	64	52	44	151	108	95	81	69	45	21	6	7
Curfew and loitering law violations	-	-	-	-	-	-	-	-	-	-	-	-	-
Runaways	-	-	-	-	-	-	-	-	-	-	-	-	-

[1] Because of rounding, the percentages may not add to 100.0.

[2] Violent crimes are offenses of murder and nonnegligent manslaughter, forcible rape, robbery, and aggravated assault. Property crimes are offenses of burglary, larceny-theft, motor vehicle theft, and arson.

Source: Crime in the United States, 2007, Federal Bureau of Investigation (2008), table 39.

Arrests by Race, 2007
(11,929 agencies; 2007 estimated population 225,477,173)

Offense charged	Total arrests					Percent distribution[1]				
	Total	White	Black	American Indian or Alaskan Native	Asian or Pacific Islander	Total	White	Black	American Indian or Alaskan Native	Asian or Pacific Islander
TOTAL	10,656,710	7,426,278	3,003,060	142,969	84,403	100.0	69.7	28.2	1.3	0.8
Murder and nonnegligent manslaughter	10,067	4,789	5,078	99	101	100.0	47.6	50.4	1.0	1.0
Forcible rape	17,058	10,984	5,708	213	153	100.0	64.4	33.5	1.2	0.9
Robbery	96,584	40,573	54,774	602	635	100.0	42.0	56.7	0.6	0.7
Aggravated assault	326,277	208,762	109,985	4,374	3,156	100.0	64.0	33.7	1.3	1.0
Burglary	228,346	156,442	68,052	2,191	1,661	100.0	68.5	29.8	1.0	0.7
Larceny-theft	894,215	610,607	261,730	11,885	9,993	100.0	68.3	29.3	1.3	1.1
Motor vehicle theft	88,843	55,229	31,765	1,041	808	100.0	62.2	35.8	1.2	0.9
Arson	11,400	8,510	2,666	119	105	100.0	74.6	23.4	1.0	0.9
Violent crime[2]	449,986	265,108	175,545	5,288	4,045	100.0	58.9	39.0	1.2	0.9
Property crime[2]	1,222,804	830,788	364,213	15,236	12,567	100.0	67.9	29.8	1.2	1.0
Other assaults	980,512	641,991	316,217	14,028	8,276	100.0	65.5	32.3	1.4	0.8
Forgery and counterfeiting	77,757	54,136	22,460	414	747	100.0	69.6	28.9	0.5	1.0
Fraud	184,446	127,377	54,575	1,369	1,125	100.0	69.1	29.6	0.7	0.6
Embezzlement	16,954	10,813	5,818	95	228	100.0	63.8	34.3	0.6	1.3
Stolen property; buying, receiving, possessing	91,937	57,870	32,570	735	762	100.0	62.9	35.4	0.8	0.8

Vandalism	220,055	166,201	48,642	3,340	1,872	100.0	75.5	22.1	1.5	0.9
Weapons; carrying, possessing, etc.	142,369	82,311	57,745	1,061	1,252	100.0	57.8	40.6	0.7	0.9
Prostitution and commercialized vice	59,307	34,190	23,251	550	1,316	100.0	57.6	39.2	0.9	2.2
Sex offenses (except forcible rape and prostitution)	32,586	45,961	15,372	633	620	100.0	73.4	24.6	1.0	1.0
Drug abuse violations	1,382,783	880,742	485,054	8,872	8,115	100.0	63.7	35.1	0.6	0.6
Gambling	9,141	2,199	6,805	20	117	100.0	24.1	74.4	0.2	1.3
Offenses against the family and children	83,437	60,124	26,090	1,686	537	100.0	68.0	29.5	1.9	0.6
Driving under the influence	1,050,303	929,453	97,472	14,251	9,627	100.0	88.5	9.3	1.4	0.9
Liquor laws	474,726	406,221	49,434	14,422	4,649	100.0	85.6	10.4	3.0	1.0
Drunkenness	449,117	375,440	62,278	8,891	2,508	100.0	83.6	13.9	2.0	0.6
Disorderly conduct	537,809	342,169	183,310	8,376	3,454	100.0	63.6	34.2	1.6	0.6
Vagrancy	25,584	15,493	9,474	501	116	100.0	60.6	37.0	2.0	0.5
All other offenses (except traffic)	2,336,233	1,969,862	905,656	40,546	20,169	100.0	67.1	30.8	1.4	0.7
Suspicion	1,571	904	649	4	14	100.0	57.5	41.3	0.3	0.9
Curfew and loitering law violations	109,575	69,950	37,532	964	1,129	100.0	63.8	34.3	0.9	1.0
Runaways	32,218	56,975	22,398	1,687	1,158	100.0	69.3	27.2	2.1	1.4

[1] Because of rounding, the percentages may not add to 100.0.

[2] Violent crimes are offenses of murder and nonnegligent manslaughter, forcible rape, robbery, and aggravated assault. Property crimes are offenses of burglary, larceny-theft, motor vehicle theft, and arson.

Source: Crime in the United States, 2007, Federal Bureau of Investigation (2008), table 43.

239

FIVE-YEAR ARREST TRENDS — TOTALS, 2003–2007
(9,746 agencies; 2007 estimated population 187,132,870; 2003 estimated population 180,729,448)

Offense charged	Number of persons arrested								
	Total all ages			Under 18 years of age			18 years of age and over		
	2003	2007	Percent change	2003	2007	Percent change	2003	2007	Percent change
TOTAL[1]	8,480,862	8,814,016	+3.9	1,370,961	1,330,889	-2.9	7,109,901	7,483,127	+5.2
Murder and nonnegligent manslaughter	7,406	7,623	+2.9	599	753	+25.7	6,807	6,870	+0.9
Forcible rape	15,619	13,699	-12.3	2,501	2,183	-12.7	13,118	11,516	-12.2
Robbery	60,487	70,536	+16.6	13,836	18,624	+34.6	46,651	51,912	+11.3
Aggravated assault	275,833	269,706	-2.2	37,231	35,102	-5.7	238,602	234,604	-1.7
Burglary	183,664	192,743	+4.9	54,171	52,595	-2.9	129,493	140,148	+8.2
Larceny-theft	728,039	735,272	+1.0	211,717	192,752	-9.0	516,322	542,520	+5.1
Motor vehicle theft	81,982	67,316	-17.9	23,945	16,679	-30.3	58,037	50,637	-12.8
Arson	10,061	9,792	-2.7	5,255	4,894	-6.9	4,806	4,898	+1.9
Violent crime[2]	359,345	361,564	+0.6	54,167	56,662	+4.6	305,178	304,902	-0.1
Property crime[2]	1,003,746	1,005,123	+0.1	295,088	266,920	-9.5	708,658	738,203	+4.2
Other assaults	783,775	813,015	+3.7	151,619	150,646	-0.6	632,156	662,369	+4.8
Forgery and counterfeiting	72,157	64,027	-11.3	3,045	1,929	-36.7	69,112	62,098	-10.1
Fraud	207,296	167,673	-19.1	5,111	4,819	-5.7	202,185	162,854	-19.5
Embezzlement	11,890	15,151	+27.4	820	1,174	+43.2	11,070	13,977	+26.3
Stolen property; buying, receiving, possessing	83,042	78,750	-5.2	16,004	14,548	-9.1	67,038	64,202	-4.2

Offense	Total 2003	Total 2007	Percent change	Male 2003	Male 2007	Percent change	Female 2003	Female 2007	Percent change
Vandalism	173,591	185,412	+6.8	69,445	71,884	+3.5	104,146	113,528	+9.0
Weapons; carrying, possessing, etc.	100,593	113,014	+12.3	23,607	26,345	+11.6	76,986	86,669	+12.6
Prostitution and commercialized vice	34,845	33,421	-4.1	722	728	+0.8	34,123	32,693	-4.2
Sex offenses (except forcible rape and prostitution)	54,249	50,696	-6.5	11,590	9,523	-17.8	42,659	41,173	-3.5
Drug abuse violations	1,002,012	1,097,267	+9.5	117,540	117,686	+0.1	884,472	979,581	+10.8
Gambling	3,512	3,004	-14.5	328	359	+9.5	3,184	2,645	-16.9
Offenses against the family and children	86,404	79,342	-8.2	4,519	3,799	-15.9	81,885	75,543	-7.7
Driving under the influence	888,660	903,244	+1.6	12,825	11,484	-10.5	875,835	891,760	+1.8
Liquor laws	388,033	390,964	+0.8	88,615	90,330	+1.9	299,413	300,634	+0.4
Drunkenness	364,149	408,141	+12.1	11,474	11,819	+3.0	352,675	396,322	+12.4
Disorderly conduct	399,596	418,957	+4.8	123,728	121,975	-1.4	275,868	296,982	+7.7
Vagrancy	17,261	13,061	-24.3	1,332	896	-32.7	15,929	12,165	-23.6
All other offenses (except traffic)	2,312,306	2,483,251	+7.4	244,982	238,424	-2.7	2,067,324	2,244,827	+8.6
Suspicion	1,163	1,423	+22.4	389	292	-24.9	774	1,131	+46.1
Curfew and loitering law violations	57,930	59,686	+3.0	57,930	59,686	+3.0	-	-	-
Runaways	76,470	69,253	-9.4	76,470	69,253	-9.4	-	-	-

[1] Does not include suspicion.

[2] Violent crimes are offenses of murder and nonnegligent manslaughter, forcible rape, robbery, and aggravated assault. Property crimes are offenses of burglary, larceny-theft, motor vehicle theft, and arson.

Source: Crime in the United States, 2007, Federal Bureau of Investigation (2008), table 34.

FIVE-YEAR ARREST TRENDS, BY SEX, 2003–2007

(9,746 agencies; 2007 estimated population 187,132,870; 2003 estimated population 180,729,448)

Offense charged	Male						Female					
	Total			Under 18			Total			Under 18		
	2003	2007	Percent change	2003	2007	Percent change	2003	2007	Percent change	2003	2007	Percent change
TOTAL[1]	6,488,366	6,656,579	+2.6	969,405	934,854	-3.6	1,992,496	2,157,437	+8.3	401,556	396,035	-1.4
Murder and nonnegligent manslaughter	6,569	6,805	+3.6	542	690	+27.3	837	818	-2.3	57	63	+10.5
Forcible rape	15,409	13,552	-12.1	2,459	2,143	-12.9	210	147	-30.0	42	40	-4.8
Robbery	54,012	62,432	+15.6	12,591	16,897	+34.2	6,475	8,104	+25.2	1,245	1,727	+38.7
Aggravated assault	218,497	212,486	-2.8	28,506	27,004	-5.3	57,336	57,220	-0.2	8,725	8,098	-7.2
Burglary	157,696	163,537	+3.7	47,626	46,231	-2.9	25,968	29,206	+12.5	6,545	6,364	-2.8
Larceny-theft	456,489	439,829	-3.6	128,945	110,134	-14.6	271,550	295,443	+8.8	82,772	82,618	-0.2
Motor vehicle theft	68,149	55,010	-19.3	19,623	13,718	-30.1	13,833	12,306	-11.0	4,322	2,961	-31.5
Arson	8,550	8,309	-2.8	4,656	4,327	-7.1	1,511	1,483	-1.9	599	567	-5.3
Violent crime[2]	294,487	295,275	+0.3	44,098	46,734	+6.0	64,858	66,289	+2.2	10,069	9,928	-1.4
Property crime[2]	690,884	666,685	-3.5	200,850	174,410	-13.2	312,862	338,438	+8.2	94,238	92,510	-1.8
Other assaults	592,533	604,611	+2.0	102,470	99,858	-2.5	191,242	208,404	+9.0	49,149	50,788	+3.3
Forgery and counterfeiting	42,999	39,268	-8.7	1,969	1,298	-34.1	29,158	24,759	-15.1	1,076	631	-41.4
Fraud	111,771	91,641	-18.0	3,363	3,056	-9.1	95,525	76,032	-20.4	1,748	1,763	+0.9
Embezzlement	5,911	7,360	+24.5	487	685	+40.7	5,979	7,791	+30.3	333	489	+46.8
Stolen property; buying, receiving, possessing	67,850	62,419	-8.0	13,543	11,834	-12.6	15,192	16,331	+7.5	2,461	2,714	+10.3

Vandalism	145,078	153,800	+6.0	59,793	62,173	+4.0	28,513	31,612	+10.9	9,652	9,711	+0.6
Weapons; carrying, possessing, etc.	92,319	104,175	+12.8	21,173	23,896	+12.9	8,274	8,835	+6.8	2,434	2,449	+0.6
Prostitution and commercialized vice	12,546	10,861	-13.4	224	167	-25.4	22,299	22,560	+1.2	498	561	+12.7
Sex offenses (except forcible rape and prostitution)	50,234	46,689	-7.1	10,504	8,617	-18.0	4,015	4,007	-0.2	1,086	906	-16.6
Drug abuse violations	813,481	882,589	+8.5	97,006	97,915	+0.9	188,531	214,678	+13.9	20,534	19,771	-3.7
Gambling	2,913	2,600	-10.7	311	346	+11.3	599	404	-32.6	17	13	-23.5
Offenses against the family and children	66,709	59,557	-10.7	2,753	2,324	-15.6	19,695	19,785	+0.5	1,766	1,475	-16.5
Driving under the influence	724,911	714,625	-1.4	10,213	8,751	-14.3	163,749	188,619	+15.2	2,612	2,733	+4.6
Liquor laws	288,242	281,189	-2.4	57,765	56,562	-2.1	99,791	109,775	+10.0	30,850	33,768	+9.5
Drunkenness	310,909	342,213	+10.1	8,746	8,758	+0.1	53,240	65,928	+23.8	2,728	3,061	+12.2
Disorderly conduct	296,046	305,441	+3.2	85,108	81,550	-4.2	103,550	113,516	+9.6	38,620	40,425	+4.7
Vagrancy	13,380	10,332	-22.8	1,003	397	-60.5	3,881	2,729	-29.7	329	199	-39.5
All other offenses (except traffic)	1,794,343	1,804,256	+6.1	177,206	174,234	-1.7	517,963	578,995	+11.8	67,776	64,190	-5.3
Suspicion	942	1,127	+19.6	298	216	-27.5	221	296	+33.9	91	76	-16.5
Curfew and loitering law violations	39,372	40,403	+2.6	39,372	40,403	+2.6	18,558	19,283	+3.9	18,558	19,283	+3.9
Runaways	31,448	30,586	-2.7	31,448	33,586	-2.7	45,022	38,667	-14.1	45,022	38,667	-14.1

[1] Does not include suspicion.

[2] Violent crimes are offenses of murder and nonnegligent manslaughter, forcible rape, robbery, and aggravated assault. Property crimes are offenses of burglary, larceny-theft, motor vehicle theft, and arson.

Source: Crime in the United States, 2007, Federal Bureau of Investigation (2008), table 35.

TEN-YEAR ARREST TRENDS—TOTALS, 1998–2007

(7,946 agencies; 2007 estimated population 171,876,948; 1998 estimated population 154,013,711)

Offense charged	Number of persons arrested								
	Total all ages			Under 18 years of age			18 years of age and over		
	1998	2007	Percent change	1998	2007	Percent change	1998	2007	Percent change
TOTAL[1]	8,397,065	8,118,197	-3.3	1,527,681	1,215,839	-20.4	6,869,384	6,902,358	+0.5
Murder and nonnegligent manslaughter	8,232	7,301	-11.3	983	753	-23.4	7,249	6,548	-9.7
Forcible rape	17,148	13,212	-23.0	2,975	2,034	-31.6	14,173	11,178	-21.1
Robbery	68,353	72,355	+5.9	18,439	19,550	+6.0	49,914	52,805	+5.8
Aggravated assault	290,851	257,464	-11.5	42,358	33,314	-21.4	248,493	224,150	-9.8
Burglary	195,696	182,552	-6.7	70,171	48,903	-30.3	125,525	133,649	+6.5
Larceny-theft	791,085	689,037	-12.9	258,540	175,561	-32.1	532,545	513,476	-3.6
Motor vehicle theft	80,925	62,766	-22.4	29,882	15,289	-48.8	51,043	47,477	-7.0
Arson	10,055	9,094	-9.6	5,407	4,391	-18.8	4,648	4,703	+1.2
Violent crime[2]	384,584	350,332	-8.9	64,755	55,651	-14.1	319,829	294,681	-7.9
Property crime[2]	1,077,761	943,449	-12.5	364,000	244,144	-32.9	713,761	699,305	-2.0
Other assaults	768,038	754,280	-1.8	138,780	138,795	*	629,258	615,485	-2.2
Forgery and counterfeiting	67,870	58,832	-13.3	4,250	1,699	-60.0	63,620	57,133	-10.2
Fraud	213,800	147,985	-30.8	6,066	4,480	-26.1	207,734	143,505	-30.9
Embezzlement	11,115	14,065	+26.5	1,018	1,072	+5.3	10,097	12,993	+28.7
Stolen property; buying, receiving, possessing	78,371	72,904	-7.0	19,869	13,230	-33.4	58,502	59,674	+2.0

Vandalism	173,617	158,815	-2.8	75,418	64,927	-13.9	98,199	103,888	+5.8
Weapons; carrying, possessing, etc.	109,533	106,080	-3.2	26,395	24,328	-7.8	83,138	81,752	-1.7
Prostitution and commercialized vice	50,082	39,081	-22.0	743	785	-5.7	49,339	38,296	-22.4
Sex offenses (except forcible rape and prostitution)	52,527	45,871	-12.7	9,531	8,106	-15.0	42,996	37,765	-12.2
Drug abuse violations	878,355	1,033,203	+17.6	116,352	109,444	-5.9	762,003	923,759	+21.2
Gambling	5,067	3,289	-35.1	495	360	-27.3	4,572	2,929	-35.9
Offenses against the family and children	85,823	71,305	-16.9	5,765	3,095	-46.3	80,058	68,210	-14.8
Driving under the influence	803,030	788,864	-1.3	11,917	9,867	-17.2	791,113	778,997	-1.5
Liquor laws	375,009	332,231	-11.4	94,257	74,948	-20.5	280,752	257,283	-8.4
Drunkenness	468,796	410,583	-12.4	15,964	11,518	-27.9	452,832	399,065	-11.9
Disorderly conduct	387,534	358,428	-7.5	101,767	104,380	+2.6	285,767	254,048	-11.1
Vagrancy	17,994	16,388	-8.9	1,805	2,719	-50.6	16,189	13,669	-15.6
All other offenses (except traffic)	2,185,863	2,267,145	+3.7	266,238	207,224	-22.2	1,919,625	2,059,921	+7.3
Suspicion	3,463	1,299	-62.5	903	255	-71.8	2,560	1,044	-59.2
Curfew and loitering law violations	104,976	73,217	-30.3	104,976	73,217	-30.3	-	-	-
Runaways	97,320	61,850	-36.4	97,320	61,850	-36.4	-	-	-

1 Does not include suspicion.

2 Violent crimes are offenses of murder and nonnegligent manslaughter, forcible rape, robbery, and aggravated assault. Property crimes are offenses of burglary, larceny-theft, motor vehicle theft, and arson.

* Less than one-tenth of 1 percent.

Source: Crime in the United States, 2007, Federal Bureau of Investigation (2008), table 32.

Ten-Year Arrest Trends, By Sex, 1998–2007

(7,946 agencies; 2007 estimated population 171,876,948; 1998 estimated population 154,013,711)

Offense charged	Male						Female					
	Total			Under 18			Total			Under 18		
	1998	2007	Percent change	1998	2007	Percent change	1998	2007	Percent change	1998	2007	Percent change
TOTAL[1]	6,550,864	6,150,145	-6.1	1,114,987	858,746	-23.0	1,846,201	1,968,052	+6.6	412,694	357,093	-13.5
Murder and nonnegligent manslaughter	7,342	6,519	-11.2	898	702	-21.8	890	782	-12.1	85	51	-40.0
Forcible rape	16,942	13,079	-22.8	2,914	2,005	-31.2	206	133	-35.4	61	29	-52.5
Robbery	61,410	64,004	+4.2	16,813	17,654	+5.0	6,943	8,351	+20.3	1,626	1,896	+16.6
Aggravated assault	234,040	202,588	-13.4	33,029	25,602	-22.5	56,811	54,876	-3.4	9,329	7,712	-17.3
Burglary	170,504	154,607	-9.3	62,217	42,872	-31.1	25,192	27,945	+10.9	7,954	6,031	-24.2
Larceny-theft	514,574	413,125	-19.7	169,452	100,042	-41.0	276,511	275,912	-0.2	89,088	75,519	-15.2
Motor vehicle theft	68,494	51,382	-25.0	24,689	12,701	-48.6	12,431	11,384	-8.4	5,193	2,588	-50.2
Arson	8,606	7,685	-10.7	4,832	3,880	-19.7	1,449	1,409	-2.8	575	511	-11.1
Violent crime[2]	319,734	286,190	-10.5	53,654	45,963	-14.3	64,850	64,142	-1.1	11,101	9,688	-12.7
Property crime[2]	762,178	626,799	-17.8	261,190	159,495	-38.9	315,583	316,650	+0.3	102,810	84,649	-17.7
Other assaults	593,042	560,655	-5.5	96,249	91,986	-4.4	174,996	193,625	+10.6	42,531	46,809	+10.1
Forgery and counterfeiting	41,508	36,217	-12.7	2,754	1,146	-58.4	26,362	22,615	-14.2	1,496	553	-63.0
Fraud	114,751	82,340	-28.2	3,969	2,849	-28.2	99,049	65,645	-33.7	2,097	1,631	-22.2
Embezzlement	5,584	6,849	+22.7	575	618	+7.5	5,531	7,216	+30.5	443	454	+2.5

Offense												
Stolen property; buying, receiving, possessing	66,132	57,865	-12.5	17,289	10,839	-37.5	12,239	15,039	+22.9	2,580	2,421	-6.2
Vandalism	147,331	139,748	-5.1	66,314	56,177	-15.3	26,286	29,067	+10.6	9,104	8,750	-3.9
Weapons; carrying, possessing, etc.	100,973	97,822	-3.1	24,048	21,999	-8.5	8,560	8,258	-3.5	2,347	2,329	-0.8
Prostitution and commercialized vice	20,745	11,485	-44.6	349	170	-51.3	29,337	27,596	-5.9	394	615	+56.1
Sex offenses (except forcible rape and prostitution)	48,658	42,369	-12.9	8,370	7,450	-16.0	3,869	3,502	-9.5	661	655	-0.8
Drug abuse violations	723,435	833,941	+15.3	99,691	91,800	-7.9	154,920	199,262	+28.6	16,661	17,644	+5.9
Gambling	4,568	2,769	-39.4	479	347	-27.6	499	520	+4.2	16	13	-18.8
Offenses against the family and children	67,843	53,754	-20.8	3,648	1,885	-48.3	17,980	17,551	-2.4	2,117	1,210	-42.8
Driving under the influence	676,911	626,371	-7.5	9,849	7,513	-23.7	126,119	162,493	+28.8	2,068	2,354	+13.8
Liquor laws	294,553	242,820	-17.6	66,251	47,505	-28.3	80,456	89,411	+11.1	28,006	27,443	-2.0
Drunkenness	409,100	345,502	-15.5	13,056	3,697	-33.4	59,696	65,081	+9.0	2,908	2,821	-3.0
Disorderly conduct	293,691	261,321	-11.0	72,357	63,051	-4.6	93,843	97,101	+3.5	29,410	35,329	+20.1
Vagrancy	14,231	12,761	-10.6	1,505	1,917	+27.4	3,713	3,627	-2.3	300	802	+167.3
All other offenses (except traffic)	1,732,271	1,744,417	+0.7	199,315	153,225	-23.1	453,592	522,728	+15.2	66,923	53,999	-19.3
Suspicion¹	2,766	1,031	-62.7	686	189	-72.4	697	268	-61.5	217	56	-69.6
Curfew and loitering law violations	73,163	51,113	-30.1	73,163	51,116	-30.1	22,101	22,101	-30.5	31,813	22,101	-30.5
Runaways	40,412	27,028	-33.1	40,412	27,028	-33.1	34,822	34,822	-38.8	56,908	34,822	-38.8

¹ Does not include suspicion.

² Violent crimes are offenses of murder and nonnegligent manslaughter, forcible rape, robbery, and aggravated assault. Property crimes are offenses of burglary, larceny-theft, motor vehicle theft, and arson.

Source: *Crime in the United States, 2007*, Federal Bureau of Investigation (2008), table 33.

APPENDIX B

IN RE GAULT ET AL.

SUPREME COURT OF
THE UNITED STATES

387 U.S. 1
December 6, 1966, Argued
May 15, 1967, Decided

PRIOR HISTORY:
APPEAL FROM THE SUPREME COURT OF ARIZONA.
DISPOSITION: 99 Ariz. 181, 407 P. 2d 760, reversed and remanded.
SYLLABUS: Appellants' 15-year-old son, Gerald Gault, was taken into custody as the result of a complaint that he had made lewd telephone calls. After hearings before a juvenile court judge, Gerald was ordered committed to the State Industrial School as a juvenile delinquent until he should reach majority. Appellants brought a habeas corpus action in the state courts to challenge the constitutionality of the Arizona Juvenile Code and the procedure actually used in Gerald's case, on the ground of denial of various procedural due process rights. The State Supreme Court affirmed dismissal of the writ. Agreeing that the constitutional guarantee of due process applies to proceedings in which juveniles are charged as delinquents, the court held that the Arizona Juvenile Code impliedly includes the requirements of due process in delinquency proceedings, and that such due process requirements were not offended by the procedure leading to Gerald's commitment. *Held:*

1. *Kent v. United States,* 383 U.S. 541, 562 (1966), held "that the [waiver] hearing must measure up to the essentials of due process and fair treatment." This view is reiterated, here in connection with a juvenile court adjudication of "delinquency," as a requirement which is part of the Due

Appendix B

Process Clause of the Fourteenth Amendment of our Constitution. The holding in this case relates only to the adjudicatory stage of the juvenile process, where commitment to a state institution may follow. When proceedings may result in incarceration in an institution of confinement, "it would be extraordinary if our Constitution did not require the procedural regularity and exercise of care implied in the phrase 'due process.'" Pp. 12–31.

2. Due process requires, in such proceedings, that adequate written notice be afforded the child and his parents or guardian. Such notice must inform them "of the specific issues that they must meet" and must be given "at the earliest practicable time, and in any event sufficiently in advance of the hearing to permit preparation." Notice here was neither timely nor adequately specific, nor was there waiver of the right to constitutionally adequate notice. Pp. 31–34.

3. In such proceedings the child and his parents must be advised of their right to be represented by counsel and, if they are unable to afford counsel, that counsel will be appointed to represent the child. Mrs. Gault's statement at the habeas corpus hearing that she had known she could employ counsel, is not "an 'intentional relinquishment or abandonment' of a fully known right." Pp. 34–42.

4. The constitutional privilege against self-incrimination is applicable in such proceedings: "an admission by the juvenile may [not] be used against him in the absence of clear and unequivocal evidence that the admission was made with knowledge that he was not obliged to speak and would not be penalized for remaining silent." "The availability of the privilege does not turn upon the type of proceeding in which its protection is invoked, but upon the nature of the statement or admission and the exposure which it invites. . . . Juvenile proceedings to determine 'delinquency,' which may lead to commitment to a state institution, must be regarded as 'criminal' for purposes of the privilege against self-incrimination." Furthermore, experience has shown that "admissions and confessions by juveniles require special caution" as to their reliability and voluntariness, and "it would indeed be surprising if the privilege against self-incrimination were available to hardened criminals but not to children." "Special problems may arise with respect to waiver of the privilege by or on behalf of children, and . . . there may well be some differences in technique—but not in principle—depending upon the age of the child and the presence and competence of parents. . . . If counsel was not present for some permissible reason when an admission was obtained, the greatest care must be taken to assure that the admission was voluntary. . . ." Gerald's admissions did not measure up to these standards, and could not properly be used as a basis for the judgment against him. Pp. 44–56.

5. Absent a valid confession, a juvenile in such proceedings must be afforded the rights of confrontation and sworn testimony of witnesses available for cross-examination. Pp. 56–57.

6. Other questions raised by appellants, including the absence of provision for appellate review of a delinquency adjudication, and a transcript of the proceedings, are not ruled upon. Pp. 57–58.

COUNSEL: Norman Dorsen argued the cause for appellants. With him on the brief were Melvin L. Wulf, Amelia D. Lewis and Daniel A. Rezneck.

Frank A. Parks, Assistant Attorney General of Arizona, argued the cause for appellee, pro hac vice, by special leave of Court. With him on the brief was Darrell F. Smith, Attorney General.

Merritt W. Green argued the cause for the Ohio Association of Juvenile Court Judges, as amicus curiae, urging affirmance. With him on the brief was Leo G. Chimo.

The Kansas Association of Probate and Juvenile Judges joined the appellee's brief and the brief of the Ohio Association of Juvenile Court Judges.

Briefs of amici curiae, urging reversal, were filed by L. Michael Getty, James J. Doherty and Marshall J. Hartman for the National Legal Aid and Defender Association, and by Edward Q. Carr, Jr., and Nanette Dembitz for the Legal Aid Society and Citizens' Committee for Children of New York, Inc.

Nicholas N. Kittrie filed a brief for the American Parents Committee, as amicus curiae.

JUDGES: Warren, Black, Douglas, Clark, Harlan, Brennan, Stewart, White, Fortas
OPINION BY: FORTAS
OPINION: MR. JUSTICE FORTAS delivered the opinion of the Court.

This is an appeal under 28 U. S. C. § 1257 (2) from a judgment of the Supreme Court of Arizona affirming the dismissal of a petition for a writ of habeas corpus. 99 Ariz. 181, 407 P. 2d 760 (1965). The petition sought the release of Gerald Francis Gault, appellants' 15-year-old son, who had been committed as a juvenile delinquent to the State Industrial School by the Juvenile Court of Gila County, Arizona. The Supreme Court of Arizona affirmed dismissal of the writ against various arguments which included an attack upon the constitutionality of the Arizona Juvenile Code because of its alleged denial of procedural due process rights to juveniles charged with being "delinquents." The court agreed that the constitutional guarantee of due process of law is applicable in such proceedings. It held that Arizona's Juvenile Code is to be read as "impliedly" implementing the "due process concept." It then proceeded to identify and describe "the particular elements which constitute due process in a juvenile hearing." It concluded that the proceedings ending in commitment of Gerald Gault did not offend those requirements. We do not agree, and we reverse. We begin with a statement of the facts.

I.

On Monday, June 8, 1964, at about 10 a. m., Gerald Francis Gault and a friend, Ronald Lewis, were taken into custody by the Sheriff of Gila County. Gerald was then still subject to a six months' probation order which had been entered on February 25, 1964, as a result of his having been in the company of another boy who had stolen a wallet from a lady's purse. The police action on June 8 was taken as the result of a verbal complaint by a neighbor of the boys, Mrs. Cook, about a telephone call made to her in which the caller or callers made lewd or indecent remarks. It will suffice for purposes of this opinion to say that the remarks or questions put to her were of the irritatingly offensive, adolescent, sex variety.

At the time Gerald was picked up, his mother and father were both at work. No notice that Gerald was being taken into custody was left at the home. No other steps were taken to advise them that their son had, in effect, been arrested. Gerald was taken to the Children's Detention Home. When his mother arrived home at about 6 o'clock, Gerald was not there. Gerald's older brother was sent to look for him at the trailer home of the Lewis family. He apparently learned then that Gerald was in custody. He so informed his mother. The two of them went to the Detention Home. The deputy probation officer, Flagg, who was also superintendent of the Detention Home, told Mrs. Gault "why Jerry was there" and said that a hearing would be held in Juvenile Court at 3 o'clock the following day, June 9.

Officer Flagg filed a petition with the court on the hearing day, June 9, 1964. It was not served on the Gaults. Indeed, none of them saw this petition until the habeas corpus hearing on August 17, 1964. The petition was entirely formal. It made no reference to any factual basis for the judicial action which it initiated. It recited only that "said minor is under the age of eighteen years, and is in need of the protection of this Honorable Court; [and that] said minor is a delinquent minor." It prayed for a hearing and an order regarding "the care and custody of said minor." Officer Flagg executed a formal affidavit in support of the petition.

On June 9, Gerald, his mother, his older brother, and Probation Officers Flagg and Henderson appeared before the Juvenile Judge in chambers. Gerald's father was not there. He was at work out of the city. Mrs. Cook, the complainant, was not there. No one was sworn at this hearing. No transcript or recording was made. No memorandum or record of the substance of the proceedings was prepared. Our information about the proceedings and the subsequent hearing on June 15, derives entirely from the testimony of the Juvenile Court Judge, Mr. and Mrs. Gault and Officer Flagg at the habeas corpus proceeding conducted two months later. From this, it appears that at the June 9 hearing Gerald was questioned by the judge about the telephone call. There was conflict as to what he said. His mother recalled that Gerald said he only dialed Mrs. Cook's number and handed the telephone to his friend, Ronald. Officer Flagg recalled that Gerald had admitted making the lewd remarks. Judge McGhee testified that Gerald "admitted making one of these [lewd] statements." At the conclusion of the hearing, the judge said he would "think about it." Gerald was taken back to the Detention Home. He was not sent to his own home with his parents. On June 11 or 12, after having been detained since June 8, Gerald was released and driven home. There is no explanation in the record as to why he was kept in the Detention Home or why he was released. At 5 p. m. on the day of Gerald's release, Mrs. Gault received a note signed by Officer Flagg. It was on plain paper, not letterhead. Its entire text was as follows:

"Mrs. Gault:
Judge McGhee has set Monday June 15, 1964 at 11:00 A. M. as the date and time for further Hearings on Gerald's delinquency."

At the appointed time on Monday, June 15, Gerald, his father and mother, Ronald Lewis and his father, and Officers Flagg and Henderson were present before Judge McGhee. Witnesses at the habeas corpus proceeding differed in their recollections of Gerald's testimony at the June 15 hearing. Mr. and Mrs. Gault recalled that Gerald again testified that he had only dialed the number and that the other boy had made the remarks. Officer Flagg agreed that at this hearing Gerald did not admit making the lewd remarks. But Judge McGhee recalled that "there was some admission again of some of the lewd statements. He—he didn't admit any of the more serious lewd statements." Again, the complainant, Mrs. Cook, was not present. Mrs. Gault asked that Mrs. Cook be present "so she could see which boy that done the talking, the dirty talking over the phone." The Juvenile Judge said "she didn't have to be present at that hearing." The judge did not speak to Mrs. Cook or communicate with her at any time. Probation Officer Flagg had talked to her once—over the telephone on June 9.

At this June 15 hearing a "referral report" made by the probation officers was filed with the court, although not disclosed to Gerald or his parents. This listed the charge as "Lewd Phone Calls." At the conclusion of the hearing, the judge committed Gerald as a juvenile delinquent to the State Industrial School "for the period of his minority [that is, until 21], unless sooner discharged by due process of law." An order to that effect was entered. It recites that "after a full hearing and due deliberation the Court finds that said minor is a delinquent child, and that said minor is of the age of 15 years."

No appeal is permitted by Arizona law in juvenile cases. On August 3, 1964, a petition for a writ of habeas corpus was filed with the Supreme Court of Arizona and referred by it to the Superior Court for hearing.

At the habeas corpus hearing on August 17, Judge McGhee was vigorously cross-examined as to the basis for his actions. He testified that he had taken into account the fact that Gerald was on probation. He was asked "under what section of . . . the code you found the boy delinquent?"

His answer is set forth in the margin. In substance, he concluded that Gerald came within ARS § 8-201-6 (a), which specifies that a "delinquent child" includes one "who has violated a law of the state or an ordinance or regulation of a political subdivision thereof." The law which Gerald was found to have violated is ARS § 13-377. This section of the Arizona Criminal Code provides that a person who "in the presence or hearing of any woman or child . . . uses vulgar, abusive or obscene language, is guilty of a misdemeanor. . . ." The penalty specified in the Criminal Code, which would apply to an adult, is $5 to $50, or imprisonment for not more than two months. The judge also testified that he acted under ARS § 8-201-6 (d) which includes in the definition of a "delinquent child" one who, as the judge phrased it, is "habitually involved in immoral matters."

Asked about the basis for his conclusion that Gerald was "habitually involved in immoral matters," the judge testified, somewhat vaguely, that two years earlier, on July 2, 1962, a "referral" was made concerning Gerald, "where the boy had stolen a baseball glove from another boy and lied to the Police Department about it." The judge said there was "no hearing," and "no accusation" relating to this incident, "because of lack of material foundation." But it seems to have remained in his mind as a relevant factor. The judge also testified that Gerald had admitted making other nuisance phone calls in the past which, as the judge recalled the boy's testimony, were "silly calls, or funny calls, or something like that."

The Superior Court dismissed the writ, and appellants sought review in the Arizona Supreme Court. That court stated that it considered appellants' assignments of error as urging (1) that the Juvenile Code, ARS § 8-201 to § 8-239, is unconstitutional because it does not require that parents and children be apprised of the specific charges, does not require proper notice of a hearing, and does not provide for an appeal; and (2) that the proceedings and order relating to Gerald constituted a denial of due process of law because of the absence of adequate notice of the charge and the hearing; failure to notify appellants of certain constitutional rights including the rights to counsel and to confrontation, and the privilege against self-incrimination; the use of unsworn hearsay testimony; and the failure to make a record of the proceedings. Appellants further asserted that it was error for the

Juvenile Court to remove Gerald from the custody of his parents without a showing and finding of their unsuitability, and alleged a miscellany of other errors under state law.

The Supreme Court handed down an elaborate and wide-ranging opinion affirming dismissal of the writ and stating the court's conclusions as to the issues raised by appellants and other aspects of the juvenile process. In their jurisdictional statement and brief in this Court, appellants do not urge upon us all of the points passed upon by the Supreme Court of Arizona. They urge that we hold the Juvenile Code of Arizona invalid on its face or as applied in this case because, contrary to the Due Process Clause of the Fourteenth Amendment, the juvenile is taken from the custody of his parents and committed to a state institution pursuant to proceedings in which the Juvenile Court has virtually unlimited discretion, and in which the following basic rights are denied:

1. Notice of the charges;
2. Right to counsel;
3. Right to confrontation and cross-examination;
4. Privilege against self-incrimination;
5. Right to a transcript of the proceedings; and
6. Right to appellate review.

We shall not consider other issues which were passed upon by the Supreme Court of Arizona. We emphasize that we indicate no opinion as to whether the decision of that court with respect to such other issues does or does not conflict with requirements of the Federal Constitution.

II.

The Supreme Court of Arizona held that due process of law is requisite to the constitutional validity of proceedings in which a court reaches the conclusion that a juvenile has been at fault, has engaged in conduct prohibited by law, or has otherwise misbehaved with the consequence that he is committed to an institution in which his freedom is curtailed. This conclusion is in accord with the decisions of a number of courts under both federal and state constitutions.

This Court has not heretofore decided the precise question. In *Kent* v. *United States*, 383 U.S. 541 (1966), we considered the requirements for a valid waiver of the "exclusive" jurisdiction of the Juvenile Court of the District of Columbia so that a juvenile could be tried in the adult criminal court of the District. Although our decision turned upon the language of the statute, we emphasized the necessity that "the basic requirements of due process and fairness" be satisfied in such proceedings. *Haley* v. *Ohio*, 332

Appendix B

U.S. 596 (1948), involved the admissibility, in a state criminal court of general jurisdiction, of a confession by a 15-year-old boy. The Court held that the Fourteenth Amendment applied to prohibit the use of the coerced confession. MR. JUSTICE DOUGLAS said, "Neither man nor child can be allowed to stand condemned by methods which flout constitutional requirements of due process of law." To the same effect is *Gallegos* v. *Colorado*, 370 U.S. 49 (1962). Accordingly, while these cases relate only to restricted aspects of the subject, they unmistakably indicate that, whatever may be their precise impact, neither the Fourteenth Amendment nor the Bill of Rights is for adults alone.

We do not in this opinion consider the impact of these constitutional provisions upon the totality of the relationship of the juvenile and the state. We do not even consider the entire process relating to juvenile "delinquents." For example, we are not here concerned with the procedures or constitutional rights applicable to the pre-judicial stages of the juvenile process, nor do we direct our attention to the post-adjudicative or dispositional process. We consider only the problems presented to us by this case. These relate to the proceedings by which a determination is made as to whether a juvenile is a "delinquent" as a result of alleged misconduct on his part, with the consequence that he may be committed to a state institution. As to these proceedings, there appears to be little current dissent from the proposition that the Due Process Clause has a role to play. The problem is to ascertain the precise impact of the due process requirement upon such proceedings.

From the inception of the juvenile court system, wide differences have been tolerated—indeed insisted upon—between the procedural rights accorded to adults and those of juveniles. In practically all jurisdictions, there are rights granted to adults which are withheld from juveniles. In addition to the specific problems involved in the present case, for example, it has been held that the juvenile is not entitled to bail, to indictment by grand jury, to a public trial or to trial by jury. It is frequent practice that rules governing the arrest and interrogation of adults by the police are not observed in the case of juveniles.

The history and theory underlying this development are well-known, but a recapitulation is necessary for purposes of this opinion. The Juvenile Court movement began in this country at the end of the last century. From the juvenile court statute adopted in Illinois in 1899, the system has spread to every State in the Union, the District of Columbia, and Puerto Rico. The constitutionality of Juvenile Court laws has been sustained in over 40 jurisdictions against a variety of attacks.

The early reformers were appalled by adult procedures and penalties, and by the fact that children could be given long prison sentences and mixed in jails with hardened criminals. They were profoundly convinced that society's duty to the child could not be confined by the concept of justice alone. They believed that society's role was not to ascertain whether the child was "guilty" or "innocent," but "What is he, how has he become what he is, and what had best be done in his interest and in the interest of the state to save him from a downward career." The child—essentially good, as they saw it—was to be made "to feel that he is the object of [the state's] care and solicitude," not that he was under arrest or on trial. The rules of criminal procedure were therefore altogether inapplicable. The apparent rigidities, technicalities, and harshness which they observed in both substantive and procedural criminal law were therefore to be discarded. The idea of crime and punishment was to be abandoned. The child was to be "treated" and "rehabilitated" and the procedures, from apprehension through institutionalization, were to be "clinical" rather than punitive.

These results were to be achieved, without coming to conceptual and constitutional grief, by insisting that the proceedings were not adversary, but that the state was proceeding as *parens patriae*. The Latin phrase proved to be a great help to those who sought to rationalize the exclusion of juveniles from the constitutional scheme; but its meaning is murky and its historic credentials are of dubious relevance. The phrase was taken from chancery practice, where, however, it was used to describe the power of the state to act *in loco parentis* for the purpose of protecting the property interests and the person of the child. But there is no trace of the doctrine in the history of criminal jurisprudence. At common law, children under seven were considered incapable of possessing criminal intent. Beyond that age, they were subjected to arrest, trial, and in theory to punishment like adult offenders. In these old days, the state was not deemed to have authority to accord them fewer procedural rights than adults.

The right of the state, as *parens patriae*, to deny to the child procedural rights available to his elders was elaborated by the assertion that a child, unlike an adult, has a right "not to liberty but to custody." He can be made to attorn to his parents, to go to school, etc. If his parents default in effectively performing their custodial functions—that is, if the child is "delinquent"—the state may intervene. In doing so, it does not deprive the child of any rights, because he has none. It merely provides the "custody" to which the child is entitled. On this basis, proceedings involving juveniles were described as "civil" not "criminal" and therefore not subject to the requirements which restrict the state when it seeks to deprive a person of his liberty.

Accordingly, the highest motives and most enlightened impulses led to a peculiar system for juveniles, unknown to our law in any comparable context. The constitutional and theoretical basis for this peculiar system is—to say the least—debatable. And in practice, as we remarked in the *Kent* case, *supra*, the results have not been entirely satisfactory. Juvenile Court history has again demonstrated that unbridled discretion, however benevolently motivated, is frequently a poor substitute for principle and procedure. In 1937, Dean Pound wrote: "The powers of the Star Chamber were a trifle in comparison with those of our juvenile courts. . . ." The absence of substantive standards has not necessarily meant that children receive careful, compassionate, individualized treatment. The absence of procedural rules based upon constitutional principle has not always produced fair, efficient, and effective procedures. Departures from established principles of due process have frequently resulted not in enlightened procedure, but in arbitrariness. The Chairman of the Pennsylvania Council of Juvenile Court Judges has recently observed: "Unfortunately, loose procedures, high-handed methods and crowded court calendars, either singly or in combination, all too often, have resulted in depriving some juveniles of fundamental rights that have resulted in a denial of due process."

Failure to observe the fundamental requirements of due process has resulted in instances, which might have been avoided, of unfairness to individuals and inadequate or inaccurate findings of fact and unfortunate prescriptions of remedy. Due process of law is the primary and indispensable foundation of individual freedom. It is the basic and essential term in the social compact which defines the rights of the individual and delimits the powers which the state may exercise. As Mr. Justice Frankfurter has said: "The history of American freedom is, in no small measure, the history of procedure." But in addition, the procedural rules which have been fashioned from the generality of due process are our best instruments for the distillation and evaluation of essential facts from the conflicting welter of data that life and our adversary methods present. It is these instruments of due process which enhance the possibility that truth will emerge from the confrontation of opposing versions and conflicting data. "Procedure is to law what 'scientific method' is to science."

It is claimed that juveniles obtain benefits from the special procedures applicable to them which more than offset the disadvantages of denial of the substance of normal due process. As we shall discuss, the observance of due process standards, intelligently and not ruthlessly administered, will not compel the States to abandon or displace any of the substantive benefits of the juvenile process. But it is important, we think, that the claimed benefits of the juvenile process should be candidly appraised. Neither sentiment nor folklore should cause us to shut our eyes, for example, to such startling findings as that reported in an exceptionally reliable study of repeaters or recidivism conducted by the Stanford Research Institute for the President's Commission on Crime in the District of Columbia. This Commission's Report states:

In fiscal 1966 approximately 66 percent of the 16- and 17-year-old juveniles referred to the court by the Youth Aid Division had been before the court previously. In 1965, 56 percent of those in the Receiving Home were repeaters. The SRI study revealed that 61 percent of the sample Juvenile Court referrals in 1965 had been previously referred at least once and that 42 percent had been referred at least twice before. Id., at 773.

Certainly, these figures and the high crime rates among juveniles to which we have referred *(supra)*, could not lead us to conclude that the absence of constitutional protections reduces crime, or that the juvenile system, functioning free of constitutional inhibitions as it has largely done, is effective to reduce crime or rehabilitate offenders. We do not mean by this to denigrate the juvenile court process or to suggest that there are not aspects of the juvenile system relating to offenders which are valuable. But the features of the juvenile system which its proponents have asserted are of unique benefit will not be impaired by constitutional domestication. For example, the commendable principles relating to the processing and treatment of juveniles separately from adults are in no way involved or affected by the procedural issues under discussion. Further, we are told that one of the important benefits of the special juvenile court procedures is that they avoid classifying the juvenile as a "criminal." The juvenile offender is now classed as a "delinquent." There is, of course, no reason why this should not continue. It is disconcerting, however, that this term has come to involve only slightly less stigma than the term "criminal" applied to adults. It is also emphasized that in practically all jurisdictions, statutes provide that an adjudication of the child as a delinquent shall not operate as a civil disability or disqualify him for civil service appointment. There is no reason why the application of due process requirements should interfere with such provisions.

Beyond this, it is frequently said that juveniles are protected by the process from disclosure of their deviational behavior. As the Supreme Court of Arizona phrased it in the present case, the summary procedures of Juvenile Courts are sometimes defended by a statement that it is the law's policy "to hide youthful errors from the full gaze of the public and bury them in the graveyard of the forgotten past." This claim of secrecy, however, is more rhetoric than reality. Disclosure of court records is discretionary with the judge in most jurisdictions. Statutory restrictions almost invariably apply only to the court records, and even as to those the evidence is that many courts routinely furnish information to the FBI and the military, and on request to government agencies and even to private employers. Of more importance are police records. In most States the police keep a complete file of juvenile "police contacts" and have complete discretion as to disclosure of juvenile records. Police departments receive requests for information from the FBI and other law-enforcement agencies, the Armed Forces, and social service agencies, and most of them generally comply. Private employers word their application forms to produce information concerning juvenile arrests and court proceedings, and in some jurisdictions information concerning juvenile police contacts is furnished private employers as well as government agencies.

In any event, there is no reason why, consistently with due process, a State cannot continue, if it deems it appropriate, to provide and to improve provision for the confidentiality of records of police contacts and court action relating to juveniles. It is interesting to note, however, that the Arizona Supreme Court used the confidentiality argument as a justification for the type of notice which is here attacked as inadequate for due process purposes. The parents were given merely general notice that their child was charged with "delinquency." No facts were specified. The Arizona court held, however, as we shall discuss, that in addition to this general "notice," the child and his parents must be advised "of the facts involved in the case" no later than the initial hearing by the judge. Obviously, this does not "bury" the word about the child's transgressions. It merely defers the time of disclosure to a point when it is of limited use to the child or his parents in preparing his defense or explanation.

Further, it is urged that the juvenile benefits from informal proceedings in the court. The early conception of the Juvenile Court proceeding was one in which a fatherly judge touched the heart and conscience of the erring youth by talking over his problems, by paternal advice and admonition, and in which, in extreme situations, benevolent and wise institutions of the State provided guidance and help "to save him from a downward career." Then, as now, goodwill and compassion were admirably prevalent. But recent studies have, with surprising unanimity, entered sharp dissent as to the validity of this gentle conception. They suggest that the appearance as well as the actuality of fairness, impartiality and orderliness—in short, the essentials of due process—may be a more impressive and more therapeutic attitude so far as the juvenile is concerned. For example, in a recent study, the sociologists Wheeler and Cottrell observe that when the procedural laxness of the *"parens patriae"* attitude is followed by stern disciplining, the contrast may have an adverse effect upon the child, who feels that he has been deceived or enticed. They conclude as follows: "Unless appropriate due process of law is followed, even the juvenile who has violated the law may not feel that he is being fairly treated and may therefore resist the rehabilitative efforts of court personnel." Of course, it is not suggested that juvenile court judges should fail appropriately to take account, in their demeanor and conduct, of the emotional and psychological attitude of the juveniles with whom they are confronted. While due process requirements will, in some instances, introduce a degree of order and regularity to Juvenile Court proceedings to determine delinquency, and in contested cases will introduce some elements of the adversary system, nothing will require that the conception of the kindly juvenile judge be replaced by its opposite, nor do we here rule upon the question whether ordinary due process requirements must be observed with respect to hearings to determine the disposition of the delinquent child.

Ultimately, however, we confront the reality of that portion of the Juvenile Court process with which we deal in this case. A boy is charged with misconduct. The boy is committed to an institution where he may be restrained of liberty for years. It is of no constitutional consequence—and of limited practical meaning—that the institution to which he is committed is called an Industrial School. The fact of the matter is that, however euphemistic the title, a "receiving home" or an "industrial school" for juveniles is an institution of confinement in which the child is incarcerated for a greater or lesser time. His world becomes "a building with whitewashed walls, regimented routine and institutional hours. . . ." Instead of mother and father and sisters and brothers and friends and classmates, his world is peopled by guards, custodians, state employees, and "delinquents" confined with him for anything from waywardness to rape and homicide.

In view of this, it would be extraordinary if our Constitution did not require the procedural regularity and the exercise of care implied in the phrase "due process." Under our Constitution, the condition of being a boy does not justify a kangaroo court. The traditional ideas of Juvenile Court procedure, indeed, contemplated that time would be available and care would be used to establish precisely what the juvenile did and why he did it—was it a prank of adolescence or a brutal act threatening serious consequences to himself or society unless corrected? Under traditional notions, one would assume that in a case like that of Gerald Gault, where the juvenile appears to have a home, a working mother and father, and an older brother, the Juvenile Judge would have made a careful inquiry and judgment as to the possibility that the boy could be disciplined and dealt with at home, despite his previous transgressions. Indeed, so far as appears in the record before us, except for some conversation with Gerald about his school work and his "wanting to go to . . . Grand Canyon with his father," the points to which the judge directed his attention were little different from those that would be involved in determining any charge of violation of a penal statute. The essential difference between Gerald's case and a normal criminal case is that safeguards available to adults were discarded in Gerald's case. The summary procedure as well as the long commitment was possible because Gerald was 15 years of age instead of over 18.

If Gerald had been over 18, he would not have been subject to Juvenile Court proceedings. For the particular offense immediately involved, the maximum punishment would have been a fine of $5 to $50, or imprisonment in jail for not more than two months. Instead, he was committed to custody for a maximum of six years. If he had been over 18 and had committed an offense to which such a sentence might apply, he would have been entitled to substantial rights under the Constitution of the United States as well as under Arizona's laws and constitution. The United States Constitution would guarantee him rights and protections with respect to arrest, search and seizure, and pretrial interrogation. It would assure him of specific notice of the charges and adequate time to decide his course of action and to prepare his defense. He would be entitled to clear advice that he could be represented by counsel, and, at least if a felony were involved, the State would be required to provide counsel if his parents were unable to afford it. If the court acted on the basis of his confession, careful procedures would be required to assure its voluntariness. If the case went to trial, confrontation and opportunity for cross-examination would be guaranteed. So wide a gulf between the State's treatment of the adult and of the child requires a bridge sturdier than mere verbiage, and reasons more persuasive than cliche can provide. As Wheeler and Cottrell have put it, "The rhetoric of the juvenile court movement has developed without any necessarily close correspondence to the realities of court and institutional routines."

In *Kent* v. *United States, supra,* we stated that the Juvenile Court Judge's exercise of the power of the state as *parens patriae* was not unlimited. We said that "the admonition to function in a 'parental' relationship is not an invitation to procedural arbitrariness." With respect to the waiver by the Juvenile Court to the adult court of jurisdiction over an offense committed by a youth, we said that "there is no place in our system of law for reaching a result of such tremendous consequences without ceremony—without hearing, without effective assistance of counsel, without a statement of reasons." We announced with respect to such waiver proceedings that while "We do not mean . . . to indicate that the hearing to be held must conform with all of the requirements of a criminal trial or even of the usual administrative hearing; but we do hold that the hearing must measure up to the essentials of due process and fair treatment." We reiterate this view, here in connection with a juvenile court adjudication of "delinquency," as a requirement which is part of the Due Process Clause of the Fourteenth Amendment of our Constitution.

We now turn to the specific issues which are presented to us in the present case.

III.

NOTICE OF CHARGES.

Appellants allege that the Arizona Juvenile Code is unconstitutional or alternatively that the proceedings before the Juvenile Court were constitutionally defective because of failure to provide adequate notice of the hearings. No notice was given to Gerald's parents when he was taken into custody on Monday, June 8. On that night, when Mrs. Gault went to the Detention Home, she was orally informed that there would be a hearing the next afternoon and was told the reason why Gerald was in custody. The only written notice Gerald's parents received at any time was a note on plain paper from Officer Flagg delivered on Thursday or Friday, June 11 or 12, to the effect that the judge had set Monday, June 15, "for further Hearings on Gerald's delinquency."

A "petition" was filed with the court on June 9 by Officer Flagg, reciting only that he was informed and believed that "said minor is a delinquent minor and that it is necessary that some order be made by the Honorable Court for said minor's welfare." The applicable Arizona statute provides for a petition to be filed in Juvenile Court, alleging in general terms that the child is "neglected, dependent or delinquent." The statute explicitly states that such a general allegation is sufficient, "without alleging the facts." There is no requirement that the petition be served and it was not served upon, given to, or shown to Gerald or his parents.

The Supreme Court of Arizona rejected appellants' claim that due process was denied because of inadequate notice. It stated that "Mrs. Gault knew the exact nature of the charge against Gerald from the day he was taken to the detention home." The court also pointed out that the Gaults appeared at the two hearings "without objection." The court held that because "the policy of the juvenile law is to hide youthful errors from the full gaze of the public and bury them in the graveyard of the forgotten past," advance notice of the specific charges or basis for taking the juvenile into custody and for the hearing is not necessary. It held that the appropriate rule is that "the infant and his parent or guardian will receive a petition only reciting a conclusion of delinquency. But no later than the initial hearing by the judge, they must be advised of the facts involved in the case. If the charges are denied, they must be given a reasonable period of time to prepare."

We cannot agree with the court's conclusion that adequate notice was given in this case. Notice, to comply with due process requirements, must be given sufficiently in advance of scheduled court proceedings so that reasonable opportunity to prepare will be afforded, and it must "set forth the alleged misconduct with particularity." It is obvious, as we have discussed above, that no purpose of shielding the child from the public stigma of knowledge of his having been taken into custody and scheduled for hearing is served by the procedure approved by the court below. The "initial hearing" in the present case was a hearing on the merits. Notice at that time is not timely; and even if there were a conceivable purpose served by the deferral proposed by the court below, it would have to yield to the requirements that the child and his parents or guardian be notified, in writing, of the specific charge or factual allegations to be considered at the hearing, and that such written notice be given at the earliest practicable time, and in any event sufficiently in advance of the hearing to permit preparation. Due process of law requires notice of the sort we have described—that is, notice which would be deemed constitutionally adequate in a civil or criminal proceeding. It does not allow a hearing to be held in which a youth's freedom and his parents' right to his custody are at stake without giving them timely notice, in advance of the hearing, of the specific issues that they must meet. Nor, in the circumstances of this case, can it reasonably be said that the requirement of notice was waived.

IV.

RIGHT TO COUNSEL.

Appellants charge that the Juvenile Court proceedings were fatally defective because the court did not advise Gerald or his parents of their right to counsel, and proceeded with the hearing, the adjudication of delinquency and the order of commitment in the absence of counsel for the child and his parents or an express waiver of the right thereto. The Supreme Court of Arizona pointed out that "there is disagreement [among the various jurisdictions] as to whether the court must advise the infant that he has a right to counsel." It noted its own decision in *Arizona State Dept. of Public Welfare* v. *Barlow*, 80 Ariz. 249, 296 P. 2d 298 (1956), to the effect "that *the parents* of an infant in a juvenile proceeding cannot be denied representation by counsel of their choosing." (Emphasis added.) It referred to a provision of the Juvenile Code which it characterized as requiring "that the probation officer shall look after the interests of neglected, delinquent and dependent children," including representing their interests in court. The court argued that "The parent and the probation officer may be relied upon to protect the infant's interests." Accordingly it rejected the proposition that "due process requires that an infant have a right to counsel." It said that juvenile courts have the discretion, but not the duty, to allow such representation; it referred specifically to the situation in which the Juvenile Court discerns conflict between the child and his parents as an instance in which this discretion might be exercised. We do not agree. Probation officers, in the Arizona scheme, are also arresting officers. They initiate proceedings and file petitions which they verify, as here, alleging the delinquency of the child; and they testify, as here, against the child. And here the probation officer was also superintendent of the Detention Home. The probation officer cannot act as counsel for the child. His role in the adjudicatory hearing, by statute and in fact, is as arresting officer and witness against the child. Nor can the judge represent the child. There is no material difference in this respect between adult and juvenile proceedings of the sort here involved. In adult proceedings, this contention has been foreclosed by decisions of this Court. A proceeding where the issue is whether the child will be found to be "delinquent" and subjected to the loss of his liberty for years is comparable in seriousness to a felony prosecution. The juvenile needs the assistance of counsel to cope with problems of law, to make skilled inquiry into the facts, to insist upon regularity of the proceedings, and to ascertain whether he has a defense and to prepare and submit it. The child "requires the guiding hand of counsel at every step in the proceedings against him." Just as in *Kent* v. *United States, supra,* at 561–562, we indicated our agreement with the United States Court of Appeals for the District of Columbia Circuit that the assistance of counsel is essential for purposes of waiver proceedings, so we hold now that it is equally essential for the determination of delinquency, carrying with it the awesome prospect of incarceration in a state institution until the juvenile reaches the age of 21.

During the last decade, court decisions, experts, and legislatures have demonstrated increasing recognition of this view. In at least one-third of the States, statutes now provide for the right of representation by retained counsel in juvenile delinquency proceedings, notice of the right, or assignment of counsel, or a combination of these. In other States, court rules have similar provisions.

The President's Crime Commission has recently recommended that in order to assure "procedural justice for the child," it is necessary that "Counsel . . . be appointed as a matter of course wherever coercive action is a possibility, without requiring any affirmative choice by child or parent." As stated by the authoritative "Standards for Juvenile and Family Courts," published by the Children's Bureau of the United States Department of Health, Education, and Welfare:

> *As a component part of a fair hearing required by due process guaranteed under the 14th amendment, notice of the right to counsel should be required at all hearings and counsel provided upon request when the family is financially unable to employ counsel. Standards, p. 57.*

This statement was "reviewed" by the National Council of Juvenile Court Judges at its 1965 Convention and they "found no fault" with it. The New York Family Court Act contains the following statement:

> *This act declares that minors have a right to the assistance of counsel of their own choosing or of law guardians in neglect proceedings under article three and in proceedings to determine juvenile delinquency and whether a person is in need of supervision under article seven. This declaration is based on a finding that counsel is often indispensable to a practical realization of due process of law and may be helpful in making reasoned determinations of fact and proper orders of disposition.*

The Act provides that "At the commencement of any hearing" under the delinquency article of the statute, the juvenile and his parent shall be advised of the juvenile's "right to be represented by counsel chosen by him or his parent . . . or by a law guardian assigned by the court. . . ." The California Act (1961) also requires appointment of counsel.

We conclude that the Due Process Clause of the Fourteenth Amendment requires that in respect of proceedings to determine delinquency which may result in commitment to an institution in which the juvenile's freedom is curtailed, the child and his parents must be notified of the child's right to be represented by counsel retained by them, or if they are unable to afford counsel, that counsel will be appointed to represent the child.

At the habeas corpus proceeding, Mrs. Gault testified that she knew that she could have appeared with counsel at the juvenile hearing. This knowledge is not a waiver of the right to counsel which she and her juvenile son had, as we have defined it. They had a right expressly to be advised that they might retain counsel and to be confronted with the need for specific consideration of whether they did or did not choose to waive the right. If they were unable to afford to employ counsel, they were entitled in view of the seriousness of the charge and the potential commitment, to appointed counsel, unless they chose waiver. Mrs. Gault's knowledge that she could employ counsel was not an "intentional relinquishment or abandonment" of a fully known right.

V.

CONFRONTATION, SELF-INCRIMINATION, CROSS-EXAMINATION.

Appellants urge that the writ of habeas corpus should have been granted because of the denial of the rights of confrontation and cross-examination in the Juvenile Court hearings, and because the privilege against self-incrimination was not observed. The Juvenile Court Judge testified at the habeas corpus hearing that he had proceeded on the basis of Gerald's admissions at the two hearings. Appellants attack this on the ground that the admissions were obtained in disregard of the privilege against self-incrimination. If the confession is disregarded, appellants argue that the delinquency conclusion, since it was fundamentally based on a finding that Gerald had made lewd remarks during the phone call to Mrs. Cook, is fatally defective for failure to accord the rights of confrontation and cross-examination which the Due Process Clause of the Fourteenth Amendment of the Federal Constitution guarantees in state proceedings generally.

Our first question, then, is whether Gerald's admission was improperly obtained and relied on as the basis of decision, in conflict with the Federal Constitution. For this purpose, it is necessary briefly to recall the relevant facts.

Mrs. Cook, the complainant, and the recipient of the alleged telephone call, was not called as a witness. Gerald's mother asked the Juvenile Court Judge why Mrs. Cook was not present and the judge replied that "she didn't have to be present." So far as appears, Mrs. Cook was spoken to only once, by Officer Flagg, and this was by telephone. The judge did not speak with her on any occasion. Gerald had been questioned by the probation officer after having been taken into custody. The exact circumstances of this questioning do not appear but any admissions Gerald may have made at this time do not appear in the record. Gerald was also questioned by the Juvenile Court Judge at each of the two hearings. The judge testified in the habeas corpus proceeding that Gerald admitted making "some of the lewd statements . . . [but not] any of the more serious lewd statements." There was conflict and uncertainty among the witnesses at the habeas corpus proceeding—the Juvenile Court Judge, Mr. and Mrs. Gault, and the probation officer—as to what Gerald did or did not admit.

We shall assume that Gerald made admissions of the sort described by the Juvenile Court Judge, as quoted above. Neither Gerald nor his parents were advised that he did not have to testify or make a statement, or that an incriminating statement might result in his commitment as a "delinquent."

The Arizona Supreme Court rejected appellants' contention that Gerald had a right to be advised that he need not incriminate himself. It said: "We think the necessary flexibility for individualized treatment will be enhanced by a rule which does not require the judge to advise the infant of a privilege against self-incrimination."

In reviewing this conclusion of Arizona's Supreme Court, we emphasize again that we are here concerned only with a proceeding to determine whether a minor is a "delinquent" and which may result in commitment to a state institution. Specifically, the question is whether, in such a proceeding, an admission by the juvenile may be used against him in the absence of clear and unequivocal evidence that the admission was made with knowledge that he was not obliged to speak and would not be penalized for remaining silent. In light of *Miranda* v. *Arizona*, 384 U.S. 436 (1966), we must also consider whether, if the privilege against self-incrimination is available, it can effectively be waived unless counsel is present or the right to counsel has been waived. It has long been recognized that the eliciting and use of confessions or admissions require careful scrutiny. Dean Wigmore states:

The ground of distrust of confessions made in certain situations is, in a rough and indefinite way, judicial experience. There has been no careful collection of statistics of untrue confessions, nor has any great number of instances been even loosely reported . . . but enough have been verified to fortify the conclusion, based on ordinary observation of human conduct, that under certain stresses a person, especially one of defective mentality or peculiar tempera-

ment, may falsely acknowledge guilt. This possibility arises wherever the innocent person is placed in such a situation that the untrue acknowledgment of guilt is at the time the more promising of two alternatives between which he is obliged to choose; that is, he chooses any risk that may be in falsely acknowledging guilt, in preference to some worse alternative associated with silence.

The principle, then, upon which a confession may be excluded is that it is, under certain conditions, testimonially untrustworthy. . . . *The essential feature is that the principle of exclusion is a testimonial one, analogous to the other principles which exclude narrations as untrustworthy. . . .*

This Court has emphasized that admissions and confessions of juveniles require special caution. In *Haley* v. *Ohio,* 332 U.S. 596, where this Court reversed the conviction of a 15-year-old boy for murder, MR. JUSTICE DOUGLAS said:

What transpired would make us pause for careful inquiry if a mature man were involved. And when, as here, a mere child—an easy victim of the law—is before us, special care in scrutinizing the record must be used. Age 15 is a tender and difficult age for a boy of any race. He cannot be judged by the more exacting standards of maturity. That which would leave a man cold and unimpressed can overawe and overwhelm a lad in his early teens. This is the period of great instability which the crisis of adolescence produces. A 15-year-old lad, questioned through the dead of night by relays of police, is a ready victim of the inquisition. Mature men possibly might stand the ordeal from midnight to 5 a. m. But we cannot believe that a lad of tender years is a match for the police in such a contest. He needs counsel and support if he is not to become the victim first of fear, then of panic. He needs someone on whom to lean lest the overpowering presence of the law, as he knows it, crush him. No friend stood at the side of this 15-year-old boy as the police, working in relays, questioned him hour after hour, from midnight until dawn. No lawyer stood guard to make sure that the police went so far and no farther, to see to it that they stopped short of the point where he became the victim of coercion. No counsel or friend was called during the critical hours of questioning.

In *Haley,* as we have discussed, the boy was convicted in an adult court, and not a juvenile court. In notable decisions, the New York Court of Appeals and the Supreme Court of New Jersey have recently considered decisions of Juvenile Courts in which boys have been adjudged "delinquent" on the basis of confessions obtained in circumstances comparable to those in *Haley.* In both instances, the State contended before its highest tribunal that constitutional requirements governing inculpatory statements applicable in adult courts do not apply to juvenile proceedings. In each case, the State's contention was rejected, and the juvenile court's determination of delinquency was set aside on the grounds of inadmissibility of the confession. *In the Matters of Gregory W. and Gerald S.*, 19 N. Y. 2d 55, 224 N. E. 2d 102 (1966) (opinion by Keating, J.), and *In the Interests of Carlo and Stasilowicz*, 48 N. J. 224, 225 A. 2d 110 (1966) (opinion by Proctor, J.).

The privilege against self-incrimination is, of course, related to the question of the safeguards necessary to assure that admissions or confessions are reasonably trustworthy, that they are not the mere fruits of fear or coercion, but are reliable expressions of the truth. The roots of the privilege are, however, far deeper. They tap the basic stream of religious and political principle because the privilege reflects the limits of the individual's attornment to the state and—in a philosophical sense—insists upon the equality of the individual and the state. In other words, the privilege has a broader and deeper thrust than the rule which prevents the use of confessions which are the product of coercion because coercion is thought to carry with it the danger of unreliability. One of its purposes is to prevent the state, whether by force or by psychological domination, from overcoming the mind and will of the person under investigation and depriving him of the freedom to decide whether to assist the state in securing his conviction. It would indeed be surprising if the privilege against self-incrimination were available to hardened criminals but not to children. The language of the Fifth Amendment, applicable to the States by operation of the Fourteenth Amendment, is unequivocal and without exception. And the scope of the privilege is comprehensive. As MR. JUSTICE WHITE, concurring, stated in *Murphy* v. *Waterfront Commission*, 378 U.S. 52, 94 (1964):

> *The privilege can be claimed in any proceeding, be it criminal or civil, administrative or judicial, investigatory or adjudicatory . . . it protects any disclosures which the witness may reasonably apprehend could be used in a criminal prosecution or which could lead to other evidence that might be so used.*" (Emphasis added.)

With respect to juveniles, both common observation and expert opinion emphasize that the "distrust of confessions made in certain situations" to which Dean Wigmore referred in the passage quoted *supra*, at 44–45, is imperative in the case of children from an early age through adolescence. In New York, for example, the recently enacted Family Court Act provides that the juvenile and his parents must be advised at the start of the hearing of his right to remain silent. The New York statute also provides that the police must attempt to communicate with the juvenile's parents before questioning him, and that absent "special circumstances" a confession may not be obtained from a child prior to notifying his parents or relatives and releasing the child either to them or to the Family Court. In *In the Matters*

Appendix B

of *Gregory W. and Gerald S.*, referred to above, the New York Court of Appeals held that the privilege against self-incrimination applies in juvenile delinquency cases and requires the exclusion of involuntary confessions, and that *People* v. *Lewis*, 260 N. Y. 171, 183 N. E. 353 {*49} (1932), holding the contrary, had been specifically overruled by statute.

The authoritative "Standards for Juvenile and Family Courts" concludes that, "Whether or not transfer to the criminal court is a possibility, certain procedures should always be followed. Before being interviewed [by the police], the child and his parents should be informed of his right to have legal counsel present and to refuse to answer questions or be fingerprinted if he should so decide."

Against the application to juveniles of the right to silence, it is argued that juvenile proceedings are "civil" and not "criminal," and therefore the privilege should not apply. It is true that the statement of the privilege in the Fifth Amendment, which is applicable to the States by reason of the Fourteenth Amendment, is that no person "shall be compelled in any *criminal case* to be a witness against himself." However, it is also clear that the availability of the privilege does not turn upon the type of proceeding in which its protection is invoked, but upon the nature of the statement or admission and the exposure which it invites. The privilege may, for example, be claimed in a civil or administrative proceeding, if the statement is or may be inculpatory.

It would be entirely unrealistic to carve out of the Fifth Amendment all statements by juveniles on the ground that these cannot lead to "criminal" involvement. In the first place, juvenile proceedings to determine "delinquency," which may lead to commitment to a state institution, must be regarded as "criminal" for purposes of the privilege against self-incrimination. To hold otherwise would be to disregard substance because of the feeble enticement of the "civil" label-of-convenience which has been attached to juvenile proceedings. Indeed, in over half of the States, there is not even assurance that the juvenile will be kept in separate institutions, apart from adult "criminals." In those States juveniles may be placed in or transferred to adult penal institutions after having been found "delinquent" by a juvenile court. For this purpose, at least, commitment is a deprivation of liberty. It is incarceration against one's will, whether it is called "criminal" or "civil." And our Constitution guarantees that no person shall be "compelled" to be a witness against himself when he is threatened with deprivation of his liberty—a command which this Court has broadly applied and generously implemented in accordance with the teaching of the history of the privilege and its great office in mankind's battle for freedom.

In addition, apart from the equivalence for this purpose of exposure to commitment as a juvenile delinquent and exposure to imprisonment as an adult offender, the fact of the matter is that there is little or no assurance in Arizona, as in most if not all of the States, that a juvenile apprehended and interrogated by the police or even by the Juvenile Court itself will remain outside of the reach of adult courts as a consequence of the offense for which he has been taken into custody. In Arizona, as in other States, provision is made for Juvenile Courts to relinquish or waive jurisdiction to the ordinary criminal courts. In the present case, when Gerald Gault was interrogated concerning violation of a section of the Arizona Criminal Code, it could not be certain that the Juvenile Court Judge would decide to "suspend" criminal prosecution in court for adults by proceeding to an adjudication in Juvenile Court.

It is also urged, as the Supreme Court of Arizona here asserted, that the juvenile and presumably his parents should not be advised of the juvenile's right to silence because confession is good for the child as the commencement of the assumed therapy of the juvenile court process, and he should be encouraged to assume an attitude of trust and confidence toward the officials of the juvenile process. This proposition has been subjected to widespread challenge on the basis of current reappraisals of the rhetoric and realities of the handling of juvenile offenders.

In fact, evidence is accumulating that confessions by juveniles do not aid in "individualized treatment," as the court below put it, and that compelling the child to answer questions, without warning or advice as to his right to remain silent, does not serve this or any other good purpose. In light of the observations of Wheeler and Cottrell, and others, it seems probable that where children are induced to confess by "paternal" urgings on the part of officials and the confession is then followed by disciplinary action, the child's reaction is likely to be hostile and adverse—the child may well feel that he has been led or tricked into confession and that despite his confession, he is being punished.

Further, authoritative opinion has cast formidable doubt upon the reliability and trustworthiness of "confessions" by children. This Court's observations in *Haley* v. *Ohio* are set forth above. The recent decision of the New York Court of Appeals referred to above, *In the Matters of Gregory W. and Gerald S.*, deals with a dramatic and, it is to be hoped, extreme example. Two 12-year-old Negro boys were taken into custody for the brutal assault and rape of two aged domestics, one of whom died as the result of the attack. One of the boys was schizophrenic and had been locked in the security ward of a mental institution at the time of the attacks. By a process that may best be described as bizarre, his confession was obtained by the police. A psychiatrist testified that the boy would admit "whatever he thought was expected so that he could get out of the immediate situation." The other 12-year-old also "confessed." Both confessions were in specific detail, albeit they contained various inconsistencies. The Court of Appeals, in an opinion

Appendix B

by Keating, J., concluded that the confessions were products of the will of the police instead of the boys. The confessions were therefore held involuntary and the order of the Appellate Division affirming the order of the Family Court adjudging the defendants to be juvenile delinquents was reversed.

A similar and equally instructive case has recently been decided by the Supreme Court of New Jersey. *In the Interests of Carlo and Stasilowicz, supra.* The body of a 10-year-old girl was found. She had been strangled. Neighborhood boys who knew the girl were questioned. The two appellants, aged 13 and 15, confessed to the police, with vivid detail and some inconsistencies. At the Juvenile Court hearing, both denied any complicity in the killing. They testified that their confessions were the product of fear and fatigue due to extensive police grilling. The Juvenile Court Judge found that the confessions were voluntary and admissible. On appeal, in an extensive opinion by Proctor, J., the Supreme Court of New Jersey reversed. It rejected the State's argument that the constitutional safeguard of voluntariness governing the use of confessions does not apply in proceedings before the Juvenile Court. It pointed out that under New Jersey court rules, juveniles under the age of 16 accused of committing a homicide are tried in a proceeding which "has all of the appurtenances of a criminal trial," including participation by the county prosecutor, and requirements that the juvenile be provided with counsel, that a stenographic record be made, etc. It also pointed out that under New Jersey law, the confinement of the boys after reaching age 21 could be extended until they had served the maximum sentence which could have been imposed on an adult for such a homicide, here found to be second-degree murder carrying up to 30 years' imprisonment. The court concluded that the confessions were involuntary, stressing that the boys, contrary to statute, were placed in the police station and there interrogated; that the parents of both boys were not allowed to see them while they were being interrogated; that inconsistencies appeared among the various statements of the boys and with the objective evidence of the crime; and that there were protracted periods of questioning. The court noted the State's contention that both boys were advised of their constitutional rights before they made their statements, but it held that this should not be given "significant weight in our determination of voluntariness." Accordingly, the judgment of the Juvenile Court was reversed.

In a recent case before the Juvenile Court of the District of Columbia, Judge Ketcham rejected the proffer of evidence as to oral statements made at police headquarters by four juveniles who had been taken into custody for alleged involvement in an assault and attempted robbery. *In the Matter of Four Youths*, Nos. 28-776-J, 28-778-J, 28-783-J, 28-859-J, Juvenile Court of the District of Columbia, April 7, 1961. The court explicitly stated that it

271

did not rest its decision on a showing that the statements were involuntary, but because they were untrustworthy. Judge Ketcham said:

> *Simply stated, the Court's decision in this case rests upon the considered opinion—after nearly four busy years on the Juvenile Court bench during which the testimony of thousands of such juveniles has been heard—that the statements of adolescents under 18 years of age who are arrested and charged with violations of law are frequently untrustworthy and often distort the truth.*

We conclude that the constitutional privilege against self-incrimination is applicable in the case of juveniles as it is with respect to adults. We appreciate that special problems may arise with respect to waiver of the privilege by or on behalf of children, and that there may well be some differences in technique—but not in principle—depending upon the age of the child and the presence and competence of parents. The participation of counsel will, of course, assist the police, Juvenile Courts and appellate tribunals in administering the privilege. If counsel was not present for some permissible reason when an admission was obtained, the greatest care must be taken to assure that the admission was voluntary, in the sense not only that it was not coerced or suggested, but also that it was not the product of ignorance of rights or of adolescent fantasy, fright or despair.

The "confession" of Gerald Gault was first obtained by Officer Flagg, out of the presence of Gerald's parents, without counsel and without advising him of his right to silence, as far as appears. The judgment of the Juvenile Court was stated by the judge to be based on Gerald's admissions in court. Neither "admission" was reduced to writing, and, to say the least, the process by which the "admissions" were obtained and received must be characterized as lacking the certainty and order which are required of proceedings of such formidable consequences. Apart from the "admissions," there was nothing upon which a judgment or finding might be based. There was no sworn testimony. Mrs. Cook, the complainant, was not present. The Arizona Supreme Court held that "sworn testimony must be required of all witnesses including police officers, probation officers and others who are part of or officially related to the juvenile court structure." We hold that this is not enough. No reason is suggested or appears for a different rule in respect of sworn testimony in juvenile courts than in adult tribunals. Absent a valid confession adequate to support the determination of the Juvenile Court, confrontation and sworn testimony by witnesses available for cross-examination were essential for a finding of "delinquency" and an order committing Gerald to a state institution for a maximum of six years.

The recommendations in the Children's Bureau's "Standards for Juvenile and Family Courts" are in general accord with our conclusions. They state that testimony should be under oath and that only competent, material and relevant evidence under rules applicable to civil cases should be admitted in evidence. The New York Family Court Act contains a similar provision.

As we said in *Kent* v. *United States*, 383 U.S. 541, 554 (1966), with respect to waiver proceedings, "there is no place in our system of law for reaching a result of such tremendous consequences without ceremony. . . ." We now hold that, absent a valid confession, a determination of delinquency and an order of commitment to a state institution cannot be sustained in the absence of sworn testimony subjected to the opportunity for cross-examination in accordance with our law and constitutional requirements.

VI.

APPELLATE REVIEW AND TRANSCRIPT OF PROCEEDINGS.

Appellants urge that the Arizona statute is unconstitutional under the Due Process Clause because, as construed by its Supreme Court, "there is no right of appeal from a juvenile court order. . . ." The court held that there is no right to a transcript because there is no right to appeal and because the proceedings are confidential and any record must be destroyed after a prescribed period of time. Whether a transcript or other recording is made, it held, is a matter for the discretion of the juvenile court.

This Court has not held that a State is required by the Federal Constitution "to provide appellate courts or a right to appellate review at all." In view of the fact that we must reverse the Supreme Court of Arizona's affirmance of the dismissal of the writ of habeas corpus for other reasons, we need not rule on this question in the present case or upon the failure to provide a transcript or recording of the hearings—or, indeed, the failure of the Juvenile Judge to state the grounds for his conclusion. Cf. *Kent* v. *United States, supra,* at 561, where we said, in the context of a decision of the juvenile court waiving jurisdiction to the adult court, which by local law, was permissible: ". . . it is incumbent upon the Juvenile Court to accompany its waiver order with a statement of the reasons or considerations therefor." As the present case illustrates, the consequences of failure to provide an appeal, to record the proceedings, or to make findings or state the grounds for the juvenile court's conclusion may be to throw a burden upon the machinery for habeas corpus, to saddle the reviewing process with the burden of attempting to reconstruct a record, and to impose upon the Juvenile Judge the unseemly duty of testifying under cross-examination as to the events that transpired in the hearings before him.

For the reasons stated, the judgment of the Supreme Court of Arizona is reversed and the cause remanded for further proceedings not inconsistent with this opinion.

It is so ordered.

CONCUR BY: BLACK; WHITE; HARLAN (In Part)
CONCUR: MR. JUSTICE BLACK, concurring.

The juvenile court laws of Arizona and other States, as the Court points out, are the result of plans promoted by humane and forward-looking people to provide a system of courts, procedures, and sanctions deemed to be less harmful and more lenient to children than to adults. For this reason such state laws generally provide less formal and less public methods for the trial of children. In line with this policy, both courts and legislators have shrunk back from labeling these laws as "criminal" and have preferred to call them "civil." This, in part, was to prevent the full application to juvenile court cases of the Bill of Rights safeguards, including notice as provided in the Sixth Amendment, the right to counsel guaranteed by the Sixth, the right against self-incrimination guaranteed by the Fifth, and the right to confrontation guaranteed by the Sixth. The Court here holds, however, that these four Bill of Rights safeguards apply to protect a juvenile accused in a juvenile court on a charge under which he can be imprisoned for a term of years. This holding strikes a well-nigh fatal blow to much that is unique about the juvenile courts in the Nation. For this reason, there is much to be said for the position of my Brother STEWART that we should not pass on all these issues until they are more squarely presented. But since the majority of the Court chooses to decide all of these questions, I must either do the same or leave my views unexpressed on the important issues determined. In these circumstances, I feel impelled to express my views.

The juvenile court planners envisaged a system that would practically immunize juveniles from "punishment" for "crimes" in an effort to save them from youthful indiscretions and stigmas due to criminal charges or convictions. I agree with the Court, however, that this exalted ideal has failed of achievement since the beginning of the system. Indeed, the state laws from the first one on contained provisions, written in emphatic terms, for arresting and charging juveniles with violations of state criminal laws, as well as for taking juveniles by force of law away from their parents and turning them over to different individuals or groups or for confinement within some state school or institution for a number of years. The latter occurred in this case. Young Gault was arrested and detained on a charge of violating an Arizona penal law by using vile and offensive language to a lady on the telephone. If an adult, he could only have been fined or imprisoned for two months for his conduct. As a juvenile, however, he was put through a more or less secret, informal hearing by the court, after which he was ordered, or, more realistically, "sentenced," to confinement in Arizona's Industrial School until he reaches 21 years of age. Thus, in a juvenile system designed to lighten or avoid punishment for criminality, he was ordered by the State to six years' confinement in what is in all but name a penitentiary or jail.

Appendix B

Where a person, infant or adult, can be seized by the State, charged, and convicted for violating a state criminal law, and then ordered by the State to be confined for six years, I think the Constitution requires that he be tried in accordance with the guarantees of all the provisions of the Bill of Rights made applicable to the States by the Fourteenth Amendment. Undoubtedly this would be true of an adult defendant, and it would be a plain denial of equal protection of the laws—an invidious discrimination—to hold that others subject to heavier punishments could, because they are children, be denied these same constitutional safeguards. I consequently agree with the Court that the Arizona law as applied here denied to the parents and their son the right of notice, right to counsel, right against self-incrimination, and right to confront the witnesses against young Gault. Appellants are entitled to these rights, not because "fairness, impartiality and orderliness—in short, the essentials of due process"—require them and not because they are "the procedural rules which have been fashioned from the generality of due process," but because they are specifically and unequivocally granted by provisions of the Fifth and Sixth Amendments which the Fourteenth Amendment makes applicable to the States.

A few words should be added because of the opinion of my Brother HARLAN who rests his concurrence and dissent on the Due Process Clause alone. He reads that clause alone as allowing this Court "to determine what forms of procedural protection are necessary to guarantee the fundamental fairness of juvenile proceedings" "in a fashion consistent with the 'traditions and conscience of our people.'" Cf. *Rochin* v. *California*, 342 U.S. 165. He believes that the Due Process Clause gives this Court the power, upon weighing a "compelling public interest," to impose on the States only those specific constitutional rights which the Court deems "imperative" and "necessary" to comport with the Court's notions of "fundamental fairness."

I cannot subscribe to any such interpretation of the Due Process Clause. Nothing in its words or its history permits it, and "fair distillations of relevant judicial history" are no substitute for the words and history of the clause itself. The phrase "due process of law" has through the years evolved as the successor in purpose and meaning to the words "law of the land" in Magna Charta which more plainly intended to call for a trial according to the existing law of the land in effect at the time an alleged offense had been committed. That provision in Magna Charta was designed to prevent defendants from being tried according to criminal laws or proclamations specifically promulgated to fit particular cases or to attach new consequences to old conduct. Nothing done since Magna Charta can be pointed to as intimating that the Due Process Clause gives courts power to fashion laws in order to meet new conditions, to fit the "decencies" of changed

275

conditions, or to keep their consciences from being shocked by legislation, state or federal.

And, of course, the existence of such awesome judicial power cannot be buttressed or created by relying on the word "procedural." Whether labeled as "procedural" or "substantive," the Bill of Rights safeguards, far from being mere "tools with which" other unspecified "rights could be fully vindicated," are the very vitals of a sound constitutional legal system designed to protect and safeguard the most cherished liberties of a free people. These safeguards were written into our Constitution not by judges but by Constitution makers. Freedom in this Nation will be far less secure the very moment that it is decided that judges can determine which of these safeguards "should" or "should not be imposed" according to their notions of what constitutional provisions are consistent with the "traditions and conscience of our people." Judges with such power, even though they profess to "proceed with restraint," will be above the Constitution, with power to write it, not merely to interpret it, which I believe to be the only power constitutionally committed to judges.

There is one ominous sentence, if not more, in my Brother HARLAN's opinion which bodes ill, in my judgment, both for legislative programs and constitutional commands. Speaking of procedural safeguards in the Bill of Rights, he says:

> *These factors in combination suggest that legislatures may properly expect only a cautious deference for their procedural judgments, but that, conversely, courts must exercise their special responsibility for procedural guarantees with care to permit ample scope for achieving the purposes of legislative programs. . . . The court should necessarily proceed with restraint.*

It is to be noted here that this case concerns Bill of Rights Amendments; that the "procedure" power my Brother HARLAN claims for the Court here relates solely to Bill of Rights safeguards; and that he is here claiming for the Court a supreme power to fashion new Bill of Rights safeguards according to the Court's notions of what fits tradition and conscience. I do not believe that the Constitution vests any such power in judges, either in the Due Process Clause or anywhere else. Consequently, I do not vote to invalidate this Arizona law on the ground that it is "unfair" but solely on the ground that it violates the Fifth and Sixth Amendments made obligatory on the States by the Fourteenth Amendment. Cf. *Pointer* v. *Texas*, 380 U.S. 400, 412 (Goldberg, J., concurring). It is enough for me that the Arizona law as here applied collides head-on with the Fifth and Sixth Amendments in the four respects mentioned. The only relevance to me of the Due Process Clause is that it would, of course, violate due process or the "law of the land" to enforce a law that collides with the Bill of Rights.

Appendix B

MR. JUSTICE WHITE, concurring.

I join the Court's opinion except for Part V. I also agree that the privilege against compelled self-incrimination applies at the adjudicatory stage of juvenile court proceedings. I do not, however, find an adequate basis in the record for determining whether that privilege was violated in this case. The Fifth Amendment protects a person from being "compelled" in any criminal proceeding to be a witness against himself. Compulsion is essential to a violation. It may be that when a judge, armed with the authority he has or which people think he has, asks questions of a party or a witness in an adjudicatory hearing, that person, especially if a minor, would feel compelled to answer, absent a warning to the contrary or similar information from some other source. The difficulty is that the record made at the habeas corpus hearing, which is the only information we have concerning the proceedings in the juvenile court, does not directly inform us whether Gerald Gault or his parents were told of Gerald's right to remain silent; nor does it reveal whether the parties were aware of the privilege from some other source, just as they were already aware that they had the right to have the help of counsel and to have witnesses on their behalf. The petition for habeas corpus did not raise the Fifth Amendment issue nor did any of the witnesses focus on it.

I have previously recorded my views with respect to what I have deemed unsound applications of the Fifth Amendment. See, for example, *Miranda* v. *Arizona*, 384 U.S. 436, 526, and *Malloy* v. *Hogan*, 378 U.S. 1, 33, dissenting opinions. These views, of course, have not prevailed. But I do hope that the Court will proceed with some care in extending the privilege, with all its vigor, to proceedings in juvenile court, particularly the nonadjudicatory stages of those proceedings.

In any event, I would not reach the Fifth Amendment issue here. I think the Court is clearly ill-advised to review this case on the basis of *Miranda* v. *Arizona*, since the adjudication of delinquency took place in 1964, long before the *Miranda* decision. See *Johnson* v. *New Jersey*, 384 U.S. 719. Under these circumstances, this case is a poor vehicle for resolving a difficult problem. Moreover, no prejudice to appellants is at stake in this regard. The judgment below must be reversed on other grounds and in the event further proceedings are to be had, Gerald Gault will have counsel available to advise him.

For somewhat similar reasons, I would not reach the questions of confrontation and cross-examination which are also dealt with in Part V of the opinion.

DISSENT BY: HARLAN (In Part); STEWART
DISSENT: MR. JUSTICE HARLAN, concurring in part and dissenting in part.

Each of the 50 States has created a system of juvenile or family courts, in which distinctive rules are employed and special consequences imposed.

The jurisdiction of these courts commonly extends both to cases which the States have withdrawn from the ordinary processes of criminal justice, and to cases which involve acts that, if performed by an adult, would not be penalized as criminal. Such courts are denominated civil, not criminal, and are characteristically said not to administer criminal penalties. One consequence of these systems, at least as Arizona construes its own, is that certain of the rights guaranteed to criminal defendants by the Constitution are withheld from juveniles. This case brings before this Court for the first time the question of what limitations the Constitution places upon the operation of such tribunals. For reasons which follow, I have concluded that the Court has gone too far in some respects, and fallen short in others, in assessing the procedural requirements demanded by the Fourteenth Amendment.

I.

I must first acknowledge that I am unable to determine with any certainty by what standards the Court decides that Arizona's juvenile courts do not satisfy the obligations of due process. The Court's premise, itself the product of reasoning which is not described, is that the "constitutional and theoretical basis" of state systems of juvenile and family courts is "debatable"; it buttresses these doubts by marshaling a body of opinion which suggests that the accomplishments of these courts have often fallen short of expectations. The Court does not indicate at what points or for what purposes such views, held either by it or by other observers, might be pertinent to the present issues. Its failure to provide any discernible standard for the measurement of due process in relation to juvenile proceedings unfortunately might be understood to mean that the Court is concerned principally with the wisdom of having such courts at all.

If this is the source of the Court's dissatisfaction, I cannot share it. I should have supposed that the constitutionality of juvenile courts was beyond proper question under the standards now employed to assess the substantive validity of state legislation under the Due Process Clause of the Fourteenth Amendment. It can scarcely be doubted that it is within the State's competence to adopt measures reasonably calculated to meet more effectively the persistent problems of juvenile delinquency; as the opinion for the Court makes abundantly plain, these are among the most vexing and ominous of the concerns which now face communities throughout the country. The proper issue here is, however, not whether the State may constitutionally treat juvenile offenders through a system of specialized courts, but whether the proceedings in Arizona's juvenile courts include procedural guarantees which satisfy the requirements of the Fourteenth Amendment. Among the first premises of our constitutional system is the obligation to conduct any proceeding in which an individual may be deprived of liberty or property in a fashion consistent with the "traditions and conscience of our people." *Snyder* v. *Massachusetts*, 291 U.S. 97, 105. The importance of these procedural guarantees is doubly intensified here. First, many of the problems with which Arizona is concerned are among those traditionally confined to the processes of criminal justice; their disposition necessarily affects in the most direct and substantial manner the liberty of individual citizens. Quite obviously, systems of specialized penal justice might permit erosion, or even evasion, of the limitations placed by the Constitution upon state criminal proceedings. Second, we must recognize that the character and consequences of many juvenile court proceedings have in fact closely resembled those of ordinary criminal trials. Nothing before us suggests that juvenile courts were intended as a device to escape constitutional constraints, but I entirely agree with the Court that we are nonetheless obliged to examine with circumspection the procedural guarantees the State has provided.

The central issue here, and the principal one upon which I am divided from the Court, is the method by which the procedural requirements of due process should be measured. It must at the outset be emphasized that the protections necessary here cannot be determined by resort to any classification of juvenile proceedings either as criminal or as civil, whether made by the State or by this Court. Both formulae are simply too imprecise to permit reasoned analysis of these difficult constitutional issues. The Court should instead measure the requirements of due process by reference both to the problems which confront the State and to the actual character of the procedural system which the State has created. The Court has for such purposes chiefly examined three connected sources: first, the "settled usages and modes of proceeding," *Murray's Lessee* v. *Hoboken Land & Improvement Co.*, 18 How. 272, 277; second, the "fundamental principles of liberty and justice which lie at the base of all our civil and political institutions," *Hebert* v. *Louisiana*, 272 U.S. 312, 316; and third, the character and requirements of the circumstances presented in each situation. *FCC* v. *WJR*, 337 U.S. 265, 277; *Yakus* v. {*69} *United States*, 321 U.S. 414. See, further, my dissenting opinion in *Poe* v. *Ullman*, 367 U.S. 497, 522, and compare my opinion concurring in the result in *Pointer* v. *Texas*, 380 U.S. 400, 408. Each of these factors is relevant to the issues here, but it is the last which demands particular examination.

The Court has repeatedly emphasized that determination of the constitutionally required procedural safeguards in any situation requires recognition both of the "interests affected" and of the "circumstances involved." *FCC* v. *WJR, supra*, at 277. In particular, a "compelling public interest" must, under our cases, be taken fully into account in assessing the validity under the due process clauses of state or federal legislation and its application. See, *e.g.*, *Yakus* v. *United States, supra*, at 442; *Bowles* v. *Willingham*, 321

U.S. 503, 520; *Miller* v. *Schoene*, 276 U.S. 272, 279. Such interests would never warrant arbitrariness or the diminution of any specifically assured constitutional right, *Home Bldg. & Loan Assn.* v. *Blaisdell*, 290 U.S. 398, 426, but they are an essential element of the context through which the legislation and proceedings under it must be read and evaluated.

No more evidence of the importance of the public interests at stake here is required than that furnished by the opinion of the Court; it indicates that "some 601,000 children under 18, or 2% of all children between 10 and 17, came before juvenile courts" in 1965, and that "about one-fifth of all arrests for serious crimes" in 1965 were of juveniles. The Court adds that the rate of juvenile crime is steadily rising. All this, as the Court suggests, indicates the importance of these due process issues, but it mirrors no less vividly that state authorities are confronted by formidable and immediate problems involving the most fundamental social values. The state legislatures have determined that the most hopeful solution for these problems is to be found in specialized courts, organized under their own rules and imposing distinctive consequences. The terms and limitations of these systems are not identical, nor are the procedural arrangements which they include, but the States are uniform in their insistence that the ordinary processes of criminal justice are inappropriate, and that relatively informal proceedings, dedicated to premises and purposes only imperfectly reflected in the criminal law, are instead necessary.

It is well settled that the Court must give the widest deference to legislative judgments that concern the character and urgency of the problems with which the State is confronted. Legislatures are, as this Court has often acknowledged, the "main guardian" of the public interest, and, within their constitutional competence, their understanding of that interest must be accepted as "well-nigh" conclusive. *Berman* v. *Parker*, 348 U.S. 26, 32. This principle does not, however, reach all the questions essential to the resolution of this case. The legislative judgments at issue here embrace assessments of the necessity and wisdom of procedural guarantees; these are questions which the Constitution has entrusted at least in part to courts, and upon which courts have been understood to possess particular competence. The fundamental issue here is, therefore, in what measure and fashion the Court must defer to legislative determinations which encompass constitutional issues of procedural protection.

It suffices for present purposes to summarize the factors which I believe to be pertinent. It must first be emphasized that the deference given to legislators upon substantive issues must realistically extend in part to ancillary procedural questions. Procedure at once reflects and creates substantive rights, and every effort of courts since the beginnings of the common law to separate the two has proved essentially futile. The distinction between them is particularly inadequate here, where the legislature's substantive preferences directly and unavoidably require judgments about procedural issues. The procedural framework is here a principal element of the substantive legislative system; meaningful deference to the latter must include a portion of deference to the former. The substantive-procedural dichotomy is, nonetheless, an indispensable tool of analysis, for it stems from fundamental limitations upon judicial authority under the Constitution. Its premise is ultimately that courts may not substitute for the judgments of legislators their own understanding of the public welfare, but must instead concern themselves with the validity under the Constitution of the methods which the legislature has selected. See, *e.g., McLean* v. *Arkansas,* 211 U.S. 539, 547; *Olsen* v. *Nebraska,* 313 U.S. 236, 246–247. The Constitution has in this manner created for courts and legislators areas of primary responsibility which are essentially congruent to their areas of special competence. Courts are thus obliged both by constitutional command and by their distinctive functions to bear particular responsibility for the measurement of procedural due process. These factors in combination suggest that legislatures may properly expect only a cautious deference for their procedural judgments, but that, conversely, courts must exercise their special responsibility for procedural guarantees with care to permit ample scope for achieving the purposes of legislative programs. Plainly, courts can exercise such care only if they have in each case first studied thoroughly the objectives and implementation of the program at stake; if, upon completion of those studies, the effect of extensive procedural restrictions upon valid legislative purposes cannot be assessed with reasonable certainty, the court should necessarily proceed with restraint.

The foregoing considerations, which I believe to be fair distillations of relevant judicial history, suggest three criteria by which the procedural requirements of due process should be measured here: first, no more restrictions should be imposed than are imperative to assure the proceedings' fundamental fairness; second, the restrictions which are imposed should be those which preserve, so far as possible, the essential elements of the State's purpose; and finally, restrictions should be chosen which will later permit the orderly selection of any additional protections which may ultimately prove necessary. In this way, the Court may guarantee the fundamental fairness of the proceeding, and yet permit the State to continue development of an effective response to the problems of juvenile crime.

II.

Measured by these criteria, only three procedural requirements should, in my opinion, now be deemed required of state juvenile courts by the Due Process Clause of the Fourteenth Amendment: first, timely notice must be provided to parents and children of the nature and terms of any juvenile court proceeding in which a determination affecting their rights or interests may be made; second, unequivocal and timely notice must be given that counsel may appear in any such proceeding in behalf of the child and its parents, and that in cases in which the child may be confined in an institution, counsel may, in circumstances of indigency, be appointed for them; and third, the court must maintain a written record, or its equivalent, adequate to permit effective review on appeal or in collateral proceedings. These requirements would guarantee to juveniles the tools with which their rights could be fully vindicated, and yet permit the States to pursue without unnecessary hindrance the purposes which they believe imperative in this field. Further, their imposition now would later permit more intelligent assessment of the necessity under the Fourteenth Amendment of additional requirements, by creating suitable records from which the character and deficiencies of juvenile proceedings could be accurately judged. I turn to consider each of these three requirements.

The Court has consistently made plain that adequate and timely notice is the fulcrum of due process, whatever the purposes of the proceeding. See, *e.g., Roller* v. *Holly*, 176 U.S. 398, 409; *Coe* v. *Armour Fertilizer Works*, 237 U.S. 413, 424. Notice is ordinarily the prerequisite to effective assertion of any constitutional or other rights; without it, vindication of those rights must be essentially fortuitous. So fundamental a protection can neither be spared here nor left to the "favor or grace" of state authorities. *Central of Georgia Ry.* v. *Wright*, 207 U.S. 127, 138; *Coe* v. *Armour Fertilizer Works*, *supra*, at 425.

Provision of counsel and of a record, like adequate notice, would permit the juvenile to assert very much more effectively his rights and defenses, both in the juvenile proceedings and upon direct or collateral review. The Court has frequently emphasized their importance in proceedings in which an individual may be deprived of his liberty, see *Gideon* v. *Wainwright*, 372 U.S. 335, and *Griffin* v. *Illinois*, 351 U.S. 12; this reasoning must include with special force those who are commonly inexperienced and immature. See *Powell* v. *Alabama*, 287 U.S. 45. The facts of this case illustrate poignantly the difficulties of review without either an adequate record or the participation of counsel in the proceeding's initial stages. At the same time, these requirements should not cause any substantial modification in the character of juvenile court proceedings: counsel, although now present in only a small percentage of juvenile cases, have apparently already appeared without incident in virtually all juvenile courts; and the maintenance of a record should not appreciably alter the conduct of these proceedings.

The question remains whether certain additional requirements, among them the privilege against self-incrimination, confrontation, and cross-examination, must now, as the Court holds, also be imposed. I share in part the views expressed in my Brother WHITE's concurring opinion, but believe that there are other, and more deep-seated, reasons to defer, at least for the present, the imposition of such requirements.

Initially, I must vouchsafe that I cannot determine with certainty the reasoning by which the Court concludes that these further requirements are now imperative. The Court begins from the premise, to which it gives force at several points, that juvenile courts need not satisfy "all of the requirements of a criminal trial." It therefore scarcely suffices to explain the selection of these particular procedural requirements for the Court to declare that juvenile court proceedings are essentially criminal, and thereupon to recall that these are requisites for a criminal trial. Nor does the Court's voucher of "authoritative opinion," which consists of four extraordinary juvenile cases, contribute materially to the solution of these issues. The Court has, even under its own premises, asked the wrong questions: the problem here is to determine what forms of procedural protection are necessary to guarantee the fundamental fairness of juvenile proceedings, and not which of the procedures now employed in criminal trials should be transplanted intact to proceedings in these specialized courts.

In my view, the Court should approach this question in terms of the criteria, described above, which emerge from the history of due process adjudication. Measured by them, there are compelling reasons at least to defer imposition of these additional requirements. First, quite unlike notice, counsel, and a record, these requirements might radically alter the character of juvenile court proceedings. The evidence from which the Court reasons that they would not is inconclusive, and other available evidence suggests that they very likely would. At the least, it is plain that these additional requirements would contribute materially to the creation in these proceedings of the atmosphere of an ordinary criminal trial, and would, even if they do no more, thereby largely frustrate a central purpose of these specialized courts. Further, these are restrictions intended to conform to the demands of an intensely adversary system of criminal justice; the broad purposes which they represent might be served in juvenile courts with equal effectiveness by procedural devices more consistent with the premises of proceedings in those courts. As the Court apparently acknowledges, the hazards of self-accusation, for example, might be avoided in juvenile proceedings without the imposition of all the requirements and limitations which surround the privilege against self-incrimination. The guarantee of adequate notice, counsel, and a record would create conditions in which suitable alternative procedures could be devised; but, unfortunately, the Court's haste to impose restrictions taken intact from criminal procedure may well seriously hamper the development of such alternatives. Surely this illustrates that prudence and the principles of the Fourteenth Amendment alike require that the Court should now impose no more procedural restrictions than are imperative to assure fundamental fairness, and that the States should instead be permitted additional opportunities to develop without unnecessary hindrance their systems of juvenile courts.

I find confirmation for these views in two ancillary considerations. First, it is clear that an uncertain, but very substantial number of the cases brought to juvenile courts involve children who are not in any sense guilty of criminal misconduct. Many of these children have simply the misfortune to be in some manner distressed; others have engaged in conduct, such as truancy, which is plainly not criminal. Efforts are now being made to develop effective, and entirely noncriminal, methods of treatment for these children. In such cases, the state authorities are in the most literal sense acting *in loco parentis*; they are, by any standard, concerned with the child's protection, and not with his punishment. I do not question that the methods employed in such cases must be consistent with the constitutional obligation to act in accordance with due process, but certainly the Fourteenth Amendment does not demand that they be constricted by the procedural guarantees devised for ordinary criminal prosecutions. Cf. *Minnesota ex rel. Pearson* v. *Probate Court*, 309 U.S. 270. It must be remembered that the various classifications of juvenile court proceedings are, as the vagaries of the available statistics illustrate, often arbitrary or ambiguous; it would therefore be imprudent, at the least, to build upon these classifications rigid systems of procedural requirements which would be applicable, or not, in accordance with the descriptive label given to the particular proceeding. It is better, it seems to me, to begin by now requiring the essential elements of fundamental fairness in juvenile courts, whatever the label given by the State to the proceeding; in this way the Court could avoid imposing unnecessarily rigid restrictions, and yet escape dependence upon classifications which may often prove to be illusory. Further, the provision of notice, counsel, and a record would permit orderly efforts to determine later whether more satisfactory classifications can be devised, and if they can, whether additional procedural requirements are necessary for them under the Fourteenth Amendment.

Second, it should not be forgotten that juvenile crime and juvenile courts are both now under earnest study throughout the country. I very much fear that this Court, by imposing these rigid procedural requirements, may inadvertently have served to discourage these efforts to find more satisfactory solutions for the problems of juvenile crime, and may thus now hamper enlightened development of the systems of juvenile courts. It is appropriate to recall that the Fourteenth Amendment does not compel the law to remain passive in the midst of change; to demand otherwise denies "every quality of the law but its age." *Hurtado* v. *California*, 110 U.S. 516, 529.

Appendix B

III.

Finally, I turn to assess the validity of this juvenile court proceeding under the criteria discussed in this opinion. Measured by them, the judgment below must, in my opinion, fall. Gerald Gault and his parents were not provided adequate notice of the terms and purposes of the proceedings in which he was adjudged delinquent; they were not advised of their rights to be represented by counsel; and no record in any form was maintained of the proceedings. It follows, for the reasons given in this opinion, that Gerald Gault was deprived of his liberty without due process of law, and I therefore concur in the judgment of the Court.

MR. JUSTICE STEWART, dissenting.

The Court today uses an obscure Arizona case as a vehicle to impose upon thousands of juvenile courts throughout the Nation restrictions that the Constitution made applicable to adversary criminal trials. I believe the Court's decision is wholly unsound as a matter of constitutional law, and sadly unwise as a matter of judicial policy.

Juvenile proceedings are not criminal trials. They are not civil trials. They are simply not adversary proceedings. Whether treating with a delinquent child, a neglected child, a defective child, or a dependent child, a juvenile proceeding's whole purpose and mission is the very opposite of the mission and purpose of a prosecution in a criminal court. The object of the one is correction of a condition. The object of the other is conviction and punishment for a criminal act.

In the last 70 years many dedicated men and women have devoted their professional lives to the enlightened task of bringing us out of the dark world of Charles Dickens in meeting our responsibilities to the child in our society. The result has been the creation in this century of a system of juvenile and family courts in each of the 50 States. There can be no denying that in many areas the performance of these agencies has fallen disappointingly short of the hopes and dreams of the courageous pioneers who first conceived them. For a variety of reasons, the reality has sometimes not even approached the ideal, and much remains to be accomplished in the administration of public juvenile and family agencies—in personnel, in planning, in financing, perhaps in the formulation of wholly new approaches.

I possess neither the specialized experience nor the expert knowledge to predict with any certainty where may lie the brightest hope for progress in dealing with the serious problems of juvenile delinquency. But I am certain that the answer does not lie in the Court's opinion in this case, which serves to convert a juvenile proceeding into a criminal prosecution.

The inflexible restrictions that the Constitution so wisely made applicable to adversary criminal trials have no inevitable place in the proceedings of those public social agencies known as juvenile or family courts. And to impose the Court's long catalog of requirements upon juvenile proceedings in every area of the country is to invite a long step backwards into the nineteenth century. In that era there were no juvenile proceedings, and a child was tried in a conventional criminal court with all the trappings of a conventional criminal trial. So it was that a 12-year-old boy named James Guild was tried in New Jersey for killing Catharine Beakes. A jury found him guilty of murder, and he was sentenced to death by hanging. The sentence was executed. It was all very constitutional.

A State in all its dealings must, of course, accord every person due process of law. And due process may require that some of the same restrictions which the Constitution has placed upon criminal trials must be imposed upon juvenile proceedings. For example, I suppose that all would agree that a brutally coerced confession could not constitutionally be considered in a juvenile court hearing. But it surely does not follow that the testimonial privilege against self-incrimination is applicable in all juvenile proceedings. Similarly, due process clearly requires timely notice of the purpose and scope of any proceedings affecting the relationship of parent and child. *Armstrong* v. *Manzo*, 380 U.S. 545. But it certainly does not follow that notice of a juvenile hearing must be framed with all the technical niceties of a criminal indictment. See *Russell* v. *United States*, 369 U.S. 749.

In any event, there is no reason to deal with issues such as these in the present case. The Supreme Court of Arizona found that the parents of Gerald Gault "knew of their right to counsel, to subpoena and cross examine witnesses, of the right to confront the witnesses against Gerald and the possible consequences of a finding of delinquency." 99 Ariz. 181, 185, 407 P. 2d 760, 763. It further found that "Mrs. Gault knew the exact nature of the charge against Gerald from the day he was taken to the detention home." 99 Ariz., at 193, 407 P. 2d, at 768. And, as MR. JUSTICE WHITE correctly points out, pp. 64–65, *ante*, no issue of compulsory self-incrimination is presented by this case.

I would dismiss the appeal.

(Footnotes omitted.)

INDEX

Locators in **boldface** indicate major treatment of topics. Locators followed by *c* indicate chronology entries. Locators followed by *b* indicate biographical entries. Locators followed by *g* indicate glossary entries.

A

ABA (American Bar Association) 95
Abbott, Grace 112*b*
absconder 122*g*
abuse 22, 36, 66
ACA (American Correctional Association) 209
accountability 89, 101c
ACLU (American Civil Liberties Union) 209
Acton, James 75
ADAM (Arrestee Drug Abuse Monitoring Program) 16
Addams, Jane 103c, 112*b*
adjudicate (term) 122*g*
adjudication 122*g*
adjudicatory hearings 46, 60, **88**, 99, 107c, 122*g*, 249
Adolescence (Hall) 7, 12, 104c
adolescent developmental psychology 7, 104c
ADR (Alternative Dispute Resolution) 85
adult correctional facilities, juveniles in **33–34**, 48, 49, 87
adult court. *See* criminal court
adult justice system. *See* criminal justice system
adults, trying juveniles as **95–96**. *See also* criminal court; criminal justice system
in ancient Rome 5

Breed v. Jones 60–61
CDC report 111c
Haley v. Ohio 267
Illinois Juvenile Court Act (1899) 43–47
juvenile justice process 84
Kent v. United States 52–54
Montana law 52
Puritan treatment of children 6
rates in 1994 109c
Stanford v. Kentucky 72–73
state legislation 80, 110c
Thompson v. Oklahoma 71–72
waiver of jurisdiction 94 95, 106c
affirm (term) 122*g*
African Americans
in adult correctional facilities 33–34
arrest trends 11
detention trends (1985–2005) 87
gang membership 23
out-of-home placement 32
pre-ajudication detention trends (1985–2005) 32
probation caseload trends (1985–2005) 32

racial slurs 29
school safety 29
school weapons trends 28
urban crime rate 4
victims of bullying at school 30
youth gangs 20, 24
aftercare 99, 122*g*
aftercare officer 122*g*
age of criminal responsibility 3, 5, 6, 100c
age of majority 107c, 122*g*
age of onset 122*g*
aggravated assault 9, 10, 28, 122*g*
aggravating factors/ circumstances 71, 73, 122*g* 123*g*
Agnew, Robert 13
Alabama Criminal Justice Information Center 214
alcohol abuse 4, **16–17**, 29. *See also* liquor law violations; substance abuse
allegations 99, 123*g*
Allender, David M. 19
Allen-Hagen, Barbara 112*b*
Alternative Dispute Resolution (ADR) 85
Altgeld, John 112*b*
American Bar Association (ABA) 95

American Bar Association
Juvenile Justice
Committee 209
American Civil Liberties
Union (ACLU) 209
American Correctional
Association (ACA) 209
appeals 123*g*
In re Gault 55, 253,
273, 275
juvenile v. criminal
justice systems 98
McKeiver v. Pennsylvania
59
apprenticeships 80, 100c
Arizona Criminal Justice
Commission 214
Arizona Supreme Court 55,
250, 253, 254, 258, 262,
263, 266, 270, 272, 273,
286
Arkansas Crime Information
Center 214
arraignment 123*g*
*Arrestee Drug Abuse
Monitoring Program
(ADAM)* 16
arrests 123*g*
by age (2007) 224*t*–
229*t*
child abuse and
delinquency 36
females, by age (2007)
230*t*–233*t*
five-year totals (2003–
2007) 240*t*–241*t*
five-year trends by sex
(2003–2007) 242*t*–
243*t*
males, by age (2007)
234*t*–237*t*
persons under 15, 18,
21, and 25 years of
age (2007) 224*t*–
229*t*
by race (2007) 238*t*–
240*t*
by sex (2003–2007)
242*t*–243*t*
10-year totals (1998–
2007) 244*t*–245*t*

10-year totals by sex
(1998–2007) 246*t*–
247*t*
totals (2003–2007)
240*t*–241t
totals by sex (1998–
2007) 246*t*–247*t*
trends (2006–2007)
111*c*
violent crime 109c
arson 123*g*
Asian Americans 20, 22, 23
assaults 9, 10, 23, 28, 123*g*
Atkins v. Virginia 74,
76–77
Augustus, John 102c, 112*b*
auto theft 4, 5, 10

B

Baca, Lee 20
balanced and restorative
justice model of correction
91, 94, 123*g*
battery 123*g*
BBBSA (Big Brothers Big
Sisters of America) 37–38
Beccaria, Cesare 14, 101c,
113*b*
Bentham, Jeremy 14, 113*b*
beyond a reasonable doubt
46, 57, 58, 107c, 123*g*
bibliography 151–206
juvenile justice system
187–206
school violence 174–
184
substance abuse 184–
187
youth gangs 165–174
Big Brothers Big Sisters of
America (BBBSA) 37–38
Bill of Rights 101c, 255,
274–276. *See also specific
amendments*
Bishop, Donna M. 113*b*
Black, Meghan C. 31
Blackmun, Harry 59, 60,
65, 71–73, 113*b*
blacks. *See* African
Americans

blended sentencing 90,
123*g*
"Blueprint for Violence
Prevention" 36–39
booking 123*g*
bootlegging 4, 8
Boston, Massachusetts
102c, 103c
Brace, Charles 102c, 113*b*
Breckinridge, Sophonisba
Preston 113*b*
Breed v. Jones **60–61**, 94,
108c
Brennan, William J. 71–74,
113*b*
Brewer, Larry Donnell 62
Breyer, Stephen G. 74, 77
Building Blocks for Youth
34
bullying 27, 29–30
burden of proof 124*g*
Bureau of Justice Statistics
107c, 207
Bureau of the Census 207
Burger, Warren 61, 113*b*
Burgess, Ernest 13
burglary 6, 8, 10–11, 124*g*
Butts, Jeffrey A. 114*b*

C

California Criminal Justice
Statistics Center 214
California Juvenile Court
Act 45–46
California Supreme Court
64, 65
Campaign for Youth Justice
209
capital offense 124*g*
capital punishment. *See*
death penalty
*Carlo and Stasilowicz, In the
Interests of* 268, 271
causes of delinquency 12–
15, **35–36**
Center for Media and Public
Affairs 35
Center for Research on
Youth and Social Policy
209

Index

Center for the Prevention of School Violence 210
Center on Juvenile and Criminal Justice 210
certiorari 124g
Chesney-Lind, Meda 114b
Chicago, Illinois
  Hull-House 103c
  Illinois Juvenile Court Act (1899) 43–44
  reform school law 103c
  sociology of delinquency 105c
  youth gangs 18, 21, 22, 105c
child abuse 36, 66
Children of the Night 210
Children's Bureau, U.S. 45, 103c, 104c
The Child Savers (Platt) 82, 107c
child-saving movement 80–81, 93, 102c, 124g
child welfare 103c, 105c
chronic offender 124g
cities 24, 27–29
classical theory 124g
club drugs 17
Cohen, Albert K. 106c, 114b
Colorado Division of Criminal Justice 214–215
Columbine High School (Littleton, Colorado) 25, 110c
commissioners 88, 124g
commitment 14, 99, 124g
Committee for Children 210
Common Sense About Kids and Guns 210
communities 13, 15, 94
community-based programs 85, 107c
community service 85, 124g
competence to stand trial 93
competency development 124g

comprehensive assessment 124g
comprehensive juvenile justice 124g
concurring opinion 124g
confessions 124g, 266–268, 270, 272
confidentiality 96–97, 124g–125g
  In re Gault 259
  juvenile v. criminal justice systems 97
  Oklahoma Publishing Co. v. District Court 63
  Smith v. Daily Mail Publishing Company 108c
  state legislation 50
confinement 31–33, 260
conflict of interest 125g
conflict resolution 84
confrontation 265, 282
Congress, U.S. 47, 49
Connecticut Office of Policy and Management 215
Consequences for Juvenile Offenders Act (2002) 49
conspiracy 125g
constitutional rights 94, 98, 257–258, 261. See also specific right, e.g.: right to counsel
Constitution of the United States 261, 276. See also amendments, e.g.: Fifth Amendment; Bill of Rights; specific amendments
Controlled Substances Act 17
cooperative supervision 125g
Cornell, Dewey 114b
correctional models/theories 93–94
corrections officer 125g
Cothern, Lynn 74
Cottrell, Leonard S., Jr. 259, 261, 270
Council of Juvenile Correctional Administrators 210

counsel, right to. See right to counsel
Court of Appeals, District of Columbia 52, 53
Court of Appeals for the Ninth Circuit 60, 75
Cox Broadcasting Company v. Cohn 62–63
crack cocaine 18
Crime in a Free Society 46
Crime in the United States 7–8
crime rate 9, 34–35
criminal court 60, 61, 94–95, 125g, 269
criminal justice process 125g
criminal justice system 14, 95–99. See also adults, trying juveniles as; juvenile justice system
Criminal Man, The (Lombroso) 12
criminal offense/offenders 125g
  detention 87
  federal requirements for treatment of 107–108c
  Juvenile Justice and Delinquency Prevention Act (1974) 82
  juvenile justice process 83
  juvenile v. criminal justice systems 97
New York Family Court Act 46
criminal records. See record entries
Crook, Shirley 76
cross-examination of witnesses 46, 56, 58, 250, 261, 265, 282
cruel and unusual punishment 125g
  Eddings v. Oklahoma 108c–109cc
  Eighth Amendment 101c

Roper v. Simmons 77
Thompson v. Oklahoma
71, 72, 109c
Wilkins v. Missouri 73
curfew 11, 125g
custody 84, 86, 125g
cyber-bullying 29–30

D
DARE (Drug Abuse
Resistance Education)
125g
death penalty **96**
Eddings v. Oklahoma 66,
67, 108c–109cc
first U.S. juvenile
execution 100c
juvenile v. criminal
justice systems 98
Roper v. Simmons 76–
77, 110c
In re Stanford 74–75
*Stanford v. Kentucky—
Wilkins v. Missouri*
73–74, 109c
Thompson v. Oklahoma
71–72, 109c
trends (1990s) 74
decriminalization 7, 94
deferred prosecution 125g
Delaware Criminal Justice
Council 215
delinquency/delinquents
adolescence 7
bonding theory of 107c
causes **12–15, 35–36**
Albert Cohen study
106c
detention trends (1985–
2005) 87
early 20th-century
theories 7
In re Gault 248–249,
255, 266, 269, 273
Illinois Juvenile Court
Act (1899) 43, 44
Juvenile Justice
and Delinquency
Prevention Act (1974)
47, 48

out-of-home placement
32
prevention **35–36**
psychological theories
104–105c
sociological studies
105c
delinquent act 99, 125g
delinquent juvenile 125g
delinquent minors 251,
262
Denver, Colorado 44, 104c
dependents 44, 46, 126g
detention **86–87,** 126g
and juveniles in criminal
justice system 95
juvenile v. criminal
justice systems 98
pre-ajudication trends
(1985–2005) 32
preventative 67–69,
109c, 131g
Schall v. Martin 67–68,
109c
trends (1985–2005) 32
detention center 126g
detention hearing 86, 126g
determinate (fixed)
sentencing 94
developmental history 97
developmental perspective
126g
developmental psychology
12–13, 95
developmental trajectories
35–36
differential association
theory of delinquency 13,
126g
direct (mandatory) filing
95, 126g
discretion 43, 50–51, 56,
88, 256–257
dismissal 89, 126g
disposition 46, **88–90,** 99,
126g
disposition hearing 126g
"disproportionate minority
contact" 48, 49
District of Columbia
52–54, 97

District of Columbia
Criminal Justice
Coordinating Council
215
diversion (informal
probation) **84–86,** 92–93,
126g
Dollard, John 13
Dorfman, Lori 34
double jeopardy 60, 61,
108c
Douglas, William O. 255,
267
Drug Abuse Resistance
Education (DARE) 126g
drug offenders
detention trends (1985–
2005) 87
juveniles in adult
correctional facilities
34
New Jersey v. T.L.O. 69
out-of-home placement
for 32
pre-ajudication
detention trends
(1985–2005) 32
probation caseload
trends (1985–2005)
32
residential placement
trends (1997–2003)
33
drug testing 75–76, 110c
drug trade 18, 23, 109c
drug use. *See* substance
abuse
drunkenness 16, 17
due process 126g. *See also*
Fourteenth Amendment
In re Gault 55, 56,
248–249, 253, 257,
259, 260, 278–280,
285, 286
Kent v. United States
52–54
McKeiver v. Pennsylvania
59
*People ex rel O'Connell v.
Turner* 82
Schall v. Martin 67–69

Index

Supreme court decisions
  affirming 80
  In re Winship 57, 58
Due Process Clause
  248–249, 254, 255, 261,
  265, 273, 275, 276, 278,
  281. *See also* Fourteenth
  Amendment

E

early-onset trajectory 35,
  126*g*
ecstasy (MDMA) 17
Eddings, Monty Lee 65, 66
Eddings v. Oklahoma **65–67,**
  108c–109c
Educational Fund to End
  Handgun Violence 210
Egley, Arlen, Jr. 19–21
Eighth Amendment 127*g*
  and death penalty 96
  Eddings v. Oklahoma 66,
    67, 108c–109cc
  ratification of 101c
  Stanford v. Kentucky—
    Wilkins v. Missouri
    72–75, 109c
  Thompson v. Oklahoma
    71, 72, 109c
  Wilkins v. Missouri 73
electronic monitoring 127*g*
Elliott, Delbert S. 114*b*
emancipation 127*g*
England 80, 100c
equal protection 55, 67,
  103c, 127*g*, 275. *See also*
  Fourteenth Amendment
escalation 126*g*
European Americans 22, 23
executions 100c, 101c
Eysenck, Hans J. 12–13

F

fact finder 127*g*
Fagan, Jeffrey 114*b*
Falco, Mathea 114*b*
families 13–14
Fare v. Michael C. **63–65,**
  108c

Farrington, David 114*b*
Federal Bureau of
  Investigation (FBI) 207
  creation of 104c
  female/male juvenile
    offender arrest ratios
    11
  and informality 84
  media coverage of crime
    35
  property crime trends
    (1998–2007) 10–11
  and UCR 7, 105c
  violent crime trends
    (1998–2007) 10
federal courts 127*g*
federal laws/legislation
  43–49. *See also specific*
  laws
Feld, Barry C. 114*b*
felonies 3–4, 127*g*
female(s)
  alcohol use at school
    29
  arrests by age (2007)
    230*t*–233*t*
  arrest trends (1998–
    1999) 11–12
  arrest trends (2005–
    2006) 5
  and bullying at school
    30
  club drugs 17
  crime rate increase from
    1960s onward 9
  crime rate trends (1998–
    2007) 10
  gang membership
    21–23
  inhalant use 17
  liquor law violations
    (1998–2007) 11
  pre-ajudication
    detention trends
    (1985–2005) 32
  probation caseload
    trends (1985–2005)
    32
  property crime arrest
    trends (1998–2007)
    10–11

runaway arrest trends
  (1998–2007) 11
  vocational training 50
  weapons at school 27
FFT (Functional Family
  Therapy) 38
field interrogation (FI)
  report 83
Fifth Amendment
  Breed v. Jones 60
  Fare v. Michael C. 64,
    65
  In re Gault 269,
    275–277
  New Jersey v. T.L.O. 70
  ratification 101c
FindLaw 211
firearms. *See* guns/gun
  violence; weapons
  violations
First Amendment 101c,
  108c
fitness (waiver) hearing. *See*
  transfer hearing
fixed sentencing. *See*
  determinate sentencing
Florida Statistical Analysis
  Center 215
Flower, Lucy Louisa Coues
  114*b*–115*b*
Fogel, David 115*b*
foreign law 77, 96, 110c
Fortas, Abe 53, 56, 115*b*,
  250–273
foster homes 102c, 127*g*
foster parent 127*g*
Fourteenth Amendment
  Eddings v. Oklahoma 66
  In re Gault 55, 249,
    254, 255, 261, 265,
    275, 278, 281, 283,
    284
  Haley v. Ohio 255
  Kent v. United States
    52–54
  McKeiver v. Pennsylvania
    59
  Nelson v. Heyne 108c
  New Jersey v. T.L.O. 70
  Oklahoma Publishing Co.
    v. District Court 62

ratification 103c
Schall v. Martin 67–69,
  108c
In re Winship 57, 58
Fourth Amendment
  Kent v. United States 53
  New Jersey v. T.L.O.
    69, 71
  Oklahoma Publishing Co.
    v. District Court 62
  ratification 101c
  Safford School District v.
    Redding 78
  Smith v. Daily Mail
    Publishing Company
    108c
  Vernonia School District
    v. Acton 75, 76,
    109c–110c
Fox, James Alan 115b
freedom of speech and press.
  See First Amendment;
  Fourth Amendment
Freud, Sigmund 12, 115b
Functional Family Therapy
  (FFT) 38

G

gang(s). *See* youth gangs
"Gangs in Middle America"
  (Allender) 19, 23
Gangs or Us 211
Gault, Gerald 54–55,
  248–254
Gault, In re **54–56**, 106c,
  248–286
  and *Breed v. Jones* 61
  and *McKeiver v.*
    Pennsylvania 59, 60
  and probation 91
  and rights for minors
    46, 106c
  and *Schall v. Martin* 69
  and *In re Winship* 57,
    58
Georgia Statistical Analysis
  Center 215
GHB (drug) 17
Ginsburg, Ruth Bader 74,
  77

Golub, Andrew 16
Goring, Charles 12, 104–
  105c, 115b
graduated sanctions 49, 90,
  127g
Greece, ancient 3
Grisso, Thomas 115b
group home 127g
guardian 127g
guns/gun violence. *See also*
  weapons violations
  gang-related homicides
    20
  homicide rate (1980s) 4
  Schall v. Martin 67
  at school **24–28**, 110c
  trends (1980s–1990s) 9
  youth gang activity 18

H

habeas corpus 55, 249, 250,
  253, 265, 266, 277
Hagedorn, John 22
Haley v. Ohio 254–255, 267
Hall, G. Stanley 7, 12,
  104c, 115b
Hamilton Fish Institute
  211
Harrell, Adele 116b
hate crimes 127g
Hawaii Crime Prevention &
  Justice Assistance Division
  215
Hawkins, J. David 116b
hearing 98, 127g
Hirschi, Travis 13–14, 107c,
  116b
Hispanics 20, 24, 28–30,
  33, 34
Holder, Eric 116b
homicide. *See* murder
Hooton, Earnest A. 12
Hoover, Herbert 4
house arrest 128g
House of Reformation
  (Boston) 81, 102c
House of Refuge (New
  York) 81
House of Representatives,
  U.S. 48

Howell, James C. "Buddy"
  18, 116b
Hunt, Karen 116b

I

Idaho Department of Law
  Enforcement 215
Illinois Criminal Justice
  Information Authority 215
Illinois Juvenile Court Act
  (1899) **43–47**, 90–91, 96,
  104c, 128g
Illinois Supreme Court 82,
  103c
immigration 4, 9
incorrigibility 6, 8, 44, 97
incorrigible minor 128g
index crimes 128g
Indiana Criminal Justice
  Institute 215–216
Indicators of School Crime and
  Safety: 2008 24, 27–30
Industrial Revolution 6–8,
  18
informality
  Colorado juvenile court
    45
  Ex parte Crouse 81
  delinquency cases 31
  diversion 84
  In re Gault 259
  Illinois Juvenile Court
    Act (1899) 44
  juvenile justice process
    84
  treatment models 93
informal probation. *See*
  diversion
Ingersoll, Sarah 116b
inhalants **17**
in loco parentis 76, 256, 284
In re... See name of party, e.g.:
  Gault, In re
intake **83–84**, 128g
international law 77, 96,
  110c
Internet research resources
  143–145
Interstate Compact on
  Juveniles 128g

Index

interstate transfer 128*g*
intervention programs 24,
  80
Iowa Statistical Analysis
  Center 216

J

Jackson, Lonnie 116*b*
jail 33, 99, 128*g*
jeopardy 60, 108c. *See also*
  double jeopardy
Johnson, Bruce D. 16
Jones, Gary 60
judges 88, 97
Judging Juveniles (Kupchik)
  98
judicial transfer 94–95,
  128*g*
jury (term) 128*g*
jury trial 46, 58–59, 97,
  101c, 107c
Justice, U.S. Department of
  7, 8, 104c, 105c, 107c
Justice Research and
  Statistics Association
  207–208
justice system
  adult. *See* adults, trying
    juveniles as; criminal
    justice system
  juvenile. *See* juvenile
    justice system
Juszkiewicz, Jolanta 33, 34
juvenile 128*g*
juvenile court 128*g*
  Jane Addams' and 103c
  establishment of 45,
    103c, 105c
  In re Gault 106c,
    255–260, 270–274,
    277–280, 283–286
  Illinois Juvenile Court
    Act (1899) 44, 104c
  and juvenile justice
    process 84
  probation caseload
    trends (1985–2005) 32
*Juvenile Court Statistics,
  2005* (Puzzanchera and
  Sickmund) 31, 87

"The Juvenile Death Penalty
  Today" (Streib) 96
juvenile delinquency 6–7,
  45, 129*g*
Juvenile Delinquency
  Prevention Act (1972)
  43, 47
Juvenile Delinquency
  Prevention and Control
  Act (1968) 47, 106c–
  108c
juvenile hall 129*g*
Juvenile Justice (Shepherd) 81
Juvenile Justice and
  Delinquency Prevention
  Act (1974) 47–48, 82–83,
  107–108c, 129*g*
  and detention 87
  and disposition 90
  juveniles in adult
    correctional facilities
    33
  passage of 46
Juvenile Justice and
  Delinquency Prevention
  Act (2002) 48–49, 82,
  110*c*
juvenile justice process
  83–96, 129*g*
  adjudicatory hearings
    88
  correctional models
    93–94
  detention 86–87
  disposition and
    treatment 88–90
  diversion 84–86
  intake 83–84
  mental health treatment
    92–93
  plea bargaining 87–88
  probation 90–92
  treatment of juveniles
    in the criminal justice
    system 95–96
  waiver of jurisdiction
    94–95
juvenile justice system
  80–99, 129*g*
  bibliography 187–206
  confidentiality 96–97

criminal justice system
  vs. 97–99
  and death penalty 96
  historical background
    80–81
  Illinois Juvenile Court
    Act (1899) 43–47
  increase in punitiveness
    110c
  Juvenile Justice
    and Delinquency
    Prevention Act (1974)
    82–83
  McKeiver v. Pennsylvania
    59
  President's 1967 task
    force report 106c
  reformatories 81–82
Juvenile Law Center 211
juvenile offenders 11–12,
  258
Juvenile Offenders and Victims
  (Snyder and Sickmund)
  32–33, 46–48, 90
juvenile probation. *See*
  probation
juveniles tried as adults. *See*
  adults, trying juveniles as

K

Kansas Criminal Justice
  Coordinating Council
  216
Keene, Charles 71
Kelly, Florence 103c, 116*b*
Kennedy, Anthony 77
Kent, Morris 52
Kentucky Justice and
  Public Safety Cabinet
  216
Kentucky Supreme Court
  73
Kent v. United States 52–54,
  106c
  and *Breed v. Jones* 61
  and *In re Gault* 56,
    248–249, 254, 256,
    261, 264, 273
  and *McKeiver v.
    Pennsylvania* 60

and probation 91
and *Schall v. Martin* 69
and *In re Winship* 58
Kerlikowske, R. Gil 116*b*–
117*b*
kidnapping 129*g*
Koch Crime Institute, The
211
Kohlberg, Lawrence 91,
117*b*
Krisberg, Barry 117*b*
Kupchik, Aaron 98

L

LAPD (Los Angeles Police
Department) 3–4
larceny-theft 5, 10–11
late-onset trajectory 35, 36,
129*g*
Lathrop, Julia Clifford 117*b*
Latinos. *See* Hispanics
laws. *See* federal laws/legisla-
tion; state laws/legislation
legal age of criminal
responsibility 3, 100c
legislation. *See* federal laws/
legislation; state laws/
legislation
Lewis, Ronald 251, 252
Life Skills Training 38
Lindsey, Ben B. 44, 45,
104c, 117*b*
liquor law violations 11, 22
Littleton, Colorado 25, 110c
Lombroso, Cesare 12, 117*b*
Los Angeles, California
in 1930s 3–4
Breed v. Jones 60
gangs in 20–22
Los Angeles Police
Department (LAPD)
3–4
Los Angeles Times, The 20
Loughran, Edward "Ned"
117*b*
Louisiana Commission
on Law Enforcement
and Administration of
Criminal Justice 216
Lubow, Bart 117*b*

M

Maine Justice Policy Center
216
males
alcohol use at school 29
and gang membership
22–23
pre-ajudication
detention trends
(1985–2005) 32
probation caseload
trends (1985–2005)
32
runaway arrest trends
(1998–2007) 11
as victims of bullying at
school 30
and weapons at school
27
malice 129*g*
mandatory filing. *See* direct
filing
manslaughter 129*g*
marijuana 16, 23, 29, 69, 70
Marshall, John 71–73
Martin, Gordon A., Jr. 117*b*
Martin, Gregory 67, 68
Maryland Justice Analysis
Center 216
Massachusetts Executive
Office of Public Safety
216
Matza, Davis 117*b*
McCord, Joan 117*b*
McKay, Henry D. 13, 105c
McKeiver, Joseph 58
McKeiver et al v. Pennsylvania
46, **58–60,** 107c
MDMA (ecstasy) 17
media coverage of juvenile
crime 26, **34–35,** 62–63,
97, 108c
mental health treatment 49,
51, **92–93**
mentoring 129*g*
Mexico 18, 101c
Michigan Justice Statistics
Center 216
Miller, Jerome G. 117*b*–
118*b*

Miller, Jody 118*b*
Miller, Neal 13
Miller, Walter B. 19
Minnesota Office of Justice
Programs 216–217
minorities 4, 238*t*–240*t*. *See
also specific minority groups,
e.g.:* African Americans
minors 129*g*
Miranda v. Arizona 64, 65,
106c, 266, 277
Miranda warning/rights 84,
98, 129*g*
misdemeanors 129*g*
Mississippi Department of
Criminal Justice 217
Missouri Statistical Analysis
Center 217
Missouri Supreme Court
73, 77
mitigating factors 66–67,
73, 88, 129*g*
Monitoring the Future (MTF)
16, 17
Montana Statistical Analysis
Center 217
Moore, Joan 22
motion 129*g*
motive 130*g*
motor vehicle theft 4, 5, 10
movies 4, 45
MTF (Monitoring the Future)
16, 17
Mueller, Robert S., III 118*b*
Multisystemic Therapy
(MST) 38
murder 130*g*
*Crime in the United
States* data 8
defined 127*g*
Eddings v. Oklahoma
65–67
Fare v. Michael C.
63–65
gang-related **20–21**
*Oklahoma Publishing
Co. v. District Court*
62–63, 108c
Roper v. Simmons 76–77
school crime trends
24–25

Index

Stanford v. Kentucky
72–73
Thompson v. Oklahoma
71–72
trends (1900–1930) 8–9
trends (1900–1935) 4
trends (1960s–1980s) 4
trends (1980s–1990s) 9
Wilkins v. Missouri 73

N

National Archive of
Criminal Justice Data 211
National Association of
Youth Courts 211
National Center for
Education Statistics
(NCES) 208
National Center for Juvenile
Justice (NCJJ) 47,
212–213
National Center on
Institutions and
Alternatives (NCIA) 212
National Clearinghouse
for Alcohol and Drug
Information 212
National Council of Juvenile
and Family Court Judges
106c, 212, 264
National Council on Crime
and Delinquency (NCCD)
36, 212
National Crime Prevention
Council 212
National Crime
Victimization Survey
(NCVS) 8, 9, 34, 107c,
130g
National Criminal Justice
Reference Service
(NJCRS) 139, 208
National Gang Crime
Research Center 212–213
*National Household Survey on
Drug Abuse* 16, 17
National Institute on Drug
Abuse 208
National Juvenile Justice
Action Plan 82–83

National Probation
Association (NPA) 91,
104c
National Resource Center
for Safe School (NRCSS)
213
National School Safety
Center 213
National Youth Gang
Center 19, 20, 213
National Youth Gang
Survey (NYGS) 19, 20
National Youth Violence
Prevention Resource
Center (NYVPRC) 213
Native American gang
members 22
NCCD (National
Council on Crime and
Delinquency) 36, 212
NCES (National Center for
Education Statistics) 208
NCIA (National Center
on Institutions and
Alternatives) 212
NCJJ (National Center
for Juvenile Justice) 47,
212–213
NCVS. *See* National Crime
Victimization Survey
Nebraska Commission on
Law Enforcement and
Criminal Justice 217
neglected children 44, 45
neighborhoods 13, 15
New Hampshire
Department of Justice
217
New Jersey 19, 26, 51,
69–71
New Jersey Department of
Law and Public Safety
217
New Jersey v. T.L.O. **69–71,**
75, 76, 79, 109c
New Marijuana Epidemic
16
New Mexico Statistical
Analysis Center 217
news media. *See* media
coverage of juvenile crime

New York Bureau of
Statistical Services 217
New York City 6–7, 102c
New York Family Court 67
New York Family Court Act
45, 46, 264–265, 268
New York State
juvenile courts 45
PINS 46
reformatories 81, 102c
In re Winship 56–58
youth gangs 19
New York Supreme Court
57
New York Times, The 3
NJCRS (National Criminal
Justice Reference Service)
139, 208
nolo contendere 66, 130g
nonpetitioned case 130g
nonsecure detention 130g
North Carolina 59
North Carolina Governor's
Crime Commission
217–218
North Dakota 45, 51
North Dakota Bureau of
Criminal Investigation
218
notice of charges 249, 261–
263, 274, 284, 285
NPA (National Probation
Association) 91, 104c
NRCSS (National Resource
Center for Safe School)
213
nurturing 6, 23
NYGS (National Youth
Gang Survey) 19, 20
NYVPRC (National Youth
Violence Prevention
Resource Center) 213

O

O'Connor, Sandra Day 72,
118*b*
O'Donnell, Christina E.
19–20
offender 130g
offense 130g

Office of Juvenile Justice
and Delinquency
Prevention (OJJDP)
130g, 208
  establishment of 108c
  Juvenile Arrests, 2007
    111c
  Juvenile Justice
    and Delinquency
    Prevention Act (1974)
    47
  juvenile offender arrest
    trends (1998–1999)
    11–12
  as research resource
    140–141
  youth violence risk
    factor study (2000)
    14–15
officer of the court 130g
Ohio Office of Criminal
  Justice Services 218
Oklahoma Court of Appeals
  71
*Oklahoma Publishing Co. v.
  District Court* **62–63,** 108c
Oklahoma Statistical
  Analysis Center 218
"once an adult, always an
  adult" 50, 52
Oregon Statistical Analysis
  Center 218
O'Toole, Mary Ellen 26–27

P

parens patriae 130g
  Ex parte Crouse 81, 102c
  In re Gault 56, 106c,
    256, 259, 261
  Illinois Juvenile Court
    Act (1899) 44
  justice model of
    correction v. 94
  juvenile proceedings 43
  Kent v. United States 54
  McKeiver v. Pennsylvania
    60, 107c
  origin of 81
  Schall v. Martin 68–69
  treatment models 93

parental responsibility laws
  130g
parents 13, 30
Park, Robert 13
parole 99, 130g
parole officer 130g
peer groups 13, 15
Pennsylvania Commission
  on Crime and
  Delinquency 218
Pennsylvania Supreme
  Court 59, 81, 102c
*People ex rel O'Connell v.
  Turner* 43, 82
perceptions of juvenile
  crime **34–35,** 45
person offenses/crimes 130g
  defined 8
  detention trends (1985–
    2005) 32, 87
  by females 9
  out-of-home placement
    for 32
  probation caseload
    trends (1985–2005) 32
  residential placement
    trends (1997–2003) 32
Persons in Need of
  Supervision (PINS) 46
petition 88, 99, 130g, 262
petitioned case 131g
placement 131g
Platt, Anthony M. 82, 107c,
  118b
plea 131g
plea bargaining **87–88,** 98,
  131g
Pointer v. Texas 276, 279
poor laws 80, 100c, 131g
Positivist School 12
Powell, Lewis 66–67, 118b
pre-adjudication detention.
  See detention
predisposition investigation
  131g
preponderance of evidence
  57, 107c, 131g
President's Commission on
  Law Enforcement and the
  Administration of Justice
  46, 106c

presumptive transfer 131g
preventative detention
  67–69, 109c, 131g
prevention of delinquency
  35–36
prison 18, 20–21, 33. *See
  also* adult correctional
  facilities, juveniles in
probable cause 68, 70, 98,
  109c, 131g
probation **31–33, 90–92,**
  131g
  California 106c
  Colorado juvenile court
    45
  community services
    107c
  and disposition 89
  and diversion 85
  establishment of system
    102c
  In re Gault 251
  Illinois Juvenile Court
    Act (1899) 44
  and juvenile courts
    105c
  and juvenile justice
    process 84
  in juvenile v. criminal
    justice systems 98
  trends (1985–2005) 32
probation officers 132g
  and adjudicatory
    hearings 88
  earliest 103c
  Fare v. Michael C. 64,
    65
  In re Gault 263
  and home detention
    87
  identification of risk
    factors by 92
  and probation 91
procedural informality 44,
  257
Prohibition 4, 8
property offense/crime
  10–11
  defined 8, 132g
  early 19th century 6
  by females 9

Index

juveniles in adult
correctional facilities
34
out-of-home placement
for 32
residential placement
trends (1997–2003) 33
Proposition 21 (California)
34
prosecutor 88, 132g
prostitution 6, 22
protective factors 132g
public defender 132g
public order offenses 32,
34, 87
public perceptions of
juvenile crime **34–35,** 45
punishment 93, 94, 97, 98
Puritanism 5–6
Puzzanchera, Charles 31,
87

Q

Quantum Opportunities
Program (QOP) 39

R

The Rand Corporation
Criminal Justice Research
213
rape 5, 30, 52, 72–73
rational choice theory 14,
132g
reasonable doubt. *See*
beyond a reasonable doubt
reasonableness 79, 109c,
132g
Rebel Without a Cause (film)
45
recidivism 132g
record, access to 51, 62,
96–97, 258
Redding, Savanna 78–79
referee 88, 132g
reformatories **81–82,** 102c,
103c
rehabilitation 132g
crime control model 94
and disposition 89

Illinois Juvenile Court
Act (1899) 44
juvenile v. criminal
justice systems 97
and probation 91
Rehnquist, William 68, 72,
77, 118b
Renwanz, Marsha 118b
research resources on
juvenile crime **139–150**
bibliographies 145–146
bookseller catalogs 146
free periodical indexes
146–149
Internet resources
143–145
legal research 149–150
library catalogs 145
NJCRS 139, 141–142
OJJDP 140–141
search engines 143–
145
residential placement 32–
33, 87, 132g
restitution 85, 94, 132g
restorative justice 50, 132g.
See also balanced and
restorative justice model
of correction
revocation 132g
revocation hearing 133g
Rhode Island 81, 102c
Rhode Island Justice
Commission 218
right to counsel. *See also*
Miranda warning/rights
in criminal justice
system 95–96
and detention 86
Fare v. Michael C. 64,
65, 108c
In re Gault 46, 56, 261,
263–266, 282–285
Kent v. United States
54
In re Winship 58
right to remain silent 64,
65. *See also Miranda*
warning/rights
right to treatment 108c,
133g

risk factors 14–15, 36, 92,
133g
robbery 133g
arrest trends (2005–
2006) 5
Breed v. Jones 60
defined 8
by females 9
by gang members 23
McKeiver v. Pennsylvania
58
Stanford v. Kentucky
72–73
Robinson, Laurie O. 118b
Rohypnol ("date rape" drug)
17
Roman law 5
Rome, ancient 5, 100c
Roper, Donald P. 77
Roper v. Simmons **76–77,**
96, 110c
runaways 133g
and child-saving
movement 81
and Juvenile Justice
and Delinquency
Prevention Act (2002)
49
Persons in Need of
Supervision (PINS)
46
and status offenders 8
trends (1983–1991;
1998–2007) 11
rural areas 22, 27–29
Ryan, Liz 118b

S

Sabol, William J. 87
*Safford Unified School
District #1 v. Redding*
78–79, 111c
sanctions 133g
San Francisco Examiner 35
Satcher, David 118b
Scalia, Antonin 72, 73,
75–77, 119b
Schall v. Martin **67–69,**
109c
Schiraldi, Vincent 34, 119b

school **24–30**
  bibliography 174–184
  bullying 29–30
  hate-related words and
    graffiti 29
  homicides 110c
  nonfatal crimes at
    28–29
  OJJDP risk factor study
    14
  safety **29–30,** 51
  shootings **24–27,** 110c
  social bonding theory of
    delinquency 13–14
  youth gangs **24**
school searches 133*g*
  juvenile v. criminal
    justice systems 98
  New Jersey v. T.L.O.
    69–71, 109c
  Safford School District v.
    Redding 78–79, 111*c*
  Vernonia School District
    v. Acton 75–76,
    109c–110c
school shootings **24–27,**
  110*c*
School Violence Resource
  Center 213–214
Schwartz, Robert G. 119*b*
sealing of juvenile record
  133*g*
search and seizure,
  unreasonable. *See* Fourth
  Amendment; school
  searches
search engines 143–145
Seattle, Washington 22–23
self-control theory 133*g*
self-defense 133*g*
self-incrimination 133*g*. *See*
  also Fifth Amendment
  Fare v. Michael C.
    64–65
  In re Gault 46, 249,
    265, 266, 268–270,
    277, 282, 283, 286
  and historic governing
    of juvenile
    proceedings 43
  New Jersey v. T.L.O. 70

self-report studies 8, 10,
  36, 133*g*
Senate, U.S. 48, 110c
sentencing 50, 99, 108c
The Sentencing Project 214
sex offenders **30–31,** 51
Shaw, Clifford R. 13, 105c,
  119*b*
shelter care 87, 133*g*
Shepherd, Robert E., Jr. 81
Sickmund, Melissa 31, 47,
  48, 87, 90, 119*b*
Simmons, Christopher 76
simple assault 10, 28, 133*g*
Simpson, O. J. 35
sin, Puritan concept of 6
Sixth Amendment 59,
  274–276
Slowikowski, Jeff 119*b*
Snyder, Harry N. 46–48,
  90
Snyder, Howard 119*b*
social bonding theory of
  delinquency 13–14, 107*c*
social history, legal facts
  v. 97
social reform 103c, 104c
sociology 13, 105c–107cc
Socrates 3
Soler, Mark 119*b*
Souter, David H. 74, 77, 78
South Carolina Planning
  and Research Division
  218
South Dakota 51, 52
South Dakota Statistical
  Analysis Center 218
specialization offenses 133*g*
Spock, Benjamin 119*b*
Standard Juvenile Court
  Act 47
standard of proof 46, 98,
  133*g*
"Standards for Juvenile and
  Family Courts" 264, 269,
  272–273
Stanford, In re 74
Stanford, Kevin Nigel
  72–74
Stanford v. Kentucky 67,
  72–73, 77, 96, 109c

Stanford v. Kentucky–Wilkins
  v. Missouri (consolidated)
  72–75
state laws/legislation **49–**
  52, 80, 96, 110c, 110*c*
status offenders/status
  offenses **11**
  California Juvenile
    Court Act 45
  defined 8, 134*g*
  detention 87
  Ex parte Crouse 81
  Illinois Juvenile Court
    Act (1899) 43
  justice model of
    correction 94
  Juvenile Justice
    and Delinquency
    Prevention Act (1974)
    48, 82
  Juvenile Justice
    and Delinquency
    Prevention Act (2002)
    49
  juvenile justice process
    83
  juvenile v. criminal
    justice systems 97
  legal category 46
  media coverage of crime
    35
  New York Family Court
    Act 46
  People ex rel O'Connell v.
    Turner 82
  Puritans and 6
  in reformatories 82
statute 134*g*
statute of limitations 134*g*
statutory rape 134*g*
statutory transfer 134*g*
Steinberg, Lawrence 120*b*
Stevens, John Paul 70–75,
  77, 120*b*
Stewart, Potter 56, 274,
  285–286
stigma 14, 50, 84, 96, 262
stock market crash (1929)
  4, 9
stop and frisk 134*g*
Streib, Victor L. 81, 96

strip searches 78, 79, 111*c*
subpoena 134*g*
substance abuse **15–17**. *See also* alcohol abuse; drug entries
    and abused children 36
    bibliography 184–187
    and female gang membership 22
    and mental illness 92
    at school 29
substance abuse treatment 49, 51
suburban schools 27, 29
supervision 134*g*
Supreme Court (state). *See under specific state, e.g.: Arizona Supreme Court*
Supreme Court, U.S. **52–79**
    Breed v. Jones 60–61, 108*c*
    clarification of juvenile law 43
    death penalty 96
    due process 80
    Eddings v. Oklahoma **65–67**, 108*c*–109*cc*
    Fare v. Michael C. **63–65**, 108*c*
    In re Gault 46, **54–56**, 106*c*, **248–286**
    Kent v. United States **52–54**, 106*c*
    McKeiver et al. v. Pennsylvania 46, **58–60**, 107*c*
    Miranda v. Arizona 106*c*
    New Jersey v. T.L.O. **69–71**, 109*c*
    Oklahoma Publishing Co. v. District Court 62–63, 108*c*
    probation decisions 91
    Roper v. Simmons **76–77**, 110*c*
    Safford School District v. Redding **78–79**, 111*c*
    Schall v. Martin **67–69**, 109*c*

Smith v. Daily Mail Publishing Company 108*c*
Stanford v. Kentucky—Wilkins v. Missouri (consolidated) **72–75**, 109*c*
Thompson v. Oklahoma 67, **71–72**, 109*c*
Vernonia School District v. Acton **75–76**, 109*c*–110*c*
In re Winship **56–58**, 107*c*
Sutherland, Edwin H. 13, 120*b*

T

Taft, William Howard 104*c*, 120*b*
taggers 134*g*
Tate, Lionel 3
teachers, as crime victims 28
technical violation 33, 134*g*
Tennessee Statistical Analysis Center 218–219
Teplin, Linda A. 15
Terry, Edward 58
Texas Department of Criminal Justice 219
theft 28, 56–58. *See also* larceny-theft
Thomas, Clarence 77, 78
Thompson, William Wayne 71
Thompson v. Oklahoma 67, **71–72**, 109*c*
Thornberry, Terence P. 120*b*
Thrasher, Frederic 105*c*, 120*b*
timely notice 46, 281–282
T.L.O. See New Jersey v. T.L.O.
transcripts 55, 134*g*, 273
transfer (waiver) hearing 60, 61, 94–95, 106*c*, 134*g*

treatment **88–90**, 105*c*, 134*g*. *See also* right to treatment
trials, juvenile v. criminal justice system 97, 99
truants/truancy 44, 46, 97, 134*g*
trying juveniles as adults. *See* adults, trying juveniles as
Twelve Tables 5

U

underage drinking. *See* alcohol abuse
Uniform Crime Reporting Program (UCR) 7–8, 105*c*, 134*g*
    drug abuse violation definition 15
    and improvement in tracking crime statistics 9
    juvenile violent crime rate (1980–2007) 9–10
    substance abuse arrest statistics (1980–2000) 15
United Nations Convention on the Rights of the Child 96
University of Alaska Anchorage Justice Center 214
unreasonable search and seizure. *See* Fourth Amendment; school searches
urban areas. *See* cities
urbanization 4, 6–9, 18, 80
USA Today 34
Utah Commission on Criminal and Juvenile Justice 219

V

vandalism 134*g*
Vermont Center for Justice Research 219

Vernonia, Oregon 75–76
Vernonia School District v.
  Acton **75–76,** 109c–110c
Vice Lords 21
victim(s) 8, 35, 94, 107c,
  135*g*
victimization 135*g*
victims' rights 50, 91
Vinter, Robert D. 120*b*
violation 135*g*
violation of parole 135*g*
violation of probation 135*g*
violence/violent crime
  8–10, 135*g*
    arrest trends 11
    female gangs 22
    increased penalties 109c
    juveniles in adult
      correctional facilities
      33–34
    media coverage 35
    public perception of 34
    at school 24, 28–29
    trends/statistics 8–10,
      24
violent offenders 97, 135*g*
Virginia Department of
  Criminal Justice Services
  219
Virginia Tech shootings 26
Vollmer, August 105c,
  120*b*

W
waiver hearing. *See* transfer
  hearing
waiver of jurisdiction **94–**
95, 98, 254
ward 135*g*

Washington, D. C. *See*
  District of Columbia
Washington Statistical
  Analysis Center 219
weapons. *See* guns/gun
  violence
weapons violations 10, 22
West Virginia Statistical
  Analysis Center 219
Wheeler, Stanton 259, 261,
  270
White, Byron 72, 120*b*–
  121*b*, 268, 277
white youth
  in adult correctional
    facilities 33, 34
  detention (1985–2005)
    87
  out-of-home placement
    32
  probation caseloads
    (1985–2005) 32
  school safety 29
  school weapons 28
  as victims of bullying
    30
  youth gang trends 20
Wickersham Commission 4
Wilkins, Heath 73
Wilkins v. Missouri 73, 109c
Wilson, John J. 121*b*
Winship, In re **56–58,** 107c
  and *Breed v. Jones* 61
  and *McKeiver v.*
    Pennsylvania 59
  and *Schall v. Martin* 69
  standard of proof 46
Winship, Samuel 56–58
Wisconsin Office of Justice
  Assistance 219

women. *See* females
Wyoming Survey and
  Analysis Center 219

Y
Yeager, Robert 63, 64
Youth Crime Watch of
  America 214
youth gangs **18–24,** 135*g*
  in 21st century 21
  bibliography 165–174
  Albert Cohen study
    106c
  defined 18
  female gangs 21–22
  first appearance 101c
  homicides and other
    crimes 20–21
  increased penalties 109c
  joining/remaining in
    22–23
  Mexican 101c
  at school 24
  sociology of 105c, 106c
  state laws 51
  Frederic Thrasher study
    105c
  trends (1970s–2007) 5,
    18–20
Youth Gangs: An Overview
  (Howell) 18
Youth Gang Survey Analysis
  (2007) 21, 22
Youth Risk Behavior Survey
  (1999) 17

Z
Zimring, Franklin E. 121*b*